Parties Long Estranged

Edited by Margaret MacMillan and Francine McKenzie

Parties Long Estranged:
Canada and Australia in the
Twentieth Century

09 08 07 06 05 04 03   5 4 3 2 1

Printed in Canada on acid-free paper. ∞

National Library of Canada Cataloguing in Publication Data

Main entry under title:

Parties long estranged : Canada and Australia in the twentieth century / edited by Margaret MacMillan and Francine McKenzie.

   Includes bibliographical references and index.
   ISBN 0-7748-0975-2 (bound); ISBN 0-7748-0976-0 (pbk)

   1. Canada – Foreign relations – Australia. 2. Australia – Foreign relations – Canada. 3. Canada – Foreign relations – 1918-1945. 4. Australia – Foreign relations – 1900-1945. 5. Canada – Foreign relations – 1945-6. Australia – Foreign relations – 1945-7. Canada – Relations – Australia. 8. Australia – Relations – Canada. I. Macmillan, Margaret Olwen. II. McKenzie, Francine, 1967-

FC251.A8P37 2003   327.71094'09'04   C2002-911338-5
F1029.5.A97P37 2003

Canadä

UBC Press gratefully acknowledges the financial support for our publishing program of the Government of Canada through the Book Publishing Industry Development Program (BPIDP), and of the Canada Council for the Arts, and the British Columbia Arts Council.

This book has been published with the help of a grant from the Humanities and Social Sciences Federation of Canada, using funds provided by the Social Sciences and Humanities Research Council of Canada.

UBC Press also gratefully acknowledges the financial assistance of the Department of Foreign Affairs and International Trade and of Ryerson University.

Printed and bound in Canada by Friesens
Set in Stone by Artegraphica Design Co. Ltd.
Copy editor: Barbara Storey
Proofreader: Gail Copeland
Indexer: Noeline Bridge

UBC Press
The University of British Columbia
2029 West Mall
Vancouver, BC V6T 1Z2
604-822-5959 / Fax: 604-822-6083
www.ubcpress.ca

Contents

Acknowledgments

This book grew out of the 1998 conference of the Australian Studies Association of North America at which Margaret MacMillan, Francine McKenzie, Galen Perras, Peter Russell, Kim Nossal, and Andrew Cooper all presented papers on various aspects of the Canadian-Australian relationship as well as the two countries' emergence as actors in the international community. We realized in conversation that there was considerable interest in the histories of Canadian and Australian foreign policies, but very little scholarship that either compared the two countries or looked at their relationship. This book has been some years in the making and owes much to the patience and good nature of its contributors, who have unfailingly and promptly returned their copy and answered all queries. In addition, the contributors have helped shape every aspect of the book, with suggestions ranging from cover design, the organization of chapters, and marketing. Special thanks to Galen Perras, who came up with our title, which so well expresses the relationship between the two former members of the British Empire, and to Chris Waters for never failing to help with our queries about Australian history and the Australian academy.

Along the way, we have incurred other debts. To Emily Andrew, our outstanding editor at UBC press; to Camilla Jenkins, our meticulous production editor; and to our previous employers, Ryerson University, in Margaret MacMillan's case, and the University of Toronto, in Francine McKenzie's, who provided us with much-needed support while this volume was being produced and vetted. Ryerson and the Canadian Department of Foreign Affairs and International Trade also generously gave us grants toward publication. Thanks to David Korth for guiding us through the rigorous process of applying for government grants. Finally we must thank the Aid to Scholarly Publications Program of the Canada Council, whose anonymous reviewers helped us and our contributors to clarify our ideas, and who also gave us a publication grant.

Parties Long Estranged

Introduction

Francine McKenzie and Margaret MacMillan

The great northern land and the huge southern island; the Big Dipper and the Southern Cross; pine trees and eucalyptus; beavers and kangaroos; the mental images reflect a difference in place and land. If Australia must come to terms with its convict settlements, Canada has its French fact, both past and present. Then there are the similarities: the dominance of the English language, English legal institutions, parliamentary government, the Queen (still), Native issues, a largely urban people who think of themselves as pioneers. So much of the history has been parallel. Canada and Australia were both explored and settled as part of the British Empire. Both fought, with pride, in world wars as British subjects.

In both countries, the achievement of nationhood has been a gentle process, one of gradual detachment from a mother country and a quest for adult identity. The growth of nationalism has followed much the same path in each country: the gradual differentiation from the parent society, the awakening sense that the land was creating a different sort of person, the tension between loyalty to the old and to the new, even a similar missing element. As Gérard Bouchard points out in a perceptive recent book, there is not, in either Australian or Canadian history, a great founding myth or act, like the American War of Independence or the conquest of the French in Canada.[1]

Canadians and Australians are separated by an immense physical distance but are close in ways that are difficult to quantify. They understand something about the other in ways that, for example, an American would not. They pay attention, as they have always done, to what the other is doing, whether it is to disapprove or to imitate. When the colonies in Australia debated federation at the start of the last century, Canada was used as an example. When the Australian Supreme Court wrestled with Native land rights, Canadian legal precedents were cited. When Canadian and Australian universities arrange faculty and student exchanges, they think of the other country. In international organizations, the United Nations for example, Australian and Canadian diplomats cooperate regularly because they often share the same viewpoints and the same values. Australians read Canadian fiction. Canadians wish that their filmmakers made more films like the Australians do, with a truly Canadian flavour. Inevitably the stereotypes creep in: at one extreme, the straitlaced Mountie hero of *Due South;* at the other, Dame Edna or Crocodile Dundee. Australians see Canadians as prissy, priggish even. Canadians, perhaps with a trace of envy, see Australians as outrageous and daring.

If there has been a sense of familiarity, relations have not been easy to cultivate and, once established, not always comfortable. In 1893, a Canadian trade minister, Mackenzie Bowell, sent to the Australasian colonies to study the possibility of increasing their mutual trade, returned to Canada empty-handed and disillusioned with the Australians. "The parties," he said bitterly, "with whom we have been so long estranged can scarcely be brought into a close relationship at a moment's notice."[2] That relationship has ranged from rivalry to resentment to partnership, and even to indifference. In the nineteenth century, within the British Empire shared legal and political institutions, a common ethnic composition, and similar problems of settlement, development, and nation-building, at once created similarities and rivalries between the two. In the formal organizations of the Empire, statesmen from both countries worked together and against each other in a process that helped to define and clarify national interests and goals. In the twentieth century, participation on the same side in wars, from the Boer to the Korean, and in the evolving British Empire produced a similar pattern of cooperation and competition.

This has not gone entirely unnoticed by historians and political scientists. John Hilliker and Greg Donaghy, two historians employed by Canada's Department of Foreign Affairs and International Trade, have completed short studies of Australian-Canadian relations, but Hilliker's piece is limited to a study of the years from 1939 to 1945, while Donaghy's publication covers more than 100 years of interaction in twenty-five pages.[3] On the whole, however, it is fair to say that scholars have been more concerned with comparisons than connections, and with the post-1945 period. Public policy, political structures and practices (federalism, the constitution), immigration, women, culture, education, legal systems, the environment, trade, the private sector, intelligence communities, the military, and Native studies are some of the areas of comparison.[4] Several scholars have taken up one of the main themes of this volume: the comparison and relations of Canada and Australia as middle powers in international affairs. Annette Baker Fox was a pioneer in the comparative study of Australia and Canada as middle powers in the late 1970s. Richard A. Higgott, Andrew F. Cooper, and Kim Richard Nossal have since followed in her footsteps in their analyses of two self-proclaimed middle powers.[5] As with all good scholarship, this work raised new questions and pointed to other areas that might profitably be explored.

It occurred to the editors of this volume that there was much interesting work being done concerning both the intersections and the parallels between the two countries that could help to define further the development and nature of each. With the end of the overwhelming presence of the Cold War and its division of so much of the world into two armed camps, it was also a good moment to look at other, less dramatic relationships – such as the one between these two white dominions of the British Empire. While geography – and this was truer in the past than the present – made direct contact difficult and fitful, Australia and Canada were brought together by a common membership in the British Empire and later the British Commonwealth. In its great crises – the Boer War and the two World Wars – they fought side by side. They learned to deal with the British as much as with their enemies, and they worked together to make sure that dominion voices were heard in the making of imperial and then commonwealth policy. In peacetime, they worked with and against London on a whole range of issues, from international communications to defence and trade. During the Cold War, the two countries shared a common perception of the threat from the Soviet Union and its allies, although they frequently differed on how to contain it. Even today, in the post-Cold War world, Australia and Canada remain linked by a shared past and by a common set of values.

That said, there are as many differences as similarities, separate paths taken as well as shared. An important objective of this collection, therefore, is to use the history of one country to better understand that of the other. We deprive ourselves of useful examples and important questions if we treat each country as unique.[6] In the past few years, there has been a real increase in comparative studies in such fields as British Empire and Commonwealth history.[7] Too often, in our opinion, scholars seeking to understand their respective national histories and developments have tended to focus on one country alone. This has led to an intellectual parochialism, as well as a tendency to overlook the ways in which developments in one country were affected by those in another. The comparative approach is shedding new light on the national histories of both countries and stimulating new questions and new research. Discussions of nationalism have usually focused on the crown colonies and their interplay with Britain, while the dominions have been overlooked. This oversight has led to the neglect of an important and complex aspect of the dominions' histories, from the colonial experience to independence, and has perpetuated ignorance of the impact of their national awakenings on the international relations of the twentieth century.

While all of the contributors have sought to bring out the comparisons between the two countries, we have not tried to force these. Nor have we tried to make more of the relationship than the evidence will bear. And, in cases where one side of the story has already been told, we have not rehashed that side at length. In Wayne Reynold's chapter on Australian nuclear policies and ambitions, the Canadian side has been brought as example and the reader has been referred to the excellent literature that already exists.

Our first section deals with nation-building. Margaret MacMillan and Francine McKenzie look at the evolution in both countries toward nationhood within the British Empire, the former in the period from 1900 to the end of the First World War, the latter from 1931 to 1945. Before 1914 Canadian and Australian statesmen met in London, generally at imperial conferences, where they clashed repeatedly over common imperial defence and foreign policies that Canadians did not want, largely for fear of antagonizing the United States, and the Australians did, for their own security against Germany and other potential enemies, possibly even the United States, in the Pacific. During the war, however, Canada and Australia found a common bond in criticizing the British management of the war. And at the Paris Peace Conference that followed, Sir Robert Borden, Canada's prime minister, worked with Billy Hughes, prime minister of Australia, to insist on separate dominion representation at the conference and on such bodies as the League of Nations. There were tensions, too; Borden deplored the Australian prime minister's antagonism to the United States.

The tensions present at the peace talks in 1919 were magnified in the interwar years. The two dominions differed on the Anglo-Japanese naval pact: the Canadians opposed its extension for fear of alienating the United States, while the Australians preferred to see its continuance as a way, in part, of keeping Japan under control. More significantly, as McKenzie points out, they differed on their respective relationships with the British Empire. While William Lyon Mackenzie King – the Canadian prime minister for much of that period – took the opportunity to stake out an independent role for Canada in foreign affairs, the Australians remained convinced that their future lay within a strong British Empire. King so resolutely opposed attempts to centralize imperial military and foreign policies that Richard Casey, one of Australia's earliest diplomats and later foreign minister, bitterly commented that "surely no one man can claim credit for having done as much as Mackenzie King to damage what remains in these autonomous days of the fabric of the British Empire. His efforts to make political capital out of his domestic nationalism are analogous to a vandal who pulls down a castle in order to build a cottage."[8] In the years after the Statute of Westminster of 1931, which granted the dominions the right to control their domestic and foreign affairs, the differences deepened. Australians and Canadians were taking different paths as they sought to reconcile their colonial pasts with their independent futures in the years between 1931 and 1945. Australia refused to ratify the Statute of Westminster; Canada, in contrast, welcomed it.

The two nations continued to channel most of their diplomatic relations through London. Though they managed, with some difficulty, to arrange trade agreements after 1918, Canadian attempts – first in 1935 and then 1937-8 – to interest Australia in diplomatic exchanges foundered. Prime Minister Joseph Lyons scotched the first approach, which he expected would be a costly and unnecessary indulgence. Mackenzie King blocked the second attempt, although his Australian counterparts were far from disappointed. In 1939 they did finally agree to exchange high commissioners, but the earlier record of failures left a residue of bitterness.

Where McKenzie and MacMillan look at the relations between Canada and Australia and between the dominions and Britain, Peter Russell looks inward, at the often-troubled relationship between settler societies and Native peoples. In the early period of settlement there was a significant difference between Australia and Canada. Where Australia was treated as a *terra nullius* – a land of no one – in which settlement could proceed without any recognition of Aboriginal rights, in British North America, the British recognized Native nations and would not permit settlement on Native lands that had not been ceded by treaty to the crown. Despite this difference in their colonial beginnings, the treatment of Native peoples in the two countries converged as they became modern, self-governing democracies. In the 1960s increased Native political awareness and mobilization helped to produce recognition of rights. Here the Canadian precedents have been a major influence on Australia.

The role of Australia and Canada as rivals, allies, and models is developed further in the second part of the book. David MacKenzie uses commercial aviation as a case study, which shows how countries facing similar challenges of geography and resources took similar measures that came out, however, to different ends. Both had state-run airlines that were quick to enter the international field; both participated in Commonwealth aviation arrangements before and after the Second World War; and both nations were determined not to be left behind in the development of civil aviation. Where they differed was in their attitudes to the Empire and to the United States. While Australia supported the idea of air links within the Empire in the 1930s, Canada saw itself as a key crossroads between the Empire and the United States. The war and the rise of the United States to superpower status brought fresh differences. The Australians, for example, looked to strong international regulations over aviation as a way of controlling the United States, while the Canadians believed they could hold their own.

Galen Perras looks at relations between the two countries over a wide range of issues during the Second World War. In a period of rapid change, Canada and Australia had more sustained contact and cooperation than ever before. As he indicates, however, this did not always go smoothly. The formal agreement in September 1939 to exchange high commissioners did not entirely overcome the mutual suspicions left over from previous decades. In 1942 there was a serious crisis when the Canadian high commissioner, Major General Victor Odlum, acting without authority, indicated to Australia that Canada would send a division there to help ward off a Japanese advance, only to have the Canadian government decline to do so. His successor, T.C. Davis, summed up his impressions of his hosts in a scathing assessment; while he found the Australians to be "a kindly friendly people," they had definitely "lived too long in solitary seclusion and security." They were, he believed, spoilt, undisciplined, lazy, and deluded.[9]

Such disturbances should not conceal the fact that, on balance, the two countries had considerable respect for each other. As they had done in the past, they continued to use the other as an example. When it came to acquiring the technology and capacity to manufacture nuclear deterrent weapons, Australia consciously set out to attain the same status that Canada had in the 1950s, as Wayne Reynolds describes in his chapter. Under the agreements reached at the Quebec Conference in 1943, Canada was allowed a limited participation in the Manhattan Project to build the American atomic bomb. When, at the end of the Second World War, it became clear to the British that the United States was not going to fulfil its commitments to share the technology, the British government decided to push ahead with its own bomb. The Australian government saw an opportunity to fill a role as a supplier of uranium, like that of Canada's with the United States.

Involvement in the Cold War brought with it the unwanted attentions of Soviet intelligence. Both Australia and Canada had major spy scandals with the defections of Vladimir Petrov and Igor Gouzenko. The revelations about Soviet spying in both countries had similar aftershocks, but in Australia there was far more condemnation of Soviet activities and the reactions of bodies responsible for postwar intelligence were different. Frank Cain explores the reasons for that difference, from the previous relations of each country to the Soviet Union to the role of American intelligence.

The early years of the Cold War also saw a rapid increase in decolonization, and Christopher Waters examines the significance of this for Canada and Australia. The emergence of the new nations of Asia presented new challenges to nations on the periphery of the Pacific, such as Australia and Canada. The decolonization process was marked by wars – in Malaya, for example, and French Indochina – and by international disputes, and was complicated, inevitably, by the Cold War itself. While Australia was much more directly involved in the consequences of decolonization in Asia, Canada was also involved, as peacekeeper and, in the case of Indochina, as a member of the International Control Commission. Australian and Canadian policy makers often consulted and exchanged views on these issues, and there are particularly interesting and important exchanges between their foreign ministers, Richard Casey and Lester Pearson.

Postwar relations did not always run smoothly. In the early years of the peace, Pearson clashed frequently with the abrasive Australian minister of external affairs, Herbert Evatt. The conflict was not just of personality, as Andrew Cooper demonstrates. Both countries were attempting to become leaders of an emerging constellation of middle powers after the Second World War. More recently Canada and Australia have bickered openly over the form and scope of the Cairns Group, which brings together agricultural producers, and Asia Pacific Economic Cooperation (APEC). While both countries have been prominent and active players in the creation and maintenance of the international trade system, particularly the General Agreement on Tariffs and Trade (GATT) and its successor, the World Trade Organization (WTO), self-interest, as Ann Capling and Kim Nossal explain, has led them on at least two occasions since 1945 to direct confrontation. During the negotiations over the International Trade Organization immediately after the war, Canada enthusiastically supported the American push for multilateral trade, while Australia, which still held to imperial preference and industrial protection, did not. The second occasion is the case of the often-bitter divergence that occurred some four decades later, when the two countries found themselves engaged in an effort to promote the liberalization of agricultural trade. Both were members of the Group of Fair Traders in Agriculture, or Cairns Group, which was formed in 1986 as the result of an Australian initiative. Canada infuriated Australia and the other members of the Group by its highly selective approach to freer trade in agricultural products. The Canadians wanted simultaneously to protect certain sectors and liberalize others.

Again, as Cooper reminds us, there is another side to the picture. The Canada-Australia diplomatic relationship is marked by multiple channels and contacts. In a variety of ways, this relationship has taken on a formal status, featuring a regular schedule of meetings at the ministerial level; top-level bureaucratic contacts around the ASEAN Regional Forum and a host of other organizations; and the formal Canada-Australia Consular Sharing Agreement. And Canadians and Australians, whether officials or ordinary citizens, tend to get on with each other. The two countries exchange considerable numbers of officials, share information, and operate together in informal working groups.

This book is a small example of that sort of cooperation. When we contacted scholars in Australia and Canada about this project, we found a welcome interest in bringing together a book that explores the relationship both over time and in a variety of areas, from the diplomatic to the legal. Considering the distances involved, we have also been pleasantly surprised at how many of us have managed to meet, often in the old imperial capital of London, sometimes in the new one of Washington, and in our own countries. Electronic mail has been invaluable for keeping us in touch and for exchanging views. The result of our collaboration is something we hope will, in its turn, lead to further research.

Notes

1 Gérard Bouchard, *Genèse des nations et cultures du Nouveau Monde* (Montreal: Boréal, 2000), 24-5, 230-7, 314-20.
2 Mackenzie Bowell, quoted in Greg Donaghy, *Parallel Paths: Canadian-Australian Relations since the 1890s* (Ottawa: Department of Foreign Affairs and International Trade, 1995), 1.
3 J.F. Hilliker, "Distant Ally: Canadian Relations with Australia during the Second World War," *Journal of Imperial and Commonwealth History* 13, 1 (1984): 46-67; Donaghy, *Parallel Paths*.
4 See, for instance, Malcolm Alexander and Brian Galligan, eds., *Comparative Political Studies: Australia and Canada* (Melbourne: Pitman, 1992); and R.L. Matthews, ed., *Public Policies in Two Federal Countries: Canada and Australia* (Canberra: Australian National University, 1982); Freda Hawkins, *Critical Years in Immigration: Canada and Australia Compared* (Montreal and Kingston: McGill-Queen's University Press, 1989).
5 Annette Baker Fox, *The Politics of Attraction: Four Middle Powers and the United States* (New York: Columbia University Press, 1977); Fox, "The Range of Choice for Middle Powers: Australia and Canada Compared," *Australian Journal of Politics and History* 26 (1980): 193-203; Andrew F. Cooper, Richard A. Higgott, and Kim Richard Nossal, *Relocating Middle Powers: Australia and Canada in a Changing World* (Vancouver: UBC Press, 1993); Andrew F. Cooper, *In between Countries: Australia, Canada, and the Search for Order in Agricultural Trade* (Montreal and Kingston: McGill-Queen's University Press, 1997); and Kim Richard Nossal, *Rain Dancing: Sanctions in Canadian and Australian Foreign Policy* (Toronto: University of Toronto Press, 1994).
6 On this point, see Bouchard, *Genèse des nations,* 12-13.
7 Marc Bloch pioneered the comparative method in an article published in 1928 in *Revue de synthèse historique:* "Pour une histoire comparée des sociétés européennes." We have used J.E. Anderson's translation of this article in Marc Bloch, *Land and Work in Medieval Europe: Selected Papers* (New York: Harper and Row, 1969), 44-81. He regarded the use of the comparative method, "easy to manipulate and yielding positive results," as a matter of pressing urgency for historians. Bloch identified two basic applications of this method: to seek universal explanations as well as "the parallel study of societies," the goal of which is to identify similarities and differences. In this volume, the contributors adopt the second approach to comparison: to examine two subjects side by side for the purpose of better understanding one or both individually.
8 R.G. Casey to S.M. Bruce, 26 April 1928, in *My Dear P.M.: R.G. Casey's Letters to S.M. Bruce 1924-1929,* ed. W.J. Hudson and Jane North (Canberra: Australian Government Publishing Service, 1980), 337.
9 T.C. Davis to N.A. Robertson, 27 December 1945, Saskatchewan Provincial Archives, James G. Gardiner Papers, reel 4210, 41887-90.

Part 1:
Decolonization and Nation Building

This study of the relations between and comparative development of Canada and Australia in the twentieth century begins by examining their evolution from colonies to nations. Their common pasts as dependencies in the British Empire largely shaped the institutions, government, cultures, and values that defined Canada and Australia. Because they were derivative societies, becoming recognizable as Canada and Australia rather than as British appendages was a drawn-out process. It also lagged far behind the nineteenth-century phenomenon of nationalism in Europe; Canada and Australia would only experience it between the two world wars. Control over external policy was the essential precondition to establishing themselves as individual and independent nations. It was the missing ingredient in their self-governance. Once Ottawa and Canberra established their authority over foreign policy and external relations, they transcended their colonial origins. The history of the independence of the two dominions belongs to a larger literature on decolonization, a literature that tends to overlook the colonies of settlement. However, the story of decolonization does not end in 1945. There is a further twist because both nations contained indigenous nations within their borders. Relations with the Aboriginal peoples date to the earliest days of the British Empire. With the independence of the dominions, their governments had to contend with the reality that they were colonizers as well as colonized. Thus the lens must be turned in to complete a study of decolonization within the dominions. In so doing, this section sketches the picture that Canada and Australia held up to the rest of the world and also fills in the backdrop, highlighting the detail and shading without which one has only a line drawing.

1

Sibling Rivalry: Australia and Canada from the Boer War to the Great War
Margaret MacMillan

"The Dominions are as jealous of each other as cats," said Sir Maurice Hankey, who, as secretary to the War Cabinet, was in a good position to see for himself.[1] And it is true that Australia and Canada were jostling for position at the Paris Peace Conference of 1919: against each other, the other dominions, the British, and the other powers. But they also worked with each other, if uneasily at times. Both countries were testing themselves at the largest, most stellar, and most uninterrupted international negotiation in memory. The peace conference allowed them to taste autonomy on the world stage, not something that could entirely be forgotten back in Sydney or Ottawa.

The experts in 1919 were divided on what the future held. Hankey – in Paris as secretary to the British Empire Delegation and then to the peace conference – and his fellow empire enthusiasts thought that the Imperial War Cabinet (the British war cabinet plus representatives from the dominions and India), which had transformed itself into the British Empire Delegation, was a major step toward an imperial cabinet and a unified Empire. Others – with gloom or enthusiasm, depending on their viewpoints – thought that the Empire had gone down the road to disintegration. Colonel Edward House, President Woodrow Wilson's closest adviser, was confident that the dominions and India were gone. And among them were the Canadians who – one is tempted to say typically – thought that it was possible to reconcile the two extremes. The Empire was becoming a United British Commonwealth, with strong and independent nations that would somehow add up to a strong and united supranational unit.

Australia, Canada, and South Africa in particular had moved a considerable way to self-government, and it was expected that India would follow in a generation or two. Moreover, dominion statesmen had grown accustomed during the war to being consulted, and heard, on matters of the highest importance. Because we now know how the story turned out, we should not assume from this that the Empire was bound to disappear. As

Francine McKenzie's chapter makes clear, even the Statute of Westminster, a decade later – often seen as the culmination of an inexorable process – is rather "an ambiguous and tentative step on the road to independence." At the time of the Paris Peace Conference, the British Empire *was* changing, but in directions that were not yet clear. That is equally true of Australia and Canada. In both countries the war had brought a heightened sense of national identity. What that meant still had to be worked out. Were Australians and Canadians still fundamentally British with an overlay of local characteristics? Were they a hybrid from British stock? Or were they something new? It would be a mistake to assume that the identity of either country had in any way gelled in 1919, and while Canadians saw themselves as a nation by the mid-1930s, Australians, so Francine McKenzie argues in her chapter, did not fully accept that status until after the Second World War.

There are clearly many factors that influence the development of national identities, and many types of identities. Benedict Anderson has introduced the useful concept of the "imagined community": any community that is larger than an individual can know directly, but that has a vitality and impact because its members assume its existence and act in accordance with what they perceive to be shared values and goals.[2] Nations such as Australia and Canada are imagined communities. Particularly in the form that became popular in the nineteenth century, they involve more than a sense of shared geography, culture, or past. They also assume a state, a state that operates as an independent agent in the world.

A small piece of the Canadian or the Australian national identity was fitted in when the members of those nations began to think of themselves as nation-states. The experience of the war and the subsequent participation in the peace negotiations contributed significantly to the development of national identities. In Paris, for six months Sir Robert Borden and Billy Hughes talked as equals, in status if not in power, to leaders of other countries; they and the other members of their delegations served on the committees and commissions that were settling the shape of the world. The British dominions had separate votes and all signed the Treaty of Versailles (and ratified it subsequently in their parliaments). All of this helped to create an assumption that there was an Australia, and there was a Canada, and that there would continue to be so.

The peace conference was important in the evolution of both countries because it forced them to define and to further their national interests. It was clear that they could not take for granted that Britain would do so. In Paris, Canada and Australia frequently worked together to pressure the British. They also opposed each other, on the League of Nations or mandates for the Pacific islands. In both cases, collaboration or confrontation, they were defining their roles as independent states. In the words of Loring Christie,

Canada's chief diplomat in Paris, who wrote a long and thoughtful memorandum on the subject, Canada had become an "international person" by the end of the peace conference. But, as he himself concluded, what that would lead to was unclear.

At the same time, paradoxically, many Australians and Canadians saw the experiences of Paris as strengthening the British Empire, so that it was too soon to talk of a clear Canadian or Australian national identity. The identity of Australians and Canadians as members of the great British Empire still exerted a formidable pull. The conflict between the imperial and the national identities – for that is what it eventually became – was not yet acute. For some time to come, those two identities were going to exist side by side. And we should remember that there were other potential identities – for Australia as the centre of a South Pacific federation, perhaps, for Canada as part of a great English-speaking union – still in people's minds.

Canada and Australia, whose evolution has been described as "parallel paths,"[3] certainly did not sail serenely toward full nationhood. Both had moved toward federation with considerable reservations. And in both there were mixed feelings of admiration and resentment toward Britain; admiration because Britain was so powerful, resentment because the British sometimes did not seem to take their concerns seriously. On the other hand, the presence of a strong United States, in the case of Canada, and an aggressively imperialistic Germany before 1914 and a potentially hostile Japan after 1919 in the case of Australia, made them appreciate the shelter of the British Empire. Even conducting foreign relations, let alone defence, was a formidable task for both dominions. They had small populations and an even smaller pool of qualified civil servants on which to draw. In the years before the war, both experienced considerable difficulty in getting good men to serve as their high commissioners in London. Only Australia and Canada even had departments of external affairs, and in 1916 Hughes abolished his department and simply ran foreign affairs out of his own office. (It was not reconstituted until 1936, and, for the most part, the Australians seem to have been content to let the British handle their external relations.)

The two peoples initially had little direct contact. Family ties, or at least those of shared background, could not count for much when communications were so slow and, in any case, tended to go through Britain. There was a Canadian-Australian steamship line running from the West Coast of Canada to New South Wales (the journey took over a month), and the first cable across the Pacific was opened by 1900. Cables were enormously expensive, which of course affected such things as newspaper reporting. Trade was insignificant. In 1911, for example, according to the Board of Trade, Canada had virtually no imports directly from its sister dominions. It exported small amounts of such commodities as preserved fish and lumber.[4] Canadian canned salmon and Australian dried apricots can scarcely have made much of an impact on the public consciousness.[5] And yet the idea of each other was present, in school atlases and stories of Empire. Canada was also important to Australia as an elder sister: sometimes as model or as path-breaker, sometimes as an example to be avoided. In the long-drawn-out debates over federalism in Australia, Canada was frequently used as an example.[6] Canada had had a high commissioner in London since 1879. In their authoritative commentary on the new federal constitution, Sir Robert Garran and Sir John Quick argued that Australia should do likewise.[7]

The Boer War

The Boer War marked a step toward a national consciousness for both countries. Joseph Chamberlain may have seen the Boer War as evidence that the bonds of Empire were drawing tighter, but, in fact, it can be seen in another way – as the occasion on which the colonials became aware of their own strengths and their own importance to Britain. As Richard Jebb noticed on a visit to Australia, "Some of the most wholehearted supporters of the sending of contingents were nationalists who knew that the undertaking of responsibility would develop national self-respect, and the respect of the authorities in London for Australian nationhood."[8] Newspaper reports, patriotic rallies, and, after the war ended, lectures, memoirs, war memorials, all helped to build up the self-confidence of Canadians, Australians, and New Zealanders. The heroic sons of Britain had rallied to its defence: "A nation is never a nation / Worthy of pride or place," boasted an Australian poet, "Till the mothers have sent their firstborn / To look death in the field in the face."[9] They had shown the Germans, among others, that the British would stand firm against aggression. They had also, at least to their own satisfaction, shown that the transplanted stock flourished in its new soil. Canadian troops were "grim, solid men as straight as poplars," stronger in fact than their British counterparts.[10] Australians had known that even before the war; after all, they had trounced the British in cricket shortly before the conflict began.[11] Indeed, it became apparent that the British also had problems in running a war. Commentaries in the colonies tended to stress British bungling and incompetence, a mild foretaste of what was to be said in the Great War.[12]

Changes within the British Empire and improved communications before 1914 provided a more sustained contact between the two dominions, at least at the élite level. From 1887 onward, colonial and then imperial conferences, as well as a Committee of Imperial Defence, met in London, providing opportunities for colonial statesmen to meet each other, usually for the first time. There was a growing tendency on the part of dominion statesmen to assert themselves. Being consulted, formally, by the British gave them a sense of importance. It also brought out into the open some of the issues that divided them, from each other and from Britain. What could be more natural and convenient than that they should occasionally meet to discuss matters of common interest before they met with the British, or communicate directly with each other without bothering to go through the Colonial Office. In 1901, for example, Wilfrid Laurier, to the annoyance of the Colonial Office, arranged a meeting with the premiers of Australia and New Zealand to discuss matters of common economic interest.[13]

British imperialists hoped to build on the conferences to bind the Empire more tightly together – perhaps through a permanent imperial council or, more modestly, with an imperial secretariat. Here the Canadian and Australian leaders had one of their first clashes. In 1907, Chamberlain and the Australian prime minister, Alfred Deakin – who was a firm advocate of a centralized body to set and implement imperial policy – tried to get an imperial secretariat through the Colonial Conference. Deakin went to his grave convinced that, before the conference met, Winston Churchill had scooped up Canada's Laurier as he arrived in London by train. While Deakin and Starr Jameson of the Cape Colony were waiting (inexplicably but perhaps symbolically at the wrong train station), Churchill was indoctrinating Laurier to oppose greater imperial unity, and Laurier in turn had led Louis Botha into error.[14] In fact, Laurier did not have the slightest intention of causing a political uproar in Canada, especially among French Canadians, who were understandably sensitive on the subject of the British Empire.

Dominion political leaders (such as Deakin and Laurier's Conservative successor, Borden) considered the British Empire to be on the leading edge of civilization and a model for future international relations. On the other hand, they also saw it, in a confused way, as a free association of powers. As Deakin wrote to Richard Jebb, a leading exponent of imperial ideas, "You have done more than anyone else to bring home the need for complete imperial decentralisation so as to secure the free play of all our self-governing powers ... In your next book you ought to preach the doctrine of recentralisation brought about by the consent of all those communities whose independent functions you have so admirably portrayed. We must have an Imperial Organisation."[15] Deakin pushed for an imperial secretariat, but he did so partly because he felt that the existing structure did not respond effectively to Australia's needs. Imperial efficiency was more immediately interesting than imperial unity; as he told the Australian parliament in 1907, there was "an absolute contrast in the problems and condition of the problems we are severally called upon to face."[16] On the whole, though, Australian political leaders – both before and after the First World War – accepted their relatively minor part in the Empire. The smallness of Australia's population and the realization that Australia depended on the British navy for its defences, as David MacKenzie points out elsewhere in this book, helped to keep the ties of Empire strong.

There can be no doubt that Borden, like Deakin, considered himself a British subject, but what he meant by that was another matter. Canadians – partly because geography put them next to a rising power, partly because it was clear that Britain would no longer defend Canada on land – had grown accustomed to thinking of their own security before the First World War. That comes across clearly in the great naval debate of 1910 over Canada's proposed contribution to imperial defence. As leader of the Opposition, Borden attacked Laurier for dismissing the German menace with "a wave of the hand and an eloquent phrase"[17] and said that Canadians stood ready to meet the challenge "with a heart no less firm than that with which our forefathers encountered the shock of the 'Invincible Armada.'"[18] In the same debate, though, he stressed the advantages of a naval contribution to imperial defence: "This would give to these dominions a voice in the control of war, because I thoroughly agree that if we are to take part in the permanent defence of this great empire we must have some control and some voice in such matters."[19] He also stressed that, in the decision on war itself, he expected the dominions to be consulted, as he argued they had been at the outbreak of the Boer War. When he visited England the following year to discuss defence, he was determined to make clear to the British that Canadian participation meant that Canada must have a voice in the shaping of imperial foreign policy.[20] Although the British gave no firm commitment, Borden professed himself satisfied: "No declaration I made was more enthusiastically and heartily received."[21] His behaviour, then, during the First World War was completely consistent. What had changed was the nature of the contribution and his assumptions about Canada's importance to the Empire. Both were bigger.

Nevertheless, before the Great War Australia and Canada were like adolescents: comfortable at home but grumbling at the mother country and threatening to leave one day. To paraphrase the joke current today in Canada about Quebec, they wanted to be independent inside a strong British Empire. And why should they give up what they had so recently acquired in the way of autonomy to a powerful federation? On the other hand, full independence was not yet tempting. As members of the British Empire, they were protected by the world's strongest navy and shared in the world's greatest power. Moreover, they had confidence in the ability of British statesmen to manage its affairs. That was about to change.

The First World War

The war had a huge psychological impact on dominion statesmen. Writings on the consequences of the First World War for colonialism have tended to concentrate on Asia and Africa and on the loss of prestige and moral authority the white masters suffered in the eyes of their black, brown, and yellow subjects. But the first-hand experience of British incompetence also shook the faith of the white subjects of the Empire that the imperial authorities were wiser and more far-seeing than they were. As Hughes of Australia put it with his usual exuberance,

> In the days before the red flood of war, the Dominion representatives had approached the portals of the Imperial Conference in the subdued and reverential spirit of worshippers entering a Buddhist temple, and ... listened to the representatives of Britain – urbane and graciously tolerant – in a mood little removed from that of devotees prostrate before its shrine. But since those far-off days there had been great changes. They, who had been children, were now grown up and had put off childish things. They were no longer impressed by lectures or flattered by being permitted to participate in ceremonious and arid debates.[22]

The Australian and Canadian governments followed a similar evolution, with growing skepticism about British leadership and an increasing irritation that they were not being informed, much less consulted. Borden complained frequently to London,[23] as did Hughes, who said that he got more information out of the newspapers than he did from the Colonial Office's secret newsletter. "The blasted Colonies want to know you know," he parodied the London officials. "We'll show 'em!"[24] By the mid-point of the war the dominions were well aware, too, of their own importance to the war effort. The dominions' and India's contributions to the British war effort were extraordinarily generous in terms of resources, war *matériel*, and manpower. Sixty thousand Canadians died and 59,000 Australians. (By comparison the United States, with a much larger population than either, lost 48,000 soldiers.) Vimy Ridge, Gallipoli, Delville Wood – these places were to become part of the fabric of nationhood. "We were content to be Colonials," according to one of the Canadians who fought at Vimy Ridge, but afterward "National spirit was born ... we were Canadians."[25] Dominion troops generally fought with their fellow countrymen, and as the war went on increasingly had their own officers and, after a period of improvisation and a certain amount of confusion, their own organizational structure.[26] Pressure for this came, not surprisingly, from the dominions themselves.[27] Indeed, the Australians used the Canadian example when arguing for their own army corps.[28] Moreover, the high commissioners of both dominions grew accustomed to consulting each other on military as well as other matters.[29]

In February 1916 Hughes passed through New Zealand and Canada on his way to London from Australia. He was invited – the first non-Canadian to be so – to sit in on the Privy Council. He and Borden discussed Pacific issues (Hughes urging Borden to establish a Pacific fleet to counter-balance Japan) and, inevitably, the conduct of the war and the long-term need for the dominions to have a voice in Empire foreign policy.[30] The two men liked each other (briefly) and thought each other's views sensible. That did not prevent a certain rivalry. When Hughes insisted on attending the 1916 inter-allied economic conference in Paris as a representative of Australia in 1916, in spite of H.H. Asquith's attempts to keep him away,[31] Canada hastily demanded that Sir George Foster, minister of trade and commerce, go as well. Foster saw his role as keeping Hughes under control, not the last time the British and Canadians would cooperate on that. As he confided to his diary on 15 June, "We are having our own time with Hughes, but are managing to keep him in fair bounds."[32]

Hughes did not manage to get to the Imperial War Cabinet and Conference of 1917 and, unreasonably, refused to send an Australian representative in his place. He came to regret this, and when the Imperial War Cabinet met again in 1918, made sure that he was there. He and Borden took the lead in pushing for a thorough investigation of the disastrous Flanders offensive of the previous summer.[33] In addition, the two men, along with Jan Smuts of South Africa, pushed for the right of dominion prime ministers to communicate directly with the British prime minister rather than going through the Colonial Office. Borden told David Lloyd George, "The idea of nationhood has developed wonderfully of late in my own Dominion; I believe the same is true of all the Dominions. Their Prime Ministers meet with British ministers on terms of equality around the Council Board."[34] Lloyd George agreed, over the plaintive objections of the Colonial Office, but in fact the change meant little at first, because he simply passed on most letters dealing with imperial matters to the Colonial Office.

By the time the war drew to an end, dominion leaders were speaking with a confidence they had not possessed in 1914. Where once they had politely requested, now they demanded. If they were not yet the equals of the British government, they had certainly moved a considerable way in that direction. Whereas Smuts of South Africa derived his status from his own personality rather than the importance of his country, Borden and Hughes were now speaking as leaders of important components of the British Empire, and of the winning side. When the Central Powers collapsed unexpectedly in the autumn of 1918, the European Allies met with an American delegation at Versailles in late October to agree on the terms of the armistice. This infuriated both Hughes and Borden, who felt that the dominions should have been consulted first. Hughes in particular also strongly objected to Wilson's fourteen points being accepted as the basis for peace negotiations.[35] He wrote to Lloyd George on 9 November that his cabinet was "surprised and indignant" at "a painful and serious breach of faith."[36] Shortly after his arrival in England, Borden visited Hankey "full of grievances and rather formidable," complaining among other things about the decision that had been taken to try the Kaiser.[37]

The Peace Conference

The dominion sense of what was due them and their feeling that the British were not taking them seriously enough in the preparations for the peace came to a head over the issue of representation at the Paris Peace Conference. When it became clear, at the meetings of the Imperial War Cabinet in late December, that the British had not considered allowing the dominions and India to attend in their own right, there was a strenuous debate. Lloyd George's suggestion that one dominion prime minister could stand in for all the rest foundered in the face of dominion *amour propre*, which was considerable. Borden, for example, refused to go to the opening plenary session of the peace conference in January 1919 because Sir William Lloyd, the prime minister of Newfoundland, was chosen to represent the British Empire as part of the British delegation.[38]

The real problem over representation, Borden wrote to his wife, was that the dominions' position had never been properly sorted out. Canada was "a nation that is not a nation. It is about time to alter it." And he noted, with a certain tone of pity, "The British Ministers are doing their best, but their best is not good enough."[39] To Hankey, he was threatening; if Canada did not have full representation at the peace conference there was nothing for it but for him "to pack his trunks, return to Canada, summon Parliament, and put the whole thing before them."[40] Borden and Hughes, and possibly Smuts, took the lead in pressuring Lloyd George, who was obliged to go to the other powers and insist that Canada, Australia, South Africa, and India have two delegates (no more, Hughes pointed out, than Belgium or Serbia), and New Zealand one to the full peace conference. On this issue, Hughes may in fact have been going against the wishes of his own cabinet. Sir Frederick Eggleston, one of the Australian delegation, claimed years later: "Immediately he arrived in Paris Borden agitated for a separate seat at the conference and began to work out a formula for a separate membership of the League and a separate signature of the peace Treaty. On this question Hughes ignored the resolution of his own cabinet and assisted the Canadians and the South Africans."[41] The British had to persuade their allies to accept separate representation for Australia and Canada and the other dominions and to accept that their own delegation would be the British Empire Delegation (and that it was known as that was a victory in itself), and that one of its five members would be chosen from a panel of dominion representatives.[42] Later on, both Hughes and Borden claimed that they had been responsible for getting the British to agree, contrary to their original position, that the dominions would also have separate representation.

In the struggle over representation, the dominion leaders, especially Borden and Hughes, had shown that they were prepared to be tough. They appealed to public opinion and warned of the unfortunate consequences in their own countries if their demands were denied.[43] The British were taken aback. Alfred Zimmern described the mood in the Foreign Office when news got out that not only did the dominions want representation but that they had views on such matters as the League of Nations: "It was very inconvenient. What was the Foreign Office to do?"[44] Harold Nicolson, a junior British diplomat, was pleasantly surprised at the reaction among Britain's allies: "this has been taken more calmly than we expected: people think that it takes us down a peg."[45]

Although the French thought that the British Empire Delegation was a sham, that the dominions and India were simply rather sophisticated puppets, in fact, it was more than that. The meetings of the Delegation – there were thirty-five meetings between 13 January and 10 June 1919 – were not simply information sessions in which the British kept their Empire happy. In that favourite phrase of diplomacy, there were frank and open exchanges of views. The British spoke quite freely of the difficulties they were encountering in negotiations with their allies, and the Empire delegates gave their views equally freely. In the course of the meetings, all the major subjects – from how to deal with Russia to the Covenant of the League of Nations to the peace terms for Germany – came up for what was often quite intense and even acrimonious discussion.[46]

And the weeks and months in Paris were important in another way: in accustoming the representatives from the different parts of the Empire to the idea that they were representing national units, that they did not have to funnel everything through the British. The dominion prime ministers sometimes met on an informal basis to discuss questions of mutual concern. On 5 February, for example, Borden called a meeting of the other dominion prime ministers on the issue of their signing the peace treaty with Germany. The meeting agreed that each dominion should give its own assent to the treaty.[47] Borden's relationship with Hughes, never warm, remained civil. They dined together and continued to work on matters of common interest. They agreed, for example, that they would coordinate their approach to diplomatic representation in Washington. The British expected that Australian and Canadian high commissioners would be attached to the British embassy. This was useful, as Borden explained to Hughes, in giving them a status greater than that of the representatives of, say, Liberia, but "Our chief concern would be to safeguard necessary independence of action and control if such a status were obtained." Hughes promised that Australia would not make any moves without consulting Canada.[48]

For the junior members, Paris gave time and opportunity to practise diplomacy and to test their own views against those from other parts of the Empire. A significant number knew each other directly or indirectly through the Round Table group (that band of Quixotes dedicated to bringing order and rationality to the British Empire). Lionel Curtis, Philip Kerr, and Lord Milner from the British delegation, Robert Garran and Eggleston from Australia, and Loring Christie from Canada had all been part of the Round Table before the war. And the physical arrangements for the British Empire Delegation meant that their members saw each other constantly, at meetings, meals, even weekly tea dances. Most lived in the Hotel Majestic, where the British had thoughtfully sacked all the French chefs and replaced them with their own.

It is clear from the minutes of the British Empire Delegation that the dominion delegates were quick to object to any attempt to diminish their status or limit their participation in the peace conference. At the Delegation meeting held on 23 January, there was a prolonged discussion of the representation of the dominions at the upcoming discussion in the Council of Ten on the disposition of the German colonies. Lloyd George reported that he had asked that the interested dominions – South Africa, Australia, and New Zealand – be allowed to attend the meeting. While Georges Clemenceau had agreed, he did not know what Wilson's position would be. Hughes at once interjected that "he did not quite follow this point as he thought it had been settled long ago that the Dominions should state their own case." He added that the dominion representatives understood that they were entitled to take part in the peace conference discussions. Borden pointed out that this was true of the formal procedure, but that the informal conversations going on in the Council of Ten were not subject to the same regulations. The difficulty, he went on, was that as far as the Council of Ten was concerned, the dominions would only be there by grace and not by right. "He was thinking, of course, of the impression created in the Dominions and particularly in Canada." While the discussion reached no conclusion, it did remind the British, yet again, that they were dealing with leaders who were answerable to their own parliaments and their own public opinions.[49]

The dominions and India did agree on one thing, and that was that they should be members not only of the League, but that they should also be eligible for election to its executive council. In addition, they wanted to adhere to the League and to the accompanying Labour Convention as individual states, not as part of the British Empire. The Americans had not intended to have dominion representation on the League Council (which was to be made up of the five great powers plus four representatives of other states that were members of the League). On the other hand, they do not seem to have worried about dominion representation in the League assembly. When the final shape of the League was settled that April, Borden met Wilson on 1 May and got his agreement to representation for the dominions in the League.[50] Clemenceau, Wilson, and Lloyd George solemnly signed a document that they interpreted the Covenant to read that representatives of the self-governing dominions might be selected or named as members of the League Council.[51]

The signing and ratification of the treaty with Germany brought a final demand by Australia, Canada, and the other dominions for recognition of their revised status. They had already insisted on being in the League on the same terms as the other smaller nations. They now made it quite clear that they wanted to sign the treaties as separate entities, not as subordinate parts of the British Empire. After a long and complicated legal dispute, the dominions, which had obtained orders in council from their own governments, signed the treaties on behalf of their own countries, although the British delegates signed for the Empire.[52] And a sort of face-saving unity was preserved when the King issued plenipotentiary powers to all the delegates. (Since none of the dominion representatives had their own seals, they hastily scoured the shops in Paris. Hughes wanted one with Hercules killing the lion, but was talked into something less tendentious.[53]) As Milner, the British Colonial Secretary, said with considerable truth, "The position of the Dominions as regards foreign policy is now a most anomalous one."[54]

Ratification brought further disputes. The Canadian government, which had taken the lead in the whole issue, announced to the Colonial Office at the end of June that it was going to submit the German treaty to parliament. That alarmed the British, who did not think it necessary or desirable and who were worried about the status of the treaty if there were too much delay. In the end the dominion parliaments ratified the treaty before France did, leaving the constitutional significance of their action unclear.[55] Milner found the whole issue intensely irritating: "Either our ratification binds the whole Empire or it does not." The insistence by Australia, Canada, and the other dominions on calling their own parliaments were "mere impotent exhibitions of the desire for an independence which, in this case, they have not really got."[56] For the dominions, ratification was yet another symbol of their changed status. When Hughes addressed the Australian parliament in September 1919 on the issue, he asserted "By this recognition Australia became a nation, and entered into a family of nations on a footing of equality. We had earned that, or rather, our soldiers had earned it for us."[57]

Questions of status, of parity, of what was owed, even perhaps of personal ambition, all played their part in the determination of the dominions to be heard in Paris. So, too, did their sense that they could not always trust the British to speak for them. Even before the war, it had often looked as though Britain put their interests second to its own. In the 1890s, when Canada had a dispute with the United States over Alaska's boundaries, the Canadians felt, with some reason, that the British government had been more concerned to improve relations with the United States than to further Canadian interests.[58] After 1902 the Anglo-Japanese naval alliance worried

Canada – where the government in its gloomiest moments saw itself fighting a war beside Japan against the United States[59] – as well as New Zealand and Australia, which also feared both Japanese power and Japanese immigration.[60] As Eggleston, a prominent Melbourne lawyer and a leading member of the Australian Round Table Movement, complained, "England is notoriously out of sympathy, and does not understand, our exclusion policy."[61]

While Canadians sympathized with the exclusion policy (after all, they had such policies of their own), they did not regard Japan as a significant military threat. For Canada, maintaining friendly relations with the United States, and between the United States and Britain, was increasingly important. In 1917 Borden told the Imperial War Cabinet that the United States and the British Empire together "could do more than anything else to maintain the peace of the world."[62] And he suggested to Lloyd George in 1918 that if the larger League of Nations did not work out, there might be one between "the two great English speaking commonwealths who share common ancestry, language and literature, who are inspired by like democratic ideals, who enjoy similar political institutions and whose united force is sufficient to ensure the peace of the world."[63]

In Paris, the Canadians saw themselves as the bridge between the two great powers. For example, there was a problem over the clause in the proposed Labour charter that dealt with the due and equitable treatment of foreign workers lawfully resident in countries. The Americans felt that it might violate states' rights; the British were afraid that if the Charter were not approved Bolshevism might spread among Europe's workers. Borden worked with Arthur Balfour and James Shotwell of the American delegation to produce a compromise.[64] When Australian intransigence on, for example, the disposition of Germany's colonies threatened to bring a breach between Britain and the United States, the Canadians were quick to offer themselves as mediators.

With perhaps an unreasoning faith that the British navy was prepared to protect them from not one but two major powers, the Australians, or at least their prime minister, chose to see the United States as almost as great a threat as Japan. (The Canadians cannot have appreciated Hughes's frequent references to those who blindly did the bidding of the United States.) Hughes told Lloyd George that "the great menace to the trade of the British Empire comes from the U.S.A.," that while the British Empire had poured out streams of blood and treasure the Americans had been busy making large profits.[65] At the peace conference he complained repeatedly that German shipping was being handed over to the United States in spite of Australia's greater need.[66] In any case, Hughes could not bear Wilson, whom he described as "the most self-centred of men."[67] He sneered at the League, calling it "Wilson's toy." Years later Hughes claimed that Wilson had snubbed him in

Washington when the Australians passed through on the way to the Imperial War Cabinet of 1918; accounts at the time record a fairly amiable meeting. Wilson, for his part, considered Hughes "a pestiferous varmint."[68]

Their relationship with the United States, and perhaps the personalities of their leaders, helped to determine the position of each country on such issues as the League and the peace settlement with Germany. Borden was for a peace of moderation: when he saw the terms proposed by the French before the peace conference opened he was horrified: "It is a most astonishing document, imposing conditions of the most rigorous character which would keep the German people under the allied nations as taskmasters for half a century ... Wilson will never stand for it, nor will I."[69] Hughes, who was friendly with Clemenceau, was outspoken in his hatred for Germany. As chairman of the committee that Lloyd George set up in November 1918 to establish British policy, Hughes went for blood. The bill for damages should be based on "justice" not what Germany could be expected to pay.[70] Foster, the Canadian delegation's economic expert who served on the committee, was scathing: "It was all guesswork and sentiment, and it is difficult to get evidence of Germany's capacity, and we have no tabulation of Allied devastation bills." Hughes, he confided to his diary, "is a talking chairman, and the committee is weak. It is all personal impression and desire – evidence there is none. To make the Hun pay to utmost, whether it leads to a generation of occupancy and direction, or not, and forgetful of the results otherwise."[71]

During the peace conference itself, Hughes gave strong support to the French demand for stiff reparations. As Hughes continued to hold out for a high sum, Lloyd George grew increasingly restless. By the end of March he was trying to get agreement on the more moderate demands outlined in his Fontainebleau Memorandum. That led to acrimonious and prolonged discussions in the meetings of the British Empire Delegation, as Hughes in particular refused to accept that the costs of the war would no longer be covered. Lloyd George wrote a very stiff letter to Hughes, who was trying to argue that he would oppose the reparations clauses but sign the treaty. "I quite understand your attitude. It is a very well known one. It is generally called 'heads I win, and tails you lose' which means that you get the full benefit from the arrangement we have painfully elaborated in compensation and especially in pensions, whereas your comrades in the Dominions, in Great Britain and in France get all the abuse."[72]

The Canadians by and large shared the British attitude that Hughes was an irritating man who threatened to disrupt the crucial relationship with the United States. Borden had long since recovered from his first favourable impression. On the train that carried much of the British Empire Delegation to Paris in January 1919, Borden and Lloyd George chatted about how to keep Hughes under control. Borden suggested that the dominion prime ministers might collectively be able to do something.[73] Temperament played a role, too. Where Hughes was volatile, frequently outrageous, determinedly informal, Borden was careful, methodical, and formal except with those closest to him. Borden, too, was always conscious of his position as leader of the senior dominion. While he was prepared, as a pragmatist, to work with Australia on areas where Australian and Canadian interests coincided, he also had a duty to the British Empire and its interests. The British duly appreciated this. Milner wrote approvingly to the Duke of Devonshire, the governor general in Canada, "Borden is very useful here. He is the only one of the Dominion P.M.'s, who, without ceasing to be a good Canadian, is capable of taking the wider view and whose judgement and influence are really useful on Imperial and International questions. He is not a showy man, but he is a man of weight. Not a provincial, as most of the Dominion Ministers still, almost inevitably are."[74] Borden no doubt would have agreed. He was never in any doubt about his own importance. When a British historian dared to leave him out of a history of the peace conference, he was furious. "I think I may safely claim that no Prime Minister of any British Dominion took more conspicuous or important a part in the work of the peace conference than I did."[75] Other leaders had given at best passive support to Canada's struggle to get due recognition for the "nationhood" of the dominions.

The proceedings in Paris served to clarify national interests for the dominions, both in relation to the British and each other. Moreover, they allowed plenty of opportunities for Hughes to promote Australia's interests and for Borden to act as mediator. For Australia, the chief menace to national security, now that Germany had gone from the Pacific, was Japan. That influenced Hughes's opposition to the Japanese desire to get a phrase in the Covenant of the League of Nations outlawing discrimination on racial grounds (the so-called "racial equality clause") and his determination to hang on to the Pacific islands, including the key territory of New Guinea, which Australia had taken from the Germans. While some of his advisers in Paris and in his own cabinet had cold feet about Hughes's intransigence,[76] it played well in Australia.[77]

On both issues, the British, against their own interests, were obliged to confront Japan. In the case of the islands, they also found themselves confronting the United States, which had come into the war on a policy of no annexations. The Canadians hastened to act as mediators. They thought Hughes was being unnecessarily confrontational on the racial equality clause. They also felt that he was exaggerating its significance when he claimed that its insertion in the League Covenant would mean that Australia would no longer be able to limit immigrants from Asia. After all, as Borden cabled back to Canada, immigration and naturalization would still be domestic concerns and, if the League should be foolish enough to try and force changes to immigration policies, Britain and the United States would veto such action.[78] Borden himself acted as a go-between in the negotiations at the end of March 1919, which tried unsuccessfully to come up with a formula that would suit both the Japanese and the Australians. On 25 March 1919, on the British suggestion, the Japanese delegates met the British Empire delegates and Borden came up with a compromise that the Japanese accepted. Hughes, whom the Japanese regarded as a peasant, rejected it. A second attempt a few days later, with Borden again acting as mediator, also failed.[79] A copy of the words the Japanese wanted – to the effect that the League Covenant recognize the principle of equality of nations and the just treatment of their nationals and that made no reference to immigration – provoked a scribbled comment from Hughes: "The Japanese wish to insert the above amendment in the Preamble. It may be *all right*. But sooner than agree to it I would walk into the Seine – or the Folies Bergères – with my clothes off."[80]

The disposition of Germany's colonies caused the most trouble within the British Empire Delegation; the matter also showed a fundamental division between the British, the French, the Italians, and Japanese on the one hand and the Americans on the other. The former wanted to hang on to what they saw as legitimate spoils of war. The Americans, of course, had come into the war with a policy against annexation. And yet again the Canadians were caught uneasily in the middle. The Canadian view also reflected their stated stance of having nothing to gain from the peace settlements. There was perhaps an element of hypocrisy in this, because the Canadian delegates from time to time toyed with the idea of claiming the French islands of St. Pierre and Miquelon or possibly swapping British Honduras for the Alaska panhandle.[81]

The Pacific islands came up for discussion on 24 January in the Council of Ten. Clemenceau, in the chair, invited Lloyd George to bring in his cannibals, Billy Hughes and Vincent Massey.[82] This was to be running joke at the conference. Hughes apparently reassured Wilson, on freedom for missionaries in New Guinea, "There are many days when the poor devils do not get half enough missionaries to eat."[83] Hughes's claim of outright annexation of the islands was based on defence – they were "as necessary to Australia as water to a city" and on Australia's payment in the war – the 90,000 casualties, the 60,000 killed, the war debt of £300 million. "Australia did not wish to be left to stagger under this load and not to feel safe."[84] (The Australians had also considered using the argument that the locals were welcoming them with open arms after the horrors of German rule, but when the Australian government carried out some inquiries in New Guinea, it found that the inhabitants had liked the German officials, who generally respected their customs.[85])

The French, who were as cynical about the League as Hughes, were sympathetic. Within the British Empire Delegation, opinion was divided, with Canada opposing annexation and New Zealand and South Africa, who had demands of their own, supporting Australia, at least initially. On 22 January Borden had talked to Woodrow Wilson, who of course, shared the Canadian view. As Borden reported to his diary, "Says world would abhor annexations and in interest of B.Emp. Hopes they will not insist and agreed with me that good relations between B.E. and U.S. best asset either c'd have."[86] Both the Canadians and the British were anxious to avoid confrontation with the United States and were therefore eager to find some face-saving compromise in the form of mandates that would ostensibly be under the control of the League of Nations. House thought that the other dominion leaders, apart from Hughes, would not stand for outright annexation. Wilson, for his part, dug in and threatened to take the whole issue to the public.[87] The 24 January meeting was followed by a series of meetings behind the scenes, involving, as Hankey put it "an infinity of delicate negotiations."[88] The compromise, worked out by House and Smuts, was to have three sorts of mandates: A, for nations nearly ready to run their own affairs; B, where the mandatory power would run them; and C (which was really annexation under another name), where the mandatory would administer the territory as part of its own, subject only to certain restrictions on the sale of alcohol and firearms.

The pressure on Hughes increased. On 29 January, there was a meeting of the British Empire Delegation, which, Borden told his diary primly, produced a "pretty warm scene."[89] Lloyd George produced the deal that had been agreed upon with House; Hughes, fighting "like a weasel,"[90] quibbled over every point until Lloyd George finally lost his temper and told him that he had been arguing his case with the United States for three days but that he did not intend to quarrel with the Americans over the Solomon Islands.[91] (That remark does not appear in the official record.) Borden supported Lloyd George. Whatever enthusiasm he had once had for his fellow dominion leader had long since evaporated: "He has very little vision beyond his own personal interests."[92]

On 30 January, there was "a first-class row." According to Lloyd George, Wilson delivered a rambling and muddled criticism of the proposed British compromise, and was noticeably rude to Hughes. "Mr Hughes was the last man I should have chosen to handle in that way."[93] Wilson ended by demanding of Hughes, "Am I to understand that if the whole civilised world asks Australia to agree to a mandate in respect of these islands, Australia is prepared still to defy the appeal of the whole civilised world? ... That's about the size of it, President Wilson."[94] Although the deal ultimately went through, it left a residue of bad feelings in the British Empire Delegation. As Philip

Kerr, Lloyd George's private secretary, complained to Milner, "the suggestion has been put out that the Prime Minister has been sacrificing the vital interests of the Dominions for the sake of the beaux yeux of America, whereas the fact is that he has fought their battles from start to finish subject only to putting pressure on them to go as far as they can in accordance with the Imperial Cabinet resolution to accept the mandatory principle and not break up the peace conference altogether." "Needless to say," Kerr added, "old Clemenceau, who hates the mandatory idea, entrenched himself behind Hughes, & egged him on!"[95] Borden went off to see House to commiserate. Hughes, they agreed, was as much a problem for the Americans as for the British Empire Delegation.[96]

The most hectic part of the Paris Peace Conference ended in June 1919 with the signing of the Treaty of Versailles with Germany. Borden had already left, leaving behind a smaller Canadian delegation. Hughes went immediately to London after he signed the treaty and headed back to Australia, which he had not seen for over a year. The governor general, Sir Ronald Munro-Ferguson, reported "Everywhere he is being received with the greatest enthusiasm and soldiers have acclaimed him as their Man, dressed him in Diggers hats, wrapped him in flags and rushed him around shoulder high." Back on the other side of the world, Milner took a dim view of the pretensions of the dominions to play an independent role in international affairs. As he saw the Empire in the autumn of 1919, it was "the old system + circumlocution and eyewash."[97] He was not quite right.

Both countries had gained an assurance and experience that could not entirely be forgotten. Their leaders had sat at the same tables as the world's statesmen, shaping the peace. Is it assuming too much, then, to argue that what happened in Paris mattered then or later to the other sides of the world? It is true that only a few people from the dominions experienced the heady atmosphere of Paris directly: the Canadians had a delegation of approximately twenty-five (if one counts the secretaries), the Australians slightly less. But there were reporters, cables, wire services, and newspapers. Dominion newspapers had become accustomed to carrying extensive foreign news during the war and the habit persisted, at least in the years immediately after 1918. The Australian press, for example, had the United Cable Service in London run by Keith Murdoch. And ratification of the Treaty of Versailles meant parliamentary debates. In other words, information and impressions about the evolving status of the country did spread downward and out, forming part of the basis for later full nationhood in both countries.

It is true that Australia did not seem concerned in the next decade to build on what had been achieved. That was a reflection, perhaps, of its relatively smaller size, the absence of an immediate threat (or a powerful neighbour), and its continuing confidence in the ability of the British Empire (and the British navy) to protect it. Canada, however, continued to move ahead to greater independence, although under Mackenzie King's direction this was by a circuitous and well-camouflaged route. In the early 1920s, Canada took little part in the European conferences and meetings that attempted to tie up the loose ends of the peace settlements. On the other hand, it made sure that it managed its relations with the United States. And in 1922, it demonstrated the limits of an imperial foreign policy when it refused to answer Lloyd George's call for dominion support for British troops at Chanak in particular and for the British position in Turkey in general. That is a story that Francine McKenzie takes up in the next chapter.

Notes

1 Stephen Roskill, *Hankey: Man of Secrets*, vol. 2, *1919-1931* (London: Collins, 1972), 30.
2 Benedict Anderson, *Imagined Communities* (London and New York: Verso, 1991).
3 Greg Donaghy, *Parallel Paths: Canadian-Australian Relations since the 1890s* (Ottawa: Department of Foreign Affairs and International Trade, 1995).
4 "Colonial Statistics, 7212119" National Archives of Canada (hereinafter NAC), Laurier Papers, vol. 744, Prepared by the Board of Trade for the 1911 Conference.
5 See Donaghy, *Parallel Paths*, 2.
6 See, for example, Luke Trainor, *British Imperialism and Australian Nationalism* (Cambridge and Melbourne: Cambridge University Press, 1994), 8; K.A. MacKirdy, "Canadian and Australian Self-Interest, the American Fact, and the Development of the Commonwealth Idea," in, *Empire and Nations: Essays in Honour of Frederic H. Soward*, ed. Harvey L. Dyck and H. Peter Krosby (Toronto: University of Toronto Press, 1969), 123-5.
7 P.G. Edwards, *Prime Ministers and Diplomats: The Making of Australian Foreign Policy 1901-1949* (Melbourne and New York: Oxford University Press, 1983), 2, 17.
8 Quoted in Charles Grimshaw, "Australian Nationalism and the Imperial Connection 1900-1914," *Australian Journal of Politics and History* 3-4 (1957-8): 164.
9 Quoted in Barbara R. Penny, "Australia's Reactions to the Boer War – a Study in Colonial Imperialism," *Journal of British Studies* 7, 1-2 (1967): 101.
10 Carman Miller, *Painting the Map Red: Canada and the South African War, 1899-1902* (Montreal and Kingston: McGill-Queen's University Press, 1993), 438.
11 Quoted in Penny, "Australia's Reactions to the Boer War," 102.
12 Miller, *Painting the Map Red*, 437.
13 John Kendle, *The Colonial and Imperial Conferences, 1887-1911* (London: Longmans, 1967), 43.
14 J.A. La Nauze, *Alfred Deakin: A Biography*, vol. 2 (Carlton: Melbourne University Press, 1965), 500-1.
15 Ibid., 476.
16 Neville Meaney, *A History of Australian Defence and Foreign Policy 1901-1923*, vol. 1, *The Search for Security in the Pacific* (Sydney: Sydney University Press, 1976), 145-6.
17 Henry Borden, ed., *Robert Laird Borden: His Memoirs*, vol. 1, *1854-1915* (Toronto: McClelland and Stewart, 1969), 128.
18 Borden, ed., *Memoirs*, 1:127.
19 Ibid., 126.
20 Ibid., 165.
21 Ibid., 190.
22 William Morris Hughes, *The Splendid Adventure; a Review of Empire Relations within and without the Commonwealth of Britannic Nations* (Toronto: Doubleday, 1928), 118.
23 George L. Cook, "Sir Robert Borden, Lloyd George, and British Military Policy, 1917-1918," *Historical Journal* 14, 2 (1971): 381.
24 L.F. Fitzhardinge, *William Morris Hughes: A Political Biography*, vol. 2, *The Little Digger 1914-1952.* (London and Sydney: Angus and Robertson Publishers, 1979), 278.

25 Quoted in Norman Hillmer and J.L. Granatstein, *Empire to Umpire: Canada and the World to the 1990s* (Toronto: Copp Clark Longman, 1994), 63.
26 C.P. Stacey, *Canada and the Age of Conflict,* vol. 1, *1867-1921* (Toronto, Buffalo, NY, London: University of Toronto Press, 1984), 194-9.
27 See, for Australia, E.M. Andrews, *The Anzac Illusion: Anglo-Australian Relations during World War I* (Cambridge: Cambridge University Press, 1993), 108-17.
28 Ibid.
29 See, for example, Perley to Borden, no date, NAC, Borden Papers, vol. 162, 88017, and Borden to Perley, 3 August 1918, NAC, Borden Papers, vol. 162, 88156.
30 Borden, ed., *Memoirs,* 2:572.
31 Fitzhardinge, *William Morris Hughes,* 2:122-8.
32 W. Stewart Wallace, *The Memoirs of The Rt. Hon. Sir George Foster* (Toronto: Macmillan Canada, 1933), 183.
33 Fitzhardinge, *William Morris Hughes,* 2:322.
34 Borden to Lloyd George, 28 June 1918, House of Lords Record Office (hereinafter HLRO), Lloyd George Papers, F/5/2/11.
35 Fitzhardinge, *William Morris Hughes,* 2:354.
36 Hughes to Lloyd George, 9 November 1918, HLRO, Lloyd George Papers, F/28/2/9.
37 Roskill, *Hankey,* 2:29.
38 Ibid., 49.
39 Robert Craig Brown, *Robert Laird Borden: A Biography,* vol. 2 (Toronto: University of Toronto Press, 1980), 152.
40 Roskill, *Hankey,* 2:29-30.
41 National Library of Australia, (hereinafter NLA), F.W. Eggleston Papers, MS 423, series 6: Peace Conference 1919, folder 30.
42 See L.F. Fitzhardinge, "Hughes, Borden, and Dominion Representation at the Paris Peace Conference," *Canadian Historical Review* 49, 2 (June 1968): 160-9.
43 See, for example, Borden's cable to Lloyd George, 2 November 1918, HLRO, Lloyd George Papers, F/15/2/24.
44 Alfred Zimmern, *The Third British Empire* (London: Oxford University Press, 1926), 30.
45 Harold Nicolson, *Peacemaking 1919* (London: Methuen, 1964), 240.
46 See Public Records Office, London UK, CAB 29, 28, The Minutes of the British Empire Delegation (hereinafter PRO, CAB 29, 28, BED).
47 See memorandum of 7 February 1919 in *Documents on Canadian External Relations,* vol. 2, *The Paris Peace Conference of 1919,* ed. R.A. MacKay (Ottawa: Department of External Affairs, 1969), 200.
48 Borden cable to White, 28 January 1919, NAC, Borden Papers, vol. 95, 50334, file 49.
49 PRO, CAB 28, 29, BED, 3.
50 Seth P. Tillman, *Anglo-American Relations at the Paris Peace Conference of 1919* (Princeton, NJ: Princeton University Press, 1961), 298.
51 6 May 1919, NAC, Borden Papers, vol. 441, file 151.
52 Philip G. Wigley, *Canada and the Transition to Commonwealth: British-Canadian Relations 1917-1926* (Cambridge: Cambridge University Press, 1977), 88-9.
53 Robert Randolph Garran, *Prosper the Commonwealth* (Sydney: Argus and Robertson, 1958), 271.
54 W.J. Hudson, *Billy Hughes in Paris: The Birth of Australian Diplomacy* (West Melbourne: Thomas Nelson [Australia] in association with the Australian Institute for International Affairs, 1978), 72.
55 See Brown, *Borden,* 2:158; Hudson, *Billy Hughes in Paris,* 71-2.
56 Milner to Balfour, 26 July 1919, Bodleian Library, Oxford, Milner Papers, Dep. 390.
57 Hudson, *Billy Hughes in Paris,* 121.
58 See, for example, Hillmer and Granatstein, *Empire to Umpire,* 24-5, and Maurice Pope, ed., *Public Servant: The Memoirs of Sir Joseph Pope* (Toronto: Oxford University Press, 1960), 86-8.
59 NAC, Borden Papers, vol. 120, file 65926.
60 See, for example, Ian H. Nish, *Alliance in Decline: a Study in Anglo-Japanese Relations 1908-23* (London: The Athlone Press, University of London, 1972), 45-6.

61 Quoted in Leonie Foster, *High Hopes: The Men and Motives of the Australian Round Table* (Carlton: Melbourne University Press, 1986), 75.
62 Lloyd George, *War Memoirs*, 6 vols. (London: Ivor Nicholson and Watson, 1934), 4:1754.
63 Borden to Lloyd George, 23 November 1918, HLRO, Lloyd George Papers, F/5/2/28.
64 Arthur Walworth, *Wilson and His Peacemakers: American Diplomacy at the Paris Peace Conference, 1919* (New York: W.W. Norton and Company, 1986), 319.
65 Hughes to Lloyd George, no date, HLRO, Lloyd George Papers, F/28/ 2/15.
66 Hughes to Lloyd George, 12 March and 19 March 1919, HLRO, Lloyd George Papers, F/28/ 3/9 and F/28/3/14.
67 Walworth, *Wilson and His Peacemakers*, 71 n. 37.
68 Stephen Bonsal, *Suitors and Suppliants* (New York: Prentice-Hall, 1946), 229.
69 Borden, *Memoirs*, 2:874.
70 See Peter Spartalis, *The Diplomatic Battles of Billy Hughes* (Sydney: Hale and Iremonger, 1983), 103-10.
71 Wallace, *The Memoirs of The Rt. Hon. Sir George Foster*, 193-4.
72 Lloyd George to Hughes, 14 April 1919, HLRO, Lloyd George Papers, F/28/3/27.
73 Entry for 11 January 1919, NAC, C1864, Borden Diary.
74 Milner to the Duke of Devonshire, 25 March 1919, Bodleian Library, Oxford, Milner Papers, Dep. 383/1.
75 NAC, Loring Christie Papers, vol. 3, file 6, folder 6.
76 See Spartalis, *The Diplomatic Battles of Billy Hughes*, ch. 6 passim.
77 See, for example, Munro-Ferguson to Milner, 15 March 1919 and 29 May 1919, Bodleian Library, Oxford, Additional Milner Papers, 706.
78 Borden to Rowell, 15 April 1919, NAC, Borden Papers, vol. 1106, file 90365.
79 Nish, *Alliance in Decline*, 270-1; Borden, ed., *Robert Laird Borden*, 1:926-8; entry for 31 March 1919, NAC, Borden Diary.
80 NLA, W.M. Hughes Papers, series 24, 1, folder 11.
81 NAC, Loring Christie Papers, vol. 7, passim.
82 Walworth, *Wilson and His Peacemakers*, 71.
83 Hudson, *Billy Hughes in Paris*, 78.
84 Cited in ibid., 93-4; Department of State, *Papers Relating to the Foreign Relations of the United States*, vol. 2, *The Paris Peace Conference 1919* (Washington: Department of State, 1942), 720-2.
85 Hudson, *Billy Hughes in Paris*, 17.
86 Entry for 22 January 1919, NAC, Borden Diary.
87 Edward Mandell House, *The Intimate Papers of Colonel House Arranged As a Narrative by Charles Seymour* (Boston and New York: Houghton Mifflin, 1926-8), 4:296.
88 Roskill, *Hankey*, 2:53.
89 Borden, ed., *Memoirs*, 2:908.
90 Alan Sharp, *The Versailles Settlement: Peacemaking in Paris, 1919* (London: Macmillan, 1991), 162.
91 Borden, ed., *Memoirs*, 2:906.
92 Entry for 29 January 1919, NAC, Borden Diary.
93 House, *The Intimate Papers of Colonel House*, 4: 299.
94 David Lloyd George, *The Truth about the Peace Treaties* (London: Victor Gollancz, 1938), 1:542; entry for 30 January 1919, NAC, Borden Diary; Stephen Bonsal, *Unfinished Business* (Garden City, NY: Doubleday Doran, 1944), 37.
95 Kerr to Milner, 31 January 1919, Bodleian Library, Oxford, Additional Milner Papers, Ms. Eng. Hist., c. 700.
96 Entry for 1 February 1919, NAC, Borden Diary.
97 R.C. Snelling, "Peacemaking, 1919: Australia, New Zealand and the British Empire Delegation at Versailles," *Journal of Imperial and Commonwealth History* 4, 1 (1975): 25.

2
Coming of Age: Independence and Foreign Policy in Canada and Australia, 1931-45
Francine McKenzie

In 1926 Prime Minister James Hertzog informed the South African Assembly that "Unless our status is acknowledged by foreign nations we simply do not exist as a nation."[1] He made this comment upon his return from an imperial conference in London where the foremost item on the agenda was the status of the dominions. In an attempt to stem the nationalist stirrings of discontented dominions (notably South Africa and the Irish Free State), a committee organized under the direction of Lord Arthur Balfour defined the nature of Anglo-Dominion relations. The Balfour Report affirmed that the dominions and Britain were equal and sovereign. The report was given legislative force in 1931 as the Statute of Westminster. But ten years later, Richard Casey, Australia's ambassador to Washington, observed that outside the British Empire and Commonwealth the dominions still appeared to be nothing more than "glorified colonies."[2] Intra-Commonwealth discussions and constitutional decrees had not resolved the confusion surrounding the dominions' relations with Britain or the concomitant ambiguity about their status.

The Canadian and Australian metamorphosis from British colonies to fully independent states was achieved when these two dominions took charge of their own foreign policies.[3] In so doing, they clarified the nature of their relationships with Britain, making the point that London did not direct their foreign policies, that they had individual interests in the world, and that they were engaged with the world beyond the confines of the Commonwealth. This also meant that no area of governance was beyond the jurisdiction of the dominion governments. There was resistance from Britain. While Britain had decentralized authority over domestic matters to Canada and Australia from the mid-nineteenth century onward, London was intent on preserving the diplomatic unity of the Empire under British direction. Indeed, the Commonwealth still appeared to be a British-led bloc in international affairs even after Britain began to cede control over external matters of a local complexion in the early 1920s. This perception had direct consequences for Canadian and Australian autonomy. As K.C. Wheare noted, the dominions' questionable control over foreign policy "allowed plenty of scope for argument about the precise status of the Members of the Common-wealth in international law."[4] The challenge for Canada and Australia was to articulate and implement distinct external policies that would make ir-refutable the claim that the dominions were independent, as well as equal and sovereign. Only then would Canada and Australia be accorded the in-ternational recognition necessary to complete their process of decolonization. Thus, foreign policy was a milestone on the road to independence.[5]

Eric Hobsbawm identifies the years 1918-50 as the time when "the nineteenth-century 'principle of nationality' triumphed."[6] These were also the years when Canada and Australia were transformed from colonies to states. In the preceding chapter, Margaret MacMillan has examined the start of their evolution toward more extensive consultation with Britain during the First World War. Canadian and Australian representation at the Paris Peace Conference signalled their willingness to play larger roles in world affairs. But the advances made during the war and at the peace conference were not clear-cut. For instance, the other leading powers tolerated Cana-dian and Australian involvement in Paris only because the British insisted. The signatures of Canadian and Australian representatives on the Treaty of Versailles were placed alongside and as a part of the British Empire Delega-tion. The standing of Canada and Australia in world affairs was contingent on their membership in a collective bloc, British-centred and London-led.

Canada's efforts to assert control over its involvement in world affairs persisted throughout the 1920s, but did not entirely succeed. For example, during the Chanak crisis of 1922, when Britain and Turkey clashed over the implementation of the Treaty of Sèvres,[7] Winston Churchill, the colonial secretary, appealed to the dominions for military support. Prime Minister Mackenzie King interpreted this plea as an attempt "to play the imperial game, to test out centralization vs. autonomy in European wars."[8] He dodged the British request for military assistance by insisting that only the Cana-dian parliament could decide whether or not to send Canadian soldiers abroad. Parliament was conveniently not then in session, and King did not recall it. British officials learned not to make demands that might be re-jected, and therefore helped preserve the appearance of diplomatic unity. When the King government decided to negotiate and ratify the Halibut Fisheries Treaty with the United States in 1923 without British involvement, the Foreign Office's first reaction was to balk at Ottawa's impudence. After sober reflection, it decided not to interfere with a bilateral agreement that it could not stop. Instead, it distinguished between local and imperial foreign policy and claimed the dominions should have responsibility only for mat-ters of a purely local nature. In this way, London diluted the significance of the Halibut Fisheries Treaty. The British could also take some comfort from the fact that American politicians did not grasp that the treaty was an important precedent in Anglo-Dominion relations. In the debate in the US Senate, American senators assumed the Halibut Fisheries Treaty was an agreement between Britain and the United States.[9] Canada also sent its own diplomats abroad – to Washington in 1927, Paris in 1928, and Tokyo in 1929. The reaction in London blended "astonishment and resentment."[10] Once again, the threat to British control over imperial foreign policy was minimized. In Washington and Paris, Canada's representatives were accredited with the resident British ambassador by their side. Britain's secretary of state for dominions affairs was satisfied that opening diplomatic offices of its own "would not denote any departure from the principle of diplomatic unity of the Empire."[11]

There were also internal restraints that prevented King from explicitly assuming control over Canadian foreign policy. He feared a backlash among English-speaking Canadians in response to the dilution of the Anglo-Canadian connection. Domestic harmony was the cardinal principle in King's foreign policy, and that meant tempering his actions. Moreover, King himself admired Britain, held British liberals like William Gladstone in the highest respect, and did not want to sever ties with the mother country, even though he resisted all attempts – perceived and real – to undermine Canadian sovereignty.[12] In fact, he intended that Canada should remain a good ally of Britain, particularly in times of war. He reassured British officials to this effect at the 1923 Imperial Conference. King noted that "If a great and clear call of duty comes, Canada will respond ... as she did in 1914."[13] Ottawa's efforts to establish authority over its foreign policy and foreign relations were temporarily stalled with the onset of the Depression, which also saw King and the Liberals go down to defeat.

Australia, on the other hand, made virtually no effort to define its own foreign policy tradition in the 1920s. Canberra responded positively to Britain's request for aid in the Chanak crisis, although Prime Minister Hughes did complain about the lack of consultation. Australia made no attempt to establish, let alone manage, external matters of a local nature. In contrast to King's efforts to disentangle Canada from a centralized imperial foreign policy, Australia's prime minister, Stanley Bruce, tried to enhance Australia's role in the framing of imperial policy. He appointed Richard Casey to act as a liaison with Britain. Casey was not long in London before he urged Bruce to "break down the proverbial silence of the Dominions" on foreign policy.[14] Bruce did not act on his advice.

In the 1920s, the perception of British control over imperial foreign policy persisted. There was no challenge to British authority from Canberra; London succeeded in containing the significance of Canadian initiatives; and Canadian advances were tempered by concerns about national unity as well as King's personal commitment to the British tie. Perhaps most importantly, the divided views of Canada and Australia perpetuated the ambiguity of the dominions' status and responsibility. As dominions, Canada and Australia belonged to the same category. The actions of one had an impact on the whole. Because Canadian and Australian actions and attitudes were conflicting, they cancelled one another out.

This chapter picks up the story in 1931. Some might think this is an unusual point of departure in an analysis of the dominions' independence, noting that Britain's passage of the Statute of Westminster in that year marked the end of the dominions' evolution from self-governing colonies to independent states. This interpretation belongs to a long tradition of overstating the significance of the Statute of Westminster.[15] While the statute did affirm the equality and sovereignty of Britain and the dominions, the word "independence" never appeared in the text. Furthermore, there was no visible change in the language used to describe the dominions after 1931. The term "dominion," regularly used since the 1907 Imperial Conference, implied British domination of Canada and Australia, as well as New Zealand and South Africa. The fact that Britain was not a dominion reinforced the inferior status of the others.[16] The term "Commonwealth" had been in use since the First World War, long before any of the dominions were independent, while the term "Empire" remained in use when discussing the dominions long after 1931. The Commonwealth was not reorganized in recognition of the dominions' sovereignty and equality. The "old dominions" and the crown colonies, like Jamaica and Kenya, had long been differentiated in imperial organization. The two tiers remained unchanged after 1931. Moreover, dominion status was not necessarily permanent. In 1934, Britain revoked Newfoundland's dominion status.[17] Perhaps most importantly, the process of constitutional negotiations perpetuated confusion. Self-government was acquired peacefully; Britain and the dominions remained close allies. The only previous example of a British colony acquiring its independence was that of the Thirteen Colonies. Waging war to overthrow British control left no doubt that the United States was separate and free. In contrast, the only war the dominions were willing to wage was to defend Britain, not to break away from it. Finally, Australia did not immediately ratify the Statute of Westminster, and Canada did so only in part. Thus the Statute of Westminster was shrouded in ambiguity. As Stephen Leacock, the famous Canadian economist and humorist, observed, "After reading ... [the Statute of Westminster] no one can tell whether the Dominions are sovereign states or not."[18] In fact, he went on to conclude the dominions were definitely not independent. Australia's constitutional lawyers in the 1930s also "found it impossible briefly and simply to describe the exact nature of the relationship between Britain and Australia and the other white dominions. All were agreed, though, that they were not foreign to each other."[19]

Canada and Australia in the 1930s: Working at Cross-Purposes

Before Canada and Australia could develop their own foreign policies, they needed the support, expertise, and infrastructure of departments devoted to foreign affairs. In the 1930s, however, their respective departments of external affairs were rudimentary. By 1939 Canada's department employed thirty officers to staff the office in Ottawa and seven posts abroad.[20] Australia's department lagged far behind, with a handful of officers and no consular offices beyond London.[21] Their departments of external affairs could not provide their governments with the advice needed to articulate individual policies. Consequently, they could not function as policy-making centres. The best they could manage were occasional utterances on international affairs, but there was neither rigour, consistency of thought, nor a philosophical foundation to their sporadic pronouncements on foreign affairs.[22] For the most part, the governments of Canada and Australia depended on British embassies for information and the Foreign Office for analysis. Hardly surprising, they saw the world much the way the British did. Even if either dominion did introduce a policy individually, such as the Canadian commitment to the appeasement of Germany in the 1930s, the overlap with the British policy meant they appeared to be following a British lead. Reliance on British sources of information prolonged the appearance, as well as the reality, of subordination to London.

It was not only size that revealed the institutional immaturity of their respective departments of external affairs. The name of the departments – External Affairs – made the same point by implying that there were two categories of relations: those that were only external and those that were truly foreign. Because neither dominion was prepared to classify Anglo-Canadian or Anglo-Australian relations as foreign, they reinforced the idea that relations with Britain were qualitatively different from those with other nations. The name also suggested that there were limits to their engagement with the wider world and that they focused only, or primarily, on those members in the external category. That left the responsibility for managing relations with the rest of the world to Britain's Foreign Office.[23]

Canada and Australia did have seats in the League of Nations, which could have served as launching pads for independent foreign policy traditions. Neither Canada nor Australia made much of this opportunity. In the Manchurian crisis of 1931-3,[24] Stanley Bruce delivered a singularly unmemorable speech. His lack of engagement reflected the views of most Australians, who at the time were more upset by a new style of bowling in cricket.[25] This was better than his muddled Canadian colleague, C.J. Cahan, who surprised all with his pro-Japanese comments. The next major challenge to the League, the Italian invasion of Ethiopia in 1935, confirmed that Ottawa and Canberra remained removed from the wider world. Bruce's contribution was on a par with his performance in the earlier crisis. He barely addressed the question of sanctions, commenting instead on issues related to food and agriculture.[26] In stark contrast, Walter Riddell, the leader of the Canadian delegation in Geneva, endorsed sanctions against Italy wholeheartedly. He even suggested adding oil to the list of embargoed items, a suggestion that the international press soon dubbed "the Canadian proposal." Mackenzie King, who returned to the prime minister's office in the midst of the crisis, was alarmed by the prominent stand taken by the Canadians in Geneva. King believed that Canada's standing in the League was too insignificant to be effective. In King's mind, Canada was "a small and distant country, not primarily responsible for what may be the outcome of league decisions."[27] Consequently, he distanced the government from Riddell, his country from the League, and removed Canada from the bright glare of the international spotlight. Neither Canada nor Australia capitalized on the opportunity provided by membership in the League of Nations to entrench their independence through the articulation of individual or well-considered policies. Instead, they confirmed that they were not yet ready for involvement in world affairs.

In contrast to Canadian and Australian self-effacement and marginalization in the League of Nations, their participation in imperial conferences perpetuated the impression that they remained attached and subordinate to Britain. Imperial gatherings of the 1930s tended to be inconclusive because of the divergent views of constituents. For instance, Australia hoped that the Empire would speak with one voice; Canada objected to all proposals involving policy centralization or automatic cooperation because both detracted from the sovereignty of the government of Canada. David MacKenzie has detected these divergent responses on the part of Canada and Australia to proposals to organize commercial aviation in the 1930s. This disagreement was clearly evident at the 1937 Imperial Conference, where the Australians preferred to work within an imperial framework and Canadian officials refused to endorse any kind of centralized coordination. Consequently, Commonwealth discussions never culminated in a single policy. However, disagreement was disguised by optimistic summaries published at the end of every meeting.[28] For instance, again at the 1937 Imperial Conference, Britain had hoped the dominions would offer their explicit support as London prepared to confront an increasingly confident and aggressive Hitler. The dominions differed on what support to extend and how to do so. Still, Neville Chamberlain, the British prime minister, claimed that the conference achieved "a general harmony of aims and policy." He went on to contrast the good relations within the Commonwealth and Empire to the deteriorating international situation. "War between us is unthinkable and if we had to consider only the countries of the British Commonwealth there would be no need of armaments for any of us."[29] This uplifting statement served two purposes. First, it masked British disappointment in not getting support from all of the dominions when it needed it most. Second, it differentiated intra-Commonwealth relations from relations between "foreign" states.

Even when the national interests of Canada and Australia came to the fore at Commonwealth meetings, the public portrayal still emphasized unity. One of the most glaring displays of Commonwealth fragmentation and dominion pursuit of self-interest occurred at the Ottawa Imperial Economic Conference of 1932. This gathering was the brainchild of Canada's prime minister, R.B. Bennett (1930-5), who believed that greater reliance on Commonwealth and imperial markets could offset the devastating effects of the Depression. The British, never keen on preferential tariffs, attended reluctantly but were hopeful that the dominions would lower their high protective tariffs against British exports. They misjudged the dominions, whose negotiators bargained single-mindedly to secure concessions that would benefit their exports, while making few reciprocal concessions. British delegates singled out Stanley Bruce, the leader of Australia's delegation, and Bennett for their ruthlessness in securing as much as possible while giving little in return. "Both Bennett and Bruce demanded further concessions – brutally and as if they were dictating terms to a beaten enemy, as indeed they were – and all were at once conceded."[30] The British delegation was thoroughly disabused of the belief in collective interests prevailing over national ones. Thus this gathering rightly belongs to the national histories of the dominions. But the public portrayal of this meeting emphasized co-operation, not discord. The very fact of coming together, against an international backdrop of mistrust and chauvinism, was more important than the results. As Stanley Baldwin, who led the British delegation, explained to the opening session, the decision to exchange preferential terms signalled a willingness to subordinate national interests to collective welfare: "it marks the point where two roads diverge, the one leading to the development of purely national interest, the other to closer imperial unity."[31] This description was totally inaccurate – but it was widely believed. Hot on the heels of the Statute of Westminster, imperial preference suggested that ties remained strong and that practical realities reinforced a Commonwealth alignment.

The description of Commonwealth meetings as family gatherings further obscured the limitations of British authority over the dominions. Even Mackenzie King, who was scrupulous about upholding Canada's independence, fell into the trap of using the family analogy. For instance, after emphasizing the differences among Britain and the dominions at the 1937 Imperial Conference, King commented on how "we have enjoyed and exercised the family privilege of free and frank speech."[32] The family construct perpetuated the historic roles of Britain and the dominions. Britain as the parent and head of the family could speak on behalf of the clan. The dominions were children, even if they were growing up. Thus the family analogy impeded the realization of Australian and Canadian independence.

Despite its attendance at imperial gatherings and the failure to distinguish itself at the League of Nations, Mackenzie King believed he had differentiated Canada from Britain. He regarded this as essential to Canada's domestic stability, even survival. King had witnessed the divisive effects of British foreign policy on English and French Canadians during the First World War. He believed his primary political task was to minimize this source of strain. His mottoes were "No Commitments" and "Parliament Will Decide," which he believed captured his commitment to preserving the sovereignty of the government of Canada. Without a doubt, King earned his reputation as a champion of Canadian sovereignty and national unity. But his tactic – adhering to a policy of inaction and non-commitment – did not positively demonstrate that Canada had a foreign policy, let alone that it controlled it. Until Ottawa affirmed its foreign policy powers by revealing what it stood for, rather than by refusing to state its views concretely, it did not fully own them.[33]

The perception of Canada as subordinate to Britain in matters of foreign policy also persisted because Canada did support Britain in its greatest test of the 1930s: going to war against Nazi Germany. King had always intended to support Britain if a fight came. It was obvious to King that morality, justice, and law were on Britain's side. He rarely said this publicly because he did not want to be accused of following Britain's lead or of being implicated in British foreign policy, especially its wars.[34] When Britain and Germany did go to war, King summoned parliament to debate whether Canada should also go to war. No vote was taken because support was overwhelming. King succeeded in bringing a united Canada into the war, thereby reconciling his domestic and external goals. Outside observers did not appreciate King's punctilious regard for Canadian authority and sovereignty. As Jay Pierrepont Moffat, the American ambassador in Ottawa confided to his diary, fighting alongside Britain reversed King's efforts to disentangle Canada from British foreign policy: "despite the outward trappings of independence, it [Canada] is, at least for the duration of the war, a mere adjunct of British foreign policy as laid down from London."[35]

Australia in the 1930s still did not try to disentangle itself from Britain. The strength of its attachment to Britain was evident in Australia's refusal to ratify the Statute of Westminster. When the attorney-general, Robert Menzies, introduced the statute to the House of Representatives in 1937, he described it as a "grave disservice" and an exercise in frustration because it attempted "to reduce to written terms something which was a matter of the spirit and not of the letter."[36] Most of Australia's elected officials agreed so completely that they decided not to endorse it at all. Hardly surprising, in the realm of foreign policy Australia continued to support a collective imperial stand in international affairs, decided upon in London. Stanley Bruce, the high commissioner to London in the 1930s, noted that there was rarely even a pretence of consultation: "What happened in ninety-nine cases out of a hundred was that the U.K. Cabinet reached a conclusion" and the dominions were implicated in the decision. Bruce complained only if a policy struck him as unwise or dangerous.[37] What he then sought was a voice in the making of imperial policy, not the separation of Australian and British policies. Either goal was unwelcome in London, which was intent on maintaining its decision-making monopoly. Despite some frustration about its exclusion, in 1939 this antipodean dominion continued to be a supporting player to Britain on the world stage.

On the eve of the Second World War, Britain still appeared to set the foreign policies of the dominions in the most vital way: deciding whether or not to go to war. In Canberra there was not a separate declaration of war. Australian politicians accepted that the British decision committed Australia to fight. Prime Minister Menzies explained the connection in a radio broadcast only a few hours after news reached Australia that Britain and Germany were at war. "Great Britain has declared war upon her [Germany], and ... as a result, Australia is also at war."[38] The way in which Australia entered the war confirmed that, eight years after Britain enacted the Statute of Westminster, Australia existed as "a major satellite in the British imperial orbit."[39]

In Washington, there was some question about whether the British declaration bound Canada, Australia, and the other dominions. The point was more than academic: the administration had to know whether to draw up one declaration of neutrality or five, that is, one each for Britain, Canada, Australia, New Zealand, and South Africa. President Roosevelt placed a call to Mackenzie King. King used this opportunity to advance Canada's constitutional status as a practically independent state by asking the president to draw up a separate declaration for Canada. Washington did so.[40] The attention King had devoted to cultivating relations with the United States had paid off in this instance. What also needs to be remembered is that President Roosevelt had to call and ask King for direction. It would have been obvious that Washington should draw up a separate declaration of neutrality for Canada had its sovereign status been established beyond question.

At the start of the Second World War, Canada exercised complete control over its foreign policy by deciding when and whether to go to war. To outside eyes, however, there remained doubt about Canadian authority. As a result, Canada's status as an independent state was not securely established. Australia, on the other hand, had not tried to gain control over its foreign policy. In the 1930s Canada and Australia were working at cross-purposes. Indeed, while King worked quietly to gain control over foreign policy and to branch out Canada's relations beyond London and the Empire and Commonwealth, Australia strove to become a larger part of a single imperial approach to foreign affairs. Australian and Canadian attitudes and goals were at odds. Not surprisingly, there was little direct contact between the two dominion governments. Despite occasional consultation at imperial meetings, there was little opportunity to work together. But lack of contact was not the real problem. Their divergent outlooks, attitudes, and objectives impeded one another's goals and meant that Canadian and Australian leaders did not turn to one another for advice, to coordinate tactics, or to seek assistance.

Canada and Australia at War: Parallel Paths

In the early years of the Second World War, the gulf separating Canadian and Australian attitudes toward and goals concerning foreign policy narrowed.[41] They agreed on the necessity and desirability of controlling all aspects of their external policy, beyond a shadow of a doubt – but for different reasons. In the perilous stage of the war after the fall of France, Canada stood as Britain's ranking ally. Canadian officials welcomed the recognition that accompanied their heavy wartime responsibilities. But with the entrance of the United States into the war, they found themselves instantly demoted and excluded, as Galen Perras's chapter details. Both Britain and the United States expected that London could represent the Commonwealth and would act as the intermediary between the United States and dominions. The realization in Ottawa of the tenuous nature of their position provoked Canadian officials to entrench their independence so as to preclude their subordination to or representation by Britain in future.

In Australia, the transition from loyal supporter to fervent nationalist was abrupt and dramatic, a product of disappointment in Britain's inability to protect Australia and the fear that Australia might be overwhelmed by the Japanese. The possibility of Australia going down to temporary defeat while Britain was preoccupied with the German advance is at the centre of a nationalist literature on Anglo-Australian relations.[42] The subsequent development of an "Australia-first" foreign policy was founded on the recognition that Britain could not be relied upon, that Australian and British interests were not compatible, and if forced to choose, the British government would ensure the security of its people first. The wartime Labor government accepted that, ultimately, it alone could guarantee that Australia remained free and safe. National interest and national boundaries obtained a clarity and discreteness of conception that they had never before enjoyed. The consequence of Canadian marginalization and Australian vulnerability was the decision of their governments to seize responsibility for their external policies and foreign relations. As Alister McIntosh, the secretary of New Zealand's Department of External Affairs wrote of Canada and Australia in 1943, they "are determined to assert their claim to equality of voice in all matters relating to the conduct of international affairs."[43]

Canada and Australia still faced obstacles, the most formidable of which was Britain's refusal to treat them as independent states. Until their oldest ally regarded them as fully independent, other governments were not likely to do so either. But Britain was not inclined to grant such recognition, principally because it was more dependent than ever on the Commonwealth to prop up its international position and as determined as ever to preserve its greatness and influence. Clement Attlee, the deputy prime minister and leader of the Labour Party, penned a memo to this effect while he served as secretary of state for dominion affairs in 1943. He accepted as "a fundamental assumption" the goal of preserving "the British Commonwealth as an international entity, recognized as such by foreign countries."[44] The idea of a united Commonwealth in world affairs was expressed as the third great power, and the unspoken assumption was that the dominions' views, interests, and voices could be subsumed within those of Britain.

Most British officials were confident that there would be collective representation and ongoing cooperation, with Britain as the natural leader of the group. Their logic reflected their own power-politics approach to international affairs. Speaking only for themselves, Canadian or Australian voices would only be "occasionally audible," whereas a representative of the Commonwealth and Empire "can rely on his voice carrying real weight all the time."[45] Ultimately, British officials were confident that "the exercise of intelligent leadership on the part of this country" would compel the dominions to follow the British lead.[46] Hence, they saw little need to acknowledge the status and standing of Canada and Australia.

Because British officials were slow to appreciate that Canada and Australia were determined to become distinct players in world affairs, they regularly offended their Canadian and Australian allies. For instance, on 24 January 1944, Lord Halifax, the ambassador in Washington, delivered a speech in Toronto in which he referred to the Commonwealth as the third great force in the postwar world. Mackenzie King responded immediately with a speech of his own, in which he affirmed that the Commonwealth would be one of many organizations with which Canada was affiliated in a new and comprehensive approach to international affairs. The third great force idea was also out of step with an Australian-New Zealand conference held only a few days before Halifax's speech, in which the antipodean dominions laid out their views about postwar planning. They did not inform London of this meeting until it was over. Australia initiated this meeting because of its exclusion from great power councils addressing the organization of the postwar world.[47] The Canberra conference was a novel experiment in bilateral relations between Australia and New Zealand and represented a departure from the standard Commonwealth configuration by shutting out Britain entirely. The Canadian and Australian repudiations of the British conception of the postwar Commonwealth confirmed that their basic outlook toward foreign policy, relations with Britain, and their roles in the international community were aligned.

British officials were quick to learn that their relations with Canada and Australia required delicate and diplomatic handling, but slow to abandon their goal of a united Commonwealth in world affairs. A close look at the language used by British officials when referring to Canada and Australia, or the dominions as a whole, reveals their persistent belief that they were led from London. For instance, politicians regularly described the war effort as British, even though the dominions donated money, materials, and men from the outset. Ernest Bevin, the wartime minister of labour and national service, labelled the period between the fall of France and the German invasion of the Soviet Union as twelve months when Britain had had to fight alone.[48] During a speech at the Mansion House on 29 May 1941, Anthony Eden lumped Britain and the dominions together. He referred only to "The countries of the British Empire and their Allies, with the United States and South America." He went on to discuss the dominions' contribution to postwar recovery under the rubric of the Empire: "The Dominions and ourselves can make our contribution to this because the British Empire will actually possess overseas enormous stocks of food and material."[49] These were not slips. They were common, and there were other variations. When discussing only the dominions, British officials would refer to the British Empire and Commonwealth. In general, the terms Empire and Commonwealth were used interchangeably. Winston Churchill was one chronic offender, who, when speaking of the British Commonwealth *and* Empire really meant the "British Commonwealth *or* Empire."[50] The semantic implications of this language reinforced the belief that Canada and Australia were subordinate to Britain and implied that the Statute of Westminster had changed nothing.

In wartime, such inaccurate terminology raised the hackles of Hume Wrong, Canada's assistant undersecretary of state for external affairs. He objected to the long-standing practice of "lumping the Dominions together ... as though the Dominions tended to possess a common interest and a common policy on all matters." One remedy would be to banish the phrase "the British Dominions," because it made the dominions faceless and indistinguishable. In particular, he wanted the British to stop referring to "Great Britain and the Dominions," which reinforced the idea of dominion subordination. Instead they should refer to "the member states of the British Commonwealth."[51] Escott Reid, the second secretary in the Department of External Affairs, also picked up on the insidious implications of nomenclature. In 1944 he drew up a twenty-four-point program to eliminate the "vestigial remnants of ... colonial subordination." He argued that the term "high commissioner" should be dropped and replaced by "ambassador." This would standardize relations between members of the Commonwealth as well as between them and foreign nations. He also recommended renaming the Department of External Affairs as the Foreign Office. His suggestions went far beyond terminology. He also believed Britain had to send out signals that it recognized its relations with the dominions as being the same as those with non-Commonwealth nations. Hence, it should transfer the responsibilities of the Dominions Office to the Foreign Office.[52]

Australian officials did not match Canadian vigilance in this particular area. They regularly conflated Australia and Britain in their public statements. For instance, Richard Casey, the Australian ambassador in Washington, referred to the American interest in "the survival of the British countries in their struggle with totalitarianism," clearly including Australia in the category of British countries.[53] Stanley Bruce, the high commissioner in London during the war, also reinforced Australia's connection to Britain. In a speech to the American and British Commonwealth Association in 1944 he said, matter-of-factly, that "we in Australia are British to the core." Throughout the speech he referred to Britain and the United States, but he used the personal pronoun "we," obviously linking Australia and Britain. When speaking of the fates of Britain and the United States, he made this conflation obvious as he referred to "the fate of our two Nations."[54] Even Australia's Labor leaders, who were eager to affirm Australian independence, regularly identified Australians as British. In a speech on the responsibilities of citizenship in 1943, well after Australia's great betrayal by Britain, Prime Minister John Curtin outlined three different manifestations of citizenship: "The full expression of these responsibilities is to be a good Australian, a good British subject and a good world citizen. They are complementary to each other."[55] The term Empire remained current in Australia, even preferable to Commonwealth, well into the 1950s, as Christopher Waters has pointed out in his chapter. However, the repeated description of Australia as British was not a reflection of enduring colonial subordination to Britain. Rather it was a response to Australia's geographic situation. It was a Pacific nation, but was unlike its neighbours ethnically and culturally. Hence, Australians could not think of themselves as Asian. The fervour of the claim that 99 percent of Australians were of British descent was an attempt to hold themselves apart from their region.[56] Thus the use of the term British was racialist, and did not mean there was a single British government. They were attached culturally, but they retained their political independence. It was "an Empire of the British race, not the British government."[57]

Clarifying the purpose of the Commonwealth was essential to the practical achievement of Canadian and Australian independence. As Hume Wrong observed, "the most important current problem in intra-Commonwealth relations is to make countries outside the Commonwealth understand what these relations actually are."[58] This was also the forum where Canada and Australia most regularly came into close contact. But the two dominions did not gravitate toward one another, despite their common objectives.

Consequently, Canadian and Australian efforts to redefine the Commonwealth were mutually reinforcing rather than coordinated. For example, it was essential in wartime to eliminate confusion about the nature of Commonwealth consultation as well as the scope of cooperation. This was important in preventing British transgressions as well as the appearance of British authority in the eyes of non-Commonwealth countries. Thus, Canada and Australia had to dispel the increasingly popular notion of the Commonwealth as an international bloc. Throughout the war, London was eager to convene Commonwealth conferences to consult on all matters, coordinate action, and preserve its association as the exclusive power base of Britain. But these were not easily organized; the dominions were uncooperative about their timing, organization, and purpose. Consequently, the first prime ministers' conference was only held in 1944, largely because of Mackenzie King's unwillingness to absent himself from Ottawa. There was, however, no consultation with Australia about monitoring Britain to ensure it did not misrepresent wartime Commonwealth meetings.

Australia helped to dispel the impression of the Commonwealth as a discrete subset of the international community in international meetings. British officials wanted to hold Commonwealth meetings on the side at international gatherings. But at the Food and Agriculture Organization conference held in Hot Springs, Virginia, in the summer of 1943, Australian officials refused to meet privately with their British colleagues, lest this create the impression of a Commonwealth bloc. Dr. Herbert Coombs, director of the Department of Postwar Reconstruction, rebuffed British overtures, claiming he was "embarrassed to come together." This frustrated British officials like Lionel Robbins, who complained that the unwillingness to consult was "a ludicrous situation."[59] On this occasion, Australia took the lead without consulting or coordinating with Canada.

When Commonwealth meetings were finally held, their achievements were minimal because of the conflicting goals and tactics of the various prime ministers. Australia and Canada adopted seemingly irreconcilable postures. At the 1944 prime ministers' meeting, Prime Minister Curtin of Australia advocated more extensive defensive cooperation among the members of the Commonwealth. King scotched the proposal, which called for more cooperation than he was comfortable with.[60] These positions were reminiscent of their roles at Commonwealth meetings in the 1930s. In fact, Australian proposals for Commonwealth cooperation and integration were not motivated by loyalty to Britain and acceptance of British leadership. Rather, Curtin wanted to revamp the Commonwealth so that it would serve as a vehicle to transport the dominion to places in international affairs that Australia could not attain by individual effort alone.[61] Thus, Curtin proposed the definition of spheres of interest, in which the dominion most interested or affected would be principally responsible for developing and implementing Commonwealth policies. This would allow Australia to take the leading role in the Pacific.

Reconstructing the Commonwealth to reflect the equality and interests of the dominions in no way weakened the organization. Quite the contrary. As Dr. Herbert Evatt, Australia's minister of external affairs, explained, continued cooperation within the Commonwealth was only made possible "by the rapid increase in status and stature" of dominions like Canada and Australia.[62] Thus Curtin and Evatt set out to reshape the Commonwealth, whereas King preferred to keep it at arm's length. Despite employing different tactics, they shared a common goal: to redefine and clarify the purpose of the Commonwealth so that it could serve their national interests and would not undermine their status as independent states. Canadian and Australian officials made little attempt to work together because they could not see that they were divided by means and not ends.

Canadian and Australian views converged over the *purpose* of Commonwealth consultation. King invoked his line of the interwar years, that consultation was limited to the simple exchange of information that facilitated cooperation where possible.[63] Australia also insisted that Commonwealth consultation must not curtail its freedom of action and opinion. Dr. Evatt issued strict instructions to ensure that, after any Commonwealth meeting ended, Britain must not try to represent Australia's view on a particular subject. After one meeting in London in 1943 to discuss postwar trade, Dr. Coombs, who regularly led Australian delegations to economic meetings, reported that nothing had been said or done to commit Australia to the British approach to postwar trade matters. He even admitted to going a little too far in defending "our freedom of action in this field."[64] But the goal was worth it: Australia's sovereignty was safe.[65]

As in the interwar years, the differences between Britain, Canada, and Australia at Commonwealth meetings – as well as the inconclusive nature of those meetings – were obscured beneath the standard public declaration about the unity of the Commonwealth. The prime ministers' meeting of 1944 ended with the usual upbeat, if bland, communiqué: "We rejoice in our inheritance of loyalties and ideals, and proclaim our sense of kinship to one another."[66] However, the significance of these public messages was becoming clearer as Canada and Australia demonstrated that the Commonwealth was not an exclusive forum or the primary focus of their foreign relations. For instance, the United States, which was deeply interested in the future of international trade, let it be known that it would welcome an invitation to a Commonwealth conference in 1943 to consider the organization of postwar trade. The British declined on the grounds that it was a family affair. Canada and Australia were quick to object, although for different reasons. Australia supported opening the meeting to American officials because they did not want to do anything to alienate the United States.[67] In the end, this did not happen, but Canberra's willingness to include American representatives demystified the Commonwealth as a closed group or a unified bloc. Canadian diplomats objected to the description of the meeting as a family gathering.[68] It was alright to keep the United States out, but Britain must not perpetuate the family image of the Commonwealth.

Not only did Canada and Australia check British attempts to harness the Commonwealth to British foreign policy, and thereby entrap them in supporting roles, they differentiated themselves from Britain and the Commonwealth by developing relations with non-Commonwealth nations. During the war, the most important ally to both Australia and Canada was the United States. Before 1939 Canada had enjoyed more extensive and harmonious relations with the United States than Australia, out of necessity as much as inclination. Geography dictated that the two nations could not be indifferent to one another, particularly in wartime. The integration of Canadian and American defences in 1940 in the Permanent Joint Board on Defence (PJBD) introduced a continental system with potentially far-reaching implications. In Britain, the PJBD was cause for alarm. It confirmed the British suspicion that America was luring Canada out of Britain's sphere. Hence Churchill's disappointed reaction to the announcement of the PJBD, even though it lessened the demands on Britain's over-taxed military resources. But he could not divert the continentalist tide. In 1941 Canada and the United States concluded the Hyde Park Agreement, which coordinated their wartime economies. Ottawa confirmed the paramountcy of the American connection when it elevated its legation in Washington to full embassy status in 1943. Thus Canada was better able to protect its interests and voice its concerns in Washington.[69] Canadian officials understood that deepening ties with the United States was an act of liberation, as it demonstrated that Canada operated independent of, even in spite of, Britain in international affairs.[70]

Australian-American relations also flourished in wartime. There was much scope to expand and improve their relations, which had been entirely acrimonious in the 1930s, poisoned by trade disputes. Australia stood so low in American eyes that Washington did not extend most-favoured-nation (MFN) treatment to it even while fascist Italy and Nazi Germany enjoyed the privilege. The first overture was the appointment of a minister to Washington in 1940: Richard Casey. It was an important step and revealed that Australia could not trust the representation of its interests to British officials in Washington. The Japanese advance was an effective inducement to further rapprochement. On 28 December 1941, Curtin, in a much-cited and regularly discussed statement, called upon the United States to come to Australia's aid. "Without any inhibitions of any kind, I make it quite clear that Australia looks to America, free of any pangs as to our traditional links or kinship with the United Kingdom."[71] Churchill's reaction was bitter. But he could do nothing to lessen the military threat to Australia. The subsequent ratification of the Statute of Westminster in 1942, and its retroactive application to 1939, reinforced the significance of Curtin's appeal. It confirmed that Australia finally accepted the principles inherent in the statute: that Australia was sovereign and fully responsible for its security. Deepening ties with the United States emphasized that Australia's wartime leaders accepted responsibility for their national interests and worked beyond and independent of Britain.

However, American recognition of the dominions' independence did not automatically follow the opening and upgrading of diplomatic offices in Washington. Americans continued to assume that Britain could speak for the dominions. As late as November 1944, American officials distributed memos to all members of the Far Eastern Committee of the United Nations Relief and Rehabilitation Agency (UNRRA), except for Australia and New Zealand. Washington sent their copies via London,[72] content to leave the briefing of the dominions to British officials. The British did not object to this practice because it reinforced their own centrality within the Commonwealth, which was consistent with their postwar aims. But this pattern of consultation was dangerous to the dominions, which were intent on gaining influence and recognition – the two went together. As a general rule, the Americans were much more willing to deal directly with Canada, with whom they had longer-standing relations. Still, they assumed that Britain exerted some influence over Canada as its historical parent.[73] For instance, when the United States and Britain drafted the principles of the Atlantic Charter, the United States left it to Britain to apprise Canada of the proposal and to consult with them, as though Canada and Britain constituted a bloc.[74] American deference to Britain in managing relations with the dominions inhibited the Canadian and Australian quest for independence. Part of the problem was that they were small powers that could be easily overlooked in the great power dynamic. But the underlying reason for their marginalization had much to do with their colonial heritage.

While American recognition came gradually, the two dominions succeeded in impressing their foreign policies with their own stamp. Their brand of internationalism helped to distinguish them from Britain. In Canada, a group of young, enthusiastic, and confident civil servants formulated a philosophy of international relations to justify their claims to inclusion and influence. It was called the functional principle. It rejected the domination of world affairs by the largest powers, but it was not an attempt to democratize international relations. Nor did it seek to delegate influence in a fixed pattern. Instead it equated capacity, contribution, and expertise with responsibility and influence.[75] Where a nation made a significant contribution or had expertise, then that nation should enjoy a commensurate influence.

The Canadians tested the functional principle by lobbying to join the executive of the Combined Food Board (CFB). Their case was compelling. Canada was second only to the United States as a supplier of food to the allied war effort. Moreover, they were included at every level of the CFB except the top one. They met with resistance, primarily from British officials whose objection was that if Canada got in, then Australia would demand inclusion. Ottawa countered by agreeing that, as soon as Australia contributed as much food as Canada, it, too, should be admitted to the executive. Over one year of lobbying paid off when Canada joined the CFB executive in October 1943. Still, the British attempted to deny that a precedent had been set or that inclusion was a form of recognition of their contribution and independence. Churchill amended the message notifying Ottawa of its executive membership so that it "cut down recognition of Canada's right to be consulted."[76] But British efforts could not deny the significance of the achievement. Canada's international personality assumed a new dimension and distinguishing traits. Canada was the champion of the right of middle-sized nations to have selective influence. This was a new role for Canada in world affairs.

Canberra also articulated a foreign policy that was explicitly geared toward the promotion of Australian goals and independence.[77] At its core was the determination to reverse the order of priorities so that Australian interests came first, Britain's lower down. An "Australian-first" approach resulted in some unpleasant disputes with Britain. For instance, Canberra took issue with the appointment of Richard Casey, Australia's first minister to Washington, as the *British* minister to the Middle East. They saw this as poaching by Britain, whereas in 1939 it would have been highly unlikely that the Australian government would have objected to one of its own representatives being singled out for such responsibility. In fact, Curtin was so indignant he threatened to block the appointment. The sniping between the two allies grew so acerbic that President Roosevelt expressed his alarm to Churchill.[78] Such disputes weakened the allied cause in the Second World War, but Canadian observers still welcomed this development, believing Australia had positioned itself on the path of sovereignty and independence: "it definitely intends to pursue a policy of greater independence of action much along the lines of Canadian policy."[79]

The emergence of an independent approach owed much to the election of the Labor Party in Australia in 1941. Labor had consistently challenged the pro-British inclinations of previous Liberal governments. Once Labor came to power, it immediately set out to complete the transition to independence. In order to be successful, Australia had to define its own voice and ensure it was heard.[80] There could be no more effective person to realize this than Herbert Evatt, foreign minister in the Labor government. He was well educated, supremely confident of his own abilities, and passionate about the cause of Australian security and independence. He also possessed a loud voice. A conventional style of diplomacy was ill-suited to Evatt's temperament, nor was it likely to achieve his objective: recognition that Australia was independent, mature, and had the ability to influence international and Commonwealth affairs. Paul Hasluck has described Evatt's diplomacy as "shin-kicking."[81] Australia could demonstrate its independence from Britain by being rude to British politicians, bureaucrats, and diplomats.[82] The British were not alone in being singled out for abrasive treatment. Evatt's diplomatic style was consistent, no matter whom he was dealing with. Without a doubt, Evatt was noticed and discussed by world leaders as no previous Australian politician ever had been. The descriptions were not always laudatory, but that was not the point. By war's end Evatt had done much to put Australia on the international map.

The expression of a new approach to international affairs was not narrowly nationalistic. Like Canada, Australia positioned itself as a middle power. Its triumphant debut in this role came at the founding conference of the United Nations in San Francisco in 1945, where Evatt objected to great power dictation of the postwar world. He insisted that unless small powers shaped the peace, no postwar settlement would be stable.[83] He went on to insist that the authority of the great powers had to be curbed. Thus, he took strong exception to the great-power veto. Instead, he advocated enlarging the contributions of the small and medium-sized members by enhancing the role of the general assembly. Although Evatt was successful in giving Australia a new international personality and function, he was less successful in revising the UN charter. He was heard, but with little effect. One of his own advisers explained why this was so. According to Paul Hasluck, Evatt adopted a position and championed it aggressively without taking into account larger international political realities. He did not understand the necessity of compromise. Consequently, he was irritated with those who did not support Australian amendments, siding instead with Britain and the United States. He called them stooges, a category to which Canada belonged.[84] But even if Evatt did not change the charter in any substantive way, he did succeed in amplifying and legitimizing the voice of small powers. Australia was rewarded with election to one of the first non-permanent seats on the UN Security Council.

In contrast to their irrepressible and flamboyant Australian colleagues, Canadian representatives to the San Francisco conference worked quietly, assiduously, and behind the scenes to help create the UN. The Canadian brand of diplomacy was the stylistic antithesis of Australia, and this was a real impediment to their burgeoning relationship. Canadian delegates were disdainful of Evatt, who railed with so little effect. Canadians prided themselves on picking their battles more wisely, and for appreciating what was possible, as opposed to what was desirable. For instance, Canada understood that relations between the United States, Britain, and the Soviet Union were extremely fragile. Agreement on the draft charter had not come easily to the big three. The great powers could not act on all of the suggestions to improve the UN because that might provoke the collapse of the great-power alliance. Canadian criticisms and contributions were framed with this in mind.

Despite a more sophisticated understanding of the international political process, Canadian officials also envied Evatt. He said what they thought and consequently got all the credit. Mackenzie King vented his frustration in his diary after Evatt was singled out for praise at the end of the conference, whereas there was no special mention of the important contributions of Canadian officials. "To me, it looked like a case where if men are nasty and rough enough, they get the credit and the decent people are left behind."[85] Australia seemed to have usurped the role Canada was meant to play as the leader of the small powers and to have stolen its seat on the Security Council. But a more flamboyant performance would have been inconsistent with the new character that Canada was defining for itself as a constructive, sensible backroom player. Incompatible diplomatic styles, mixed with mutual envy, limited the scope for cooperation between Canada and Australia on the world stage.

Even if they enjoyed little success in amending the UN charter, the roles played by Canada and Australia at the San Francisco conference were effective in distancing themselves from Britain and entrenching their individuality and independence. Their success was evident when Lord Halifax, Britain's ambassador in Washington, complained to Prime Minister Smuts of South Africa of the embarrassing "exhibition the Empire was making in the presence of the Americans and other countries" because of the active and vocal role of Evatt, as well as that of Prime Minister Peter Fraser of New Zealand. Smuts disagreed with his gloomy view, insisting that it was "on the whole very good" that "other nations should see that each part of the Empire really managed and we were not following just one particular course."[86] This was deeply disappointing to the British, who wanted to lead a united Commonwealth into the peace. Canada and Australia, in their own ways, made it clear that the Commonwealth would not function as a bloc in world affairs. Britain's acceptance of the limits of its authority over the dominions and its inability to use the Commonwealth as the exclusive instrument of British foreign policy granted recognition, albeit grudgingly, that Canada and Australia were sovereign states. Lord Cranborne, the secretary of state for dominion affairs, commented that the San Francisco meeting demonstrated that Australia, and even New Zealand, were following the Canadian lead of disentangling themselves from Britain: "First, Canada, and now, as appeared at San Francisco, Australia and New Zealand, are beginning to show the most disturbing signs of moving away from the conception of a Commonwealth acting together to that of independent countries, bound to us and each other only by the most shadowy ties. Dr. Evatt is only a particularly repulsive representative of a not at all uncommon point of view in his own and the other Empire countries."[87]

Despite Cranborne's pessimistic assessment of the state of the Commonwealth, the determination of the Canadian and Australian governments to carve out individual niches for themselves in world affairs did not translate into rupture with Britain. Both continued to believe that the Commonwealth was, or should be, a useful association of nations. The difficulty was that membership in the Commonwealth had compromised their independence and status. They had to distinguish between "acting as a unit" and "acting in unison."[88] Part of the purpose of behaving separately in international affairs was to clarify the confusion surrounding the relationship between Britain and the dominions. If the rest of the world understood that Britain, Canada, and Australia were sovereign, equal, and independent allies, then membership in the Commonwealth would no longer engender confusion and ambiguity. Thus they had to disentangle themselves from Britain in world affairs so that they would be able to work together in the Commonwealth, as well as other international forums.

The development of more extensive ties with the United States reinforced the appeal for Canada and Australia of maintaining close relations with Britain. Although Canadian officials initially saw their relationship with the United States as a form of emancipation, they soon learned that their neighbour could be as oblivious to their interests and opinions as Britain. Having cleared the colonial hurdle, they still had to overcome the realities of power politics. Maintaining a working relationship with Britain acted as a counterweight to the American relationship. Australians also cherished their relationship with Britain; despite the wartime rapprochement, they were deeply suspicious of the United States. Their apprehension was rooted in an historic mistrust of American capital.[89] Direct contact between Americans and Australians during the war deepened this suspicion. Moreover, Australian politicians and diplomats, like their Canadian counterparts, discovered through close contact with the United States that the difficulty in making themselves heard was a problem of stature as well as status. Working with Britain and the Commonwealth, as long as it was on Australian terms, would enhance their standing in Washington. Although Evatt was despised in London, and accused by his compatriots of being "probably a secessionist,"[90] he was satisfied with shaking the Commonwealth up and did not try to break it apart.

The Canadian and Australian desire to maintain close contact with Britain and the Commonwealth was cold comfort in London. Although Britain would likely remain the hub of the Commonwealth, it was clear that London could not manage that association to serve its own ends. From the

Canadian and Australian points of view, however, cooperation with Britain and association in the Commonwealth was much less problematic after 1945. There was less confusion among outsiders about the workings of the Commonwealth. And British frustration in its dealings with Canada and Australia was all the evidence needed to demonstrate convincingly that they were not appendages of British foreign policy. Moreover, they had impressed their own views upon their external policies and distinguished themselves in the international community so that they could no longer be ignored or mistaken as subordinate to Britain. Their independence was beyond question, and the reason this was so was that Canada and Australia assumed all of the responsibilities of sovereignty. However, the challenge did not end there. Having entrenched their independence, these two dominions also wanted to be relevant and influential in international affairs. To do so they would have to learn to compensate for their relatively small size in a world dominated by superpowers and once-great powers. But before they could reasonably attempt to shape the course of world affairs, they had to come to terms with their colonial pasts. By war's end they had done so in one overwhelmingly important area – that of managing their own foreign affairs.

Conclusion: Canada and Australia As Middle Powers

The emergence of Canada and Australia as independent states required that they have complete control over foreign policy. As Escott Reid complained in 1942, the dominions were themselves primarily responsible for their underdeveloped standing in the world. Their refusal to assume responsibility for foreign policy prolonged and testified to their immaturity and resulted in other nations regarding them as dependents. "We are being treated as children because we have refused to behave as adults. An adult makes his own decisions; he accepts responsibility for his own decisions ... We have taken a positive pleasure in trying not to influence the course of history."[91] The timing of the Canadian and Australian affirmation of independence, during the Second World War, when the Commonwealth war effort validated the connection to Britain, seems ironic at first glance. But the wartime revival of the Commonwealth threatened to have a regressive effect on Anglo-Dominion relations. Canada and Australia could lose what gains they had made in the interwar years unless they were anchored to their existence and acceptance as discrete states.

The story of the dominions' independence was also a tale of struggle against British resistance. Until their oldest ally regarded them as true equals, other states would be slow to acknowledge that these two dominions no longer fell within Britain's purview. Thus British recognition was essential to securing general recognition, without which Canadian and Australian claims to independence would ring hollow. However, the struggle to limit and clarify their relations with Britain did not mean their relations with Britain were at an end. Cooperation with Britain would persist, but only because the dominions had eliminated confusion about their connection with Britain. Indeed, they proved to be tenacious allies. In Australia's case, its determination to stand unquestioningly by Britain endured until the Suez Crisis of 1956. But there was a fundamental difference between being a loyal ally and a subservient pawn. If the dominions chose to work with Britain, they did so voluntarily. Moreover, this aspect of the history of the dominions' emergence as autonomous states tells only one side of the story. It concentrates on securing political and international independence. These two nations also needed to develop individual civic identities, which would involve patriating their Britishness. That was a more drawn-out and subtle process.[92]

This study of Canada and Australia emphasizes comparisons more than relations, a product of respecting the historical record. Individually, although not in concert, they became states in fact, recognized as distinct from Britain. They adopted different tactics even if their ultimate goals overlapped. Moreover, they generally misunderstood one another and believed they were working at cross-purposes. This was particularly evident in the Commonwealth, where Australia teamed up with New Zealand to overhaul its structure and purpose. To Canadian eyes this appeared to be another attempt at centralization, which robbed them of their autonomy. Thus they did not see eye to eye. Contrasting diplomatic styles – from the self-effacing backroom diplomacy favoured by Canadian diplomats to the shin-kicking, soapbox diatribe at which Evatt excelled – disguised substantive agreement. Their relations were also limited because they viewed one another as rivals. The middle-power category was a new one in the international hierarchy. It was not clear that they could both excel. One's gain seemed to represent a loss for the other. Thus there was a competitiveness between Canada and Australia that impeded cooperative relations.

But even if relations were limited, their awareness of one another was great because Australia and Canada also acted as reference points for one another as they defined and moved toward middle-power roles and identities. Measured against the other's progress, they could gauge whether or not they were moving in the right direction and at a fast enough pace. They could also learn from one another how to avoid, circumvent, or overcome obstacles as they confronted the same challenges. Estrangement did not entail lack of interest. In fact, one's gain was a direct benefit to the other when it came to entrenching their autonomy. The dominions constituted an eclectic group, but it was still assumed that there was one set of rules for all. Consequently, an advance made by one dominion affected all the others. So Canada and Australia pushed and pulled one another down the road to independence; at war's end, although their successes were individual, they were mutually reinforcing. As they turned to the next challenge in foreign affairs – to assert real influence in the international community – they would realize the benefits of cooperation that the chapters in the next section examine. But in 1945 they remained accidental allies.

Notes

1 Sara Pienaar, *South Africa and International Relations between the Two World Wars: The League of Nations Dimension* (Johannesburg: Witwatersrand University Press, 1987), 21.

2 "Text of an address on the occasion of the annual Feast at Eliot House, Cambridge, Mass., by Mr. R.G. Casey, Australian Minister to the United States on the Evening of March 20th, 1941," Franklin Delano Roosevelt Library (hereinafter FDRL), Winant Papers, box 222, folder: Speeches by Members of the British Government.

3 This logic also applies to South Africa and New Zealand. I have included them in my study of Anglo-Dominion relations in the 1940s: *Redefining the Bonds of the Commonwealth, 1939-1948: The Politics of Preference* (Basingstoke: Palgrave, 2002).

4 K.C. Wheare, *The Constitutional Structure of the Commonwealth*, (1960; reprint, Oxford: Clarendon Press, 1969), 55.

5 Although there is a vast literature on the subject of nationalism, little attention has been paid to the way that states acquired sovereignty and standing in the international community, a fundamental part of the process of becoming independent.

6 See E.J. Hobsbawm, *Nations and Nationalism since 1780: Programme, Myth, Reality* (Cambridge: Canto, 1990), ch. 5, "The Apogee of Nationalism, 1918-1950" for an elaboration of his general argument.

7 This was the peace treaty concluded with Turkey at the Paris Peace Conference.

8 Quoted in Charles Stacey, *Canada and the Age of Conflict*, vol. 2, *1921-1948, The Mackenzie King Era* (Toronto: University of Toronto Press, 1981), 23. Stacey denied that the British were trying to assert their authority over Canada and the other dominions. Rather, he concluded that the clash was a product of Britain's sloppy handling of relations with King in particular, and of lack of interest in the management of relations with the dominions in general. For his analysis, see 2:17-31.

9 John Herd Thompson and Stephen J. Randall, *Canada and the United States: Ambivalent Allies* (Montreal and Kingston: McGill-Queen's University Press, 1994), 105.

10 R.F. Holland, *Britain and the Commonwealth Alliance, 1918-1939* (London: Macmillan, 1981), 74.

11 Amery to Skelton, 11 May 1929, *Documents on Canadian External Relations*, vol. 4, *1926-1930*, ed. Alex I. Inglis (Ottawa: Department of External Affairs, 1971), 76-7. For more information on the opening of Canada's embassy in Japan, see John Meehan, "From Ally to Menace: Canadian Attitudes and Policies toward Japanese Imperialism, 1929-1939" (PhD diss., University of Toronto, 2000), 16-76.

12 Charles Stacey, "Mackenzie King's Personal Atlantic Triangle," *Mackenzie King and the Atlantic Triangle*, 1976 Joanne Goodman Lectures (Toronto: Macmillan of Canada, 1976), 19, 21. Stacey described King's attitudes toward Britain as "those of a good Victorian and a good colonial." King's closest adviser on foreign policy in the 1920s and 1930s was O.D. Skelton, who became undersecretary of state for external affairs in 1925. Skelton was much more critical of the British connection and willing to act more boldly in distancing Canada from Britain. For an analysis of Skelton's attitudes toward relations with Britain, see Norman Hillmer, "The Anglo-Canadian Neurosis: The Case of O.D. Skelton" in *Britain and Canada: Survey of a Changing Relationship*, ed. Peter Lyon (London: Frank Cass, 1976), 61-84.

13 Stacey, "The Hermit Kingdom, 1921-1930," *Mackenzie King and the Atlantic Triangle*, 35. J.L. Granatstein and R. Bothwell make the same point about King being determined to stand by Britain in a major war in "'A Self-Evident National Duty': Canadian Foreign Policy 1935-1939," in *Canadian Foreign Policy: Historical Readings*, ed. J.L. Granatstein (Toronto: Copp Clark Pitman, 1993), 159.

14 W.J. Hudson, *Casey* (Melbourne: Oxford University Press, 1986), 69.

15 An examination of the British understanding of the consequences of the statute raises more doubt about its significance. The British endorsed the Statute of Westminster because they believed they were simply replacing formal ties with voluntary ones, which they did not doubt would be as strong. Unofficial links, such as finance and emigration, would perpetuate cooperation with Britain. London believed it was merely sacrificing the form of control in order to retain the substance of it. See John Darwin, "Imperialism in Decline? Tendencies in British Imperial Policy between the Wars," *The Historical Journal* 23, 3 (1980): 662-7. As Darwin observed, "the price of constitutional equality would be little more than an exaggerated deference to the prejudices and susceptibilities of dominion politicians," 667; P.J. Cain and A.G. Hopkins, *British Imperialism: Crisis and Deconstruction 1914-1990* (London: Longman, 1993), 109, note that dominions remained dependent on the UK economically and militarily, except for Canada.

16 Wheare, *The Constitutional Structure of the Commonwealth*, 6-16.

17 A Commission of Government was established to restore order to Newfoundland's financial affairs, after which responsible government was supposed to return. The Commission of Government was directly responsible to the Dominions Office. For an explanation of Newfoundland's economic and political development, consult the introduction in David Mackenzie, *Inside the Atlantic Triangle: Canada and the Entrance of Newfoundland into Confederation, 1939-1949* (Toronto: University of Toronto Press, 1986).

18 Stephen Leacock, *Back to Prosperity: The Great Opportunity of the Empire Conference* (Toronto: Macmillan, 1932), 28.

19 Hudson, *Casey*, 103.

20 See John Hilliker, *Canada's Department of External Affairs*, vol. 1, *The Early Years, 1909-1946* (Montreal and Kingston: McGill-Queen's University Press, 1990) for information about the growth of the department. There are several useful memoirs covering the early history of the department. See Maurice Pope, ed., *Public Servant: The Memoirs of Sir Joseph Pope* (Toronto: Oxford University Press, 1960); Lester B. Pearson, *Mike: The Memoirs of the Rt. Hon. Lester B. Pearson*, vol. 1, *1897-1948* (Toronto: University of Toronto Press, 1972); Hugh L. Keenleyside, *The Memoirs of Hugh L. Keenleyside*, vol. 1, *Hammer the Golden Day* (Toronto: McClelland and Stewart, 1981). J.L. Granatstein's biography of Norman Robertson, *A Man of Influence: Norman A. Robertson and Canadian Statecraft* (Toronto: Deneau, 1981) is also helpful.

21 The Australian Department of External Affairs did not have its own secretary until November 1935; it had been a part of the Prime Minister's Department before then. David Lee is currently completing an official history of the Department of External Affairs.

22 P.G. Edwards, *Prime Ministers and Diplomats: The Making of Australian Foreign Policy, 1901-1949* (Melbourne: Oxford University Press, 1993), 66.

23 Australia renamed it the Department of Foreign Affairs and Trade in 1970; Canada likewise changed the name to the Department of Foreign Affairs and International Trade in 1993.

24 Japan invaded Manchuria and established a puppet state of Manchukuo under the titular authority of Pu Yi, China's last emperor, who had been deposed in 1911.

25 Cecil Edwards, *Bruce of Melbourne, A Man of Two Worlds* (London: Heinemann, 1965), 224.

26 Ibid., 236.

27 Nicholas Mansergh, ed., *Documents and Speeches of British Commonwealth Affairs 1931-1952*, vol. 1 (London: Oxford University Press, 1953), 147.

28 J.D.B. Miller, *Britain and the Old Dominions* (London: Chatto and Windus, 1966), 155-6.

29 Mansergh, ed., *Documents and Speeches*, 1:170-1.

30 Joe Garner, *The Commonwealth Office 1925-68* (London: Heinemann, 1978), 106.

31 Mansergh, ed., *Documents and Speeches*, 1:122.

32 Ibid., 171, 172.

33 J.L. Granatstein and Norman Hillmer, *Empire to Umpire: Canada and the World to the 1990s* (Toronto: Copp Clark Longman, 1994).

34 King did remark in January 1939 that an attack on Britain would put Canada at war; criticism followed. In March 1939, following Germany's seizure of Czechoslovakia, King stated that aggression against Britain would represent aggression against the entire Commonwealth. The backlash was sharp and divided. The French press speculated whether Quebec's

MPs should quit the government. The English press blasted King for not making a strong enough commitment to Britain. King's fears about national unity and the divisive impact of foreign policy on relations between French and English Canadians were more than justified by this response. See H. Blair Neatby, *William Lyon Mackenzie King: The Prism of Unity, 1932-1939* (Toronto: University of Toronto Press, 1976), 297-9.

35 Diary entry for 21 December 1940, in *The Moffat Papers: Selections from the Diplomatic Journals of Jay Pierrepont Moffat, 1919-1943*, ed. Nancy Harvison Hooker (Cambridge, MA: Harvard University Press, 1956), 342.

36 Mansergh, ed., *Documents and Speeches*, 1:21.

37 Edwards, *Bruce of Melbourne*, 233.

38 Mansergh, ed., *Documents and Speeches*, 1:479.

39 Carl Bridge, ed., *From Munich to Vietnam: Australia's Relations with Britain and the United States since the 1930s* (Carlton: Melbourne University Press, 1991), 3.

40 Memo, 6 September 1939, FDRL, Berle Papers, box 211, Diary September-October 1939.

41 Greg Donaghy's short and useful survey of Canadian-Australian relations is called *Parallel Paths: Canadian-Australian Relations since the 1890s* (Ottawa: Department of Foreign Affairs and International Trade, 1995).

42 See especially David Day, *The Great Betrayal: Britain, Australia and the Onset of the Pacific War, 1939-1942* (London: Angus and Robertson, 1988).

43 McIntosh to Berendsen, 6 November 1943, in *Undiplomatic Dialogue: Letters between Carl Berendsen and Alister McIntosh 1943-1952*, ed. Ian McGibbon (Auckland: Auckland University Press, 1993), 35.

44 Memo by Secretary of State for Dominion Affairs, "The Relationship of the British Commonwealth to the Post-War International Organisation," 15 June 1943, Public Records Office, London, UK (hereinafter PRO), PREM4, 30, 3, W.P. (43), 244.

45 Minutes by Ronald, 31 December 1942, PRO, FO371, file 35362.

46 Minutes by Gladwyn Jebb, 28 December 1942, PRO, FO371, file 35362.

47 Evatt was particularly irate about his exclusion from the Cairo conference, to which Chiang K'ai-shek had been invited.

48 "The Rt. Hon. Ernest Bevin, M.P., Minister of Labour and National Service, Speaking at Shipley, Yorkshire, on Sunday, 12th April 1942," FDRL, Winant Papers, box 185, file: Bevin, Ernest.

49 "Mr. Eden at the Mansion House, 29 May 1941," FDRL, Winant Papers, box 194, file: Eden, Anthony.

50 Wheare, *The Constitutional Structure of the Commonwealth*, 5. Italics added.

51 Hume Wrong, memorandum, "Some comments on intra-Commonwealth relations," 17 August 1943, National Archives of Canada (hereinafter NAC), RG25, vol. 3263, file 6133-40, part 1.

52 "Twenty-Four Point Programme for the Abolition of the Vestigial Remnants of Canada's Former Status of Colonial Subordination and for the Creation of Appropriate Symbols of Canadian Nationhood," memo by Escott Reid, 21 March 1944, NAC, Escott Reid Papers, MG31 E46.

53 "Address by Mr. R.G. Casey, 20 March 1941," FDRL.

54 "Notes of Speech by the Rt. Hon. S.M. Bruce to the American and British Commonwealth Association," 12 December 1944, FDRL, Winant Papers, box 183, file: Australia – High Commissioner, Bruce, S.M.

55 Mansergh, ed., *Documents and Speeches*, 1:565.

56 Nicholas Mansergh, *Survey of British Commonwealth Affairs*, vol. 3, *Problems of External Policy 1931-1939* (London: Oxford University Press, 1952), 137. This statistic exaggerates the number of Australians who were British. About 90 percent were, but the 99 percent figure was bandied about as popular lore.

57 David Day, "Pearl Harbor to Nagasaki," in *Munich to Vietnam*, ed., Bridge, 67.

58 Wrong, "Some comments on intra-Commonwealth relations."

59 "Lionel Robbins: Hot Springs and After, May-June 1943," 5-7 June 1943, in *The Wartime Diaries of Lionel Robbins and James Meade 1943-45*, ed. Susan Howson and D.E. Moggridge (Basingstoke: Macmillan, 1990), ch. 1, 56.

60   Paul Hasluck, *Government and the People 1942-1945* (Canberra: Australian War Memorial, 1970), 478.
61   Nicholas Mansergh, *Survey of British Commonwealth Affairs*, vol. 4, *Problems of Wartime Co-operation and Post-War Change, 1939-1952* (London: Oxford University Press, 1958), 168-9.
62   Douglas Copeland, "Australia's Attitude to British Commonwealth Relations," *International Journal* 3, 1 (1947-8): 41.
63   Heather J. Harvey, *Consultation and Cooperation in the Commonwealth* (London: Oxford University Press, 1952), 84.
64   Coombs to Chifley, 12 July 1943, Australian Archives (hereinafter AA), Department of Treasury, Main series files, A571, 61, file: 1944, 1109 part 1.
65   Meade Diary, 10 June 1945, London School of Economics Archives. James Meade described the experience of Leslie Melville, who attended an economic conference of the Commonwealth. Evatt reprimanded Melville for saying that Australia would not give up any imperial preferences in future tariff negotiations unless there were far-reaching concessions. This went too far for Evatt, who insisted that Australia be absolutely uncommitted with respect to changing preferential tariffs.
66   Mansergh, ed., *Documents and Speeches*, 1:586
67   Coombs to Melville, telegram no. E.68, 10 May 1943, AA, Department of Treasury, Main series files, A571, 61, file: 1944, 1109C part 2; Department of External Affairs to Prime Minister, teleprinter draft message, 27 April 1943, AA, Department of Treasury, Main series files, A571, 61, file: 1944, 1109 part 2.
68   Secretary of State for External Affairs to Canadian High Commissioner in London, tel. 1101, 25 June 1943, *Documents on Canadian External Relations*, vol. 9, *1942-1943*, ed. John F. Hilliker (Ottawa: Department of External Affairs, 1980), 678-9.
69   King to House of Commons, 12 November 1940, in *Documents and Speeches*, ed. Mansergh, 1:548.
70   Author interview with Charles Ritchie, Ottawa, 24 September 1992.
71   Cited in *Documents and Speeches*, ed. Mansergh, 1:550.
72   McGibbon, ed., *Undiplomatic Dialogue*, 91.
73   Memo to Hull from Berle, 28 August 1942, FDRL, Berle Papers, Box 58, Hull, Cordell – January-August 1942.
74   Memo of conversation between Berle and Hume Wrong re joint declaration of the Atlantic Charter, 31 December 1941, FDRL, Berle Papers, box 213, file: Diary December 12-31, 1941.
75   J.L. Granatstein, *The Ottawa Men: The Civil Service Mandarins 1935-1957* (Toronto: Oxford University Press, 1982), 92.
76   Minutes by Berle, 15 October 1943, FDRL, Official file series 4281, file: Winant, John G. 1941-1944.
77   Roger Bell, *Unequal Allies: Australian-American Relations and the Pacific War* (Carlton: Melbourne University Press, 1977). Bell dates the articulation of Australia's own role and personality in world affairs to 1941-6.
78   Roosevelt to Churchill, tel. 127, FDRL, Hopkins Papers, box 136, file: Winston S. Churchill (folder 1), 22 March 1942.
79   Davies to Robertson, letter, 23 June 1944, NAC, RG25, 89-90, 029, box 4, 4-G(s), part 2.
80   Paul Hasluck, *Diplomatic Witness: Australian Foreign Affairs, 1941-47* (Carlton: Melbourne University Press, 1980), 28.
81   Hasluck, *Government and the People 1942-1945*, 629.
82   Hasluck, *Diplomatic Witness*, 42.
83   Evatt's comments cited in "Voice for Small Nations in Making of Peace," January 1945, FDRL, Winant Papers, box 183, file: Australia – High Commissioner, Bruce, S.M. Jan. 45.
84   Hasluck, *Diplomatic Witness*, 195.
85   Mackenzie King diary, microfilm reel 219, 26 June 1945, 642. Thanks to Kathy Rasmussen for finding this passage for me.
86   Ibid., 24 June 1945, 631-2. Thanks again to Kathy Rasmussen.
87   David Day, *Reluctant Nation: Australia and the Allied Defeat of Japan 1942-1945* (Oxford: Oxford University Press, 1992), 280.
88   Pearson to Robertson, 1 February 1944, NAC, RG25, vol. 3263, file 6133-40, part 1.

89 Peter Love, *Labor and the Money Power: Australian Labour Populism 1890-1950* (Carlton: Melbourne University Press, 1984).

90 J.M. McCarthy, "Australia: A View from Whitehall 1939-1945," *Australian Outlook* 28, 3 (1974): 326. Note that it was Australians who described him as "probably a secessionist."

91 Denis Smith, *Diplomacy of Fear: Canada and the Cold War, 1941-48* (Toronto: University of Toronto Press, 1988), 17.

92 Many historians have tackled the slippery subject of dominions' nationalism, in particular how the British heritage of Canada and Australia contributed to individual identities, as well as making them a part of Greater Britain. See Carl Berger, *Sense of Power: Studies in the ideas of Canadian Imperialism, 1867-1914* (Toronto: University of Toronto Press, 1970). Also consult John Eddy and Deryck Schreuder, *The Rise of Colonial Nationalism: Australia, New Zealand, Canada and South Africa First Assert Their Nationalities, 1880-1914* (Sydney, Wellington, London, and Boston: Oxford University Press, 1988).

3
Colonization of Indigenous Peoples: The Movement toward New Relationships
Peter H. Russell

Australia and Canada have each passed through their own process of evolving from British colonies to independent nations. They have overcome the ambivalence about acquiring an independent identity that Francine McKenzie's essay shows they had earlier in this century. But now, having reached maturity as sovereign nation-states, both countries are challenged by the peoples who have been colonized within their own boundaries. The challengers are the Indigenous peoples[1] who inhabited and governed the lands and waters of Australia and Canada for many centuries before the arrival of the Europeans. Today these first peoples seek to establish a postcolonial relationship based on mutual consent rather than force. Their insistence on being recognized and respected as peoples with collective rights to land and self-government is certainly a material and practical challenge. More profoundly, it is a challenge that jars the prevailing sense of identity and accomplishment of the dominant majorities in Australia and in Canada. Until this challenge is met in a manner that is just and consensual, a heavy cloud will hang over the legitimacy of what these two countries have achieved.

Given Australia's and Canada's common experience as former British colonies and the dominant British influence on their laws and institutions, one would expect to find marked similarities in their relationships with Indigenous peoples. However, it is the differences that really stand out. While in each case the broad picture of colonization – political and cultural domination and massive dispossession – is the same, there are important and instructive differences. The two countries, following the assertion of British sovereignty, moved along parallel colonizing paths in their relationship with Indigenous peoples. But as they moved along these paths, virtually in total isolation from each other, major differences in laws, institutions, and attitudes developed. Only in the contemporary period, when Australia and Canada – and the world – confront the challenge of working out a post-imperial relationship with Indigenous peoples, is there much interaction.

Today this interaction is as much between Indigenous peoples from the two countries as between policy makers, jurists, and opinion leaders in the dominant societies. Because this interaction occurs so late in the day, it is heavily freighted with the baggage of very different histories.

This essay will trace and analyze the main differences between Australia and Canada that grew up in the process of colonization. It will attempt to show how these differences condition what the two countries can learn from one another, or take from one another, as they endeavour to establish a postcolonial relationship with Indigenous peoples. In the end, it will argue that, despite these differences of the past and present, globalization of the political struggle of Indigenous peoples puts Australia and Canada on converging paths.

A Contrast in Imperial Foundations

Relations between British authorities and the Indigenous peoples of Australia and Canada began on very different footings of law and policy. Indeed, it is the great and distinctive misfortune of the aboriginal peoples[2] of Australia that, from the earliest British contact their land was treated by Britain as a *terra nullius* (a land of no one) under international law.[3] The British colonies in Australia were considered to be pure "colonies of settlement" established on uninhabited wastelands. Although the hundreds of thousands of aboriginal peoples who actually inhabited these wastelands at the time the British discovered them[4] never for a moment accepted this view of the situation, the *terra nullius* doctrine was not effectively challenged in the settler society's courts until the decision of Australia's High Court in the *Mabo* case in 1992[5] – 204 years after the founding of the first British settlement in Australia. Even today, the *terra nullius* outlook is still being challenged politically.

In North America, the British never had the option of ignoring Native societies as if, for practical purposes, they did not exist. English settlement, which began in America in the early 1600s on a very small and tentative basis, depended on a successful "intercourse" with Amerindian nations. Treaties were the instrument of choice for both the British and the First Nations in regularizing their relationship. Treaties were used for a variety of purposes: to secure friendly relations, to establish trading partnerships and military alliances, to delineate the boundaries of European settlement, to fix the terms on which Europeans could enter Native territory, and sometimes to arrange for the purchase of Native lands for European settlement. Given the rough equality of power between Europeans and the Indian nations, and the familiarity of each with treaty-like agreements in international relations, treaties were a natural way of ordering the relationship between their societies. Indeed, the latter part of the eighteenth century was the era of treaties. The emerging nation-states of Europe were turning increasingly to treaties as the means of ordering both their relations with one another as well as with the Indigenous peoples they encountered in Africa, Asia, and North America. The Indigenous nations and confederacies of North America were never more actively involved in this extended world-wide treaty system than in the period between the end of the Seven Years War and the beginning of the American Revolution. Between 1763 and 1774 North American Indian nations and confederacies were signatories to thirty treaties.[6]

Underlying these treaty relationships with Indigenous nations were conflicting motives and assumptions. Whereas the British (and other European powers) viewed them as temporary instruments of pacification to protect the foothold their people had established before advancing further and increasing the area of their occupation, the Amerindians hoped that, through the treaties, they could obtain permanent boundaries and long-term security from further encroachment. Moreover, the British assumption that they had established legal sovereignty over the Indigenous peoples and their lands was never clearly articulated and was altogether at odds with the Indians' view that, while they may have agreed to cede part of their territory to the Europeans, they had not surrendered their political independence. Indians viewed the treaties as agreements between nations of equal status; Britain (like other European powers) viewed the Indian nations as subordinate to them in the sense that they aimed to deny them the right to have international relations with any other external power.[7] Later on, toward the end of the eighteenth century and in the early decades of the nineteenth, when the rough equilibrium of power between the settlers and the Indigenous peoples broke down, these conflicting understandings of the treaty relationship would come to the surface. A recent United Nations study of treaties with Indigenous peoples shows how, through their "domestication," they became instruments of colonialism.[8]

Nonetheless, the treaty relationship did embody a very different foundation for settler-Indigenous relations in Canada as compared with Australia. British colonies in North America were never pure colonies of settlement. The classic distinction in English law – summed up authoritatively in Blackstone's *Commentaries on the Laws of England*[9] – between colonies of settlement and colonies obtained through conquest or cession, though clear enough in theory, did not fit the realities of North America. A colony of settlement was one established through the occupation of uninhabited land to which the settlers brought all the applicable English law. In colonies acquired through conquest and session, the laws of the Indigenous peoples continued until altered by the new sovereign. The British colonies in North America did not fall neatly into either of these categories, but combined features of conquered and settled colonies: "Regarded initially as conquests by the Crown, they eventually in most instances assumed the characteristics of settled colonies, with English law and representative institutions, at least so far as the settler communities were concerned. However the Indians stood in a different position. Generally speaking, they retained an autonomous status living under their own laws and political structures and dealing directly with the Crown and its emissaries on a communal basis."[10]

Thus, at the time Captain Cook came into contact with Indigenous peoples in New Zealand and Australia, Aboriginal peoples in North America living outside areas of European settlement enjoyed full powers of internal self-government and dealt with Europeans on a nation-to-nation basis.

In 1763 the British government issued a royal proclamation on its governance of the vast areas of North America ceded to Britain by France at the end of the Seven Years War. The proclamation established the boundaries of Quebec and set out British policy with respect to Indian lands beyond the settled colonies. It referred to the Aboriginal peoples as "the several Nations or Tribes with whom We are connected" and acknowledged that these nations and tribes were "in Possession of such Parts of our Dominions and Territories as, not having been ceded to or purchased by Us, are reserved to them."[11] The royal proclamation went on to explain that the government aimed to put an end to the "great Frauds and Abuses" committed in purchasing Native lands so that "the Indians may be convinced of our Justice and determined Resolution to remove all reasonable Cause of Discontent." To this end, the King, with the advice of his Privy Council did "strictly enjoin and require, that no private Person do presume to make any purchase from the said Indians of any Lands reserved to the said Indians, within those parts of our Colonies where, We have thought proper to allow Settlement; but that, if at any Time any of the Said Indians should be inclined to dispose of the said Lands, the same shall be Purchased only for Us, in our Name, at some public Meeting or Assembly of the said Indians."[12]

Thus the proclamation recognized Indigenous peoples as nations in possession of all the lands beyond the frontier of European settlement in North America and laid down the rule that no further settlement was to take place on Indian lands until such time as Indians, in a public and responsible way, agreed to cede more land to the crown.

When Captain Cook set out in 1768, just five years after the royal proclamation, on his first great voyage of discovery to the southern hemisphere, it was logical that the instructions he was given by the British government would contemplate relationships with Native peoples not unlike those entered into in North America. And they did. When the *Endeavour* cleared Plymouth Sound and Cook opened his secret instructions from the Admiralty, he read that, among the other things he was enjoined to do when he found the vast and rich southern continent that was thought to occupy the high latitudes of the Pacific, he was "with the Consent of the Natives to take possession of Convenient Situations in the Country in the Name of the King of Great Britain; or, if you find the Country uninhabited take Possession for his Majesty by setting up Proper Marks and Inscriptions, as first discoverers and possessors."[13]

Note that these instructions contained two options, and that the first – making agreements with Native peoples on the terms of settlement – sounds much like the treaty arrangements with Amerindians. But it was the second approach – treating the newfound lands as uninhabited – that was actually followed when British settlement began in 1788, just eighteen years after Cook landed at Botany Bay.

This *terra nullius* policy was never announced or promulgated as official British policy in Australia. If it had, it would have sounded ridiculous; from the moment an Aboriginal man threw a stone at Cook's longboat as he attempted the first British landing on Australian soil, the British knew this land was inhabited.[14] Again, when Captain Bligh, charting a course through the Torres Strait, was confronted by a flotilla of canoes full of warriors, he, too, knew that the islands in this strait he claimed as "new jewels in Britannia's crown" were not unoccupied.[15] Why then did the *terra nullius* approach become so entrenched in Australia?

The beginning of an answer to this question is to observe that the legal doctrine of establishing pure colonies of settlement on uninhabited lands did not assume the total absence of human life from the land in question before the settlers arrived. Rather, it meant that – from the perspective of the colonizers – the people the settlers encountered were too uncivilized, too low on the scale of human existence to count as organized nations with which a European state could make political agreements.[16] This legal doctrine was reinforced by the dominant political philosophy of the day, which is well represented by John Locke's *Second Treatise of Government*. According to Locke, property rights in land come into existence only when man mixes his labour with the earth by cultivating it. Cook, oblivious as most Europeans were to Aboriginal methods of land management, clearly expressed this view when he reported that Aborigines did not practise agriculture nor have domesticated animals and concluded that their land is "in the pure state of Nature, the Industry of Man (having) had nothing to do with any part of it."[17]

It would be a mistake to attribute the treatment of Aboriginal peoples and their lands in the formative years of Australian settlement as driven entirely by legal doctrine or political philosophy. Indeed, it was not until 1889, in the case of *Cooper v. Stuart*, that the Imperial Supreme Court, the Judicial Committee of the Privy Council, endorsed the view that New South Wales was "a Colony which consisted of a tract of territory practically unoccupied, without settled inhabitants or settled law, at the time it was peacefully annexed to the British dominions."[18] It was not until Mr. Justice Blackburn's decision in the 1971 *Cape Gove* case[19] that an Australian court explicitly endorsed this view – and Blackburn's decision stood only until 1992, when the High Court of Australia overturned it in the *Mabo* case.[20] The *terra nullius* doctrine is best understood as a useful legal fiction with which to justify the political and economic objectives of the settlers. As Henry Reynolds has observed, "The theory of an uninhabited continent was just too convenient to surrender lightly. Consequently the gap between law and reality, law and colonial experience grew progressively wider."[21]

As settlers moving inland from the coast encountered Aboriginal people wherever they went and were often fiercely resisted by them, the gap between legal theory and reality that Reynolds speaks of became increasingly evident. But this did not result in a shift to the kind of relationship with Indigenous peoples that developed in the early days of settlement in North America.

The key to the distinctive character of European-Aboriginal relations in Australia is not to be found in law or in philosophy, but in the peculiar circumstances of contact and settlement in Australia. The circumstances of the inauguration of British settlement were indeed peculiar – in Robert Hughes's words "the largest forced exile of citizens at the behest of a European government in pre-modern history."[22] The arrival in Port Jackson on 26 January 1788 of eleven ships carrying over 1,000 British citizens, most of them convicts, followed in the immediately ensuing years by thousands more,[23] meant that right from the beginning the Australian colonies were developed as colonies of settlement. Unlike North America – or, for that matter, New Zealand – large-scale European settlement in Australia was not preceded by a long period in which European powers aimed more at exploiting resources and establishing trading relationships than on planting large instant settlements of their own people.

European settlement in North America developed much more gradually. Through the first two centuries of contact there was more mutuality of interest and more parity of power in settler-Aboriginal relations than occurred in Australia. The Royal Proclamation of 1763 was issued at a time when an uprising led by Pontiac threatened to push the British out of the North American Midwest. Between 16 May and 20 June 1763, nine British forts fell.[24] Officially recognizing Aboriginal rights on unsettled lands was a military imperative. A year later, when William Johnson, the northern superintendent of Indian Affairs, read the proclamation to 2,000 chiefs representing over twenty-four nations gathered at Niagara, he was careful to skirt any assertion of British sovereignty, concentrating instead on sealing a treaty of alliance with the First Nations.[25] One further reason the British had for entering into treaty relationships with Indigenous peoples both in North America, and later on in New Zealand, was that treaties were seen as a way of excluding other rival European powers from establishing relationships with Indigenous peoples. In Australia, however, once the convicts arrived and settlement began, there was not the same level of apprehension of rival

European powers or any sense that formal alliances with the Native inhabitants were needed to protect strategic interests.

Whatever the reasons for the disinclination of the British to enter into treaty-like relations with Indigenous peoples in Australia, the absence of such relationships in the early years of settlement has had profound consequences. It is in the political culture of Australia more than in its laws that these consequences have had the most enduring effect. The non-recognition of Aboriginal peoples as official policy at the beginning of British settlement has meant that these peoples, as collective political entities, have been excluded from much of white Australia's history. This is why, after the High Court in 1992 swept away *terra nullius* as legal doctrine, "white" Australia was so ill-prepared to work on a new relationship based on recognition of the collective rights of aboriginal peoples to land and self-government.[26] In Canada (as in New Zealand), while it is surely not proving to be easy to build a postcolonial relationship with Indigenous peoples, the historical consciousness of these countries is more open to such an undertaking than is Australia's.

Differences within a Common Experience of Dispossession and Subjugation

Despite important initial differences, relations between the settler society and Indigenous peoples in Australia and Canada were soon on parallel paths. In both countries, from the late eighteenth and early nineteenth centuries until well after the Second World War in the twentieth century, the common experience of Indigenous peoples in Australia and in Canada was one of massive dispossession and political subjugation.

The key to the change in the Canadian relationship was the massive influx of settlers following the American revolutionary war. Loyalists from the American colonies and British immigrants flooded into the Maritimes and Upper Canada. In the latter colony, by 1812, settlers outnumbered Natives by ten to one in an area where just thirty years earlier there had been but a handful of white soldiers and traders.[27] Canada, in the eyes of its imperial authorities and of its own settler population, was firmly set on becoming – like Australia – a pure colony of settlement. In this vision there was no room for the partnership kind of relationship that had flourished during the period of the fur trade and early treaty-making. Canada – along with the other three "English-settler" societies, Australia, New Zealand, and the United States – was on its way to establishing its own distinctive model of colonial expansion: the building of new European societies in which the Indigenous peoples were reduced to small, marginalized populations whose fate, in the eyes of the colonizers, was to be either assimilated or eliminated.

While the broad contours of relations with Indigenous peoples in Australia and Canada during this long period of colonialism were roughly the same, there were some notable points of divergence – one relating to law and treaties, a second to the locus of political control, and a third to attitudes. All three have important consequences for contemporary efforts at decolonization. All three leave Australia at something of a disadvantage in this struggle.

In Canada, the original foundations of law and policy in relation to Aboriginal peoples remained in place in theory, but were largely ignored or subverted in practice. The Proclamation of 1763, with its recognition of the Indian nations and their possession of their own lands, was never rescinded. Indeed, it survived as part of Canada's legacy of pre-Confederation imperial law and eventually, in 1982, was inscribed as an Aboriginal magna carta in Canada's modern Constitution. But once the balance of military power turned clearly in their favour, the colonial authorities did not hesitate to give full force to the sovereign power they had previously been wary of asserting. The main instrument for regulating relations with Native peoples was not nation-to-nation treaties but top-down legislation unilaterally imposed by Canadian legislators. This legislation – the Indian Act of 1876 and the earlier legislation on which it was built – resembled in its basic objective the Protection legislation that the Australian colonies, beginning with Victoria, began to adopt in the latter part of the nineteenth century.[28] The aim was "to protect" Natives by segregating them on reserves where, by being "civilized" and Christianized, they would be prepared for assimilation into the dominant society.

Aboriginal peoples in Australia and Canada may well have had rights to land and self-government – they certainly did under their own laws – but in neither country during this long period of colonial domination did they use the courts to vindicate these rights. The era in which they would look for help in the white man's courts did not come until the 1970s. When Canadian courts dealt with Aboriginal issues, it was in cases brought by settlers to defend their property rights or to impose the settlers' criminal law on Native peoples. In most of these cases, Canadian judges usually displayed a stunning ignorance of imperial law and practice. Sidney Harring's recent study of the treatment of Aboriginal issues in nineteenth-century Canadian courts shows that John Beverley Robinson "whose legal mind dominated Upper Canadian jurisprudence in the middle of the nineteenth century" displayed a lack of "any consciousness of the legal issues presented by the presence of the colonies 12,000 native people."[29] Ironically, Robinson's American counterpart, the great US Chief Justice, John Marshall, had a much greater appreciation of the significance of the Proclamation of 1763 and other British precedents for the recognition of Native peoples' rights.[30] In the 1888 *St. Catherine's Milling* case, when the Judicial Committee of the Privy Council rendered a decision (in the context of a federal-provincial dispute) on Indian land rights, though it did not deny that Indians had enjoyed property rights, it reduced "tenure" of their lands to "a personal and usufructuary right" and referred to their possession "such as it was" as depending entirely on the 1763 proclamation.[31]

All this points to Australian and Canadian convergence on legal recognition of Aboriginal rights. Still, there were differences. In the Australian courts there was not even the belittling and demeaning recognition of Indigenous property rights that the Privy Council granted Canadian Indians. More than that, there were occasional glimpses in the Canadian cases of a larger and more generous view. In 1867, a Quebec Superior Court judge, Justice Monk, recognized the validity of a Cree marriage between a Cree woman and an English trader. Justice Monk invoked the American jurisprudence of Chief Justice Marshall, who had acknowledged that "history furnishes no example, from the first settlement of our country, *of any attempt on the part of the Crown to interfere with the internal affairs of the Indians.*"[32] And when *St. Catherine's Milling* was before the Supreme Court of Canada, at least the dissenting justices invoked the Marshallian doctrine and advanced a more robust version of Native peoples' property rights.[33] Thus, in contrast to Australia, there remained in Canadian legal history a doctrine of Aboriginal rights that could be revived in a more enlightened age.

The same kind of difference is evident in the way the lands of Aboriginal people were taken over by the settlers. In Australia the crown granted land to settlers without prior purchase of the land from its Native occupants. When John Batman came over from Van Dieman's Land (Tasmania) in 1835 to Port Phillip Bay (near present-day Melbourne) and purchased 600,000 acres from Aborigines, his "treaty" was firmly rejected both by the local governor and the colonial secretary.[34] In Canada, on the other hand, treaties remained the principal means of obtaining additional lands for settlement and development. Nevertheless, treaties became essentially instruments for legalizing dispossession rather than forging partnerships with Indigenous nations. Their printed versions (in English only) bore little resemblance to what was agreed upon in oral negotiations. Typically, they included clauses in which the Aboriginal signatories were purported to have agreed to "cede, release, surrender and yield up to the Government of the Dominion of Canada, for his Majesty the King and His successors forever, all their rights, titles and privileges whatsoever" over vast tracts of land.[35] In return, Indians were granted tiny, postage-stamp reserves, small annual annuities, and a few tools and trinkets. Through treaties of this kind the frontier of settlement, agriculture, and resource development advanced westward through Ontario across the prairies and into a large wedge of the Northwest Territories. British Columbia was the great exception: from the time it became a

Canadian province in 1871 right up to the 1990s, it resisted the treaty process, treating its territory in effect as a *terra nullius*.[36]

The practical effect of the treaties negotiated with Canadian Indians in the nineteenth and early twentieth century was massive dispossession. The Royal Commission on Aboriginal Peoples, reporting in 1996, presents a stark measure of that dispossession when it observes at the opening of its chapter on Lands and Resources that south of the sixtieth parallel (the boundary between the northern territories and the provinces) "Lands acknowledged as Aboriginal ... (mainly reserves) make up less than one half of one per cent of the Canadian land mass."[37] The commission points out that the comparable figure for the United States (excluding Alaska) is 3 percent. One half of 1 percent is not a whole lot better than the Australian *terra nullius*.

On the other hand, for Aboriginal peoples in Canada there was a significant positive side to these treaties. The treaties were nation-to-nation agreements. As such, they entailed recognition by the incoming settler-state of the nationhood of the Aboriginal signatories and their collective ownership of their traditional lands. It is essential to bear in mind that it was the settler-state's interpretation of these treaties – an interpretation that relied entirely on the written text – that resulted in massive dispossession. Later in the twentieth century, the Supreme Court of Canada would increase considerably the value of treaty rights by incorporating into Canadian law a piece of American jurisprudence requiring that a treaty "be construed, not according to the technical meaning of its words to learned lawyers, but in the sense in which they would naturally be understood by the Indians."[38] Today, treaty-making – the renewal of old treaties according to the mutual understanding of both parties, and the negotiation of new treaties with Aboriginal peoples who are still on their traditional lands but were never parties to so-called "land cession" treaties (mostly in the northern territories, British Columbia, northern Quebec, and Labrador) – is at the heart of efforts to restructure the relationship with Aboriginal peoples in Canada.[39] This means that the federal government in Canada, unlike its counterpart in Australia, accepts that it has a responsibility for working out consensual agreements with Aboriginal peoples on sharing land and resources.[40] This is the positive legacy of the treaty-making process in Canada.

This relates directly to the second point of divergence between Australian and Canadian colonialism – the locus of settler-state control. In imperial relationships with Aboriginal peoples, there is evidence of an iron law at work that goes roughly like this: the further the policy-making authority is from the Native peoples, the more liberal (or less oppressive) it is likely to be. In the first part of the nineteenth century, when Britain was still nominally in control of Aboriginal policy in Australia and Canada, Colonial Office officials and parliamentarians in London were concerned about securing the interests of Native peoples from encroachments of the settlers. This was never so evident as in 1837, when the British House of Commons, moved by the same surge of liberalism that had inspired the abolition of slavery, established a Select Committee on Aborigines. The committee was extremely critical of the treatment of Native peoples in Australia and in Canada (as well as in other British colonies). Its first recommendation was to make Aboriginal relations the exclusive responsibility of the executive government in the colonies. It warned against giving local legislatures any responsibility in this area because "the settlers in almost every colony, having either disputes to adjust with native tribes, or claims to urge against them, the representative body is virtually a party, and therefore ought not to be the judge in such controversies."[41]

Over the next few decades, as Britain relaxed its imperial controls over its colonies of settlement, the direction of Aboriginal affairs in Australia and Canada came under the control of governments in the colonies that were increasingly responsive to settler interests. It was the way in which Britain relinquished responsibility for Aboriginal relations to local authorities that established an important difference between Australia and Canada. In 1867, when Canada became a federation with self-government in its internal affairs, section 91(24) of its Constitution assigned exclusive jurisdiction over "Indians, and Lands reserved for the Indians" to the federal parliament. During this same period in Australia, the governments and legislatures of the individual colonies were assuming the lead in making aboriginal policy. When the Australian federation was formed in 1901, its Constitution, unlike Canada's, did not assign responsibility for aboriginal affairs to the new federal parliament. Quite the contrary; section 51(26) of the Australian Constitution empowered the Commonwealth to legislate for the "people of any race, other than the aboriginal race in any State, for whom it is deemed necessary to make special laws." The states of the federation retained the powers they had been exercising as colonies in relation to Aborigines and Torres Strait Islanders.[42]

This difference in constitutional arrangements was not simply the accidental result of historical timing. With the royal proclamation as a strong historical precedent for a uniform Aboriginal policy and the practice of crown treaty-making with Native peoples, it was logical for control over that policy to remain centralized in Canada. Certainly this is what Aboriginal peoples in Canada wanted: they have viewed formal relationships with provincial governments as not in keeping with their ideal of maintaining nation-to-nation relationships. Indeed, many First Nations in Canada have insisted that their treaty relationship is still with the *British* crown. In Australia colonial policy in aboriginal affairs was more decentralized than in Canada and remained that way after federation. The Commonwealth government became marginally involved in aboriginal policy in 1911 when it took over control of the Northern Territory. But it did not have any Australia-wide legislative authority in this field until the 1967 referendum, which removed the constitutional prohibition against Commonwealth legislation in relation to people of "the aboriginal race." Even then, the states retained their power to legislate in this area, although under the rule of federal paramountcy, their laws in case of a conflict must give way to the Commonwealth's.

The states' retention for so long of control over aboriginal policy left Native peoples in Australia more exposed to the aggression of local settlers than were the Aboriginals in Canada. The consequences were most severe in Queensland and Western Australia, the states with the largest aboriginal populations.[43] The more long-term consequence is that in the contemporary era Canberra's mandate to take the lead in reforming aboriginal relations is not nearly as strong as Ottawa's. Even in Canada, the federal government, despite its having exclusive legislative jurisdiction, cannot accomplish major reforms without provincial cooperation. This is evident when modern treaty-making moves south of the sixtieth parallel.[44] The impact of the land, self-government, and the fiscal implications of these modern comprehensive agreements on vital provincial interests requires provincial participation. Still, it is the federal government that leads, and is expected to lead the process. In Australia, however, after the High Court's 1992 decision in *Mabo* swept away *terra nullius*, the Commonwealth government encountered a great deal of resistance from the states in giving legislative effect to a nation-wide system of aboriginal land rights. Federalism continues to be a stronger restraint on national efforts at restructuring relations with aboriginal peoples in Australia than it does in Canada.

The third point of divergence is the centrality of race in the way white Australians have thought about Aborigines and Torres Strait Islanders – and, sadly, in the way they have encouraged Australia's Indigenous people to think about themselves. A Canadian observer is apt to be struck by the reference in section 51(26) of Australia's Constitution to "the aboriginal race." That section, which is now the basis for Commonwealth legislation in relation to Aborigines and Torres Strait Islanders continues to be referred to as "the race power." Australian public discourse about Indigenous peoples is much more saturated with the language of race than is the case in Canada. As Francine McKenzie points out, there was a racialist sense to Australians identifying themselves as British and therefore not Asian. The comparative point that is being made here is not about racism but about the distinctive and pervasive Australian conceptualization of diverse Native peoples as one race.

If we think of racism as simply a strong belief in the superiority of one's own culture, there has not been much difference historically between Australia and Canada in the extent to which racist assumptions permeated the treatment of Indigenous peoples. In Canada as in Australia, the ideological engine for subjugating and attempting to assimilate Indigenous peoples was the Europeans' belief in their own inherent superiority. As Edward Said has written, it was "the almost metaphysical obligation to rule subordinate, inferior, less advanced peoples" that "allowed decent men and women to accept that their native peoples *should* be subjugated."[45] His words apply as much to the colonizers of Native peoples in Canada as in Australia. It was this belief, for instance, that served as the rationale for forcibly removing Aboriginal children from their families to be brought up in an environment where they had a better chance of being "civilized" – a policy that was vigorously carried out in both countries through much of the twentieth century.[46]

It is in terms of the pseudo-scientific racism that emerged in nineteenth-century European thought – which attributed the most important and fixed differences among human beings to physical, biologically determined features – that the distinctive quality of Australian racism can be seen.[47] In Australia, when this way of classifying human beings was combined with social Darwinism, much of the intellectual leadership in white society became convinced that the Aborigines were not just an inferior race but a "doomed race."[48] It was this kind of thinking that prompted Australian authorities, in removing children from Aboriginal communities, to focus on mixed bloods. Full bloods, it was assumed, were doomed, whereas there might be some hope of salvaging a decent future for those who had at least one white parent or grandparent. This pseudo-scientific brand of racism, with its emphasis on blood and its fatalistic belief that "savage races" were doomed to extinction, did not penetrate Canadian white society to the same degree. There was, to be sure, a great deal of attention to blood quantum in administering the Indian Act, but Natives were also identified as belonging to nations or tribes with different languages, cultures, and histories. Nor was there the same phobia in Canada about mixing bloodlines. The Métis, a people of mixed Aboriginal and non-Aboriginal ancestry whose sense of national identity was forged through resistance to Canada's western expansion, today are recognized constitutionally as one of Canada's Aboriginal peoples.[49]

White Australia's overwhelming historic tendency to conceptualize Indigenous peoples in biological racial terms continues to stand as a barrier against recognizing Indigenous peoples as societies with diverse and evolving cultures. The one thing Indigenous societies share is their common political experience of oppression and resistance. Thinking about others in terms of blood and biology engenders a blindness to the fluidity and diversity of culture. In Canada, while this kind of thinking about Aboriginal peoples continues to be heard in popular discourse, it is countered by the success of First Nations, the Métis, and Inuit peoples in gaining recognition of their distinct identities. This difference has produced a political climate in Canada that makes it easier than it is in Australia to restructure relationships with Indigenous peoples in ways "that accommodate the diverse Aboriginal identities associated with place or region."[50] Conceptualizing aboriginal peoples as primarily belonging to "a" race makes it more difficult to recognize rights to self-determination and self-government for the historical societies on which aboriginal peoples found their identity.

Globalization and the Winds of Change

The decolonization process that got under way following the Second World War marked the beginning of a new set of possibilities for Native peoples. The first stage of decolonization was aimed at the dismantling of European rule over Asian, African, Caribbean, and Pacific peoples. But it would not be long before those relentless and, in the long term, irresistible winds of change that led to decolonization in the "Third World" would begin to affect the conditions of the "Fourth World" – the colonized Indigenous "Third World" within the "First World."[51]

Two interacting features of the politics of decolonization had a decisive effect on the political environment of Indigenous peoples in both Australia and Canada. The first was the beginning of an effective challenge to racist thinking among Europeans. Racism by no means disappeared, but was now hotly contested within European societies – at the very least as entitling Europeans to rule other peoples or discriminate against them. The second decisive feature of decolonization was its global character. Just as the building of the European empires was a globalizing political phenomenon, the dismantling of those empires was and is, inevitably, a global process. This global dimension was most evident in the establishment of the United Nations and its commitment to universal standards of human rights. Australia's and Canada's active participation in the founding of the United Nations and their support for the first stage of decolonization would soon have unanticipated spill-over effects on relations with Indigenous peoples.

In the 1950s and 1960s, within the dominant societies of Australia and Canada, there was scarcely a glimmer of recognition that Indigenous minorities were colonized peoples within their countries. Decolonization was understood as granting Third World majorities the right to self-rule. The principle of the self-determination of peoples, inscribed in Article 1 of the UN Charter, applied overseas but not to colonies within. However, the spirit of anti-racism and the principle of securing equal rights to all regardless of colour or creed, which resonated through the United Nations Declaration of Human Rights and provided the ethical inspiration for decolonization, were a crucial stimulus to the beginning of efforts to reform Indigenous relations in Australia and Canada. In both countries these efforts took the same form: ending official discrimination against Native people and granting them full rights of citizenship. Aboriginal citizens became fully enfranchised at the federal level in Canada in 1960, and in Australia in 1962.[52] In Australia, the culmination of this process was the 1967 referendum that removed not only the bar against Commonwealth legislation in relation to aboriginal Australians, but also section 127 of the Constitution, which had stipulated that "aboriginal natives" were not to be counted in determining the census of a state or the Commonwealth.

A civil-rights approach to reforming aboriginal relations was a natural and relatively easy step for the dominant societies in Australia and Canada to take. After all, for them it meant simply extending principles of Western liberalism central to their own identity to Indigenous peoples. An unprecedented "yes" vote of over 90 percent for the 1967 referendum demonstrated how willing white Australia now was to share full citizenship with Aborigines and Torres Strait Islanders.

If sharing full citizenship as individual Australian or Canadian citizens was the sum total of Indigenous peoples' aspirations, our story would end right here. But of course that was not and is not the case in either country. In both countries Indigenous people welcomed the end of official state discrimination. Most of them valued access to the political, educational, and economic institutions of the mainstream society. Many had already mastered the skills needed to operate effectively in that society and, to that extent, had integrated with it. But in neither country had Indigenous peoples ever abandoned their desire to have the Europeans and other newcomers respect their spiritual and proprietorial attachment to their lands, or their laws and governance of their own affairs. If full and equal access to the rights and opportunities of the society the settlers had built meant that Indigenous peoples had to abandon their own societies and the elements of them so crucial to their well-being and identity, then for most it would be too great a price to pay. When full and equal citizenship on exactly the same terms as all other Australians or Canadians is the only reform on offer, it is profoundly assimilationist, and the great majority of Indigenous people in both countries view it as a continuation of their colonization. Full and equal access for *individuals* of aboriginal descent to the democratic rights and economic opportunities of the mainstream society – the integrationist approach – was not something to be spurned. This approach, however, held the promise of being part of a postcolonial relationship only if it could be combined with an autonomist approach recognizing the *collective* right of Aboriginal peoples to survive and develop as distinct, self-governing communities on or in connection with traditional lands and waters.[53]

The inadequacy of the liberal, civil-rights approach as the basis for reaching a consensual accommodation with Aboriginal peoples became crystal clear in Canada in 1969. In June of that year, Prime Minister Pierre Trudeau and his Indian Affairs minister, Jean Chrétien, issued a White Paper proposing a new

Aboriginal policy. The crux of this policy was that Indian people would have "full and equal participation in the cultural, social, economic and political life of Canada" but they would have to give up any claims to special status or rights as Aboriginal peoples.[54] Even traditional treaty rights would eventually have to be abandoned. The largest and most representative group of Aboriginal leaders ever assembled were flown to Ottawa to respond to the White Paper. To the government's great discomfort, this gathering of Aboriginal people, in no uncertain terms, rejected the White Paper as the basis for an acceptable restructuring of their relationship with Canada.[55]

The White Man's Courts Become the Agents of Change

From the late 1960s right up to the present day, aboriginal issues have been major items on the political agenda of Australia and Canada. In both countries the central issue has been how to respond to the autonomist dimension of Indigenous peoples' aspirations. Both countries have struggled with the challenge of working out arrangements that recognize aboriginal citizens as "citizens plus" – the plus being recognition that aboriginal peoples have a special status and special rights that other citizens do not have. In this modern era, Indigenous peoples in both countries, as never before, have resorted to the courts of the dominant society to claim the recognition they seek. This has occurred at a point in the history of both countries – and in the development of liberal democracy generally – that has witnessed the emergence of the courts as a major site for the vindication of minority rights. Thus the judiciaries of Australia and Canada, and above all their highest courts – the High Court of Australia and the Supreme Court of Canada – have come to play a leadership role in defining and arbitrating disputes about aboriginal rights.

In Canada it was the Supreme Court's 1973 decision in the *Calder* case[56] that had a catalytic effect on Aboriginal relations. In this case, the Nisga'a people sought a declaration that they had Aboriginal title to their ancestral lands in the Nass River valley of northwestern British Columbia. It was a claim they had been trying to have adjudicated since 1913.[57] In the late 1960s they finally got to argue their case before the British Columbia courts, only to have their claim roundly rejected at both the trial and appeal levels. But on appeal to the Supreme Court of Canada they were much more successful. The Supreme Court's response to the Nisga'a claim resuscitated the doctrine of Native title in Canadian law – and politics. All six of the judges who dealt with the issue on its merits not only recognized that Native title was well established in Canadian law but recognized, as the British Privy Council had not, that Native title to land was not a creation of the British or Canadian authorities but was founded on "original and previous possession" of the land. Though the judges entertained no doubts about Canada's sovereign power to extinguish Native title, they split, three-to-three, on whether the Nisga'a's title had been extinguished.

The political reaction to the Supreme Court decision was immediate and positive. The government of Canada, still presided over by Pierre Trudeau, accepted the position of the three judges who found that the Nisga'a still had title to their lands. Instead of simply extinguishing the Nisga'a title by legislation (which at that time it had the power under Canada's Constitution to do), the Trudeau government announced a new policy on Native land claims: it would negotiate comprehensive land settlement agreements not only with the Nisga'a but with all other Aboriginal peoples who had not entered into land-cession treaties in the past and who were still occupying at least a portion of their ancestral lands.[58] The announcement ushered in a new era of modern treaty-making in Canada. To appreciate the turn-around in policy, bear in mind that it was Pierre Trudeau who just four years earlier had bluntly stated, "We say we won't recognize aboriginal rights."[59] And to understand how favourable the general political environment in Canada was for such a turnaround, it is important to observe that both the Conservatives and the NDP, the major opposition parties to the right and left of the Trudeau Liberals, fully supported the new policy.

Just as *Calder* was making its way through the British Columbia courts, an Australian case very much parallel to it came before Justice Blackburn of the Federal Court. The case was brought by three Aboriginal clans on the Gove Peninsula in the northeastern corner of Arnhem Land, who claimed that the Commonwealth's lease of part of their lands to Nabalco for bauxite mining violated their common-law Native title. This was the first time in Australian history that a Native group had brought such a claim before a "white man's court." The result was very negative: Justice Blackburn invoked the *terra nullius* doctrine to dismiss the Gove peoples' claim. Since Australia was a pure colony of settlement, Blackburn felt obliged by the legal precedents to accept the view that when the Europeans arrived, it was a territory occupied, in Blackstone's words, by "uncivilized inhabitants in a primitive state of society" lacking any rights recognized by common law.[60] But Blackburn went further and held that even in colonies like Canada, where the crown had acquired Native lands by cession and purchase, Native peoples had no rights except those subsequently granted or recognized by the European sovereign. In reaching this conclusion, Blackburn followed the British Columbia courts' negative treatment of common-law Native title in *Calder*. Two years later, Blackburn's understanding of the common-law doctrine of Native title was explicitly repudiated in the Supreme Court of Canada by Justice Emmett Hall and two other judges. But his decision was not appealed and stood as "good law" in Australia until the High Court overturned it twenty-one years later in *Mabo*.

Despite its negative outcome as a legal ruling, the Blackburn decision had positive political effects. The Whitlam Labor government, which came to power shortly after the decision, established a royal commission headed by A.E. Woodward, the Aboriginal claimants' lawyer in the *Cape Gove* case.[61] The Woodward Commission led to legislation – introduced by Labor, but eventually enacted by the Fraser Liberal government in 1976 – that established a statutory process whereby Aboriginal communities in the Northern Territory could acquire control over traditional lands. Though the legislation – at the philosophical and symbolic levels – fails to recognize the Aboriginal peoples' pre-contact ownership of their lands, at the practical level it has served as a vehicle through which nearly 50 percent of the Northern Territory has been brought under the management of Aboriginal Land Councils.[62] Similar legislation in South Australia, enacted in 1981, gave control over much of the state's northwest desert country to its traditional owners, the Pitjantjatjara people.[63]

Thus Aboriginal relations in Australia were beginning to move, albeit somewhat haltingly, toward some combination of integration and autonomy. "Assimilation" was giving way to "integration" in Commonwealth policy statements, and Labor was now talking about "self-determination."[64] Through the land councils, the establishment of Aboriginal medical, legal, and welfare service agencies in the cities,[65] and the incorporation of Aboriginal associations,[66] Indigenous communities in Australia were gaining political recognition and a measure of self-government. A committee of white Australians chaired by Nugget Coombs, chair of the Council for Aboriginal Affairs from 1967 to 1976, began to float the idea of a treaty – a grand treaty of reconciliation between black and white Australians.[67] But this movement was also beginning to encounter political opposition. When Prime Minister Robert Hawke, in 1987, indicated his interest in moving forward with the general concept of a treaty or compact, he was aggressively attacked by the Leader of the Opposition, John Howard, who branded the treaty "a recipe for separatism."[68] During this same period, Hawke dropped his commitment to extend land-rights legislation nationwide when the proposal came under attack from the Western Australia Labor government. The Hawke government did introduce one reform: the turning-over of primary responsibility for the delivery of federal programs for Indigenous peoples to the Aboriginal and Torres Strait Islander Commission (ATSIC) made up predominantly of persons elected to regional Aboriginal and Torres Strait Islander councils.[69] This was clearly more a measure of integration than of autonomy.

In Canada, Aboriginal affairs benefited from a more harmonious meshing of judicial decisions and mainstream politics. After *Calder* Aboriginal peoples were able to take advantage of Canada's intense involvement in constitutional politics provoked by the threat of Quebec separatism. The continuing constitutional debate gave Canada's Aboriginal peoples an exceptional opportunity to negotiate, on a pan-Canadian basis, their status and rights in the Canadian federation.[70] Accommodating Aboriginal nationalism posed as serious a challenge to Canadians as accommodating Quebec nationalism (and to none more than Pierre Trudeau). Still, because of the historic encounter with Quebec and the treaty tradition with Aboriginal peoples, the idea of recognizing "nations within" encountered less resistance from the prevailing liberalism than was (and is) the case in Australia. The payoff came in 1982, when the package of constitutional amendments adopted as part of the patriation of the Canadian Constitution (making it entirely independent of Britain) included a clause stating that "the existing aboriginal and treaty rights of the aboriginal peoples of Canada are hereby recognized and affirmed."[71]

Thus Canada became the first of the English-settler countries to recognize Aboriginal rights in its Constitution. For Aboriginal leaders and non-Aboriginal governments alike this constitutional recognition of Aboriginal rights was disturbingly vague. Still, it meant that in Canada the question now would be not *whether* Aboriginal peoples were to enjoy special rights but rather what those rights would mean.

Though on Aboriginal issues there remained a significant gulf in law, policy, and opinion between white Australia and white Canada, the same could not be said of Indigenous peoples in the two countries. As never before, Indigenous peoples around the world were now in touch with one another. These contacts were facilitated as much by the growth of the international human rights movement as by the new technologies of air travel and telecommunications. One can trace the development of this global dimension of Aboriginal politics from the first meeting of the Arctic Peoples Conference at Copenhagen in 1973, through the establishment of the World Council of Indigenous Peoples to the emergence of a Working Group on Indigenous Populations at the United Nations and the production of a Draft Declaration on the Rights of Indigenous Peoples to be ratified by the UN by 2004, the final year of what the UN has identified as the Decade for the World's Indigenous Peoples.[72] Globalization has also had its informal side, through networking and exchanges of visits among Indigenous peoples. Meeting with Indigenous peoples who have had some success in recovering control over their communities and a better stake in their traditional lands and waters – notably in Greenland and North America – has had the important consequence of raising the sights of Indigenous Australians as to what might be achieved in their own country.[73] While local circumstances might well require variations in institutional and constitutional solutions, nonetheless the international community's response to the shared aspirations of Aboriginal peoples was now establishing universal benchmarks of principle in Aboriginal relations. This development would make it impossible for Australia to remain the settler country of *terra nullius*.

The Judicial Revolution of *Mabo*

The influence of these globalizing forces can be clearly seen in the High Court of Australia's 1992 decision in the second *Mabo* case. *Mabo* was truly a judicial revolution.[74] The High Court, in a six-to-one decision, overturned Justice Blackburn's decision in the *Cape Gove* case, and with it the doctrine of *terra nullius*. The High Court adopted the essential elements of Native title jurisprudence articulated by justices of the Canadian Supreme Court in *Calder*. The majority found that, in Australia, Native title exists at common law – not only for Eddie Mabo and the Torres Strait Islanders, the claimants in the case, but for all of Australia's aboriginal peoples – and has its source in Native pre-contact connection to and occupation of the land. The Australian justices followed their Canadian colleagues in holding that Native title, though not created by acts of the settler regime, is vulnerable to regulation and extinguishment by the sovereign authority of the settler state, but to be valid "the exercise of a power to extinguish native title must reveal a clear and plain intention to do so."[75] In abandoning the legal fiction that Australia was a pure colony of settlement, the High Court justices made it clear that they were responding to changes in international and domestic political values. Justice Gerard Brennan put it this way: "Whatever the justification advanced in earlier days for refusing to recognize the rights and interests in land of the indigenous inhabitants of settled colonies, an unjust and discriminatory doctrine of that kind can no longer be accepted. The expectations of the international community accord in this respect with the contemporary values of the Australian people."[76] The political fallout of this decision was soon to demonstrate that Justice Brennan was overly optimistic about the transformation of Australian attitudes to aboriginal peoples.

That a judicial revolution could not – overnight, or by itself – effect a political reformation became evident when the Labor government of Paul Keating introduced legislation to facilitate the registration and settlement of Native title claims. The Native Title Act,[77] a dense 127-page statute with 253 sections, validated the extinguishment of Native title over all land that, at the time the Act came into force, was privately owned or taken for a public use incompatible with aboriginal tenure. To claim title to any of the remaining land, Aboriginals and Torres Strait Islanders would have to establish, through a special tribunal process, their continuing connection with the land since first European contact, and even then they would have only a right to negotiate with those proposing "future acts" on their land. Though for many aboriginal Australians the Act was a bitter pill to swallow, for many other Australians it was much too much. The Act, in total contrast to the 1967 referendum, was the centre of bitter political controversy. It was opposed by the Liberal-National opposition, by the state premiers, and by the mining and pastoral industries. After months of passionate and divisive debate that had all the marks of one of Canada's mega-constitutional rounds, the Act was finally passed by parliament at the end of 1993.[78]

Three years later, in the *Wik* case,[79] the High Court dropped the second shoe of its judicial revolution. The case involved a question left hanging after the Native Title Act: did the granting of pastoral leases automatically extinguish aboriginal title? Much was at stake in answering this question. A full 42 percent of Australia's land mass was leased for cattle grazing and sheep farming. With a major decline in the pastoral industry, pastoral lease holders (many of whom were foreign and domestic corporations) were looking to mining and industrial agriculture as the economic future of their land. Neither pastoralists nor mining companies wanted the encumbrance of having to negotiate new developments with Native title holders. On the other hand, these pastoral range lands continued to be of vital spiritual, economic, and recreational value for a great many aboriginal Australians. The court, divided this time four-to-three, held that pastoral leases did not automatically extinguish Native title. In effect, the court's ruling meant that a regime of coexistence could prevail on Australia's range lands so long as Native title holders did not interfere with the activities for which pastoral leases had been issued. New uses of pastoral lands, such as mining, would, however, be subject to Native title holders' right to negotiate.

Wik brought on "another season of political storm and legal fog as intense as that which followed *Mabo*."[80] Between *Mabo* and *Wik*, the political pendulum had swung to the right in Australia, and a Liberal-National government led by John Howard was now in power in Canberra. Howard and the deputy prime minister, Tim Fischer – leader of the National Party, which draws its support from rural white Australia – led a political attack on the decision, and on the court. The Howard government argued that a regime of coexistence on pastoral lands subjected industrial interests to too much uncertainty. Howard promised a "ten point plan" to amend the Native Title Act in ways that would greatly diminish and circumscribe Native title on lands subject to pastoral leases. For instance, Native title holders would lose the right to negotiate with companies granted exploration and mining rights on pastoral lands.[81] In September 1997, after months of stormy debate and sporadic negotiations with the National Indigenous Working Group on Native Title – a coalition representing all of the major Indigenous organizations in Australia – Howard introduced a 293-page package of amendments to the Native Title Act. For the next nine months, the so-called "*Wik* legislation" was the centre of yet another turbulent national debate over aboriginal rights. At one point, when the *Wik* bill was blocked in the Senate, where – as is normal in Australia – the government did not have a majority, Howard threatened to call an election on the issue. A double dissolution of both houses of parliament was averted only when the government struck a deal with Senator Brian Harradine, an independent who held the balance of power in the Senate.[82] The government did back down a bit from the full force of its plan to reduce Native rights: on the critical issue of Native title holders' right to negotiate with mining interests, the right would not be eliminated but would be subject to state-based tribunals and regulatory systems.[83]

While all this had been going on in Australia, Aboriginal relations in Canada were moving in a different direction and responding to different political rhythms. The direction of government policy was not to roll back rights won in the courts, but to accommodate Aboriginal rights through negotiated agreements with Aboriginal peoples. Frequently relations with Aboriginal communities explode into heated political controversy and become major media events. But the politics of Aboriginal rights was not carried on in Canada at the same continuing level of intensity as it was in Australia through most of the 1990s. This is, in part, because the Aboriginal issue in Canada is often eclipsed by (and sometimes brought into) the Quebec issue. It is also because, unlike Australia, Aboriginal rights have not become – at least at the national level – a major issue of partisan politics.

The best exemplar of these Canadian trends is the Royal Commission on Aboriginal Peoples. The immediate impetus for establishing the commission was the Oka crisis. The Mohawks on two reserves near Montreal resisted the expansion of a golf course onto a sacred burial ground by maintaining an armed standoff with the police and the army for the entire summer of 1990.[84] Aboriginal communities in other parts of Canada began to initiate civil disobedience actions in support of the Mohawks. In response, Conservative Prime Minister Brian Mulroney asked Brian Dickson, the recently retired Chief Justice of Canada, to draw up the terms of reference and select the members of a wide-ranging royal commission on Aboriginal issues. Just before retiring, Dickson had co-authored the Supreme Court's decision in *Sparrow*. In this, the court's first interpretation of the "existing aboriginal rights" recognized and affirmed in the 1982 constitutional amendment, the justices made it clear that "a generous, liberal interpretation of the words in the constitutional provision is demanded."[85] The terms of reference of Canada's Royal Commission on Aboriginal Peoples were even more comprehensive than those of Australia's Inquiry into Aboriginal Deaths in Custody.[86] A majority of the commissioners (four out of seven) were Aboriginal persons. It was the first time in any settler society that Aboriginal and non-Aboriginal leaders, through broad consultation with their communities, had jointly reviewed their past relationship and agreed to a plan for the future.

That plan, as set out in the commission's massive five-volume *Final Report,* covered both integration and autonomy concerns.[87] An extensive set of recommendations addressed the need to bring the living standards of Aboriginal Canadians into line with those enjoyed by their fellow citizens, particularly in relation to health, education, and economic opportunity. Other recommendations called for restructuring relationships with Aboriginal peoples through treaty-like agreements that recognize their inherent right to self-government and hold the prospect of enabling them to become more self-sufficient and in control of traditional lands. By the time the commission had completed its report in 1996, the Chrétien Liberals had replaced the Mulroney Conservatives in Ottawa. Though it took another election and a new minister, Jane Stewart, to formulate the Chrétien government's formal response to the commission, when it came it was very positive. The government fully committed itself to the commission's idea of "a circle of well-being in which self-government, economic self-reliance, healing and a partnership of equal respect are the key building blocks."[88] This Aboriginal Action Plan was prefaced by a Statement of Reconciliation, in which the government of Canada officially apologized for past actions based on "attitudes of racial and cultural superiority" that "led to a suppression of Aboriginal culture and values" and in particular for the "pain and distress" resulting from the residential school system.[89] The apology was backed by committing a third of a billion dollars to an Aboriginal healing fund. This Canadian response was in stark contrast to Prime Minister Howard's performance a few months earlier at a Reconciliation Conference in Melbourne, when he refused to give an official apology in response to the *Stolen Generations* report.[90]

But by the late 1990s there were signs of a political backlash building against the gains Indigenous peoples were making in Canada. When the Supreme Court of Canada decided the *Delgamuukw* case in late 1997,[91] for the first time one of its decisions on Aboriginal rights became the focus of a major political controversy. In this case the Supreme Court, drawing on its own previous decisions and the Australian High Court's decision in *Mabo*, spelled out more comprehensively than ever before just what Native title to land entails. The crux of its decision was that Native title is a full right of property ownership very close to ownership in fee simple – the fullest estate that can exist in common law. In Chief Justice Antonio Lamer's words, "What aboriginal title confers is the right to the land itself."[92] But this is not an absolute right: it is subject to "infringement" by the sovereign power of the crown, a power that can be used for important public purposes such as the building of infrastructure, economic development, and settlement. However, the court also stipulated that at the very least such infringements cannot be done without compensation and consultation, and where the infringement is very serious, to be justifiable, the interests of Native title holders must be given priority in the development and "may require the full consent of an aboriginal nation."[93] Though the court saw its doctrine of Native title as an instrument for reconciling Aboriginal and non-Aboriginal societies in Canada, it was not universally received in this spirit. It was attacked by a number of prominent columnists, especially in British Columbia, and nationally by Preston Manning, leader of the Reform Party.[94] Indeed, the Reform Party and its successor, the Canadian Alliance Party, which now forms the official opposition in the Canadian parliament, espouses a classical form of liberalism. Unlike Canada's traditional parties of the left and right, including the Conservatives, the Alliance has little tolerance for accommodating the collective rights of founding peoples. On Aboriginal issues, the Alliance sounds very much like the Liberal-National coalition in Australia.

The *Delgamuukw* case was brought to court by two British Columbia First Nations, the Gitskan and the Wet'suwet'en. British Columbia is the part of Canada with the most unsettled claims, where Aboriginal land claims pose the greatest threat to non-Aboriginal economic interests. It is no coincidence that British Columbia is also the part of Canada in which recognition of the First Nations' right to self-determination is most severely contested. In a nutshell, British Columbia, as noted earlier, is the part of Canada most like Australia in its Aboriginal politics.[95] In the 1990s the province finally agreed to take part in the treaty process and signed an agreement with Aboriginal representatives and the federal government, setting up the British Columbia Treaty Commission.[96] The commission presides over a modern treaty-making process in which fifty-four First Nations are currently taking part.[97] Though the province's initial decision to enter into the treaty process had broad political support, Aboriginal politics in British Columbia has taken on a distinctly Australian flavour, as the media and public become more aware of what treaties with First Nations might actually entail.

This became abundantly clear in the political struggle over the ratification of the Nisga'a Final Agreement. Since the conclusion of the *Calder* case in 1973, the Nisga'a had been endeavouring to negotiate a modern treaty. In 1998 they signed an agreement with the Canadian and British Columbia governments.[98] Under the agreement, the Nisga'a have ownership and control over approximately 10 percent of their traditional lands, and the Nisga'a government has jurisdiction over a wide range of matters, including language and culture, health, social welfare, education, and public order. In most areas of law-making, federal or provincial laws prevail over conflicting Nisga'a law. But in matters essential to their collective life as a people – including their constitution, language, culture, management of their own lands, and citizenship in the Nisga'a Nation – Nisga'a laws prevail over conflicting federal or provincial laws. In effect, the Nisga'a are now recognized as having a share of Canadian sovereignty. While the majority of Nisga'a supported the agreement, a significant number thought it gave away too much land and self-government. Nearly 30 percent opposed it in the Nisga'a referendum ratifying the agreement. But in the ratification processes that took place in the British Columbia legislative assembly and the Canadian parliament, the agreement was vigorously opposed by non-Native politi-cians, who argued that it gave far too much to the Nisga'a. Political leaders and editorial writers on the political right focused their attack on the agree-ment's paving the way for what they referred to as "racially based" govern-ments with sovereign powers.[99] The agreement was ratified by the British Columbia legislature, but only after the NDP government invoked closure on debate. Early in 2000 the federal parliament completed the ratification process, but not without a lengthy examination in the Senate that indi-cated anxiety among the government's own supporters about the implica-tions of the agreement for Canadian sovereignty.

Ratification did not end the battle over the Nisga'a Agreement. Gordon Campbell, leader of the opposition British Columbia Liberal Party, assisted by two former members of the Supreme Court of Canada, initiated a court challenge against the agreement on the grounds that it unconstitutionally recognized Nisga'a sovereignty. In July 2000, Justice Williamson of British Columbia's highest trial court rejected the challenge and held that the form-ing of Canada in 1867 did not extinguish the Aboriginal peoples' right to govern their own societies.[100] In May 2001, Mr. Campbell's Liberals won a landslide election victory and took power in British Columbia. Though Brit-ish Columbia does not have the constitutional power to unilaterally revoke the Nisga'a Agreement, the Liberals promised a province-wide referendum on the BC treaty process.

Backlash has not been confined to the far West. At the other end of the country, the Supreme Court of Canada's 1999 decision in the *Marshall* case sparked a major battle over fishing rights in Atlantic Canada. The Supreme Court found that federal fishing regulations contravened the rights of the Maliseet and Mi'kmaq peoples to fish for a modest livelihood, secured in eighteenth-century treaties with the crown.[101] The court's decision enraged non-Native fishers in New Brunswick and Nova Scotia, who remained sub-ject to regulatory restrictions. The Supreme Court refused their demand for a re-hearing, but did so in a decision that emphasized the limited nature of the Aboriginal people's treaty right, including its vulnerability to justifiable government regulation.[102]

The debates over the Nisga'a Agreement and the Supreme Court deci-sions in *Delgamuukw* and *Marshall* demonstrate that, while Canada's tradi-tional political, judicial, and Aboriginal elites have reached a point at which consensus on a new relationship is possible, there is not yet a consensus in the Canadian body politic on the nature of this relationship. Since its ini-tial reaction to the royal commission report, the federal government has given no effective national leadership on Aboriginal policy. The loudest voices in non-Native politics on these issues have been those of right-wing leaders and thinkers who want to roll policy back to the assimilation era.[103]

It appears that further advance toward decolonization will depend on Aboriginal initiatives.[104]

Conclusion

Australia and Canada have moved along the path from colony to nation scarcely noticing that, all along, there were colonized peoples within. Now, well established as sovereign democratic states, their sense of achievement is jarred by the survival – despite everything – of these "nations within" and their political mobilization through the global forces of modernity.

Building a postcolonial, non-imperial relationship with this "Fourth World" is a tougher challenge, mentally and constitutionally, than decolonization of the "Third World." The political-constitutional formula for decolonization in the Third World was simple: the dismantling of European rule and the dominance of the settler minority. But in countries like Australia and Canada, where the settlers and their descendants are the vast majority of the population, this solution is obviously not possible. These countries are now as much homelands to their settler majorities as they are to their Indigenous minorities. The Indigenous peoples and the relative newcomers are fated to live together, sharing a common citizenship and sovereign rule over a common territory. The challenge of moving to a postcolonial relationship is to work out ways of sharing land and citizenship that, instead of being based on the power of the stronger, are truly consensual.

Historically, Canada has had something of a head start over Australia in meeting this challenge. Not suffering from the blinding handicap of *terra nullius*, settlers and their governments in Canada recognized much earlier that Indigenous populations constituted peoples with collective identities and rights. The High Court has eliminated *terra nullius* as legal doctrine, but a judicial decision alone, particularly one coming so late in the day, cannot transform prevailing political attitudes.

A further handicap arising from Australia's historical legacy is the relative weakness of its national government in aboriginal affairs. Even under Labor, the Commonwealth government – instead of trying to negotiate new relationships with Indigenous peoples – has relied on the highly legalistic processes of the Native Title Act and the mediating efforts of the National Native Title Tribunal to generate solutions to aboriginal land claims. This has resulted in a mountain of litigation and a molehill of settlements.[105] Partly influenced by Canada's comprehensive land-claim process, the Native Title Act provides for "regional settlements."[106] Though recent amendments strengthen this part of the Act, there is no sign that Canberra will emulate Ottawa in taking responsibility for furthering the process of achieving such agreements. Under the Liberal-National coalition, the public body that has played the strongest role in reaching a consensual relationship with Indigenous peoples is the Reconciliation Council, established by the Hawke Labor government and constituted of leaders from the aboriginal and non-aboriginal communities. But in contrast to the Chrétien government's Aboriginal Action Plan, the Howard government became antagonistic toward the Reconciliation Council.[107]

The contrast should not be overdrawn. In some respects real progress has been made in Australian aboriginal relations. Though state and Commonwealth legislation respecting aboriginal sacred sites leaves much to be desired[108] – especially after the High Court upheld Commonwealth legislation prohibiting application of its Heritage Act to Hindmarsh Bridge[109] – still Australia is ahead of Canada, which at both federal and provincial levels has done next to nothing in this area, as witnessed by the Oka crisis. Aboriginals and Torres Strait Islanders may, as yet, have had little success after *Mabo* in vindicating Native title rights, but through the statutory land councils of the Northern Territory, Queensland, South Australia, and Western Australia, much land has been brought under aboriginal control. The legislative response to *Mabo*, in addition to the Native Title Act, included the establishment of a land fund generating $100 million a year for purchasing and servicing lands for Indigenous Australians,[110] and an Aboriginal and Torres Strait Islander social justice commissioner, who has acted as an independent and national monitor of progress in securing the rights and interests of Indigenous peoples.[111] Canada has no such agencies. Nor has Canada achieved anything close to the citizen involvement in reconciliation activities facilitated by the Reconciliation Council.[112] That Australia is making more progress through processes that have an organic, grassroots rather than state-directed character is evident in negotiations between mining companies and Aboriginal communities. Some of these have resulted in agreements that give Indigenous communities a share in the benefits and control of resource developments on their country.[113] On the big-ticket item of regional autonomy for the Torres Strait Islanders – who, like the Inuit of Canada's Eastern Arctic, constitute the great majority of the population in the most remote northeast corner of the country and for whom Canada's Nunavut has served as a model – Australia is inching toward a Canadian-style solution.[114] In 1997 an all-party committee of the Commonwealth government issued a report calling for measures that will increase the autonomy and "economic independence" of the Islanders.[115]

In Australia and Canada Indigenous peoples constitute a very small proportion of their countries' populations – just under 2 percent in Australia and just under 3 percent in Canada. Given the imperatives of democratic politics, the rights these minorities have won in the courts will not be secure and effectively implemented until both sides of mainstream politics accept their full significance. Agreement with Indigenous peoples on a postcolonial relationship requires a broad political consensus within the non-aboriginal majority. That consensus has not yet been reached in Australia, and in Canada – particularly in British Columbia – is still being forged.[116]

The Howard government's rollback of land rights in the *Wik* legislation was a bitter disappointment for aboriginal peoples and their supporters in the white community. But it should be observed that, after his re-election in 1998, Howard made reconciliation with Indigenous Australians a top priority for his second term. Though the prime minister could not find it in himself to acknowledge the Indigenous peoples' ownership of Australia before the Europeans arrived, at least he could support a new constitutional preamble in the 1999 Referendum "honouring Aborigines and Torres Strait Islanders, the nation's first people, for their deep kinship with their lands and for their ancient and continuing cultures which enrich the life of our country."[117] That the preamble (along with the republic) failed to win the necessary majority should not be taken as an indication that a majority of Australians are opposed to moving toward a more consensual relationship with Aborigines and Torres Strait Islanders.[118] Clear evidence of public support for a new relationship was the event that concluded the Reconciliation Council's ten-year mandate, Corroboree 2000. On Mabo Day, 3 June 2000, the most comprehensive gathering of political leaders in Australian history – aboriginal and non-aboriginal – met in Sydney's Opera House and committed themselves to reconciliation.[119] This was followed the next day by the largest public demonstration in Australian history – the march of over a quarter of a million people across the Sydney Harbour Bridge in support of reconciliation, followed by similar marches in cities all around the country. Of course the marchers, like the politicians, have differing conceptions of what is required for "reconciliation." But these events left no doubt that working toward a consensual relationship has become the defining moral issue of Australian politics.

There are two further reasons for a measure of optimism about the long-term prospects of Indigenous decolonization in Australia and Canada. One is the pressure of those international forces earlier alluded to and to which Australia is, inescapably, vulnerable. Because of the *Wik* legislation, Australia became the first Western nation to be asked by the United Nations Committee on the Elimination of Racial Discrimination to explain its policies on race. In March 1999 the UN committee reprimanded Australia for its treatment of Native title and urged its government to re-open talks with aboriginal representatives.[120] At the 1996 session of the UN committee working on the Draft Declaration on the Rights of Indigenous Peoples, Canada finally accepted "a right to self-determination for Indigenous peoples which respects the political, constitutional and territorial integrity of democratic states."[121] Australia – which, under the Keating government, had worked closely with Canada at the UN on these issues – could not take this step under the Howard government. Instead, Australia urged the United Nations to abandon the principle of self-determination for Indigenous peoples, even with the Canadian caveat attached, and adopt "self-management" as the standard for aboriginal autonomy.[122]

It is most unlikely that Australia will get its way on this matter. In March 2000 Australia was raked over the coals by the UN Committee on the Elimination of Racial Discrimination for its treatment of Indigenous peoples. The committee expressed concern about "the apparent lack of confidence by the indigenous community in the process of reconciliation," and urged that Australia "take measures to ensure that the reconciliation process was conducted on the basis of robust engagement and effective leadership."[123] Later, in July 2000, Leslie Luck – Australia's Permanent Representative to the UN – found himself on the carpet before the UN's Human Rights Commission. He stated that "Australia believed in self-determination of people to handle their own affairs at local and regional levels."[124] Prime Minister Howard, with some support in the popular press, has expressed resentment of Australia's treatment before these UN human rights bodies. Nonetheless, the very seriousness with which his government has taken this UN criticism shows that it very much fears being seen as a racist pariah by the international community.

The other reason for optimism is the strength of aboriginal leadership in both countries. Geoff Clark, the first elected chair of ATSIC (the Aboriginal and Torres Strait Islander Commission) has emerged as a strong national leader. Since Corroboree 2000, he has been insisting that Indigenous peoples' relationship with the Australian state be based on a treaty-like agreement. In Canada Mathew Coon Come, the grand chief of the Assembly of First Nations, is providing the Canada-wide leadership so needed at a time when the federal government shows signs of losing its interest – and perhaps its nerve – in building a postcolonial relationship with Aboriginal peoples. In the early years of the twenty-first century, the struggle for decolonization in both countries has reached a point analogous to that of Third World decolonization forty years earlier, when the main initiatives are taken by Indigenous leaders. During this century, Australia and Canada, each in their own way, will bend and adapt to the relentless, decolonizing winds of change as surely as the most reluctant European powers did when they blew through the Third World in the last century.

Notes

1 Indigenous peoples are referred to here in the sense of the working definition adopted at the United Nations: "Indigenous communities, peoples and nations are those which, having a historical continuity with pre-invasion and pre-colonial societies that developed on their territories, consider themselves distinct from other sectors of the societies now on

their territories, or parts of them. They form at present non-dominant sectors of society and are determined to preserve, develop and transmit their ethnic identity, as the basis of their continued existence as peoples, in accordance with their own cultural patterns, social institutions and legal systems." See Catherine J. Irons, "Indigenous Peoples and Self Determination: Challenging State Sovereignty," *Case Western Reserve Journal of International Law* 24, 2 (1992): 99.

2 In the Australian context, when aboriginal is written in the lower case, it refers to all of Australia's Indigenous peoples – mainland Aboriginals and Torres Strait Islanders. Aboriginal written in the upper case refers to the Indigenous peoples of mainland Australia. In the Canadian context, a different usage is favoured by Indigenous leaders and writers. Aboriginal written in the upper case in Canada refers to all of Canada's Indigenous peoples – Indian, Inuit, and Métis.

3 Alex C. Castles, *An Australian Legal History* (Sydney: The Law Book Company, 1982), ch. 2.

4 The aboriginal population in 1788 is estimated to have been 314,500. David Horton, ed., *The Encyclopaedia of Aboriginal Australia* (Canberra: The Australian Institute of Aboriginal and Torres Strait Islanders Studies, 1994), 1299.

5 *Mabo v. Queensland* (no. 2) (1992), 175 C.L.R. 1.

6 Dorothy V. Jones, *License for Empire: Colonization by Treaty in Early America* (Chicago: University of Chicago Press, 1982), 6.

7 This was the crux of US Chief Justice John Marshall's view of Aboriginal nations as "domestic dependent nations," which he articulated in *Cherokee Nation v. State of Georgia* 30 U.S. (5 Pet.), 1 (1831).

8 Miguel Alfonso Martinez, *Final Report of Special Rapporteur of Study on Treaties, Agreements and other Constructive Arrangements between States and Indigenous Populations,* tabled at the UN Indigenous Working Group, Geneva, 29 July 1998.

9 William Blackstone, *Commentaries on the Laws of England,* vol. 1 (1765-9; reprint, Chicago: University of Chicago Press, 1979), 104-5.

10 Brian Slattery, *The Land Rights of Indigenous Canadian Peoples, As Affected by the Crown's Acquisition of Their Territories* (Saskatoon: Native Law Centre, University of Saskatoon, 1979), 4.

11 Bradford W. Morse, *Aboriginal Peoples and the Law: Indian, Métis and Inuit Rights in Canada* (Ottawa: Carleton University Press, 1985), 2.

12 Ibid., 3-54.

13 J.C. Beaglehole, ed., *The Journals of Captain James Cook on His Voyages of Discovery,* vol. 1, *The Voyage of the Endeavour, 1768-1771* (Cambridge: Cambridge University Press, 1967), ccixxxiii.

14 C.M.H. Clark, *A History of Australia,* vol. 1 (London and New York: Cambridge University Press, 1962), 9.

15 Nonie Sharp, *Stars of Tagai: The Torres Strait Islanders* (Canberra: Aboriginal Studies Press, 1993), 4.

16 M.F. Lindley, *The Acquisition and Government of Backward Territories in International Law* (New York: Negro University Press, 1926), 1.

17 Quoted in Alan Frost, *Botany Bay Mirages: Illusions of Australia's Convict Beginnings* (Carlton: Melbourne University Press, 1994), 185.

18 *Cooper v. Stuart* (1889) App Cas 286, at 291.

19 *Milirrpum v. Nabalco Pty. Ltd.* (1971), 17 F.L.R. 141.

20 *Mabo v. Queensland* (no. 2) (1992), 175 C.L.R. 1.

21 Henry Reynolds, *The Law of the Land* (Ringwood, Victoria: Penguin Books, 1988), 32.

22 Robert Hughes, *The Fatal Shore* (London: Pan Books, 1987), 2.

23 According to Manning Clark, between 26 January 1788 and 20 November 1823, 37,606 convicts embarked for New South Wales. Clark, *History of Australia,* 1:90.

24 Olive B. Dickason, *Canada's First Nations: A History of Founding Peoples from the Earliest Times* (Toronto: McClelland and Stewart, 1992), 183.

25 John Burrows, "Wampum at Niagara: The Royal Proclamation, Canadian Legal History and Self-Government," in *Aboriginal and Treaty Rights in Canada: Essays on Law, Equality and Respect for Difference,* ed. Michael Asch (Vancouver: UBC Press, 1997), 155-72.

26   See Bain Attwood, ed., *In the Age of Mabo: History, Aborigines and Australia* (St. Leonards, NSW: Allen and Unwin, 1996).
27   J.R. Miller, *Skyscrapers Hide the Heavens: A History of Indian-White Relations in Canada* (Toronto: University of Toronto Press, 1989), 92.
28   For an analysis of the Indian Act and its background, see Royal Commission on Aboriginal Peoples, *Report*, vol. 1, *Looking Forward, Looking Back* (Ottawa: Canada Communication Group, 1996), ch. 9. For an account of early legislation in the Australian colonies, see Ann McGrath, ed., *Contested Ground: Australian Aborigines under the British Crown* (St. Leonards, NSW: Allen and Unwin, 1995).
29   Sidney L. Harring, *White Man's Law: Native People in Nineteenth-Century Canadian Jurisprudence* (Toronto: University of Toronto Press, 1998), 62-3.
30   For a discussion of Marshall's decisions in comparative perspective, see Peter H. Russell, "High Courts and the Rights of Aboriginal Peoples," *Saskatchewan Law Review* 61 (1998): 247-76.
31   *St. Catherine's Milling and Lumber Co. v. The Queen*, (1888), 14 A.C. 46, at 54.
32   Emphasis supplied by Justice Monk. For a discussion of this case, see Royal Commission on Aboriginal Peoples, *Report*, vol. 2 (part 1), *Restructuring the Relationship* (Ottawa: Canada Communication Group, 1996), 87-8.
33   *St. Catherine's Milling and Lumber Co. v. The Queen*, (1887), 13 S.C.R. 577.
34   Castles, *An Australian Legal History*, 8-31.
35   This is from the 1905 Treaty 9, covering two-thirds of present-day Ontario. See Patrick Macklem, "The Impact of Treaty 9 on Natural Resource Development in Northern Ontario," in *Aboriginal and Treaty Rights in Canada*, ed. Michael Asch (Vancouver: UBC Press, 1997), ch. 5.
36   There were some early colonial treaties on Vancouver Island and Treaty 8 in 1899, covering much of northern Alberta and part of the Northwest Territories, also took in the northeast corner of British Columbia. See Paul Tennant, *Aboriginal Peoples and Politics: The Indian Land Question in British Columbia, 1849-1989* (Vancouver: UBC Press, 1990), chs. 2 and 5.
37   Royal Commission on Aboriginal Peoples, *Report*, 2:22.
38   *R. v. Sioui*, [1990], 1 S.C.R. 1025.
39   Royal Commission on Aboriginal Peoples, *Report*, 2: ch. 2, Treaties.
40   For the government of Canada's response to the royal commission, see Minister of Indian Affairs and Northern Development, *Gathering Strength – Canada's Aboriginal Action Plan* (Ottawa: Department of Indian Affairs and Northern Development, 1997).
41   House of Commons, *Report from the Select Committee on Aborigines (British Settlements)*, 26 June 1837, 7.
42   For a comparison of constitutional provisions, see Council for Aboriginal Reconciliation, *The Position of Indigenous People in National Constitutions* (Canberra: Commonwealth Government Printer, 1993).
43   See, for instance, the account of Queensland's administration of aboriginal affairs in Rosalind Kidd, *The Way We Civilize: Aboriginal Affairs – the Untold Story* (St. Lucia: University of Queensland Press, 1997), and the account of the Forrest River massacre in Western Australia in Bruce Elder, *Blood on the Wattle* (French's Forest, NSW: National Book Publishers, 1988), ch. 11.
44   Quebec was a party to the James Bay and Northern Quebec Agreement of 1975 and the Northeastern Quebec Agreement of 1978, along with Canada and the Aboriginal parties. The only other modern treaty in a province is the Nisga'a Agreement in British Columbia, discussed below.
45   Edward Said, *Culture and Imperialism* (New York: Vintage Books, 1994), 10.
46   For Australia, see Human Rights and Equal Opportunity Commission, *Bringing Them Home: Report of the National Inquiry into the Separation of Aboriginal and Torres Strait Islander Children from their Families* (Canberra: Australian Government Publishing Service, 1997). For Canada, see Royal Commission on Aboriginal Peoples, *Report*, 1: ch. 10.
47   See Michael Banton, *The Idea of Race* (London: Tavistock, 1977).
48   See Russell McGregor, *Imagined Destinies: Aboriginal Australians and the Doomed Race Theory, 1880-1939* (Carlton: Melbourne University Press, 1997).

49   See Donald Purich, *The Métis* (Toronto: James Lorimer, 1988). In 1996, the Royal Commission on Aboriginal Peoples, *Report*, 1:16, reported that, of Canada's estimated Aboriginal population of 819,000, 18.7 percent (152,800) were Métis.

50   Geoffrey Stokes, "Citizenship and Aboriginality: Two Conceptions of Identity in Aboriginal Political Thought," in *The Politics of Identity in Australia*, ed. Geoffrey Stokes (Cambridge: Cambridge University Press, 1997), 70.

51   For a discussion of the "Fourth World" in world politics, see Franke Wilmer, *The Indigenous Voice in World Politics* (London: Sage, 1993).

52   For Canada, see Royal Commission on Aboriginal Peoples, *Report*, 1:99-300, and for Australia, see John Chesterton and Brian Galligan, *Citizens without Rights: Aborigines and Australian Citizenship* (Cambridge: Cambridge University Press, 1997). The franchise for Indigenous peoples was not put on the same footing as for non-Natives until 1983, when the Commonwealth made it compulsory for Aborigines and Islanders to enrol and vote in elections. The franchise was fully extended at the provincial level in Canada when Quebec removed restrictions in 1969, and at the state level in Australia when Queensland did the same in 1965.

53   On the need to work out a balance between the integrationist and autonomist approach, see Peter H. Russell, "Aboriginal Nationalism – Prospects for Decolonization," *Pacifica Review* 8 (1996): 7-67.

54   Department of Indian Affairs and Northern Development, *Statement of the Government of Canada on Indian Policy* (Ottawa: Queen's Printer, 1969).

55   Ibid.

56   *Calder v. British Columbia*, [1973] S.C.R. 313.

57   For an account by the Nisga'a's lawyer, see Thomas R. Berger, *Fragile Freedoms: Human Rights and Dissent in Canada* (Toronto: Irwin, 1981), ch. 8.

58   For an account of the new policy and its implementation, see Task Force to Review Comprehensive Claims Policy, *Living Treaties: Lasting Agreements* (Ottawa: Department of Indian Affairs and Northern Development, 1981).

59   Quoted in Michael Asch, *Home and Native Land: Aboriginal Rights and the Canadian Constitution* (Toronto: Methuen, 1984), 9.

60   *Milirrpum v. Nabalco* (1971), 17 F.L.R. 141, at 201.

61   Kenneth Maddock, *Your Land Is Our Land: Aboriginal Land Rights* (Ringwood, Victoria: Penguin Books, 1983).

62   For an account of what has been accomplished under the Act, see Galarrwuy Yunupingu, ed., *Our Land Is Our Life: Land Rights – Past, Present and Future* (St. Lucia, Queensland: University of Queensland Press, 1997).

63   David Day, *Claiming a Continent: A History of Australia* (Sydney: Angus and Robertson, 1996), 48.

64   Scott Bennett, *Aborigines and Political Power* (Sydney: Allen and Unwin, 1989), 3-4.

65   Richard Broome, *Aboriginal Australians* (Sydney: Allen and Unwin, 1982), ch. 11.

66   H.C. Coombs, *Aboriginal Autonomy: Issues and Strategies* (Cambridge: Cambridge University Press, 1994), ch. 15.

67   Judith Wright, *We Call for a Treaty* (Sydney: Fontana, 1985).

68   Frank Brennan, *Sharing the Country: The Case for an Agreement between Black and White Australians* (Ringwood, Victoria: Penguin, 1991), 9.

69   Aboriginal and Torres Strait Islander Commission Act 1989 (Cwth.), no. 150 of 1989.

70   This point is more fully developed in Peter H. Russell, *Constitutional Odyssey: Can Canadians Become a Sovereign People?* 2nd ed. (Toronto: University of Toronto Press, 1993), 4-95.

71   Section 35 of the *Constitution Act, 1982*, being Schedule B to the *Canada Act* (U.K.). 1982, c. 11.

72   For a brief overview, see Peter H. Russell, "The Global Dimensions of Aboriginal Politics," in *Education for Australia's International Future*, ed. Rodney Sullivan, Claire Smith, Lesley Jackman, and Anne Smith (Townsville, Queensland: James Cook University, 1998). For an account of UN developments, see Sarah Pritchard, ed., *Indigenous Peoples, the United Nations and Human Rights* (Leichhardt, NSW: Federation Press, 1998).

73   For an account of this tendency, see Peter Jull, "An Aboriginal Policy for the Millennium: The Three Social Justice Reports," *Australian Indigenous Law Reporter* 1, 1 (1996): 1-13.

74 See M.A. Stephenson and Suri Ratnapala, eds., *Mabo: A Judicial Revolution: The Aboriginal Land Rights Decision and Its Impact on Australian Law* (St. Lucia, Queensland: University of Queensland Press, 1993).

75 *Mabo v. Queensland* (no. 2) (1992), 175 C.L.R. 1, at 64.

76 Ibid., 2.

77 Native Title Act (Cwth.), no. 110 of 1993.

78 See Frank Brennan, *One Land, One Nation: Mabo – Towards 2000* (St. Lucia, Queensland: University of Queensland Press, 1995).

79 *Wik Peoples v. Queensland* (1996), 141 A.L.R. 129.

80 Peter H. Russell, "High Courts and the Rights of Aboriginal Peoples: The Limits of Judicial Independence," *Saskatchewan Law Review* 61 (1998): 268.

81 Richard Bartlett, "A Return to Dispossession and Discrimination: The Ten Point Plan," *University of Western Australia Law Review* 27 (1997): 44.

82 Margo Kingston, James Woodford, and Michael Seccombe, "Wik Deal Scuttles Race Poll," *Sydney Morning Herald,* 2 July 1998.

83 The government also scrapped its proposed six-year sunset clause on making all Native title claims. For a full analysis, see Paul Burke, "Evaluating the Native Title Amendment Act 1998," *Australian Indigenous Law Reporter* 3, 3 (1998): 333-56.

84 Geoffrey York and Loreen Pindera, *Peoples of the Pines: The Warriors and the Legacy of Oka* (Toronto: Little Brown, 1991).

85 *Sparrow v. The Queen,* [1990] 1 S.C.R. 1075, at 1106.

86 Royal Commission into Aboriginal Deaths in Custody, *National Report: Overview and Recommendations* (Canberra: Australian Government Publishing Service, 1991).

87 Royal Commission on Aboriginal Peoples, *Report,* vol. 5, *Renewal: A Twenty-Year Commitment* (Ottawa: Canada Communication Group, 1996).

88 Minister of Indian Affairs and Northern Development, *Gathering Strength,* 2.

89 Ibid.

90 John Short and Georgina Windsor, "Howard Warns Blacks to Back Off," *Australian,* 26 May 1977. (The *Stolen Generations* report is the 1997 report of the Human Rights and Equal Opportunity Commission, entitled *Bringing them Home: Report of the National Inquiry into the Separation of Aboriginal and Torres Strait Islander Children from Their Families*.)

91 *Delgamuukw v. British Columbia,* [1997] 3 S.C.R. 1010.

92 Ibid., 52.

93 Ibid., 65.

94 See, for instance, Preston Manning, "Parliament, Not Judges, Must Make the Law of the Land," *Globe and Mail,* 16 June 1998, A23.

95 Tennant, *Aboriginal Peoples and Politics.*

96 Christopher McKee, *Treaty Talks in British Columbia: Negotiating a Mutually Beneficial Process* (Vancouver: UBC Press, 1996).

97 British Columbia Treaty Commission, *Update,* newsletter, February 1999.

98 *Nisga'a Final Agreement* (Ottawa: Federal Treaty Negotiation Office, 1998).

99 See, for instance, Andrew Coyne, "The Nisga'a Land Treaty: Sword or Shield?" *Cité Libre* 27 (Spring 1999): 8-59.

100 *Campbell et al. v. A. G. British Columbia et al.* [2000] 189 D.L.R. (4th) 333, p. 355.

101 *R. v. Marshall,* [1999] 1 S.C.R. 1075.

102 *R. v. Marshall II,* [1999] 3 S.C.R. 533.

103 See, for instance, Tom Flanagan, *First Nations? Second Thoughts* (Montreal and Kingston: McGill-Queen's University Press, 2000).

104 For a leading example of the thinking of the new generation of Aboriginal leaders in Canada, see Taiaiake Alfred, *Peace, Power, Righteousness: An Indigenous Manifesto* (Toronto: Oxford University Press, 1999).

105 The first successful claim occurred in October 1996, when a small Aboriginal group in New South Wales received A$738,000 in compensation for recognition of their Native title. It was not until November 1997 that an Aboriginal community in Australia – at Hopevale in Queensland – was actually granted land under the Native Title Act. Australian Institute of Aboriginal and Torres Strait Islanders Studies, *Land Title Newsletter,* no. 6 (1997), 97.

106 See Burke, "Evaluating the Native Title Amendment Act 1998," 339.

107 Claire Harvey, "Council Counting Down to Consensus," *Australian,* 5 March 1999.

108 Elizabeth Evatt, "Overview of State and Territory Aboriginal Heritage Legislation," *Indigenous Law Bulletin* 4, 16 (1998): 4-8.

109 Garth Nettheim, "The Hindmarsh Bridge Act Case," *Indigenous Law Bulletin* 4, 12 (1998): 7.

110 Minister of Aboriginal and Torres Strait Islander Affairs, *Aboriginal and Torres Strait Islander Land Fund: An Act of Good Faith* (Canberra: Australian Government Publishing Service, 1995).

111 For an example of its work, see Aboriginal and Torres Strait Islanders Social Justice Commissioner, *Fourth Report, 1996* (Canberra: Australian Government Publishing Service, 1996).

112 For an account of its activities, see Australian Reconciliation Council, *The Path to Reconciliation: Issues for a People's Movement* (Canberra: Australian Government Publishing Service, 1997).

113 Ciaran O'Faircheallaigh, "Negotiations between Mining Companies and Aboriginal Communities: Process and Structure," *Centre for Aboriginal Economic Policy Research* no. 86 (1995): 1-20.

114 Peter Jull, "The Political Future of Torres Strait," *Indigenous Law Bulletin* 4, 7 (1997): 4-9.

115 House of Representatives Standing Committee on Aboriginal and Torres Strait Islander Affairs, *Torres Strait Islanders: A New Deal* (Canberra: AGPS, 1997).

116 A Canadian survey shows support for Aboriginal self-determination at the 70 percent level. See Paul M. Sniderman, Joseph F. Fletcher, Peter H. Russell, and Philip E. Tetlock, *Clash of Rights: Liberty, Equality and Legitimacy in Pluralist Democracy* (New Haven, CT: Yale University Press, 1996), 30-147.

117 Constitutional Centenary Foundation, "1999 Referendum: A New Preamble," Constitutional Centenary Foundation, Carlton, Victoria, September 1999.

118 For an account of the 1999 Referendum, see George Williams, "Why Australia Kept the Queen," *Saskatchewan Law Review* 63, 2 (2000): 477-501.

119 For an account, see Peter H. Russell, "Corroboree 2000-A Nation Defining Event," *Arena Journal* 15 (2000): 5-38.

120 Brendan Nicholson and Michael Gordon, "UN Slams Australia on Native Title," *Age,* 20 March 1999.

121 Sarah Pritchard, "The United Nations and the Making of a Declaration of Indigenous Rights," *Indigenous Law Bulletin* 3, 89 (1997): 8.

122 Mick Dodson and Sarah Pritchard, "Recent Developments in Indigenous Policy," *Indigenous Law Bulletin* 4, 15 (1998): 4-6.

123 United Nations press release, 24 March 2000, morning.

124 United Nations press release, Human Rights Committee, 69th session, 20 July 2000, afternoon.

Part 2:
Rivals, Allies, and Models

Canada and Australia first came together as colonies in the British Empire. The imperial link brought irregular contact that highlighted their differences as much as their common interests and views. As the Empire evolved into the Commonwealth, it endured as one of the main forums in which Canadian-Australian relations developed. Indeed their relationship has flourished largely through this and other international organizations, such as the United Nations, as well as specialized agencies like the International Civil Aviation Organization, the General Agreement on Tariffs and Trade, and the Cairns Group of agricultural producers. Canada and Australia have gravitated toward one another on the world stage and found opportunity for contact, if not always cooperation.

Direct relations, however, have not been inconsequential. Despite differences over specific issues, as well as more fundamental clashes over points of view, objectives, and interests, Canada and Australia have leaned toward one another, learned from one another, worked out tactics, supported one another, and talked over common challenges. Technological advances and the global economy have broadened and facilitated their relations throughout the twentieth century. While Australia has not been on a par with Britain and the United States as an ally of Canada, and Canada is not on a par with Britain and the United States as an ally of Australia, the importance of Canadian-Australian relations is undeniable. Where relations with the United States and the United Kingdom have been forced on these two dominions by circumstances beyond their control, including history, economic development, and the Cold War, Canadian-Australian relations are interesting because they are largely self-selected. Underscored by a sense of kinship that is real as much as imagined, cooperation has been enduring and multifaceted. Their relations are also valuable for scholars seeking insights into national interests, national identities, and the roles played by nations outside the superpower or major power categories. Canada and Australia could never claim to belong to the same category as the United States or even a weakened Britain. Still, they have made real contributions to the international community. The following chapters cover Canadian-Australian relations broadly from the 1920s to the 1990s, demonstrating their scope, depth, and limitations. They also confirm that there has been conflict, acrimony, and rivalry. Even so they constitute a special international relationship that brings out their essential differences and enduring compatibility.

4
Australia and Canada in the World of International Commercial Aviation
David MacKenzie

Throughout the twentieth century, Australians and Canadians looked to the evolution of international commercial aviation with enthusiasm and optimism. At the same time, both nations have exhibited attitudes toward international aviation displaying a mixture of smugness and naïveté. "It is hardly an exaggeration," two Australians wrote in 1951, "to say that in the pre-war years Australia was the most air-minded nation in the world."[1] Similarly, Grant Dexter, a Canadian journalist, wrote of his country during the Second World War: "There is no need of argument to demonstrate the importance of civil aviation to this country. All that is necessary is to look at a map of the world, preferably a global map. In terms of international flying, geography makes Canada one of the key crossroads of the world."[2] Less than two years later, in the wake of the creation of the International Civil Aviation Organization and the International Air Transport Authority, both of which were located in Montreal, one Canadian magazine boasted that "Montreal became the air capital of the world."[3] However much truth or wishful thinking such statements may have contained, they reflected the widespread sense of confidence found in both countries.

Australia and Canada may have been small nations in many ways, but when it came to international commercial aviation they had big ideas, concerns, hopes, and dreams. On the surface they appeared to be natural allies because they had so much in common, in that both suffered from what one Australian historian called the "tyranny of distance."[4] Both were countries with large land masses and small populations huddled largely in a few urban centres. So much of their respective territories were sparsely populated and, unlike the European states, vast distances separated their major cities. From the wilderness of the Canadian north to the Australian outback, the advent of air flight offered the promise of swifter transportation, better communications with remote regions, the opening up and economic development of new areas and industries, and, to some dreamers and visionaries,

even the promise of nation building. In both countries civil aviation operations expanded for very practical reasons – in terms of mail delivery and
various emergency services – and both nations saw the advent of a new
twentieth-century adventurer: the bush pilot.

There were other similarities. Australia and Canada shared British traditions and language and developed similar political institutions and economic systems. More specifically in aviation terms, they both established
national airlines to act as their "chosen instruments" in international aviation diplomacy. Their populations embraced the idea and challenge of air
flight, and their governments reflected the belief that they had important
roles to play and contributions to make in the unfolding drama of international civil aviation. Moreover, both had to come to terms with the rise of
the United States in the world of commercial aviation, and had to build a
strong relationship with the Americans and attempt to use it to their advantage. Finally, Australia and Canada shared a connection to Great Britain
and the Empire-Commonwealth, and it was the imperial relationship that
actually brought Australia and Canada into aviation diplomacy early in the
twentieth century.

The governments and people of Australia and Canada quickly understood
the value of commercial aviation. Transportation has always been vital for
the expansion and development of societies, and aviation – because of the
way speed can overwhelm geography – provided a unique tool for improved
communications and closer personal contact between governments, states,
and individuals. Equally, the military potential of aviation was not lost on
Australians or Canadians; a commercial aircraft can carry soldiers as easily
as paying customers, a peacetime air service can quickly assume military
dress, and a commercial pilot can change into a military uniform. Most
important, the links between national interest, economic development, and
national prestige were clear, especially for small nations searching for a role
to play on the world stage. As one American author wrote, "every nation
with a claim to a prominent position in the world community has deemed
it necessary to take an active part in its [aviation's] development by generous governmental encouragement and assistance in almost every imagina-
ble form."[5] This was as true for Australia and Canada as it was for the United
States, Great Britain, or any other modern nation. Ultimately, aviation was
filled with possibilities, and it sparked the imaginations of millions of Australians, Canadians, and others around the world.

Despite these great similarities, however, Australia and Canada developed
quite different policies when it came to the development of international
civil aviation. Examining these differences in a comparative framework helps
to shed some light on the distinct ways that Australians and Canadians
viewed their relations with Great Britain and the United States and, more
generally, how they reacted to the unfolding of events in the international

community in the twentieth century. Their interests collided directly only a few times, and for the most part their relationship evolved not from their own initiative but rather from their reaction to technological innovation and the emergence of great-power rivalries, in particular between Great Britain and the United States. The Australian-Canadian relationship, and the development of their differing international aviation policies, is the focus of this chapter.

The Beginnings of a Relationship

The same factors that made it so hard to fly between Australia and Canada made it difficult and perhaps even unnecessary to have extensive diplomatic and economic relations. Canada and Australia were linked through membership in the British Empire, but that link ran through London, not directly between Canberra and Ottawa. For Australians and Canadians, the imperial relationship was really two relationships: Anglo-Australian and Anglo-Canadian. When the two nations interacted with each other, it was usually in an imperial context.

Things began to change in the late nineteenth century, but only very slowly. The westward expansion of Canada – symbolized by the completion of the Canadian Pacific Railway in 1885 – awoke many Canadians to their Pacific dimension, and made some look across the Pacific for trade and commerce purposes, sparking some public enthusiasm for cable and steamship connections with Australia and New Zealand.[6] But even here there were limits to the optimism of expanding contacts. "I do not anticipate any great immediate results from our visit to Australia," wrote Mackenzie Bowell, the leader of the first Canadian trade mission to Australia in 1893. "The parties with whom we have been estranged so long can scarcely be brought into a close relationship at a moment's notice."[7]

The trappings of a closer relationship began to emerge, however. A Canadian trade commissioner was sent to the Australian territories in 1894 (Australia reciprocated with a trade commissioner to Ottawa only in 1929), a steamship service was inaugurated, and trade began to grow slowly, leading to trade agreements in 1925 and 1931.[8] Ann Capling and Kim Richard Nossal explore the trading relationship in more detail in their chapter, but it is clear that trade between the two countries paled in comparison to their individual trade relationships with Great Britain and, increasingly for them both, with the United States. The latter was particularly true for the Canadians, and compared to the growth of the Canadian-American economic relationship, Australian-Canadian trade was relatively insignificant.

Australia and Canada also had dissimilar views on the evolution of the Empire itself, despite some constitutional collaboration during the Great War. As Margaret MacMillan and Francine McKenzie demonstrate in their chapters, the Australians – for security reasons and, more generally, thanks to their closer ties to the United Kingdom – were more hesitant than the Canadians in the movement toward dominion autonomy. The Canadians, with their North American outlook and internal linguistic diversity, were more determined to carve out an autonomous foreign policy. These tensions never led to a diplomatic rupture – although they did spark very heated discussions in 1921 over the possible renewal of the Anglo-Japanese Alliance – but they did punctuate the evolving imperial relationship from the turn of the century to the passage of the Statute of Westminster in 1931.[9] Things were not much different when it came to the development of international civil aviation. The two countries showed a similar pattern of development, but they came to international civil aviation with different perspectives and interests. In addition, both worked with Britain and then with the United States, rather than with each other.

Australia was a natural for aviation. In addition to its vast size and economic prosperity, it was a relatively flat country blessed with excellent weather for flying – a temperate climate, with little snow, ice, and fog.[10] As with the Canadians, the Australian government became involved with commercial aviation at an early stage through the use of subsidies and regulation. The first flights took place in Australia in 1910, and in 1914 a Melbourne-Sydney airmail route was inaugurated, but it was not until the 1920s that aviation really took off. An Air Navigation Act was passed in December 1920, and a Controller of Civil Aviation was established to advise the government on aviation matters. The Controller did not specifically determine routes, but did oversee the subsidies given to commercial operators, and therefore exercised considerable influence. The first regular air service (Geraldton-Derby, Western Australia) appeared in 1921, and was followed by several others in subsequent years. In 1926, the first Australia-England return flight was made.[11]

In November 1920, Queensland and Northern Territory Aerial Services Ltd. (Qantas) was created, with Sir Hudson Fysh as chairman (a post he held for nearly half a century) and using two surplus aircraft from the First World War.[12] Originally, Qantas operated in areas of Australia that were remote or where using other forms of transportation was difficult, but by the early 1930s it had developed into Australia's chosen instrument in the air, even though it remained, at first, privately owned.[13] By 1938 regular Australian air services flew more than 42,000,000 passenger miles.[14]

The names of the people and places were different, but the Canadian experience was not dissimilar. The first flight of the *Silver Dart* in Baddeck, Nova Scotia, took place in 1909, and although regular services did not appear at first, during the First World War the Canadian government began to examine aviation issues, while a rudimentary aircraft industry was created and hundreds of Canadians served in the Royal Flying Corp.[15] An Air Board to regulate civil aviation was established in 1919, and by the 1920s the Canadian government had shed its earlier indifference toward aviation.[16]

The primary focus of the early development of aviation was not on inter-city services, but rather on the opening up of the north. Canada's north – enormous, economically undeveloped, and sparsely populated – acted as a magnet for adventurers and entrepreneurs in the interwar period, and avia-tion provided the means to explore and develop it. Within a few years, one bureaucrat could argue that, thanks to aviation, "more has been learned of northern Canada during the past ten years than in the preceding three hun-dred. The forester, surveyor, geologist, prospector, mining engineer; the clergy, the doctors, the nurses, the police; in fact, all whose activities lie in northern Canada find their task greatly lightened, their range of action multiplied many times and their efficiency increased by the use of aircraft."[17]

In 1928 a New York-Montreal mail and passenger service was established, and by the early 1930s most of the major cities had fully equipped munici-pal airports and some cross-border services had been introduced by small, private airline companies. In 1937 the Canadian government took a major step with the creation of Trans-Canada Air Lines (TCA), a government-owned, government-operated national airline that would act as Canada's chosen instrument in the international field.[18] TCA's first regularly scheduled service was inaugurated in September of that year, linking Seattle, Washington, with Vancouver.

Australia and Canada moved into the realm of international commercial aviation easily. It was a relatively smooth extension of national services for Australia to make connections with New Zealand and various Pacific islands, and for Canada to inaugurate services with the United States and Newfound-land. But at first neither state considered as a high priority the extension of services to each other. The Australian government naturally focused first on its own region and then to mail and passenger services to India or Singa-pore, with a view to connecting Australia with Great Britain. Similarly, the Canadians looked east across the Atlantic and south to the United States when it came to the expansion of services. Even when they looked across the Pacific, Australians and Canadians were not looking at each other; the Australians saw the Pacific route within an imperial framework, while the Canadians dreamed of services to Tokyo, Hong Kong, and Shanghai, not Sydney, Brisbane, or Melbourne.[19]

It was the British government and its imperial aviation policy, however, that brought Australians and Canadians into contact in aviation affairs. The potential value of commercial aviation for the Empire was quickly grasped in the United Kingdom (and among the other colonial powers) after the First World War. It was a matter of prestige, one observer wrote in 1945, and "no nation could afford to neglect the air."[20] The creation in

1924 of Imperial Airways – a privately owned but government-backed company – gave the British government its chosen instrument in the international field, and before the end of the decade Imperial Airways had established services to the Continent, Africa, and as far as Karachi. By 1933 services had been extended to New Delhi and Cape Town.[21] The appearance of several European state-run airlines (in Germany, France, the Netherlands, and the Soviet Union, for example) made the competition for European routes quite fierce, while outside of Europe the rise of Pan American Airways – the American company backed by the United States government – presented a formidable rival to British interests.[22] In the increasingly competitive world of international aviation diplomacy, Britain's vast colonial empire became its trump card, and within that framework the dominions took on special importance.

As early as the First World War the British government had begun to involve Australia, Canada, and the other dominions in discussions and planning for imperial civil aviation. This process continued after the war, and aviation was a regular point of discussion at the interwar Imperial conferences.[23] Throughout this period, British policy was remarkably consistent: first, to keep the Empire together and British influence within it strong; second, to seek Commonwealth collaboration in creating a global imperial network of air services; and third, to keep American competition at bay.[24]

One way to keep the dominions in and the Americans out was to establish an "All-Red Route," encircling the globe through a chain of imperial possessions, including both the colonies and the dominions. The idea became feasible in the 1930s, and this global network became the focus of imperial discussions in that decade. Plans for an Empire Air Mail Scheme, for example, were unveiled in 1934 and discussed – unsuccessfully – for the rest of the decade.

The Australians and Canadians were both involved in these discussions, although their focus differed: the Canadians on the Atlantic, the Australians on the Pacific. The Australians were especially interested in participating in the "All-Red Route," and the extension of the Imperial Airways service to Singapore made this possible. In 1934 a regular airmail service between Britain and Australia began operations, and that same year negotiations between Qantas and Imperial Airways led to the creation of Qantas Empire Airways, a joint company that would operate the Australian section of the air service. (In 1938, Tasman Empire Airways was created to operate services across the Tasman Sea.) What began as a weekly service in 1934 had, by 1938, expanded into a three-times-per-week service.[25] This method of Commonwealth collaboration and joint operating companies set a pattern that Australia and Great Britain supported through the Second World War. Similar arrangements were made by Imperial Airways, leading to the formation, with India, of Indian Trans-Continental Airways and, with Ireland, of Aer Lingus Teoranta.

The Canadians were interested in a similar arrangement for the Atlantic service at first, but as the 1930s wore on, they became less sanguine about the possibilities of Commonwealth collaboration. The British wanted an imperial transatlantic service routed through Montreal – one that could be expanded across Canada and ultimately become the western link in a future trans-Pacific service.[26] Before the creation of TCA in 1937, the Canadians could not operate a transatlantic service on their own, even if they had wanted to, and they had little to offer Britain other than the fact that their territory was a valuable piece of real estate in any imperial scheme for a global network. Equally important, the British anticipated extremely tough competition from the United States on the proposed transatlantic service, and the fact that the shortest route across the Atlantic (often referred to as the "direct route") crossed Canadian airspace made it vital to keep the Canadians onside. If nothing else, having the Canadians involved in a Commonwealth scheme would strengthen the British position in future Anglo-American discussions for a transatlantic service.

In 1935 the pieces of the puzzle came together, and representatives from Canada, Great Britain, and Ireland agreed to the creation of a Joint Operating Company to establish a Commonwealth transatlantic service. It was a joint company, but it was controlled by Britain and Imperial Airways: the UK retained 51 percent of the capital stock in the new company, while Ireland and Canada received 24.5 percent each; the British would appoint the chair of the board of directors; and most of the costs for the company's operations would be paid for by Britain. It was an open-ended agreement, but no regular service was established by the Joint Operating Company before the outbreak of war in 1939. Following the expansion of TCA into a national service, the Canadians became restless with the existing arrangements, and in 1943 they broke them and established their own TCA transatlantic service.[27]

Fairly early in the imperial discussions, a fundamental difference in perspective appeared between Australia and Canada. Francine McKenzie examines this issue in a more general way in her chapter, and she notes how both nations pursued their own national interests – the Australians doing it within the imperial framework, while the Canadians acted more on their own. The same was true for international commercial aviation. The Australians, for reasons of security and prestige, wanted to ensure two things: first, that air services would fly to Australia and connect it to the outside world; and second, that Australia would have a role to play in the services within its region and connecting it to the outside world. The imperial connection, which was already strong, could provide both. By participating in a joint imperial arrangement, Australia could tap into the imperial network while at the same time participating in the Australian leg of the "All-Red Route."

The Canadians saw it differently. What Canada had to offer was the fact that it lay on the flight path of the two great global air routes: across the north Atlantic, connecting the United States and Great Britain, and across the North Pacific, connecting the United States with Japan and the rest of Asia. The British were interested in Canada for this very reason; Canada was a destination in itself, but it could also be an important part of the larger British plans for imperial aviation, especially in its growing rivalry with the United States. But for the Canadians, turning this geographical advantage to Canada's benefit did not automatically have an imperial dimension. Indeed, it was widely believed that Canada would be better able to pursue its interests independently. In other words, Canada was a transit nation – a place that many others would want to fly over but not necessarily stop at on their way to somewhere else. Australia, on the other hand, was a terminal nation – a state that others might wish to fly to but not often have to fly across to get somewhere else. In this respect, Australia had more in common with South Africa and Canada had more in common with Ireland than they did with each other.[28]

These different attitudes were revealed at the 1937 Imperial Conference. The conference was staged in an effort to achieve some kind of Commonwealth unity in the face of the deteriorating international situation, and one area for cooperation was commercial aviation. A committee on civil air communications was established, chaired by Sir Archdale Parkhill, the Australian minister of defence, to discuss mutual aviation issues. The British were the only ones prepared for the discussions, and they were keen on achieving and maintaining Commonwealth cooperation and consultation on the establishment of joint air services, and on the use of British aircraft throughout the Commonwealth. In their conference paper, the British government called for the creation of "a trunk route right round the world with arterial and subsidiary services radiating in all directions from important points."[29] This was the "All-Red Route" and would involve Ireland, Newfoundland, Canada, New Zealand, Australia, India, and a variety of British islands in the Atlantic and Pacific Oceans, as well as subsidiary services from Britain to South Africa and across Africa to South America.[30]

Neither the Australians nor the Canadians were willing to completely submerge their own airlines or the air services to their countries in a British-controlled imperial system, and, after much debate, they agreed to a system of "local control" over services to their respective countries. But the Canadians were adamant that any conference resolutions on aviation should stay clear of any endorsement of a common Commonwealth policy, and here there were some differences with the Australians. The Australians could see some advantage in joining together to negotiate; for example, in negotiations with the Americans for a Pacific service, Australia could benefit from British support. The Canadians, conversely, were insistent that they have complete control over any negotiations with the United States that concerned them, so as to ensure that their interests were not "sacrificed" for some larger imperial aim. At one point, Parkhill asked Canadian prime minister Mackenzie King what was wrong with Commonwealth members combining to negotiate with foreigners on each other's behalf, and King responded sharply that "it almost seems as if they had different ideas of the British Commonwealth."[31] In the end, the committee produced a document that endorsed cooperation between Commonwealth states, but did not make it mandatory.[32]

At the 1937 Imperial Conference, the establishment of a trans-Pacific service was discussed but there was little progress made. The Pacific route posed special and difficult problems for everyone; first, you had to survey and then negotiate a practical route, and second, you had to develop airplanes that could fly it. Technology solved the latter problem by the mid-1930s with the introduction of the large, American-manufactured flying boats that could fly up to 3,200 kilometres non-stop.[33] It was up to governments and diplomats to negotiate the former.

The United States was in a strong position in the Pacific. The Americans had the airplanes and, whereas in the Atlantic it was possible to establish an all-British route, in the Pacific all routes would likely have to fly through Hawaii, which gave the Americans a strong negotiating position right at the start. And, as the international situation deteriorated in the Pacific, they became more determined to have things their way. Pan American launched a trans-Pacific airmail service in 1934 and it was expanded as the decade progressed.[34] Later, during the war, when the British began to explore the possibility of bypassing Hawaii by using Clipperton Island as a base, the two countries nearly came to blows as the Americans moved into the island and warned the British to stay away.[35]

The Australians and Canadians found themselves very much the observers during these developments. Both were interested in a trans-Pacific service, but neither had the economic strength, the technological know-how, nor the diplomatic skills to pull it off. As a result, when the Second World War began in 1939, there was no Pacific service linking Australia and Canada. More important, on the eve of some of the greatest changes in the development of international civil aviation, the two countries were moving in increasingly different directions.

The Second World War
The outbreak of the Second World War began a process of change in the Australian-Canadian relationship and in the way they both viewed international civil aviation. Australia and Canada found themselves as allies in a common cause, and the opportunity for improved and closer relations

appeared very real. High commissioners were exchanged, putting the relationship on a more formal foundation, and, generally, the war provided the
opportunity for Australians and Canadians to meet and work together, more
so than in the past. But there were limits to this new-found relationship.
For the Canadians, the key theatre in the war was across the Atlantic, and
the principal enemy was Hitler's Germany – the war against Japan was very
much a secondary consideration, and the Mackenzie King government was
reluctant to become heavily involved in it. For the Australians, obviously,
the focus was Japan. After the December 1941 Japanese attack on Pearl Harbor
and Hong Kong, fears of a Japanese invasion ran high in Australia. Lack of
interest from Canada was hardly of great import in the big scheme of things,
but it did little to help improve relations between the two nations.[36]

More importantly, however, Australia and Canada became allies by default because they were both small powers having to deal with the great
powers – in particular, the United States and, thanks to the imperial relationship, Great Britain – and almost inevitably they came to share many
worries and fears for the future. Although on opposite sides of the globe,
Australia and Canada were concerned about the rise of American power,
and for security reasons both tried to establish a stronger relationship with
the United States. At the same time, both were determined to have a voice
in the postwar era and not be relegated to obscurity by their much stronger
allies. As Paul Hasluck, an official in the Australian Department of External
Affairs put it, neither Australia nor Canada wanted a "peace dominated by
Britain and America."[37]

If there was one area that seemed to offer potential opportunity for the
development of Australian-Canadian cooperation, it was in planning for
the postwar era, and, in particular, for postwar international organizations.
Australia and Canada were emerging as two of the new middle powers, with
a broad sense of internationalism but also looking out for their own security and economic interests. Differences between the two nations remained,
but mutual interest as middle powers led to some cooperation; as one Canadian explained, "there developed a collaboration in international organizations so habitual that it was taken for granted by the 1950s."[38]

Few areas in postwar planning received more attention than international
aviation, because of its obvious link to security, defence, and economic prosperity.[39] The international competition and rivalries from before the war
and the destructive power of aviation unleashed during the war made it
clear that no nation could ignore aviation's potential benefits – or its haz-
ards. People were certain of the value of aviation, but to make matters more
difficult, in an age of rapid technological change, no one could know for
sure how it would develop in the postwar world. The British worried that
the Americans would use commercial aviation as a springboard to world
economic domination; the Americans suspected the British of carving out a

global network by using their Empire to block American expansion; the Australians and Canadians worried about them both and wondered where they would fit in once the war had ended. The postwar planners in all these nations, therefore, invested great faith in the future of aviation – as well as time, effort, and determination not to fall behind in its development or implementation.

Planning for the postwar world began long before the war ended, even though international civil aviation itself almost disappeared during the war. Most international services were eliminated or curtailed, especially in Europe and between the European states and their colonial possessions. In Britain, Imperial Airways was submerged into British Overseas Airway Corporation (BOAC) in 1940, but few civilian services survived the first year of the war, although a few colonial routes were maintained.[40] In Australia international services were severely reduced, while Canada was a bit of an exception in that it inaugurated a transatlantic service during the war, but even this service was designed for military purposes.

It was the Americans who emerged as the world leader in aviation during the war, using their prewar strength and the unique wartime circumstances to forge an enormous advantage over all rivals. The United States had a strong internal aviation system, with several competing airlines, and American dominance in the field of aircraft production was furthered by the combination of economic strength and technological revolution in aircraft design and performance.[41] Pan Am did not shrink once the war began, it developed new routes through the Caribbean and Latin America and to Africa, and other American airlines tried to push their way into the international market.[42]

To many in Britain it appeared that the Americans might dominate postwar commercial aviation if action were not taken to prevent it. And the way to check the Americans was through imperial solidarity. The Americans had the airplanes and the economic clout, but Britain still had its Empire, and this global array of potential landing sites and bases could be used to advantage when negotiating with the Americans. As a result, as the war progressed, it became even more important for London to bring the dominions into aviation discussions with a view to hammering out a joint Commonwealth policy.[43]

To this end, the British government invited the Australians, Canadians, and other dominion representatives to a series of preliminary and informal discussions on postwar aviation, beginning in February 1943. These discussions focused on the concept of "internationalization" of international aviation – an idea that meant different things to different people, although it was usually thought of as some kind of international control and regulation of international aviation. Supporters of internationalization ranged from those who believed it meant a strict regulation of international air services to those who believed that there should be a single international airline company to own and operate all the main international air services after the war.[44]

Differences between the Australians and Canadians surfaced early in the Commonwealth aviation discussions held in London in October 1943. The major disagreement came over this issue of internationalization. Some Canadians were enthusiastic about the possibility of a "World Airways," but the government and the Cabinet War Committee – which made the decisions on these matters – were decidedly cool.[45] It seemed so impractical to try to arrange for the international control and operation of international commercial aviation. In addition, the Canadians believed that, given their geographical location, the expansion of TCA and the Royal Canadian Air Force, the training of thousands of Canadians as pilots and ground crew under the British Commonwealth Air Training Plan, and the emergence of a domestic aircraft industry, that Canada would be able to hold its own in the postwar competition for international air travel. But most importantly, every pronouncement out of Washington made it clear that the Americans would have nothing to do with the idea, and the British had begun to waver on the issue as well. Likewise, the Canadians turned against internationalization, although there was still strong support for the regulation of air travel – to ensure that smaller nations like Canada were not swamped by the great powers like the United States.[46]

The Australians came out in favour of internationalization, and stuck with it long after most other nations had turned to other proposals. In Canberra there was a close link made between internationalization and postwar security in general. If Australia was not to be bypassed or forced to live in an American-dominated world, some control of aviation was necessary. During the war, Australians found themselves increasingly dependent on the United States to provide aircraft and to maintain connections with the outside world, and there was little desire to maintain such a relationship after the war had ended. "The real solution," wrote A.B. Corbett, the Australian Director-General of Civil Aviation in 1943, "is an international body representing and supported by all the nations; set up by the Peace Conference as a World Authority, or a World Civil Aviation Department of Civil Service to own and operate all international air trade routes, drawing its aircraft, pilots, mechanics, servants, from the member nations to serve under one World authority, and distributing any profits and any benefits fairly among its member nations."[47] Internationalization seemed to offer an alternative, if only to prevent the outbreak of cutthroat competition that would tend to work against Australian interests. As a result, while the Canadians were moving away from internationalization, John Curtin's Labor government informed its high commissioner, Stanley Bruce, the Australian representative at the Commonwealth discussions, that Australia was looking for "as large a measure of international collaboration in civil aviation as possible."[48]

Other differences appeared during the Commonwealth talks, particularly over the proposal for imperial solidarity. The Australians had been more supportive of imperial collaboration in the 1930s, and these prewar attitudes survived through the war. Conversely, the Canadian opposition to such collaboration became even stronger during the war, especially when it came to negotiating with the United States. Imperial interests were not always the same as Canadian interests, and it was feared that Canadian needs might be sacrificed to achieve some larger imperial goal in Anglo-American negotiations. For the Canadians, the answer to American competition was not to submerge Canadian aviation policy in an imperial one, but, rather, to move toward a more autonomous role in an aviation world that was regulated by some international aviation authority.[49] As C.D. Howe, the Canadian minister in charge of commercial aviation policy, put it: "Through our geographical position, if for no other reason, Canada will have an important place in postwar civil aviation, provided we are able to work out our own situation apart from that of the United Kingdom."[50]

It made for interesting but not very successful triangular discussions, with the Canadians and Australians on opposing sides of the two main issues of the day – internationalization and imperial solidarity. The British team – led by Canadian-born Lord Beaverbrook – was unhappy with both dominions. As Lord Privy Seal and the cabinet member in charge of Britain's commercial aviation negotiations, Beaverbrook hoped to achieve some kind of imperial unity before opening discussions with the Americans. But Canadian recalcitrance on this issue made it almost impossible. Indeed, the Canadians were talking about holding their own independent discussions with the Americans. Moreover, the British already had moved away from internationalization and found the Australians a little difficult. But Beaverbrook quickly dispensed with the idea during the Commonwealth discussions by burying it in a subcommittee, much to Bruce's surprise.[51]

In the wake of the failure of the Commonwealth discussions, the Australians, British, and Canadians began preparing their separate proposals for the much-anticipated international aviation conference. These documents revealed that the Australians and Canadians had much in common, but they also underlined the basic differences between them. Both wanted a role to play in aviation and, to ensure and preserve this role, they agreed on the need for an international regulatory body and on the need to reserve internal services for each nation. Beyond that, however, differences appeared. The Canadians wanted a much less powerful international authority than the Australians, and their "Tentative and Preliminary Draft of an International Air Transport Convention" gave the new international body regulatory powers only.[52] Australia, on the other hand, reconfirmed its support for internationalization in the influential 1944 Anzac Agreement with New Zealand, which stated that "air services using the international air trunk routes should be operated by an International Air Transport Authority" that should own all the aircraft and regulate the international air routes of the future.[53]

Neither country achieved complete success at the International Civil Aviation Conference held in Chicago in November 1944. Over fifty nations participated, but the conference was largely controlled by the Americans and overshadowed by difficult Anglo-American disputes on the control and regulation of postwar international air services. The Canadians fared better than the Australians, largely because the Americans were completely opposed to internationalization and the Australian proposals were quickly dismissed. Moreover, the Canadian proposals had some useful ideas for the regulation of international aviation, and the Canadians also made themselves useful in bringing together the British and American teams.[54]

The Chicago air conference was a success in that it produced the International Civil Aviation Organization (ICAO) and established the technical rules for the operation of postwar international air services. But it was much less of a success in producing the hoped-for multilateral agreement on the regulation of those air services. Anglo-American disagreement on traffic rights, rates, and service frequencies led to a breakdown in negotiations and, in the end, the regulatory agreements that were produced were relatively toothless. Hopes for a multilateral air agreement ran high for several more years, especially among many Australians and Canadians, but the failure at Chicago meant that postwar commercial aviation would unfold in a competitive environment. Furthermore, the 1946 Anglo-American Bermuda Agreement virtually ensured that most future aviation agreements would be bilateral rather than multilateral in nature.[55] Neither the Australians nor the Canadians were completely happy with these arrangements, and both were left to defend their own interests in the postwar era.

The Postwar Era

The end of the war sparked a new beginning for international commercial aviation. As the Germans and Japanese were pushed out of their conquered territories, old airlines and services were revived both within Europe and between Europe and its former colonies. Old rivalries reappeared, too. The American expansion continued from the war, and bilateral aviation agreements were signed with many nations in Latin America, the Pacific, Europe, and Asia. BOAC's colonial services were re-established, as were direct connections with continental Europe, and in 1946 BOAC inaugurated a transatlantic service to New York. Qantas revived some of its dormant services, and the Canadians turned their wartime transatlantic service into a civilian one, following it with agreements with the Americans, Irish, and several Caribbean states. Passenger services increased significantly in both countries and began to rival other forms of transportation. In 1948, for example, Canadian airplanes carried one-tenth the traffic of Canadian railways; twelve years later, air-passenger traffic surpassed train travel.[56]

Australian support for the idea of internationalization remained fairly high. In November 1947 an ICAO conference was held in Geneva in one last attempt to hammer out a multilateral aviation agreement. The idea was nearly dead by this time, but, in its instructions to the Australian delegation, Canberra maintained its commitment to internationalization, stating that "this objective must be constantly borne in mind and the Australian Government is unlikely to subscribe to any arrangement which jeopardises this objective."[57] The Canadians and Australians still could not agree, and the Americans, British, and French also had their own distinct views. Within days the Australians reported home: "Although no vote has yet been taken conference appears to have accepted that full multilateral agreement is not possible at this stage and discussion is now centring on how much should be included in multilateral and how much left to subsequent bilateral negotiation."[58] The Geneva Conference ended with no agreement signed, and the tacit acknowledgment that there would be no multilateral agreement.[59]

With the demise of internationalization as an achievable goal, reality dictated the negotiation of bilateral agreements for specific routes, rights, and rates. The Australians were forced to retreat to their fallback position, that of local control over air services in and out of Australia and Commonwealth collaboration on the international trunk routes – in particular, on the hoped for trans-Pacific service. Commonwealth collaboration provided for some safety in numbers. John Curtin, for one, was convinced; as one Australian historian put it, "Curtin wanted the Commonwealth to formulate a united approach in civil aviation so that the Americans could not pick the Dominions off one at a time as they had been attempting to do."[60]

The vehicle for the promotion of future Commonwealth collaboration (to be used in conjunction with other existing diplomatic channels) was to be the Commonwealth Air Transport Council (CATC), established near the end of the war. Representatives from Australia, Britain, Canada, India, New Zealand, Newfoundland, and South Africa met in Montreal in October and December 1944 (just prior to and following the Chicago Conference) and agreed that problems would continue in aviation regardless of the outcome at Chicago. Indeed, with the subsequent failure at Chicago to achieve a multilateral aviation agreement, it appeared more important than ever to establish some kind of permanent machinery for Commonwealth consultation on aviation affairs. Dealings with the Americans would likely be difficult in the coming months; the various members of the Commonwealth were eager to establish air services connecting their nations; and, for the

British, there was a desire to get some agreement to purchase Common-wealth (British) aircraft. In addition, Australia, Britain, and Canada were now all members of the new ICAO, and for some it was considered neces-sary to meet prior to ICAO general assemblies to hammer out a joint Com-monwealth policy.[61]

The CATC held its first meeting in London in July 1945. It was an advi-sory body, with a small secretariat and newsletter set up to discuss aviation matters of common interest to Commonwealth members. It had no powers to enforce decisions, only to discuss, exchange information, and inform gov-ernments of its resolutions. Proposals to make it more powerful – including the decision to hold compulsory Commonwealth discussions prior to bi-lateral negotiations with non-Commonwealth states and an agreement on standard clauses that *all* Commonwealth governments would subscribe to in future air agreements – were vetoed by the Canadians, who again found themselves in opposition to the Australian delegates and consistently re-fused to give the new body anything more than advisory functions. But the lack of enthusiasm from the Canadians was not enough to scuttle the CATC; for the Australians, British, and others, it would furnish the opportunity to enhance relationships among all the other Commonwealth members.[62]

The CATC could also help in the negotiation of the one Commonwealth route that remained to be agreed upon: the trans-Pacific service connecting Australia, Canada, and Britain. The war had put on hold the plans for a Pacific service, but by 1946 the time appeared right to open negotiations again. It would be the first time that Australia and Canada negotiated di-rectly in commercial aviation, and it would re-open some of the divisions between them, especially over the question of Commonwealth collabora-tion and the joint operation of air services.

During the war, there had been some preliminary discussions for a Pacific air service. Beaverbrook and Howe had talked about it in 1943, and the latter informed the British that Canada had no interest in a Commonwealth-run Pacific service. Howe repeated this message at the December 1944 Com-monwealth meetings in Montreal. What the Canadians had in mind was for Canada to operate the Canada-Hawaii section, with the Australians or a joint British-Australian company operating the Hawaii-Australia part of the service. If a division of services was impossible, then the Canadians insisted on two parallel services; one a Commonwealth collaboration and the other run by TCA.[63] Canadian policy remained consistent into the postwar era, and was in many ways contrary to the Australian ideal of Commonwealth cooperation.

Proposals for a Pacific service were formally discussed at the first meeting of the CATC in London in 1945. These talks did not progress beyond gen-eralities, and no real progress could be made until landing rights at Hawaii were secured from the Americans.[64] In the interim, at a conference in Wellington, New Zealand, in February 1946, representatives from Australia, New Zealand, Britain, Fiji, and the Western Pacific High Commission agreed to the incorporation of British Commonwealth Pacific Airlines (BCPA), a joint operating company to manage the Pacific service. Control of BCPA was divided between Australia (50 percent), Britain (30 percent), and New Zealand (20 percent).[65] The Australians supported this joint Commonwealth arrangement, as they had most Imperial-Commonwealth ventures in the past, regardless of how the Canadians felt about it. This conference also produced the South Pacific Air Transport Council (SPATC), established on the CATC model to handle regional aviation issues.[66] The Canadians sent an observer to the conference but were not involved in the creation of BCPA. They joined the SPATC in 1948.[67]

Once landing rights at Hawaii were obtained, the negotiations for a bilateral Australian-Canadian Pacific air-service agreement were resumed, and an agreement was signed on 11 June 1946.[68] There would be two airlines operating the service, and the two countries granted each other the right to operate a Sydney-Vancouver air service and agreed to divide the traffic roughly in half. BCPA was designated by the Australians to run their service; operations began in the summer and were in full swing by May 1947. To the surprise of many on both sides of the Pacific, the Canadians designated a private company – Canadian Pacific Air Lines – to operate the Canadian service. The decision was made more for domestic reasons than relations with the Pacific states, but it did worry the Australians and New Zealanders; they wondered if a private company could operate the service effectively without large government subsidies.[69] The differences were aired at a November 1948 meeting of the SPATC, which was attended by the Canadians, including the president of Canadian Pacific Air Lines. The Australians and New Zealanders protested that having a private company operate the service would make it harder for it to cooperate with BCPA, and they hoped that the Canadians would change their minds.[70] The Canadians remained firm, however, and a Canadian Pacific service was inaugurated in the middle of 1949, and a second Pacific service – to Japan – opened later that year.[71]

With the opening of the Pacific service, aviation relations between Australia and Canada reached a plateau, and in subsequent years began to diminish. International negotiations had failed to produce a multilateral aviation agreement, and most nations pursued their individual policies on a bilateral basis. The Australians and Canadians turned the focus of their attention to other nations and to parts of the world where they wanted to fly. Although BCPA was disbanded in 1954 and replaced by a cooperative arrangement between Qantas and BOAC, Australia continued to participate in several other Commonwealth ventures with, for example, New Zealand,

Fiji, Malaya, and others. The principle of Commonwealth cooperation remained strong in Australia into the 1960s.[72]

Attempts were made to foster closer aviation relations between Australia and Canada over the years, but with little success. The relationship itself has experienced many difficult times from the 1960s to the present, and these difficulties quite probably influenced aviation relations.[73] Even more important, however, was the fact that Australia and Canada had relatively few people who wanted to fly to each others' countries, and aviation relations inevitably suffered as a result. The two nations became world leaders in aviation – but not by flying to each other. For the Canadians, the Pacific soon came to be dominated by services to Japan, Hong Kong, and other locations on the Pacific Rim. For the Australians, traffic to London was always the most important, and a Pacific service through the United States was a much more valuable prize for Canberra.

By 1958 Australia had acquired rights through San Francisco, and from that time the Qantas world service went via the United States. It created a kind of paradox for the Australians, mixing their desire for Commonwealth collaboration with the fact that flying to Canada or over Canada was increasingly less important in the Australian scheme of things – they still wanted the collaboration, but the need for doing so seemed much less pressing. For example, Australian and Canadian representatives discussed closer cooperation in Melbourne in April 1959, and the report of the Australian delegation said it all, perhaps unintentionally: "Now that Australia has a route through the United States to Europe we have very little real interest in Canadian traffic rights except for the value that a Canadian polar route might have as an escape route in the event that something went wrong with our rights in the United States." But, the report added, the Canadians appeared more open to Commonwealth collaboration and "in the interests of drawing [them] into closer cooperation in civil aviation matters we showed a willingness to broaden the discussions with the Canadians."[74]

Australia and Canada have amended their aviation relationship over the years, but even with the great changes in international commercial aviation that came with the rise of charter-class service, the oil crisis of the 1970s, and the spread of international terrorism, it has never achieved a place of prominence in their relationship. The relative decline in their aviation relations appears even greater when compared to the continued interest of the two countries in domestic and international civil aviation. Over the years, international aviation has maintained its importance, "affecting the way governments view one another, the way individual citizens view their own and foreign countries, and in a variety of direct and indirect connections the security arrangements by which we live."[75] Australians and Canadians acknowledged the importance of commercial aviation, and their governments worked to expand air services at home and abroad, focusing considerable diplomatic attention on ICAO,[76] but bilateral relations continued to decline.

At first the CATC remained and, despite its relative impotence, it provided the Australians and Canadians – along with their membership in ICAO – with the permanent machinery for their aviation relationship to evolve and develop. Even here, however, it was a relationship in decline: meetings of the CATC were held irregularly, and by the 1950s they were usually scheduled only in advance of meetings of ICAO. And, as the major aviation disputes between the great powers were settled, the CATC evolved into what was essentially a body for the exchange of technical information. Membership grew in inverse proportion to the function of the CATC: as Britain decolonized, new states were invited to join, enlarging the membership to nearly forty by the 1970s; but over the years, the CATC had less and less to do, and its role was increasingly overshadowed by the much larger ICAO. Indeed the CATC nearly disappeared by the late 1960s, only to be revived – by the Mulroney government and others – in the 1980s. It is clearly a moribund organization, however; there were no meetings in the 1990s.

Conclusion

The decline of the CATC is symptomatic of the Australian-Canadian aviation relationship. Other chapters in this book examine the many areas in which Australia and Canada have cooperated and grown closer in the international community, but this has not always been the case with respect to commercial aviation. Since the Second World War, the bonds of Commonwealth have become weaker, and Australians and Canadians have not always moved in the same direction in pursuit of their economic and security needs. The importance of their regions – Asia-Pacific for the Australians, North America for the Canadians – has risen in significance in the last few decades, and these factors have been reflected in their aviation relations. Even with the great boom in air traffic across the Pacific, making it one of the world's most travelled routes, there has been relatively little increase in traffic between Australia and Canada.

When it came to the evolution of international commercial aviation, Australia and Canada saw the world from very different perspectives, and these differing vantage points were reflected in their aviation policies. Thanks to their geographical locations and to the neighbours that surrounded them, fundamental differences emerged – even on the basic issues of allowing other states to fly over their airspace. Because few would need to fly over Australia, the Australians were willing to give this right away without much of a fight; but for the Canadians, their airspace promised to be a popular route and, consequently, it was a vital concern to Ottawa and not to be negotiated away without gaining something in return.[77] At the same time, when it came to the more delicate issue of picking up passengers in countries other than where a service began or ended, the Canadians, at first, were less determined to secure extra landing rights, since most of their services would be direct ones – to New York, London, or Bermuda. For the Australians, who eyed the long Sydney-London route that needed frequent stops along the way, the right to pick up additional passengers became an issue of vital importance.[78]

As several chapters in this book have demonstrated, Australia and Canada had – and still do have – much in common, and throughout the twentieth century they shared many of the same basic security needs, often viewing the world in similar ways. But these similarities could not hide the major differences in international commercial aviation, especially when it came to relations with Great Britain and the United States. The imperial relationship always meant something different to Australians than it did to Canadians, and however much they tried in the 1930s, during the war, and through the 1950s and 1960s, the gulf was too vast to bridge. There was room for friendship and even, at times, cooperation, but at no time was it possible to establish a convergence between Australia and Canada in Commonwealth aviation policies.

Equally, in their dealings with the United States, the world's major air power in civil aviation, Australia and Canada could not agree. Australian concern over the United States was global – how to further Australia's security needs in the Pacific in an American-dominated world. For the Canadians, the concern was regional, in that Canadians share a 4,800-kilometre border with the United States; this close proximity was a factor in almost all aspects of Canada's international aviation policy, including those parts that concerned the Commonwealth and Australia.

However much Australia and Canada may have wanted to become close allies and partners in the development of international commercial aviation, geographical location, regional security concerns, the historical legacy of the imperial relationship, and economic advantage combined to make it virtually impossible. The fact that they came into contact at all in the early years was something of an historical accident, in that they were both former colonies of Great Britain. Their direct connections were minor in comparison to their individual bilateral relations with Britain, and it was only because of this British connection that Australia and Canada were introduced to the world of aviation diplomacy. The great distance between Australia and Canada and the relative weakness of both countries compared to Britain and the United States made direct aviation relations necessary only on rare occasions. Australia and Canada may have been "distant allies" travelling on "parallel paths," but in the world of international commercial aviation, they were worlds apart.[79]

Notes

1 Their conclusion was based on route mileage per one million population. The Netherlands and Belgium came second and third, respectively; Canada placed fourth. See D.M. Hocking and C.P. Haddon-Cave, *Air Transport in Australia* (Sydney: Angus and Robertson, 1951), 36.

2 Grant Dexter, *Canada and the Building of Peace* (Toronto: Canadian Institute of International Affairs, 1944), 112.

3 "Men of 46 Airlines Meet in Montreal," *Canadian Aviation* 18 (1945): 103.

4 Geoffrey Blainey, quoted in Garth Stevenson, *The Politics of Canada's Airlines from Diefenbaker to Mulroney* (Toronto: University of Toronto Press, 1987), 3.

5 Oliver James Lissitzyn, *International Air Transport and National Policy* (New York: Council on Foreign Relations, 1942), 14.

6 For a general background of the Australian-Canadian relationship, see Greg Donaghy, *Parallel Paths: Canadian-Australian Relations since the 1890s* (Ottawa: Department of Foreign Affairs and International Trade, 1995), 1. See also K.A. MacKirdy, "Canadian and Australian Self-Interest, the American Fact, and the Development of the Commonwealth Idea," in *Empire and Nations: Essays in Honour of Frederic H. Soward*, ed. Harvey L. Dyck and H. Peter Krosby (Toronto: University of Toronto Press, 1969), 116-32.

7 Mackenzie Bowell, quoted in Donaghy, *Parallel Paths*, 1.

8 Ibid., 2-9.

9 For the outline of Australian-Canadian relations in the imperial setting, see Philip Wigley, *Canada and the Transition to Commonwealth, 1917-1926* (Cambridge: Cambridge University Press, 1977); and Nicholas Mansergh, *The Commonwealth Experience* (New York: Praeger, 1969). For a recent look at Australia and the Empire, see David McIntyre, "Australia, New Zealand, and the Pacific Islands," in *The Oxford History of the British Empire*, vol. 4, *The Twentieth Century*, ed. Judith M. Brown and Wm. Roger Louis (Oxford: Oxford University Press, 1999), 667-92.

10 J.E. Richardson, "American Influence on the Air Transport Industry," in *Contemporary Australia: Studies in History, Politics, and Economics*, ed. Richard Preston (Durham, NC: Duke University, 1969), 521-2.

11 David Corbett, *Politics and the Airlines* (Toronto: University of Toronto Press, 1965), 19-21. For another general review, see the Report of Inter-Departmental Committee, "Civil Aviation Policy and Organization during the War and Post-War Period" (December 1943), 1-6, Australian Archives (hereinafter AA), Department of Defence, Central Office, Sir Frederick Shedden Collection, A5954, 1, 1979, 159.

12 Hocking and Haddon-Cave, *Air Transport in Australia*, 35.

13 Corbett, *Politics and the Airlines*, 21; Report of Inter-Departmental Committee (December 1943), 4-5.

14 Report of Inter-Departmental Committee (December 1943), 6. The equivalent is 67,200,000 kilometres.

15 See Fred Gaffen, "Canada's Military Aircraft Industry: Its Birth, Growth and Fortunes," *Canadian Defence Quarterly* 15, 2 (1985): 48-53; and S.F. Wise, "The Borden Government and the Formation of a Canadian Flying Corps, 1911-1916," in *Policy by Other Means: Essays in Honour of C.P. Stacey*, ed. Michael Cross and Robert Bothwell (Toronto: Clarke, Irwin, 1972), 121-44.

16 On the development of civil aviation in Canada, see the early chapters in J.R.K. Main, *Voyageurs of the Air: A History of Civil Aviation in Canada, 1858-1967* (Ottawa: Queen's Printer, 1967), and Margaret Mattson, "The Growth and Protection of Canadian Civil and Commercial Aviation, 1918-1930" (PhD diss., University of Western Ontario, 1978).

17 J.A. Wilson, "The World's Airway System," *The Engineering Journal* (December 1936): 15-16. See also Wilson's "The Expansion of Aviation into Arctic and Sub-Arctic Canada," *Canadian Geographical Journal* 41 (1950): 130-41.

18 See C.A. Ashley, *The First Twenty-five Years: A Study of Trans-Canada Air Lines* (Toronto: Macmillan, 1963), 5-10; Philip Smith, *It Seems Like Only Yesterday: Air Canada, the First 50 Years* (Toronto: McClelland and Stewart, 1986), 31-61.

19 Corbett, *Politics and the Airlines*, 19-21; J.A. Wilson memo, "Trans-Pacific Airways," 9 November 1933, Directorate of History, Department of National Defence, Ottawa, J.A. Wilson Papers, 76, 271, folder E, file E1.

20 Harold Stannard, "Civil Aviation: An Historical Background," *International Affairs* 21, 4 (1945): 499. See also Roger Beaumont, "A New Lease on Empire: Air Policing, 1919-1939," *Aerospace Historian* 26, 2 (1979): 84-90.

21 Corbett, *Politics and the Airlines*, 26-33; see also Robert McCormack, "Imperialism, Air Transport and Colonial Development: Kenya, 1920-46," *Journal of Imperial and Commonwealth History* 17, 3 (1989): 374-95.

22 On international rivalry in commercial aviation before the Second World War, see – among others – Marc Dierikx, "Struggle for Prominence: Clashing Dutch and British Interests on the Colonial Air Routes, 1918-42," *Journal of Contemporary History* 26, 2 (1991): 333-51; Wesley P. Newton, "International Aviation Rivalry in Latin America, 1919-1927," *Journal of Inter-American Studies* 7, 3 (1965): 345-56; and Stephen James Randall, "Colombia, the United States, and Interamerican Aviation Rivalry, 1927-1940," *Journal of Interamerican Studies and World Affairs* 14, 3 (1972): 297-324.

23 See Mattson, "Growth and Protection," 8-16; Norman Hillmer, "Mackenzie King, Canadian Air Policy, and the Imperial Conference of 1923," *High Flight* 1, 5 (1981): 189-93, 196. See also Robert McCormack, "Missed Opportunities: Winston Churchill, the Air Ministry, and Africa, 1919-1921," *International History Review* 11, 2 (1989): 205-28, and "Inter-Imperial Communications" (1932), Directorate of History, Department of National Defence, J.A. Wilson Papers, 76, 271, folder C, file C8.

24 On the evolution of British policy, see Alan Dobson, *Peaceful Air Warfare: The United States, Britain, and the Politics of International Aviation* (Oxford: Clarendon Press, 1991), 15-49, and Robin Higham, *Britain's Imperial Air Routes 1918-1939: The Story of Britain's Overseas Airlines* (Hamden, CT: Shoestring Press, 1961), 41-8. See also John Cooper, "Some Historic Phases of British International Civil Aviation Policy," *International Affairs* 23, 2 (1947): 189-201, and Peter Fearon, "The Growth of Aviation in Britain," *Journal of Contemporary History* 20, 1 (1985): 21-40.

25 Corbett, *Politics and the Airlines*, 21; Higham, *Britain's Imperial Air Routes*, 85-7.

26 Dobson, *Peaceful Air Warfare*, 114.

27 On the 1935 agreement, see David MacKenzie, *Canada and International Civil Aviation, 1932-1948* (Toronto: University of Toronto Press, 1989), 49-51, 87-92; on the negotiations with the United States on a transatlantic service, see Higham, *Britain's Imperial Air Routes*, 182-202.

28 See, for example, Robert McCormack, "Man with a Mission: Oswald Pirow and South African Airways, 1933-1939," *Journal of African History* 20 (1979): 543-57, and David MacKenzie, "Ireland, Canada and Atlantic Aviation, 1935-45: A Comparative Study," *Canadian Journal of Irish Studies* 18, 1 (1992): 31-47.

29 "The Commonwealth Air Route round the World," February 1937, National Archives of Canada (hereinafter NAC), W.L.M. King Papers, MG26 J4, vol. 177, file F1637, E (37), 4.

30 MacKenzie, *Canada and International Civil Aviation*, 60-70. See also H.V. Hodson, "The Imperial Conference," *International Affairs* 16, 5 (1937): 660. More generally on the issue of Commonwealth cooperation, see Rainer Tamchina, "In Search of Common Causes: The Imperial Conference of 1937," *Journal of Imperial and Commonwealth History* 1, 1 (1972): 79-105.

31 Quoted in MacKenzie, *Canada and International Civil Aviation*, 68.

32 The committee resolution can be found in MacKenzie, *Canada and International Civil Aviation*, 255. The committee documents and minutes can be found in NAC, W.L.M. King Papers, MG26 J4, vol. 177, file F1637.

33 See "D," "Pacific Airways" *Foreign Affairs* 18, 1 (1939): 60-9, and Grayson Kirk, "Wings over the Pacific," *Foreign Affairs* 20, 2 (1942): 293-302.

34 On Pan Am and US policy generally, see Marylin Bender and Selig Altschul, *The Chosen Instrument* (New York: Simon and Schuster, 1982), and Carl Solberg, *Conquest of the Skies: A History of Commercial Aviation in America* (Boston: Little, Brown, 1979).

35 See M. Ruth Megaw, "The Scramble for the Pacific: Anglo-United States Rivalry in the 1930s," *Historical Studies* 17, 69 (1977): 458-73, and David Day, "P.G. Taylor and the Alternative Pacific Air Route, 1939-45," *Australian Journal of Politics and History* 32, 1 (1986): 6-19.

36 Donaghy, *Parallel Paths*, 10-11; see also J.F. Hilliker, "Distant Ally: Canadian Relations with Australia during the Second World War," *Journal of Imperial and Commonwealth History* 13, 1 (1984): 46-67, and David Day, "Anzacs on the Run: The View from Whitehall, 1941-42," *Journal of Imperial and Commonwealth History* 14, 3 (1986): 187-202.

37 Paul Hasluck, *Diplomatic Witness: Australian Foreign Affairs, 1941-1947* (Carlton: Melbourne University Press, 1980), 80. See also Trevor Reese, *Australia, New Zealand, and the United States: A Survey of International Relations, 1941-1968* (London: Oxford University Press, under the auspices of the Royal Institute of International Affairs, 1969), 31-3; J.L. Granatstein and Norman Hillmer, *For Better or for Worse: Canada and the United States to the 1990s* (Toronto: Copp Clark Pitman, 1991), 133-62, and David Day, *Reluctant Nation: Australia and the Allied Defeat of Japan, 1942-45* (Melbourne: Oxford University Press, 1992), 145-6, 181.

38 Quoted in Donaghy, *Parallel Paths*, 11.

39 For a detailed examination of Australian-Canadian postwar planning for international aviation, see David MacKenzie, "Wartime Planning for Post-war Commercial Aviation: Australia and Canada Compared," *Journal of Imperial and Commonwealth History* 26, 3 (1998): 50-70.

40 See Robert McCormack, "War and Change: Air Transport in British Africa, 1939-1946," *Canadian Journal of History* 24, 3 (December 1989): 341-59.

41 See R.K. Smith, "The Intercontinental Airliner and the Essence of Airplane Performance, 1929-1939," *Technology and Culture* 24, 3 (July 1983): 428-49, and John M. Wilson, "The Shape of Things to Come: The Military Impact of World War II on Civil Aviation," *Aerospace Historian* 28, 4 (1981): 262-7.

42 See Deborah Ray, "The Takoradi Route: Roosevelt's Prewar Venture beyond the Western Hemisphere," *Journal of American History* 62, 2 (1975): 340-58, and David Haglund, "'Delousing' Scadta: The Role of Pan-American Airways in U.S. Aviation Diplomacy in Colombia, 1939-1940," *Aerospace Historian* 30, 3 (1983): 177-90.

43 See MacKenzie, *Canada and International Civil Aviation*, 126-7; see also Dobson, *Peaceful Air Warfare*, 130-8.

44 On British policy, see Christopher Brewin, "British Plans for International Operating Agencies for Civil Aviation," *International History Review* 4, 1 (1982): 91-110.

45 Escott Reid, "The Internationalization of Civil Aviation," 24 December 1942, NAC, Escott Reid Papers, MG31 E46, vol. 10, file 37.

46 Cabinet War Committee minutes, 6 October 1943, NAC, RG2 7c, vol. 14.

47 A.B. Corbett memo, "Post War Civil Aviation," 12 August 1943, AA, Department of External Affairs (hereinafter DEA), Correspondence files, 1943-4, A989, 1, 43, 735, 832, 1, part 1.

48 Commonwealth Government to Bruce, telegram 146, 8 October 1943, AA, A989, 1, 43, 735, 832, 1, part 1.

49 On the evolution of Canadian wartime policy, see MacKenzie, *Canada and International Civil Aviation*, 119-26.

50 Howe to Norman Robertson, 8 February 1943, NAC, RG2 series 18, vol. 18, file A-15-1-A (vol. 1).

51 MacKenzie, "Wartime Planning," 57-8. On the discussions, see "British Commonwealth Conversations," 11-13 October 1943, NAC, RG2 series 18, vol. 52, file a-15-1 (w), part 1.

52 Cabinet Document 693, "A Tentative and Preliminary Draft of an International Air Transport Convention," 8 January 1944, NAC, Privy Council Office, reel 4576.

53 *Australian-New Zealand Agreement 1944*, 21 January 1944, taken from W.J. Hudson, ed., *Documents on Australian Foreign Policy 1937-49*, vol. 7, *1944* (Canberra: Australian Government Publishing Service, 1988), doc. 26.

54 On the Chicago Conference, see David MacKenzie, "An 'Ambitious Dream': The Chicago Conference and the Quest for Multilateralism in International Air Transport," *Diplomacy and Statecraft* 2, 2 (1991): 270-93; Dobson, *Peaceful Air Warfare*, 151-72; Escott Reid, *Radical Mandarin: The Memoirs of Escott Reid* (Toronto: University of Toronto Press, 1989), 170-89;

John Andrew Miller, "Air Diplomacy: The Chicago Aviation Conference of 1944 in Anglo-American Wartime Relations and Postwar Planning," (PhD diss., Yale University, 1971); and Edward Warner, "The Chicago Conference: Accomplishments and Unfinished Business," *Foreign Affairs* 23, 3 (1945): 406-21. The conference documents can be found in *Proceedings of the International Civil Aviation Conference, Chicago, Illinois, November 1 – December 7, 1944*, 2 vols. (Washington, DC: Department of State, 1948).

55 On Bermuda, see David MacKenzie, "The Bermuda Conference and Anglo-American Aviation Relations at the End of the Second World War," *Journal of Transport History* 12, 1 (1991): 61-73; and John Cooper, "The Bermuda Plan: World Pattern for Air Transport," *Foreign Affairs* 25, 1 (1946): 59-71.

56 Stevenson, *The Politics of Canada's Airlines*, 12.

57 E.C. Johnston (Director-General of Civil Aviation), "Instructions to Delegation to Commission on Multilateral Agreement on Air Transport Rights," 31 October 1947, AA, DEA, Correspondence files, A1838, 1, 890, 36, 5.

58 Australian Delegation to Department of External Affairs, Canberra, 7 November 1947, AA, DEA, Correspondence files, A1838, 1, 890, 36, 5.

59 See John Cooper, "The Proposed Multilateral Agreement on Commercial Rights in International Civil Air Transport," *Journal of Air Law and Commerce* 14, 2 (1947): 125-49; and R.J.G. McClurkin, "The Geneva Commission on a Multilateral Air Transport Agreement," *Journal of Air Law and Commerce* 15, 1 (1948): 39-46.

60 Day, *Reluctant Nation*, 224.

61 On the CATC, see David MacKenzie, "The Rise and Fall of the Commonwealth Air Transport Council: A Canadian Perspective," *Journal of Imperial and Commonwealth History* 21, 1 (1993): 105-25. The Montreal conference documents can be found in NAC, RG2 series 18, vol. 52, file A-15-1 (w), part 1. See also "After Chicago: Imperial Interests in Civil Aviation" *Round Table* 35 (March 1945): 130-6.

62 MacKenzie, "Rise and Fall," 112-13.

63 MacKenzie, *Canada and International Civil Aviation*, 203.

64 High commissioner for Canada in Great Britain to secretary of state for external affairs, Canada, t. 1959, 13 July 1945, NAC, C.D. Howe Papers, MG27 III B20, vol. 98, file 61-6 (15).

65 Corbett, *Politics and the Airlines*, 96-7.

66 Minister for external affairs, Wellington, New Zealand, to secretary of state for external affairs, Ottawa, t. 4, 6 March 1946, NAC, C.D. Howe Papers, MG27 III B20, vol. 98, file 61-6 (15).

67 MacKenzie, *Canada and International Civil Aviation*, 245-51.

68 "Agreement between Canada and Australia for Air Services between the Two Countries," 11 June 1946, NAC, RG2 series 18, vol. 55, file A-15-1-J 1944-47.

69 See the text of an Australian government press release: High commissioner for Canada in Australia to secretary of state for external affairs, Ottawa, telegram 71, 4 August 1948, NAC, RG2 series 18, vol. 55, file A-15-1-J 1948.

70 High commissioner for Canada in New Zealand to secretary of state for external affairs, Canada, telegram 231, 29 November 1948, NAC, RG2 series 18, vol. 55, file A-15-1-J 1948.

71 On Canadian Pacific, see D.M. Bain, *Canadian Pacific Air Lines: Its History and Aircraft* (Calgary: Cal/oka, 1987).

72 See Corbett, *Politics and the Airlines*, 97; also Department of Civil Aviation, Melbourne, "International Air Traffic Rights," November 1960, AA, DEA, Correspondence files, A1838, 1, 717, 1, part 1.

73 On problems in the relationship, see, for example, Donaghy, *Parallel Paths*, 15-18, and Andrew Cooper, "Australia and Canada View the Pacific," in *Canada among Nations 1997: Asia Pacific Face-Off*, ed. Fen Osler Hampson, Maureen Appel Molot, and Martin Rudner (Ottawa: Carleton University Press, 1997), 145-63.

74 "Notes for Cabinet by Minister of Civil Aviation on: Development of Commonwealth Co-operative Arrangements in International Air Transport and Overseas Air Negotiations to be Undertaken in Europe in July/August, 1959," Summer 1959, AA, DEA, Correspondence files, A1838, 1, 716, 52, 6, 2.

75 Andreas Lowenfeld, "A New Takeoff for International Air Transport," *Foreign Affairs* 54, 1 (1975): 36. See also Alan Dobson, "Aspects of Anglo-American Diplomacy 1976-93," *Diplomacy and Statecraft* 4, 2 (1993): 235-57, and Eugene Sochor, *The Politics of International Aviation* (Basingstoke: Macmillan, 1991).

76 See, for example, "Report of the Tenth Session of the Assembly of the International Civil Aviation Organisation held at Caracas, Venezuela," June-July 1956, AA, DEA, Correspondence files, A1838, 1, 717, 31, 10.

77 Location lost some of its advantages with the introduction of jet aircraft: "They could fly non-stop from New York to most gateways in Europe, so that travellers could forget about Shannon, Gander or Goose Bay ('No Goose, No Gander,' boasted El Al when it began non-stop flights), and the once-crucial airports were only used by local passengers ... while the Canadians and Irish lost trump cards in the bargaining for landing rights." Anthony Sampson, *Empires of the Sky: The Politics, Contests and Cartels of World Airlines* (London: Hodder and Stoughton, 1984), 110.

78 See Hocking and Haddon-Cave, *Air Transport in Australia*, 158-9.

79 See Hilliker, "Distant Ally," and Donaghy, *Parallel Paths*.

5

"She Should Have Thought of Herself First": Canada and Military Aid to Australia, 1939-45

Galen Perras

Australian historian Jeffrey Grey asserts that "much of the military history of Canada in the twentieth century is also written in terms which are strikingly familiar to Australian readers, and which speak of similar concerns in the development of that dominion," adding that "war is something that we go away to fight, generally of our own volition."[1] But in the Second World War, while hundreds of thousands of Canadians fought in Europe and the north Atlantic, just a few hundred Canadians served in the Antipodes, despite concerted efforts by key Australian and Canadian officials to dispatch many more Canadian troops. Not surprisingly then, few Canadian historians have paid much attention to Canadian-Australian relations between 1939 and 1945. R.G. Haycock discusses Major General Victor Odlum's quixotic attempt to bring a Canadian division to Australia in early 1942, while John Hilliker offers a good short analysis of the Canadian-Australian relationship in the Second World War.[2] Hilliker, an official historian at the Canadian Department of Foreign Affairs and International Trade, focuses on Canada's relationship with Australia within the context of the Allied wartime alliance. Most importantly, Hilliker's account, while admitting that Canada and Australia were distant allies, puts a rather good face on things. I will argue that the situation was far more dire – that senior Canadian and Australian politicians and policy makers often found the other side difficult at best and deliberately obstructionist or dishonest at worst, and that this unhappy state of affairs continued well into the postwar period. Mostly uninterested in the strategic realities of the Asia-Pacific region, Canadian decision-makers remained utterly fixated upon the European conflict, at Australia's expense. Forced to confront Australia's needs after Canadian high commissioner Odlum foolishly offered Canberra military assistance in early 1942, Canadian leaders declined to make timely or clear decisions regarding Australia. Odlum's disastrous promise was the low point of an often testy bilateral relationship, but the die was cast before 1942 and would continue beyond the war's end, a relationship constrained by vastly different geostrategic circumstances, radically different national political-diplomatic styles, and personality clashes.

Early Days

Initially, Australia and Canada had some things in common when the Second World War erupted. Having encouraged the appeasement of Adolf Hitler, Prime Ministers Robert Menzies and William Lyon Mackenzie King greeted Britain's declaration of war on Germany on 3 September 1939 with little enthusiasm. Menzies had warned Australians on 25 August 1939 that involvement in a European conflagration was unavoidable, as "the destruction or defeat of Great Britain would be the destruction or defeat of the British Empire and would leave us with a precarious tenure of our own independence." Because Australia had not ratified the 1931 Statute of Westminster, when news of Britain's belligerence arrived Menzies had no choice; Australia was at war. Concerned that Japan might take advantage of Europe's conflict, Menzies wanted to avoid dispatching substantial forces overseas – only to see that hope dashed when New Zealand's prompt troop offer and growing domestic public pressure compelled him to send much of Australia's navy and three army divisions to the Middle East.[3] Though he had consistently refused to commit to Britain in advance, in order not to alienate French Canada, King was determined that Canada would stand by Britain against Germany. Utterly determined to avoid the racial divisiveness engendered by the First World War, King recalled parliament for a formal debate before Canada declared war against Germany on 10 September 1939. King would have preferred a war of limited liability, providing raw materials, weapons, and air crew while avoiding a costly land battle. But Canada's military and people had other ideas. When Britain asked for Canadian ground and air forces for European service, King had to acknowledge the request. By December 1939 a Canadian army division had arrived in Britain, and more would follow after the disasters that befell Allied arms in 1940.

September 1939 also witnessed two examples of Australian-Canadian cooperation. On 13 September, the Australian and Canadian high commissioners to Britain – Stanley Bruce and Vincent Massey – discussed a training plan to churn out air crew, a proposal Britain eagerly favoured – if the dominions carried much of the cost. Hard bargaining procured a deal in mid-December 1939, but the British Commonwealth Air Training Plan's paternity remains in dispute. Massey claims the idea, Bruce's biographer avers that the Australian sired the plan, while the official history of the Royal Canadian Air Force (RCAF) states that Bruce and Massey jointly offered the scheme.[4] And when King also suggested swapping high commissioners at an early date, Menzies agreed, after ascertaining that Britain did not object.[5] Charles J. Burchell arrived in Australia in December 1939, while former general and politician William Glasgow landed in Ottawa in March 1940. While

King thought that Burchell's primary qualification was his attendance at a 1938 British Commonwealth Relations Conference in Sydney, he feared that Burchell looked on the appointment "as a quasi pleasure trip, satisfying a certain social ambition at this time" – not an egregious offence, as King expected diplomats to be nothing more than his mouthpieces. Burchell averaged three speeches a week until his July 1941 recall to Canada, and, according to an American diplomat, undoubtedly had done much to foster Canadian-Australian relations.[6]

A busier Glasgow had to deal with the Canadian government's civilian and military agencies, Britain's high commission in Ottawa, Australia's new legation in Washington, and submit regular accounts of Canada's political scene to Canberra. He keenly followed the August 1940 creation of the Canadian-American Permanent Joint Board on Defence (PJBD), as Australia had been seeking a similar arrangement with America since the 1930s. Though King aide Leonard Brockington favoured adding Britain, Australia, and New Zealand to the PJBD, Secretary of State Cordell Hull declared his country was not ready for a military alliance in the Pacific.[7]

Other Australian initiatives fared poorly. Glasgow's notion of exchanging military information and unit dispositions found support from the Canadian chiefs of staff (COS) and defence minister J.L. Ralston. But Canada's army balked at Glasgow's suggestion that such a liaison could be handled by Australia's air liaison office in Ottawa and its naval attaché in Washington, wanting instead an Australian military attaché in Washington to handle purely army matters. When Glasgow thought the amount of work would not justify the appointment, Canada agreed to bimonthly liaison letters.[8]

The second initiative is less easily traceable. Australia had committed three divisions to the Middle East, plus two brigades at Singapore, by early 1941. So, when an Anglo-Japanese war scare arose in February 1941, Australia's war cabinet asked Bruce if any of Canada's inactive 60,000 British-based soldiers might be sent down under. Though he did not know Canada's official attitude, Bruce had little doubt, given reports of restive Canadian troops, that Canada "would agree that the utilisation of Canadians was the most effective and expeditious method of reinforcing the Far East." There seems to be no record that Bruce broached the subject with Canadian authorities, however. O.D. Skelton, undersecretary of state for external affairs, had rejected an invitation in October 1940 to attend a conference dealing with south Pacific defence cooperation, as well as rejecting the notion that Canada should commit forces to that region. King had sent a naval officer to the Singapore-based meeting, but also had opposed sending units to the South Pacific, and dismissed a proposal to dispatch Canadian soldiers to North Africa, as "the logical thing was to have Canadians continue to defend Britain, and not to begin to play the role of those who want Empire war."[9]

On 24 January 1941 Menzies embarked upon an exhaustive tour that took him to Singapore, the Middle East, Britain, and North America before returning home in May. By April, with German troops advancing on Egypt and threatening to annihilate imperial forces in Greece, Menzies – concerned that Britain's war cabinet could not restrain Winston Churchill – wanted to revive the Imperial War Cabinet (IWC), which had brought dominion leaders to London in 1917-18 to direct the imperial war effort. Menzies viewed King as a key ally, having lobbied the Canadian prime minister to secure American aid for the failing Allied cause in 1940. When he first met King in Ottawa on 7 May 1941, though he found King both pleasant and cooperative, Menzies pronounced that the Canadian had "no *burning* zeal for the cause, and [was] a politician who possibly prefers to lead from behind." King thought that Menzies possessed a "splendid presence, great vigour ... a wonderful gift for speaking" and "many of the qualities of a great leader." Yet King opined that Menzies "nevertheless is thinking pretty much of Menzies most of the time," and priggishly offered that Menzies's affection for "the environments of high society, palaces, etc., ... will cost him, perhaps, dearly in the end." More importantly, believing that Menzies "would rather be on the War Cabinet in London than Prime Minister of Australia," and clearly recalling Prime Minister Robert Borden's extended sojourns in Britain in 1917-18, King also worried about domestic political repercussions if he spent too much time in London. If special circumstances dictated the need for imperial leaders to make "great decisions," then King might consider travelling to Britain.[10] Churchill was not very interested, either, in a revived IWC, but under considerable pressure after the Greek and North African debacles, he agreed to arrange a special conference with dominion leaders in July. Complaining that it was unfair for him to have to choose between Canadian unity and Churchill's wishes, King told Churchill that avoiding a repetition of Canada's 1917 conscription crisis and his close relationship with Roosevelt dictated that he must remain at home. These protests had the desired effect, as Dominions Secretary Lord Cranborne declared that the conference was off for the moment.[11]

Menzies's resignation on 28 August 1941 only convinced King he had been correct to concentrate on domestic politics,[12] but as the resignation drama was unfolding, a Labor member of the house of representatives asked army minister Percy Spender if Canada had troops in the Middle East, or if the Canadian army had seen any action anywhere. Spender's response was blunt; "My answer to the first part of the question is, not that I am aware of; and to the second part, that I believe Canadian troops were in service during the evacuation of Dunkirk." R.G. Casey, Australia's minister in Washington, had an even harsher opinion. Arguing that Canada had "fallen between two stools," he claimed that it "does not seem to have developed into a self-confident nation – but to have, quite unnecessarily, I think, developed rather a 'poor relation' complex – through close proximity to the vast population and wealth of the United States."[13]

A New War

King replaced Burchell with Major General Victor Odlum. The general had been a Canadian divisional commander in Britain until 1941, and King told Odlum that his military experience would show Australia and Britain that Canada was making a real contribution in the Pacific if he took the Canberra position.[14] Certainly King desired to rid himself of the troublesome and well-connected general, and Odlum, who had been badgering the prime minister for a meaningful military appointment, soon made King regret his decision. Meeting with Australian General Thomas Blamey in Egypt in December 1941, Odlum remarked that Canada should send troops to the Antipodes as "a hammer stroke for Empire solidarity." In Canberra on 10 January 1942, he relayed to Ottawa that Australia faced a real military emergency, and that the subject of Canadian military aid had been raised. King reminded Odlum that only Canada's Cabinet War Committee (CWC) could determine troop dispositions, and warned the general "that cabinet is zealous in guarding its prerogative of deciding all questions of war policy including disposition of man-power and allied problems."[15]

That admonition arrived after Odlum's attendance at the 12 January 1942 meeting of the Australian Advisory War Council (AWC). Australia's army had 270,000 troops at home, but most were poorly trained and badly armed militia. Just 373 obsolete aircraft sat in Australia, while the navy could muster only five ships in home waters. Though Australia's military had commented that the new threat was "merely another incident in the present war," Labor Prime Minister John Curtin, in the job only since October, ordered the chiefs of staff to take another look. That assessment, ready on 11 December 1941 – one day after the Royal Navy had lost two capital ships to a Japanese air attack near Malaya – anticipated that Japan might contemplate a direct move on Australia if it captured Singapore.[16]

Japan's victories were Curtin's nightmare come true, as he had warned in 1936 against counting "upon the competence, let alone the readiness, of British statesmen to send forces to our aid" in a major conflict. Churchill twice had promised Australia, in 1940, that if Japan seriously threatened, Britain would cut its Mediterranean losses and "proceed to your aid sacrificing every interest except only defence position of this island [Britain] on which all depends." But on 11 December 1941, the British doubted that Australia would face a large-scale threat until after Japan had consolidated its position, adding ominously, "[We] must not forget that Germany ... is still the main enemy."[17] With Japan besieging Malaya and Hong Kong, Curtin had started looking elsewhere for assistance. As the Americans already had diverted 2,400 army air force personnel and ninety air planes to Australia, also on 11 December, Curtin appealed privately to Roosevelt for aid, as Australia's military resources were insufficient to defend "the Pacific Islands in which you and we are vitally interested." But when that request and a subsequent entreaty made to Roosevelt and Churchill on 23 December went unheeded, Curtin informed the Melbourne *Herald* that he refused "to accept the dictum that the Pacific struggle must be treated as a subordinate segment of the general conflict," adding that "without any inhibitions of any kind, I make it quite clear that Australia looks to America, free of any pangs as to our traditional links or kinship with the United Kingdom."[18]

Although Curtin's precise motivations remain in dispute,[19] the new Anglo-American combined chiefs of staff confirmed in late December that Germany had to be dealt with first. Then on 29 December, the Australian chiefs remarked that the American Pacific fleet, "on which we based great hopes is unable or unwilling to assist," while Churchill hammered home the last nail with a 9 January 1942 telegram to Canberra, stating that Australia's defence "rests primarily with you."[20] So, just as Curtin was considering repatriating Australian divisions from the Middle East, Odlum told the AWC on 12 January that he had been instructed to discuss the most appropriate form that Canadian aid might take. He then added that, as it was contrary to Canadian policy to send small dispersed detachments abroad, an entire army division likely could be provided.[21]

In 1944 Odlum conceded that he had "learned to see things, not as they are, but as they ought to be, or, rather, as my fancy would like them to be." This admission has led Kim Richard Nossal to describe the general as prone to ignoring discrepant information, inclined toward wishful thinking, able to reinterpret information to fit pre-existing attitudes and beliefs, desirous of changing minds, and craving social support.[22] Odlum's ability to see things as they ought to be must have been particularly acute on 12 January 1942 for King had not authorized him to offer Canadian forces to Australia. Furthermore, on 17 January, Odlum advised King that "nothing had been promised but goodwill and sympathy based on common interest in the Pacific and knowledge of the existing threat." But on 15 January the *New York Times* had quoted Odlum as stating that "Canada's interest in the defense of Australia was the primary reason for the despatching of two Canadian divisions to Hong Kong. She can do more if Australia wants. Australia only has to say the word." Indeed, on 13 January, Odlum had told the Australians that, if they could show a real need for Canadian troops in Australia, Canada might be able to find some forces, whereupon they requested planes, armoured vehicles, anti-aircraft guns, crewed warships, and Canadian troops to act as a general reserve.[23]

Exactly why Odlum led the Australians to believe that Canadian help would be forthcoming is not clear. R.G. Haycock argues that the general, "more imbued with the myth of Empire than the realities of coalition war," had said "far too much about things of which he knew too little."[24] Odlum definitely had gotten the impression that Australia's press viewed Canada as a "spoiled child doing just as England wishes," and that he was just "another brass hat from Whitehall filled with the English point of view." Furthermore, having vehemently protested his removal from command in Britain and complaining that he expected "to die of slow motion, internal explosion or spontaneous combustion" in Canberra's "placid atmosphere," Odlum had begun peppering King with plaintive requests for re-assignment.[25] So, if Odlum was hoping to bring troops to Australia, troops he likely hoped to lead, King's subsequent actions further confused an already muddled situation. Upon reading the *Times* piece, King gently reminded the general that only the CWC could dispatch forces to Australia. Yet he fed Odlum's delusional fire by remarking that, while the threat to Canada was "only less immediate than that to Australia and cannot be overlooked in deciding [the] most effective disposition of available forces," some "consideration will be given to suggestions contained in your telegrams" pending further instructions "not to raise expectations which might prove impossible to fulfill."[26]

Many of King's advisers seemed quite intent on keeping expectations low. When the CWC discussed Australia on 14 January, still reeling from the loss of nearly 2,000 Canadian soldiers in Hong Kong and pondering a politically dangerous spring referendum that would void King's promise not to use draftees overseas, it was in no mood to consider new commitments. Air defence minister C.G. Power made clear that troop dispositions were not Odlum's concern and that Australian aid was premature. Two weeks later, the three defence ministers announced that none of their services favoured meeting the Australian military wish-list, either because the requested equipment was in short supply, or because, as Ralston explained, it would be unwise to act independently of the combined chiefs. The CWC thus decided to place the matter before the combined chiefs.[27]

Yet Glasgow came away from a 17 January chat with King convinced that Canada was "favourably disposed toward rendering assistance wherever possible in the Pacific area" – as long as Southwest Pacific commander Field Marshal Wavell made the request. Further encouragement was offered on 26 January, when opposition leader R.B. Hanson demanded a Canadian division for Australia. Australian reporters quoted King as replying that Canada would give Australia "every possible help in men and machines in the present crisis." But the official Hansard transcript (edited by King) states only that Canada was anxious "to cooperate in every possible way in affording such assistance as can be effectively given," and that the Australians "may be receiving some assistance of the kind from Canada at present, and that we shall be able to add considerable assistance to them in those particulars, and possibly in other ways, as time goes on."[28]

King's comments about meeting Australia's needs certainly had been "cloaked in the typical pall of Mackenzie King's ambiguous language – a language with which Mr. Curtin's government had precious little experience."[29] Curtin happily cabled King on 28 January to say that "nothing would please us better than to have the active cooperation of Canadian forces in the Pacific theatre of war which is so vital to all British countries as well as ourselves." Curtin needed encouragement, as the Malayan campaign – where 20,000 Australian troops were fighting – was going very badly. Noting on 29 January that Australia had just seven not completely trained or equipped divisions and 460 mostly second-line aircraft to protect itself and the northern island screen, Australia's chiefs ruled that their forces could not meet a Japanese attack against either the mainland or the islands. In such dismal circumstances, they thought any additional force "must increase our security and provide a greater deterrent against attack," and repeated their request for Canadian warships and army and air force units.[30]

Curtin had already asked Britain for 250 planes and demanded the repatriation of Australia's Middle Eastern divisions. American forces were arriving in Australia in dribs and drabs, but Roosevelt had told Casey that he had little anxiety for Australia's security. Appalled by American indifference to his nation's fate, Curtin viewed King's apparent willingness to send forces with considerable relief. But when news of the CWC's willingness to provide only some air crew reached Australia on 3 February, External Affairs Minister H.V. Evatt asked Odlum to transmit the latest pessimistic Australian military appreciation to Ottawa.[31] Odlum did so on 5 February, and two days later responded to King's 21 January message. His ability to reinterpret information to fit pre-existing beliefs intact, Odlum judged from "reading between the lines" that Canadian forces likely would arrive in Australia soon. Convinced that his presence in Australia constituted "a waste of public funds" if no troops were sent, Odlum told King that only Canadian soldiers would fit the bill: British troops could not be employed "because everything they would do would be wrong"; Indian soldiers would be unwelcome and unwilling to serve in view of the white Australia policy; and America's contribution would not be of much value for some time to come. Intent on driving his point home, Odlum breathlessly reported a week later that Curtin's government might have to move to elude capture, and pronounced that a Canadian declaration of imminent help "would have an electric effect here."[32]

King, however, was certain Canada's own crisis had arrived. Canada's military had played down the Japanese threat after December 1941, averring that it should not alter Canada's commitment to Germany's defeat, even if temporary weakness on the west coast "must be accepted under present circumstances." But when some Canadian officers warned in February that Japanese attacks upon North America were possible, a rattled King

– worried that Japan might make some landing on Canada's coast – argued that Canadians did "not want to see large numbers of men sent overseas in addition to those already there before U.S. troops begin to be landed on either British or European soil."[33] Determined to build a formidable Canadian fighting force in Europe, General Kenneth Stuart, chief of the General Staff, asserted on 19 February that Japan likely would not divert major units to attack North America and that Canadian preparations were adequate to deal with anticipated small enemy raids. But by March's end, claiming that his job was in jeopardy, Stuart formed two additional home defence divisions.[34]

Having ruled on 12 February that no further action regarding Australia's request was called for at present, the CWC reconsidered once Odlum's messages arrived. Still believing that the combined chiefs should handle the matter, Ralston was willing to offer a brigade. Naval minister Angus Macdonald emphatically opposed dispatching even a token naval force to the South Pacific, leaving Power to offer a compromise; canvassing the Canadian chiefs about troops and providing six Catalina flying boats to Australia.[35] Losing the home defence battle and intent upon scuttling Britain's proposal to garrison the Falkland Islands with Canadians, Stuart and the other chiefs decided that any assistance to Australia was impracticable in view of other commitments and needs, and instructed their joint subcommittee to support that position. Asserting that Canada's basic commitments included self-defence, maintenance of Britain's supply lines, and the general war effort, the subcommittee declared that the deteriorating Atlantic situation and the increased threat to Canada's west coast mitigated against providing substantial aid to Australia. Six minesweepers might be sent, but as dispatching air crew and troops would come at the expense of home defence and the army overseas, the matter should be handled by the combined chiefs.[36]

This reasonable position satisfied the CWC but utterly failed to placate Canberra, especially after 17,000 Australians surrendered when Singapore fell on 15 February 1942. Two days later, Curtin authorized the mobilization of all resources for the defence of Australia. On 19 February, Japanese warplanes bombed the northern town of Darwin, killing almost 250 Australians and blasting its air base "off the face of the earth."[37] Those defeats, according to D.M. Horner, created an air of panic over the government, Curtin, and some portions of the Australian populace. Claiming on 27 February that Japan could invade Australia if it so desired, the Australian chiefs believed that a minimum of twenty-five divisions were required, ten of which would have to come from allied states. Eight days later they predicted Japanese attacks upon Port Moresby in New Guinea by mid-March, Darwin and New Caledonia in April, and a possible invasion of Southeast Australia in May.[38] Meeting this threat seemed impossible, for the three Middle Eastern divisions were not expected home before late March. Curtin hoped that the

United States might provide 100,000 soldiers, especially after the deputy American commander in Australia had noted on 4 March that the successful defence of Australia itself was questionable. Some 80,000 American soldiers were in Australia by March, but most were support troops, as Roosevelt had told Curtin on 20 February that Australia's vital centres were not in immediate danger. Chief army planner Brigadier General Dwight Eisenhower had ruled on 28 February that, while retaining Australia and stopping Japan in the South Pacific were highly desirable, neither was immediately vital to the war's successful outcome.[39]

A desperate Evatt put aside a crippling fear of flying to go to North America in March to change some minds. Odlum relayed that Evatt wished to meet King "so that Canadian-Australian views, though divergent, might be harmonized." But Glasgow cautioned Norman Robertson, the undersecretary of state, that Evatt "had been rather violent over the telephone, complaining that Canada was not rallying to Australia's aid in the present crisis in the way that Australia had a right to expect." Robertson hoped that Evatt would meet the CWC first, so he would understand Canada's position before he gave a "mischievous speech" on the air[40] – but he had reasons to fear mischief. First, Burchell had described Evatt as able but insincere, a man quite willing to "sacrifice anything and anybody to satisfy his own ambition." (Evatt, for his part, thought that Australia needed an unpopular man such as himself, as it was the "unpopular man who gets things done because he does not have to worry about what people think of him."[41]) Second, just days before Evatt's scheduled arrival, Howard Green, Vancouver's Conservative member of parliament, announced that "it would be very much better to fight Japan in Australia rather than Vancouver" and had publicly demanded at least a token Canadian force for the Antipodes. King had responded by blaming Odlum for speaking on his own, and then noting that, since Canadians should serve where they would do the most good, "it did not appear to be in the interests of the combined war effort that Canada should undertake at this time the sending of an expeditionary force to Australia."[42]

Believing that Australia had one month to live,[43] Evatt first sought to convince Roosevelt to send Australia more resources and to form a council in Washington to direct the Pacific war. Planning to arrive in Ottawa in early April, on 24 March Evatt gave Glasgow a letter requesting Canadian weapons and an armoured division. Ralston again wanted the matter handled by the combined chiefs, while C.D. Howe, the powerful munitions and supply minister, bluntly stated that Australia's needs could not be met without affecting existing equipment allocations to Britain and America and suggested that Australia should approach the Munitions Assignment Board (MAB) in Washington.[44] Events in Washington, however, gave Evatt hope that Canada would *have* to help. April Fool's Day witnessed the inaugural meeting of the Pacific War Council (PWC), established by Roosevelt to furnish a formal ministerial forum for consultation with smaller countries.[45] Roosevelt singled out Canada, asserting that he had brought it into the PWC because he thought Canada might do more in the Pacific. Though Hume Wrong, of the Department of External Affairs (DEA) hoped that Canada had not been purposefully singled out, State Department official John Hickerson revealed that Roosevelt had deliberately done so "solely with the [political] object of playing up Canada's part in the Council vis-à-vis the members from 'down under.'" Wrong should have seen it coming, for Undersecretary of State Sumner Welles had told Canadian minister Leighton McCarthy on 26 March that Roosevelt had discussed Australia's inability to comprehend why Canada continued to send troops to Britain rather than to Australia.[46]

Pleased by Roosevelt's intervention, Evatt already had put to King "very strongly" that Canada should help Australia with munitions allocations and aircraft supply, something that he intended to emphasize when he met King in Ottawa on 8 April. Convinced that Evatt's introductory letter revealed "a sort of inferior complex, an over-sensitiveness and touchiness," to his surprise, King found Evatt "sincere and a fine type of man." Then, when Evatt presented his case, King – who had opened the meeting by outlining Canada's extensive military commitments and declaring that British Columbians would panic if Canadian soldiers went to Australia – confessed a tremendous sympathy for Evatt's point of view. Even Howe thought that Australia's equipment demands could be met by diverting production already allocated to Britain and America. Sympathy's shelf life is frequently short, though, and when the CWC reconvened on 9 April without Evatt, King claimed – while acknowledging the great moral value Canadian assistance might have – that Evatt had suggested Canada need provide only a small radar unit for Australian service. Though Ralston again offered a brigade, the indecisive ministers sent the matter to the Chiefs of Staff (COS). Their response was blunt; as Canada's defences had not yet met COS and combined chiefs standards, the chiefs argued that Canada should not divert any home defence resources.[47]

Back in Washington, Evatt cabled Curtin that Canada would support Australian initiatives to alter MAB allocations and "was now prepared to make more direct contribution to Australia in the form of certain equipment other than aircraft." But when Evatt heard that Howe had withdrawn his aid offer, he entreated King to save the situation. King did not oblige. At the 15 April PWC meeting, he sympathized with Australia but said that Canada's military commitments and domestic political problems had made it increasingly difficult for Canada to comply with Australia's requests. As to helping Evatt to alter munitions allocation – while King believed that MAB membership was desirable, he clearly did not want to offend the Americans, and stated that Canada "would not wish this representation on the score of being there to protect the interests of any particular part of the Empire."[48]

While a betrayed Evatt doubted that Canada would get an MAB seat and pondered obtaining Churchill's help to force the release of the needed equipment, more bad news was on the way. On 28 April – the day after a majority of Canadians had released their government from its pledge not to use draftees overseas – King, knowing that the crucial province of Quebec had voted 73 percent against the alteration, finally gave Evatt an unequivocal answer. No Canadian troops would be sent to Australia, but King promised to do everything possible to strengthen the defences of Australia and New Zealand once Canada sat on the MAB.[49] King's fervent hope that the Australians "could be trusted to deprecate the criticism of the amount of Canadian aid" appeared to be granted. On 17 May, Evatt expressed appreciation for King's kind message and a desire to finalize the munition matter. Odlum, too, reported that Canberra had no intention of pressing for direct assistance from Canada; "that phase is past." No doubt Evatt's restrained reaction had been influenced by the turning back of a Japanese fleet in the Coral Sea in early May by the US Navy. Also helpful was Odlum's recall to Ottawa in September 1942. Still, Odlum lobbied hard for aid for Australia until the end, raised the matter twice with General Douglas MacArthur, and warned King that Labor might punish his inaction by reducing postwar imports of Canadian newsprint and automobiles.[50]

The Post-Odlum Period
Odlum's legacy was not so easily forgotten. When Ottawa gave Britain a billion-dollar credit in August 1942, the Australians feared that having to go through Britain might obstruct access to the Canadian funds. When Ottawa declined to renegotiate the deal, Evatt, "in a very bad temper," informed Acting High Commissioner E.B. Rogers that Canada "was tied to Mr. Churchill's apron strings," referred "to Canadians and the Canadian Government in particular in most offensive terms," and complained about Canada's empty gestures to Australia. Later that day, Evatt "sarcastically" denounced Canada in front of Canberra's diplomatic community and spoke of Odlum "in very disparaging terms, saying that he (General Odlum) had offered Australia as many as ten divisions at one time or another." Though Evatt explained that his remarks had been made jokingly,[51] intent on repairing bilateral ties but without adding to Canada's heavy burden, King replaced Odlum with T.C. Davis, as he "could be relied on to avoid the misunderstandings of the sort that had arisen after Odlum's arrival in Canberra." Arriving in Australia in December 1942, Davis understood that he "should not directly or indirectly or by any suggestion or implication promise anything," but, finding his nation's stock at a rather low ebb, he stated that Canada would not lay down its arms until Japan had been crushed. King

quickly ordered Davis to refrain "from any statement which might be interpreted as implying the participation of Canadian forces against Japan since
as you know we are committed to employment of our army and bulk of air
force in [the] European theatre."[52]

Believing that recent favourable press reports about Canada indicated matters were improving, Davis soon found reason for concern. Though he had
uttered "not the slightest hint of complaint against Canada," Curtin remarked on 15 January 1943 that there was no point in "complaining that
Australia had been let down for there had been and still were physical obstacles (mainly shortage of shipping) preventing despatch of assistance on a
large scale." By month's end, after hearing more complaints about Canada,
Davis convinced King to let him emphasize that Canada was not a military
free agent, but an ally subject to the direction of the combined chiefs.[53]
Davis was pleased to report on 2 March that Curtin not only appreciated
Ottawa's reasons for declining assistance, he had "nothing in mind at the
moment with regard to help to Australia but that Evatt would be in a position to discuss the matter fully when he arrived." Viewing Evatt as one of
the government's strong men and likely to be "a leading factor in the life of
this country over many years to come," Davis judged it critical that Evatt's
unflattering impressions of Canada be broken down. But he failed to speak
with Evatt before the Australian minister left on another extended trip on 1
April. Though the men met at various social gatherings, Evatt limited their
contact to handshakes and formal greetings, while Davis continued to hear
second-hand that Evatt rarely missed an opportunity to expound upon Canadian perfidy.[54]

Having been told by Odlum in January that his efforts to educate Ottawa
about the Pacific conflict had struck a stone wall, Curtin had responded on
19 March that it was "difficult to educate one country to accept the view
that it would probably make a greater contribution to the defeat of the
common enemy if it took some further risk itself and detaches some additional Forces to aid a partner in a distant theatre." Though it is unclear
whether Davis was party to that complaint, he asked Robertson to consider
allocating some RCAF squadrons to Australia, both for the immediate moral
effect as well as Canada's future status in the region. Robertson tersely responded that such a plan was not desirable at present; if Canada used the
RCAF in the Pacific in 1943, it would be confined to Alaska.[55] Robertson did
convince a reluctant King to provide a brigade group to retake Kiska in the
Aleutian Islands. Part of a new DEA generation that did not shrink from a
greater global role, Robertson favoured the Aleutian role – not only to improve relations with the United States and to balance America's massive
military presence in Northwest Canada, but also to remind Australia and
New Zealand that the United States "was not the only American country
helping in the Pacific war."[56]

Evatt's return to Ottawa in July 1943 offered an opportunity to see if relations were improving. Prospects seemed surprisingly good, as an Evatt aide called the day before his superior's arrival with a tantalizing offer; if Canada praised Australia's war effort and "the value such opportunities for personal contact between Commonwealth statesmen as Dr. Evatt's visit to Ottawa provided," Evatt would tell the Canadian press how tremendously impressed Australia was by Canada's war effort. Evatt delivered. He thanked the CWC for considering the provision of Mutual Aid money to Australia, predicted genuine consultation in the postwar world, mentioned the Canadian army's participation in the Sicilian campaign, praised Canada's essential "but less spectacular" war production effort, and averred that "Australia's relationship with Canada must be closer." But when asked if he was satisfied with Canadian aid to Australia and whether Canadian troops would be welcomed in Australia after Germany's defeat, Evatt emphasized the desperate plight his country had endured in 1942, stated that Canadian forces would be welcomed now, and predicted that "Canadians would be in action in the Pacific long before Hitler is beaten."[57]

While a cynical Hume Wrong offered that Evatt was less interested in Mutual Aid money than in saying "that he had been to Canada and to get some Canadian material for public quotation during the [Australian] election campaign," he advised King to emphasize how the Aleutian offensive aided Australia when he announced the 15 August invasion to Canadians. Obliging, King declared that "just as the control achieved by the United States, Australian and New Zealand forces in New Guinea, the Solomons and elsewhere in the Southwest Pacific is aiding in the defence of Canada, so the control of the Aleutian Islands in the North Pacific by United States and Canadian forces will aid in the defence of Australia and New Zealand."[58] Few Australians seemed impressed, though, when 5,000 Canadians and 30,000 American troops discovered that Japan's garrison had departed Kiska in late July. Moreover, given that Roosevelt had claimed in 1942 that public pressure to retake the Aleutians had interfered with plans to attack Japanese positions near Australia, and then had added in July 1943 that recapturing Kiska was necessary only on psychological grounds, few Australians thought much of Canada's Aleutian expedition. Australian newspapers mentioned Kiska but omitted King's message, while Blamey told Davis that "he regretted the Canadian troops were not in this theatre of war – not so much because of the actual need for them in military operations – but as a gesture which would enhance the prestige of Canada in Australia and make for better feeling between Australia and Canada."[59]

Better feelings were mostly absent over the next few months. On 1 October, most unhappy with its limited influence upon Allied strategy-making, Curtin's government opted to concentrate Australia's military effort in the Pacific, even "at the expense of commitments in other theatres." Though the Australians deemed it "imperative that this view be accepted by the United Kingdom and the other Dominions, especially New Zealand and Canada," Canada offered little support, and indeed did not respond specifically to the statement. DEA official John Holmes, reacting to Evatt's 14 October speech that had laid out Australia's foreign policy goals, praised Evatt's emphasis on international cooperation, as it "might very well form the basis of a Canadian policy." However, while it sought to make its "influence felt through Commonwealth channels," Canada was not committed "to the policy of *joint* Commonwealth action," especially in the Pacific, as later events would amply demonstrate.[60]

Nor did Canberra find Ottawa very cooperative on a strictly bilateral issue. By December 1943 Mutual Aid negotiations verged on collapse over Canada's demand for lower Australian tariffs at war's end. Although the matter was resolved in February 1944 – Ottawa agreed to provide aid sufficient to cover Australia's wartime trade deficit with Canada, just over $91 million – Evatt accused Canada of driving a hard bargain and doing little "to help Australia which was bearing the brunt of the Pacific war."[61] King felt no inclination to ease Australia's burden. Discussing Canada's contribution to an invasion of Japan with Power on 5 January 1944, King thought that Canada was obligated to participate but was certain of two things: that Canadians would "get little credit for anything we do, either on the part of the U.S. or Great Britain"; and that excepting British Columbians, Canadians would be unenthusiastic about "going on with the war against Japan." While Power was eager to employ the RCAF in the Pacific to repatriate Canadians serving in Britain, he and King, who already had scotched the plans of Ken Stuart, chief of the Canadian general staff, to send troops to the Kurile Islands, "agreed that there really was no place for sending any army over the Pacific," a decision the CWC ratified two days later.[62]

Still, King was coming under considerable pressure to fight in the Pacific. DEA officer Hugh Keenleyside, concerned about the scale, intensity, and permanence of America's military effort in Northwest Canada, had suggested in July 1943 that Canada should participate in additional Pacific operations, to balance the American presence and to acquire a strong voice for Canada in the regional peace settlement. The Royal Canadian Navy (RCN) also was pushing an ambitious program to acquire Tribal destroyers, cruisers, and even aircraft carriers so that it could operate with the Royal Navy in the Pacific and cement postwar blue-water status. Lastly, Britain – seeking to prevent America from getting all the credit for Japan's defeat while limiting its contribution – wanted the dominions to provide considerable forces for the last assault upon Japan.[63] Canada had agreed, in 1943, to cooperate with the Lethbridge Mission, a British investigation of the most effective way to prosecute the Japanese war, and reconsidered a September 1942 Australian proposal to attach Canadian observers to Australian forces in the

Southwest Pacific. Major General Maurice Pope, who would become the CWC's major military adviser in August 1944, had advocated sending observers to the South Pacific in May 1943, in case Canada found it opportune to fight there, and now the army was listening. Twenty Canadian officers (the first of ninety-nine) were split between Australian and American units by early 1944. Then, in April, the CWC sent a small radar unit (seventy-three men) to Australia.[64]

But when the dominion prime ministers finally met with Churchill in London in May 1944, Curtin wanted improved and permanent imperial consultative machinery and military cooperation in the Southwest Pacific. Having decisively rejected a similar suggestion from Lord Halifax (Britain's ambassador to the United States) in January 1944, King refused to countenance any centralization schemes. He also pointedly remarked that neither Britain nor Canada had finalized their Pacific plans before declining to sign a statement claiming that the leaders had agreed on the future conduct of the war with Germany and Japan.[65] Intent on pressing their case, Curtin and Blamey followed King back to Ottawa. Much to King's irritation, Curtin said very little about Canada's war effort, preferring to discuss Australia's plight in 1942. Things worsened when Curtin responded to a reporter's question about whether he was satisfied with the results of the London parley. According to the *Sydney Morning Herald*'s correspondent, he "looked at Mr. King and said that the only man in that state of mind was the man 'who sat on the right hand of the almighty.'" Blamey accomplished little as well, outlining Australia's strategic situation and ending with a solicitation for more Canadian officers to visit the south Pacific.[66]

Blamey's request fell on deaf ears. After Halifax's speech King had ensured that an aide memoire sent to Britain in February 1944 made very clear that his commitment to the Japanese war would be determined by Canada's place as a Pacific nation, Commonwealth membership, a desire to defeat Japan, and a "close and common interest with the United States." Most important, Pope had stated that "the importance which the northwestern route to Asia, across Canada, may assume in the later stages of the war," might "render it advisable for Canada to play her part in the Japanese war in very close cooperation with the United States, at any rate in certain operational areas." Finding the notion of fighting in the South Pacific quite fantastic, Pope had reminded the army's chief Pacific planner that, given American prewar concerns about Canada's ability to defend British Columbia, the dominion's interests would be served best by operating with America in the North Pacific. Lieutenant Colonel J.H. Jenkins, worried that Americans would be displeased by a proportionately inadequate Canadian contribution and judging that Canadians lacked the jungle warfare skills needed in Southeast Asia, therefore recommended selecting a division to fight with the Americans in China or Japan.[67] The CWC ordered the Canadian chiefs,

Norman Robertson, the undersecretary of state for external affairs, and CWC Secretary A.D.P. Heeney to recommend alternatives. Though Stuart favoured fighting with the British in Southeast Asia and the RCAF and navy preferred to operate with British units given common weapons and doctrines, the ad hoc committee ruled that, as Britain was "apparently committed to no particular long-term strategy for the assault upon Japan," Canadian and Commonwealth interests "might be better served if the Canadian contribution to the war against Japan were made in an 'American' theater, namely the North or West Pacific." Accordingly, the CWC told Britain that it preferred to make its major military contribution in the North Pacific.[68]

While the British would try until the war's last days to alter this decision, Curtin reacted bitterly. Though he admired Canada's economic effort and regarded King "with considerable awe," when some Canadian parliamentarians came to Canberra on 9 July, Curtin, asked if a Canadian expeditionary force should be sent to Australia, snapped, "I don't care what Canada does. We had a (Canadian) High Commissioner here who wanted to help us. He went home and never came back." Eight days later, when Curtin informed his parliament of what had transpired in London, he acknowledged King's praise for Australia's martial effort, but noted enviously that "Canada has not been directly threatened in this war" and added that he did "not seek to convert my friend, Mr. Mackenzie King, to my point of view."[69] Military attaché Colonel M. Cosgrave's response was to prompt the United States to ask Canada to send three RCAF squadrons to Australia. Though the Americans proved cooperative, Wrong termed the initiative an unfortunate misunderstanding prompted by Cosgrave's exuberance. Power was willing to grant Cosgrave's desire, as the RCAF's home defence establishment was being substantially reduced, but citing the costs of switching to American-made planes (at least $35 million just for the capital outlay), Howe said it would be much cheaper just to release the surplus personnel. King, who had been willing to consider a token force, took refuge in a nondecision; nothing could be decided until Canada had finalized its Pacific role.[70]

Not yet done, Davis wrote King on 9 August to argue that Canada's relationship with Australia called for some kind of Canadian military contribution in the South Pacific, even if the North Pacific was more appropriate for "geographical and other reasons." Noting that Britain was considering basing four divisions in Australia, Davis reasoned that some Canadians currently fighting in Italy might be attached to that force, for, regardless of what Canada did in Europe, "you will have a hard time in the future to convince Australians that we had much to do with the war in this area unless Canadian forces are actively based on this continent." This lobbying failed, for basing troops in Australia was not the central point of the debate in Canada's cabinet. King told his more imperially minded ministers on 31 August "that it would be inappropriate and undesirable for Canadian forces to participate in the southern theatre of operations," only to have Angus Macdonald argue on 13 September that "the enemy must be fought wherever he was, regardless of geography." Convinced that Macdonald supported British plans for a Southeast Asian campaign designed solely to salvage imperial prestige, King threatened to resign unless the CWC agreed to send forces only to the central or North Pacific. King's victory was complete when Churchill told him at the September Quebec Conference that he did not think it "appropriate or necessary to have Canadians serving in the tropical or semi-tropical areas of Southeast Asia."[71]

Few Australians were surprised. An Australian officer who had visited Ottawa in early August had found few Canadian officers who expected to see Pacific action, except in China, and then only after Germany's final defeat. And while Australia had lacked formal representation at Quebec, Lieutenant General John Lavarack of Australia's military mission in Washington had correctly predicted that Canada would not employ its military assets south of the equator. In turn, Glasgow doubted that Canadians were "prepared for the sacrifices which the Canadian government may call upon them to make." Putting the blame squarely upon King's rounded shoulders, Glasgow feared that once Germany had been beaten, a war-weary Canadian military would need months to rest and prepare before it could fight in the Pacific. Strongly believing that Australia had a "responsibility to ensure that the Canadian people do not forget Hong Kong and that their desire for revenge is maintained," Glasgow recommended pressing Canada to take concrete action, to feed intelligence and training memoranda "designed to 'sell' the idea of a Pacific War to the Canadian Staff," and adding a press attaché to the Ottawa high commission to get Australia's point of view out to Canadians.[72]

If Glasgow sent those recommendations to Canberra, it does not seem that Curtin's government, already scaling back its own military effort, was much interested. Still, Cosgrave, the focus of repeated queries from American, Dutch, and Australian officers about the likelihood of Canadian assistance in the South Pacific, recommended attaching more observers to Australian units in order to improve political and trade relations with Canberra. But even after Germany finally surrendered on 8 May 1945, Canada – which had committed a division to an American-led invasion of Japan slated for 1946 – had done nothing about Australia. Davis told King that Australians, noticing Canada's rapid demobilization, were "bound to feel that we are not doing our share in the Pacific" unless Canada made a concerted effort to relay the facts. Assuming that Canadian forces operating in the Pacific would not be based in Australia, Davis advised Ottawa to heavily publicize the dispatch of forces to other theatres, to play up Mutual Aid, and suggested that King and other prominent Canadians visit Australia soon. Japan's surrender in mid-August 1945 rendered a response meaningless.[73]

Conclusion

Two questions must be addressed: what had brought about this unhappy chapter; and did it inflict lasting consequences upon the bilateral connection? In the first case, one is tempted to accept John Hilliker's understated argument that Odlum "was not the best spokesman ... for a country disinclined to commit forces to the war in the Pacific."[74] Had Odlum not promised Canadian aid when he lacked the authority to do so, Australian-Canadian relations might have fared somewhat better. But King must shoulder much of the blame for the fiasco. First, he had appointed the ill-qualified Odlum. And once Odlum had said that Canadian assistance was Australia's for the asking, King, having told a British diplomat in 1938 "that his experience of political life had taught him that any success he had attained had been due far more to avoiding action rather than taking action,"[75] resorted to his traditional practice of issuing statements so convoluted and ambiguously qualified that both proponents and opponents of Australian aid felt assured King was on their side. King's tactics were unfortunate for two reasons. The Australians had been desperate in 1942, and thus gave Odlum's nonsense too much credence. American minister Nelson Johnson had noted in January 1942 that the Australians "were in a state of funk and yelling for help, now, from the United States while they cast blame on the British for failures in the past, some of which they share responsibility for," while another American likened Australia to a panicked boy forced to confront a bully after his protective older brother had collapsed.[76] Australian historians John Robertson and Glyn Harper argue that Curtin's government greatly exaggerated the Japanese threat in 1942, with Harper claiming that the "error" was deliberate for domestic political reasons. But former Evatt aide Alan Renouf relays that Canberra had been profoundly shaken by Allied defeats and highly inaccurate British and American assessments of Japanese capabilities. Moreover, Henry P. Frei demonstrates that, until its stunning June 1942 Midway Island defeat, Japan was considering invading Australia.[77]

Although some Australian politicians were very familiar with King's evasive ways and obsession with Canadian unity, Curtin and Evatt, in power only since October 1941, were not. They were accustomed to a political culture that valued and encouraged plain speaking and confrontation and had given birth to an adversarial diplomatic style described by J.D.B. Miller as having made Australians "a formidable foe" but one that could also render them "somewhat muscle-bound in our advocacy of fixed positions." Canada's foreign policy style, as Norman Hillmer aptly points out, has tended to be about what Canadians *"might* do, or what others *ought* to do, or what they were *not* going to do,"[78] and one cannot find a better description of King's foreign policy in the Second World War. R.G. Haycock maintains that much of the wartime unpleasantness resulted from the rapid expansion of dominion diplomatic corps.[79] Certainly a more experienced diplomat would have easily avoided Odlum's gross errors, but Jay Pierrepont Moffat, the American consul-general in Sydney from 1935 to 1937 and minister to Canada from 1940 until 1943, blamed Australian inexperience for much of the trouble. In May 1941, Moffat described Australia as "still in the adolescent stage" of political development. Canada, however, was a "post-graduate who has just completed his doctor's thesis," adding that "if a process required seven steps the average Australian could never see more than two at most; the Canadian can see at least five, sometimes six and occasionally all seven."[80]

But emphasizing diplomatic growing pains avoids the fact that Canada and Australia faced extraordinarily different geostrategic circumstances, circumstances that were not compatible. In peacetime, stuck cheek to jowl with the American colossus, Canada was impervious to any major military assault except one emanating from America, and that attack long had been regarded as unimaginable on both sides of the forty-ninth parallel. So as "Canadians have always felt that theirs is about the safest country in the world,"[81] insulated from the physical and psychological pressures that beset Australia's small and distant society, they focused upon national unity at the expense of imperial cooperation. This was not an unreasonable tradeoff, especially given that Canada's French-English political divide had always made imperial cooperation problematic. Still, geographical good fortune had blinded Canadians to the problems of others. In 1940 Burchell had reported that Australians viewed the PJBD's creation "with universal approval which is not unmixed with envy," while Moffat commented in 1942 that "the unfortunate reaction of all too many Canadians to Australia's present plight is that she should have thought of herself first and not denuded her own territory by sending so many of her soldiers abroad."[82] Canadians seemed to have forgotten that they had denuded their defences to protect Britain in the desperate summer of 1940, only to have Roosevelt come to Canada's rescue with the PJBD. In the war itself, Canadian interests were naturally focused on the Atlantic and on Europe, while Australia's were equally naturally focused on the South Pacific and Asia.

Did Canada's failure to aid Australia militarily have a lasting effect on bilateral relations? Certainly it did while Evatt remained on the scene. When various national delegations converged in San Francisco in 1945 to hammer out the United Nations charter, Canada's refusal to back Evatt's attempt to block a great-power veto on the new Security Council led Evatt to angrily label Canada's representative "an American stooge" and "pawn in the move to defeat the Australian case." Delegation member Charles Ritchie responded by calling Evatt "insufferably megalomaniacal and irresponsible," while Maurice Pope explained his negotiating strategy at the Paris Peace Conference simply as "I wait till that bastard [Evatt] takes his position then [I] take the opposite."[83] Two years later, when Evatt organized a Commonwealth conference to provide input into the Japanese peace settlement, Canada agreed to participate – though Wrong and Robertson thought that Evatt had arranged the gathering to advance his personal agenda. Placing relations with America above ties to Australia, and convinced that Canada was in a better position than Britain to absorb domestic criticism, Wrong wanted to kill Evatt's notion of a coordinated Commonwealth position. Canada's cabinet agreed, describing the Canberra conference only as an exploratory exchange of views.[84]

Australians had few warm feelings for Canada, either. In 1946, Canada and Australia competed for a Security Council seat, and the Australian and New Zealand delegations, believing that Canada's selection would be "unacceptable" to Australian and New Zealand public opinion, tried unsuccessfully to convince Canada to withdraw its bid. Australia won the election, a victory that Canadian diplomat Lester Pearson attributed to the fact that the combative Evatt had won the affection of smaller nations by standing up to the great powers. In terms of security arrangements, the Australians, who were very much interested in building multinational defence systems after 1945, so as to avoid the isolation they had felt in early 1942, had learned a lesson. When the Council of Defence considered postwar military plans, Prime Minister J.B. Chifley dismissed Canada as "non co-operative."[85]

The departure of King and Evatt from power – King retired in 1948, Labor lost the 1949 election – offered fence-mending opportunities. As minister for external affairs in 1951, R.G. Casey thought that Canada and Australia could become "an effective force for the reconciliation of interests between the United States and Britain and an element of stability in the United Nations and the world in general," a subject Christopher Waters explores in this volume. The path was anything but smooth. During difficult General Agreement on Tariffs and Trade negotiations in 1955, Australian delegate Allan Westerman drew attention to Canada's sanctimonious attitude by remarking that "unlike Canada, Australia is not without sin."[86] Perhaps the noted Canadian historian A.R.M. Lower put matters best in 1939. Asked to outline Canada's role in a potential Pacific conflict, Lower thought that while Canadians would be "excited about a Japanese conquest" of Australia and New Zealand, Canada's "slender political relationship" with those antipodean dominions made them appear closer than they really were.[87]

Notes

1 Jeffrey Grey, *A Military History of Australia* (Cambridge: Cambridge University Press, 1990), 4.
2 R.G. Haycock, "The 'Myth' of Imperial Defence: Australian-Canadian Bilateral Military Cooperation, 1942," *War & Society* 21 (May 1984): 65-84; and J.F. Hilliker, "Distant Ally: Canadian Relations with Australia during the Second World War," *Journal of Imperial and Commonwealth History* 13, 1 (1984): 46-67.
3 John Robertson, "The Distant War: Australia and Imperial Defence, 1919-41," in *Australia: Two Centuries of War and Peace*, ed. M. McKernan and M. Browne (Canberra and Sydney: Australian War Memorial and Allen and Unwin Australia, 1988), 224-5; and Glyn Harper, "Threat Perceptions and Politics: The Deployment of Australian and New Zealand Ground Forces in the Second World War," *Journal of the Australian War Memorial* 20 (April 1992): 36.
4 Vincent Massey, *What's Past Is Prologue: The Memoirs of the Right Honourable Vincent Massey, C.H.* (Toronto: Macmillan, 1963), 303-4; Cecil Edwards, *Bruce of Melbourne: Man of Two Worlds* (London: Heinemann, 1965), 277-8; and W.A.B. Douglas, *The Creation of a National Air Force: The Official History of the Royal Canadian Air Force,* vol. 2 (Toronto: University of Toronto Press and Department of National Defence, 1986), 205.
5 W.L.M. King to Robert Menzies, 3 September 1939, Australian Archives, ACT (hereinafter AA), Department of External Affairs, series A981, item Australia 151; Menzies to Bruce, 5 September 1939, ibid.; Bruce to Menzies, 5 September 1939, ibid.; Menzies to King, 6 September 1939, ibid.
6 King to Charles J. Burchell, 17 October 1939, National Archives of Canada (hereinafter NAC), RG25, vol. 1944, file 763. A high commissioner for King was "merely the agent of the government, with no right to raise foreign policy issues or to make public statements about them." King diary, 24 November 1939, NAC, W.L.M. King Papers, MG26 J13; John Hilliker, *Canada's Department of External Affairs,* vol. 1, *The Early Years, 1909-1946* (Montreal and Kingston: McGill-Queen's University Press, 1990), 184; and Australia, John R. Minter to Secretary of State Cordell Hull, 22 July 1941, National Archives Records Administration (hereinafter NARA), Military Intelligence Division Regional File 1922-44, RG165, file 3600.
7 William Glasgow to the Minister for External Affairs John McEwan, 23 September 1940, Flinders University of Australia (FUA), H.V. Evatt Papers, Despatches and Correspondence, file External Relations Canada-Australian Legation, Ottawa 1940; Jay Pierrepont Moffat memorandum of conversation with Leonard Brockington, 19 August 1940, NARA, Department of State Records, Matthews-Hickerson File, RG59, reel 5; and Lord Casey, *Personal Experience 1939-1946* (London: Constable and Company, 1962), 59.
8 Glasgow to Casey, 19 February 1941, AA, Department of External Affairs, series A3300, 7, item 158; Minutes of the Canadian Defence Council, 31 January 1941, NAC, RG24, reel C8295; Noel Deschamps, Australian high commission, Ottawa, to Colonel J.C. Murchie, 10 February 1941, ibid.; and Frederick Shedden to Acting Prime Minister Arthur Fadden, 15 April 1941, AA, Department of Defence Coordination, series A816, 1, item 12, 301, 26.
9 Fadden to Bruce, 12 February 1941, AA, Frederick Shedden Papers, series A5954, 1, item 527, 13; Bruce to Fadden, 12 February 1941, ibid., 15; Skelton to King, "Singapore Conference," 11 October 1940, NAC, RG25, vol. 779, file 380; King to Skelton, "Singapore Conference," 11 October 1940, NAC, W.L.M. King Papers, Correspondence, MG26 J1, vol. 284, file C-IJ Campbell 1940; and King diary, 4 December 1940, NAC, W.L.M. King Papers, MG26 J13.
10 Menzies to King, 22 May 1940, NAC, W.L.M. King Papers, Memoranda and Notes, MG26 J4, C281473-74; A.W. Martin and Patsy Hardy, eds., *Dark and Hurrying Days: Menzies' 1941 Diary* (Canberra: National Library of Australia, 1993), 8 May 1941, 124-5; and King diary, 7 May 1941, NAC, W.L.M. King Papers, MG26 J13.
11 58th conclusion, Cabinet Meeting, 9 June 1941, Public Records Office, London, UK (hereinafter PRO), CAB 65, 18, WM (41); Churchill to King, 21 June 1941, PRO, DO35, 999; King diary, 27 June 1941, NAC, W.L.M. King Papers, MG26 J13; King to Churchill, 16 June 1941, PRO, DO35, 999; and Lord Cranborne to Churchill, 17 June 1941, ibid.
12 King diary, 27 and 30 August 1941, NAC, W.L.M. King Papers, MG26 J13.

13 Percy Spender quoted in E.B. Rogers to King, 29 August 1941, NAC, RG25, vol. 2560, file 3939-L-40; and Casey to Stewart, 11 June 1941, AA, series A5954, 1, item 435, 9.

14 King to Odlum, 10 October 1941, NAC, Victor Odlum Papers, MG30 E300, vol. 57, file 57-24.

15 Odlum to King, 18 December 1941, NAC, W.L.M. King Papers, MG26 J1, vol. 313, file Odlum-Patt; Odlum to King, 10 January 1942, NAC, J.L. Ralston Papers, MG27 III B11, vol. 38, file Australia Gen (Secret); and King to Odlum, 12 January 1942, NAC, W.L.M. King Papers, MG26 J1, vol. 331, file O'Connell-Purdy.

16 D.M. Horner, "Defending Australia in 1942," *War and Society* 11 (May 1993): 2-3; D.M. Horner, *High Command: Australia and Allied Strategy 1939-1945* (Sydney: Allen and Unwin, 1982), 142; and "Defence of Australia and Adjacent Areas – Appreciation by Australian Chiefs of Staff," 11 December 1941, AA, series A2671, item 14, 301, 227.

17 John Curtin, quoted in Robertson, "The Distant War," 225; Churchill to the prime ministers of Australia and New Zealand, 8 August 1940, attached to WM (40), 222nd conclusion, 11 August 1940, PRO, CAB 65, 15; Churchill to Menzies, 23 December 1940, attached to COS (40), 1069, 30 December 1940, PRO, Chiefs of Staff Committee Records, Memoranda, CAB 80, 24; and D.M. Horner, "Australia under the Threat of Invasion," in *Australia: Two Centuries of War and Peace*, ed. McKernan and Browne, 249.

18 Department of the Navy to Shedden, 11 December 1941, AA, series A5954, box 535; Curtin to Roosevelt and Churchill, 23 December 1941, ibid., and Roger J. Bell, *Unequal Allies: Australia-American Relations and the Pacific War* (Carlton: Melbourne University Press, 1977), 44.

19 D.M. Horner argues that a frustrated Curtin was demonstrating that "the strategic situation looked different from Canberra than it did from Washington," while David Day alleges that Curtin issued "a panic-stricken and general plea for help" intended to embarrass Churchill: Horner, "Australia under the Threat of Invasion," 247-9; and David Day, *The Great Betrayal: Britain, Australia and the Onset of the Pacific War* (New York: W.W. Norton, 1989), 227-9.

20 Combined chiefs of staff, "American-British Grand Strategy," ABC-4, CS-1 WW-1 (Final), 31 December 1941, NARA, Joint Chiefs of Staff Records, Decimal File 1942-1945, RG218, file CCS 320.2 (1-28-42); Australian chiefs of staff report, 29 December 1941, AA, series A2671, item 445, 1941; and Churchill to Curtin, 9 January 1942, AA, series A5954, 1, item 463, 3.

21 Horner, "Australia under the Threat of Invasion," 250; and AWC minutes, 12 January 1942, AA, series A5954, 46, item 813, 2.

22 Odlum, quoted in Hilliker, *Canada's Department of External Affairs*, 1:264; and Kim Richard Nossal, "Chunking Prism: Cognitive Process and Intelligence Failure," *International Journal* 32 (Summer 1977): 559-76.

23 Odlum to King, 17 January 1942, NAC, W.L.M. King Papers, MG26 J1, vol. 331, file O'Connell-Purdy; "War Issues Studied by Australian Board," *New York Times*, 15 January 1942; Chiefs of staff, "Australian-Canadian Cooperation in the Pacific," 15 January 1942, AA, series A2670, 1, item 31, 1942; AWC minute 683, 20 January 1942, AA, series A5954, 46, item 813, 2; and War Cabinet minutes 1718, 20 January 1942, AA, series A2670, 1, item 31, 1942.

24 Haycock, "The 'Myth' of Imperial Defence," 79.

25 Odlum to King, 17 January and 21 February 1942, NAC, W.L.M. King Papers, MG26 J1, vol. 331, file O'Connell-Purdy; RB (Lord), Odlum to Bennett, 29 April 1942, NAC, Victor Odlum Papers, MG30 E300, vol. 1, file Bennett.

26 King to Odlum, 20 January 1942, NAC, RG25, vol. 819, file 676.

27 CWC minutes, 14 and 20 January 1942, NAC, Privy Council Office Records, Minutes and Documents of the Cabinet War Committee, RG2 7c, vol. 8; and Kenneth Stuart, "Australian Request for Military Aid from Canada," 27 January 1942, NAC, J.L. Ralston Papers, MG27 III B11, vol. 38, file Australia Gen (Secret).

28 Glasgow to Department of External Affairs Canberra, 17 January 1942, AA, series A3095, 1, item 35, 9; R.B. Hanson speech, House of Commons, Canada, *Debates*, 26 January 1942, 21-2; "Want to Send Canadian Division to Australia," *The Argus* (Melbourne), 28 January

1942; "Canadian Division for Australia Urged," *Sydney Herald*, 27 January 1942; and King speech, House of Commons, Canada, *Debates*, 26 January 1942, 42-3.

29 Haycock, "The 'Myth' of Imperial Defence," 69.

30 Curtin to King, 28 January 1942, AA, series A5954, 1, item 581, 16; and Chiefs of staff, "Australian-Canadian Cooperation in the Pacific – Appreciation of Defence of Australia and Adjacent Areas," 29 January 1942, AA, series A2670, 1, item 31, 1942.

31 Curtin to Churchill, 25 January 1942, AA, Stanley Bruce Papers, series M100; Casey to H.V. Evatt, 24 January 1942, AA, series A3300, item 219; Chiefs of staff, "Australian-Canadian Cooperation in the Pacific," 3 February 1942, AA, series A2670, 1, item 31, 1942; and War Cabinet minutes 1853, 5 February 1942, ibid.

32 Odlum to King, 5, 7, and 14 February 1942, NAC, W.L.M. King Papers, MG26 J1, vol. 331, file O'Connell-Purdy.

33 Chiefs of staff committee (COS), "Monthly Appreciation – January 15th 1942," Directorate of History and Heritage (hereinafter DHH), Department of National Defence (DND), Kardex File 193.000 (D3); Commanding officer Pacific Command to Stuart, 6 February 1942, NAC, RG24, vol. 13282, file 4; "Appreciation of Possible Japanese Action on the Pacific Coast by Intelligence, Pacific Command," 16 February 1942, DHH, DND, Kardex File 322.009 (D157); and King diary, 11 December 1941, NAC, W.L.M. King Papers, MG26 J13.

34 C.P. Stacey, *Arms, Men and Governments: The War Policies of Canada 1939-1945* (Ottawa: Department of National Defence, 1970), 47n.

35 CWC minutes, 12 and 18 February 1942, NAC, RG2 7c, vol. 8; and King to Odlum, 19 February 1942, NAC, W.L.M. King Papers, MG26 J1, vol. 331, file O'Connell-Purdy.

36 145th COS meeting minutes, 24 February 1942, NAC, RG24, vol. 8081, file NSS 1272-2 (vol. 6); and COS to the CWC, 3 March 1942, NAC, RG2 7c, vol. 8. See also Galen Roger Perras, "As Lambs to the Slaughter: Canada and the Garrisoning of the Falkland Islands, 1942," *War and Society* 14 (May 1996): 73-97.

37 Day, *The Great Betrayal*, 261; and Henry P. Frei, *Japan's Southward Advance and Australia: From the Sixteenth Century to World War II* (Carlton: Melbourne University Press, 1991), 132-3.

38 Horner, "Australia under the Threat of Invasion," 256-8; and Chiefs of staff, "Probable Immediate Japanese Moves in the Proposed New ANZAC Area," 5 March 1942, AA, series A2671, item 143, 1942.

39 Curtin to F.M. Forde, 24 January 1942, AA, series A5954, 1, item 581, 16; Julian Barnes quoted in D.M. Horner, *Crisis of Command: Australian Generalship and the Japanese Threat, 1941-1943* (Canberra: Australian National University Press, 1978), 46-7; Roosevelt quoted in Maurice Matloff and Edwin M. Snell, *Strategic Planning for Coalition Warfare 1941-1942* (Washington, DC: Department of the Army, 1953), 131; and Dwight Eisenhower to General George C. Marshall, "Strategic Conceptions and Their Application to the Southwest Pacific," 28 February 1942, in *The Papers of Dwight David Eisenhower*, vol. 1, *The War Years*, ed. Alfred D. Chandler (Baltimore: Johns Hopkins University Press, 1970), 149-55.

40 Odlum to King, 11 March 1942, NAC, W.L.M. King Papers, MG26 J1, vol. 331, file O'Connell-Purdy; and Robertson to King, 23 March 1942, NAC, RG25, vol. 2168, file 53-MP-40.

41 NAC, RG25, vol. 2736, file 329-40, part 1; and Evatt, quoted in Coral Bell, *Dependent Ally: A Study in Australian Foreign Policy* (Melbourne: Oxford University Press, 1988), 24.

42 Howard Green statements, House of Commons, Canada, *Debates*, 23-4 March 1942, 1558 and 1610; and King statements, House of Commons, Canada, *Debates*, 25-6 March 1942, 1632 and 1645.

43 Evatt, quoted in Norman Harper, *A Great and Powerful Friend: A Study of Australian American Relations between 1900 and 1975* (St. Lucia, Queensland: University of Queensland Press, 1987), 112.

44 CWC minutes, 26 March and 1 April 1942, NAC, RG2 7c, vol. 9.

45 Stanley W. Dziuban, *Military Relations between Canada and the United States 1939-1945* (Washington, DC: Department of the Army, 1959), 67-8. Roosevelt intended the PWC "to disseminate information as to the progress of operations in the Pacific – and, secondly, to give me a chance to keep everybody happy by telling stories and doing most of the talking"; Robert Dallek, *Franklin D. Roosevelt and American Foreign Policy, 1932-1945*

(New York: Oxford University Press, 1979), 355. Though he thought that the PWC "really was of no particular benefit," Evatt unsuccessfully tried to revive it in 1944-5 so that it could play a role in "all Pacific war matters including Armistice and post-hostility matters"; Evatt quoted in Harper, *A Great and Powerful Friend*, 110; and Evatt to Frederic Eggleston, 19 December 1944, in "Pacific War Council," 1946, Australian War Memorial Archives, Australian War Memorial Records, AWM68, series 3 DRL8052, 184, item 419, 45, 13.

46 PWC minutes, 1 April 1942, NAC, Privy Council Office Records, RG2, vol. 3, file W-29-1; Hume Wrong to King, 2 April 1942, ibid.; PWC minutes memorandum, 3 April 1942, Franklin Delano Roosevelt Library (hereinafter FDRL), Franklin Roosevelt Map Room files, box 168, 1 April 1941; Pope diary, 2 April 1942, NAC, Maurice Arthur Pope Papers, MG27 III F4, vol. 1; and Leighton McCarthy to Robertson, 26 March 1942, NAC, RG25, vol. 2961, file 35.

47 Evatt to Curtin, 1 April 1942, General Douglas MacArthur Foundation (hereinafter GDMF), Records of General Headquarters United States Army Forces Pacific, RG4, reel 586; King diary, 27 March and 8 April 1942, NAC, W.L.M. King Papers, MG26 J13; Howe to King, 13 April 1942, in *Documents on Canadian External Relations*, vol. 9, *1942-1943*, ed. John F. Hilliker (hereinafter *DCER*) (Ottawa: Department of External Affairs, 1980), 1039; CWC minutes, 9 April 1942, NAC, RG2 7c, vol. 9; King diary, 9 April 1942, NAC, W.L.M. King Papers, MG26 J13; and COS to the CWC, 10 April 1942, NAC, RG2 7c, vol. 9.

48 Evatt to Curtin, 14 April 1942, AA, series A5954, 1, item 581, 17; Evatt to King, 14 April 1942, *DCER*, 9:1040; and King memorandum, 15 April 1942, NAC, W.L.M. King Papers, MG26 J13.

49 Evatt to Curtin, 18 April 1942, AA, series A3300, 7, item 23; and King to Evatt, 28 April 1942, NAC, W.L.M. King Papers, MG26 J4, vol. 348, file C240280.

50 King to Odlum, 28 April 1942, NAC, RG25, vol. 819, file 376; Evatt to King, 17 May 1942, *DCER*, 9:1042; Odlum to King, 20 May 1942, NAC, J.L. Ralston Papers, MG27 III B11, vol. 38, file Australia Gen (Secret); Odlum to King, 12 August 1942, ibid.; Odlum to MacArthur, 25 June 1942, GDMF, Douglas MacArthur Private Correspondence 1932-1964, RG10, reel 333; Odlum, "Memorandum of a conversation with General Douglas MacArthur, USA, at HQ, South-west Pacific Area, on Saturday, August 8, 1942," NAC, Victor Odlum Papers, MG30 E300, vol. 7, file MacArthur Douglas; and Odlum to King, 1 June 1942, NAC, W.L.M. King Papers, MG26 J1, vol. 331, file O'Connell-Purdy.

51 Rogers to King, 13 October 1942, in *DCER*, 9:376; and Rogers to Robertson, 20 October 1942, NAC, RG25, vol. 3116, file 4533-40.

52 Hilliker, *Canada's Department of External Affairs*, 1:266; T.C. Davis to King, 11 January 1943 and 4 June 1945, NAC, RG25, vol. 3116, file 4533-40; and King to Davis, 8 January 1943, ibid.

53 Davis to King, 15 January 1943, NAC, W.L.M. King Papers, MG26 J1, vol. 339, file Coleman-Duckworth; Rulon HD to Davis TC, Davis to King, 29 January 1943, ibid.; and King to Davis, 1 February 1943, ibid. See also "Canada's War Effort. New Commissioner Arrives," *Sydney Morning Herald*, 31 December 1942; and "Fraternal Gesture," *The Argus* (Melbourne), 10 February 1943.

54 Davis to King, 2 March 1943, NAC, W.L.M. King Papers, MG26 J1, vol. 339, file Coleman-Duckworth; Davis to Robertson, 2 March 1943, NAC, RG25, vol. 2453, file 250-1943; and Davis to Robertson, 3 April 1943, NAC, RG25, vol. 2168, file 53-MP-40.

55 Odlum to Curtin, 23 January 1943, GDMF, RG4, reel 587; Curtin to Odlum, 19 March 1943, AA, series A5954, 1, item 581, 16; Davis to Robertson, 23 March 1943, NAC, RG25, vol. 348, file C240289; and Robertson to Davis, 15 April 1943, ibid., file C240290.

56 Robertson to King, 27 May 1943, NAC, W.L.M. King Papers, MG26 J4, vol. 348, file 3770; and CWC minutes, 27 May 1943, NAC, RG2 7c, vol. 13.

57 Robertson to King, 14 July 1943, NAC, W.L.M. King Papers, MG26 J4, vol. 348, file C240302; CWC minutes, 15 July 1943, NAC, RG2 7c, vol. 13; "Statement to Press Conference by Dr. H.V. Evatt, Australian Foreign Minister at Press Gallery, Parliament House at 3 P.M., July 15th, 1943," NAC, RG25, vol. 2168, file 53-MP-40; and John W. Holmes to Wrong, 15 July 1943, ibid.

58 Wrong to Davis, 10 August 1943, NAC, RG25, vol. 2168, file 53-MP-40; Wrong to Robertson, 14 August 1943, NAC, RG25, vol. 3236, file 5639-40; and "Broadcast by the Prime Minister

the Rt. Hon. W.L. Mackenzie King on participation of Canadian forces in Alaska and the Aleutians," 21 August 1943, NAC, W.L.M. King Papers, MG26 J4, vol. 361, file 3853.

59 Australian legation Washington to External Canberra, 23 June 1942, AA, series A3300, 7, item 229; Australian Legation Washington to External Canberra, 21 July 1943, ibid.; "Japanese Loss," Melbourne *Age*, 23 August 1943; "Another Aleutian Island Recaptured," *Sydney Morning Herald*, 24 August 1943; "Kiska Opens Short Route to Japan," *The Argus* (Melbourne), 24 August 1943; and Davis to Robertson, 24 August 1943, NAC, RG25, vol. 2453, file 250-1943.

60 War Cabinet minute 3065, 1 October 1943, AA, series A2673, vol. 13; and Holmes, "Notes on a speech by Dr. Evatt, October 14th, 43," 22 October 1943, *DCER*, 9:1042-4.

61 S.J. Butlin and C.B. Schedvin, *War Economy 1942-1945* (Canberra: Australian War Memorial, 1977), 467; and Davis to King, 18 December 1943, NAC, W.L.M. King Papers, MG26 J1, vol. 339, file Coleman-Duckworth.

62 King diary, 5 and 7 January 1944, NAC, W.L.M. King Papers, MG26 J13. The obligation notion arose when Roosevelt said that Allied resources, including Canadian, would be shifted to the Pacific after Germany's defeat; PWC minutes, 11 August 1943, NAC, RG2, vol. 14, file W-29-1.

63 Keenleyside to King, "Canadian-American Relations in the Northwest," 29 July 1943, NAC, W.L.M. King Papers, MG26 J1, vol. 337, file BA-BL 1943. Roger Sarty discusses the interplay between the Canadian services and Britain in "The Ghosts of Fisher and Jellicoe: The Royal Canadian Navy and the Quebec Conferences," in *The Second Quebec Conference Revisited*, ed. David B. Woolner (New York: St. Martin's Press, 1998), 143-70; and Galen Roger Perras, "Once Bitten, Twice Shy: The Origins of the Canadian Army Pacific Force," in *Uncertain Horizons: Canadians and Their World in 1945*, ed. Greg Donaghy (Ottawa: Canadian Committee for the History of the Second World War, 1997), 77-99.

64 220 Military Mission meeting minutes, 17 August 1943, DHH, DND, Kardex File 112.21009 (D197); Pope to Stuart, 24 May 1943, NAC, Maurice Arthur Pope Papers, MG27 III F4, vol. 1; and C.P. Stacey, *Six Years of War: The Army in Canada, Britain and the Pacific* (Ottawa: Department of National Defence, 1966), 507-10. For the original observer proposal, see Colonel M. Cosgrave to Odlum, 28 September 1942, NAC, Victor Odlum Papers, MG30 E300, vol. 57, file 57-24.

65 14th meeting, Dominion Prime Ministers 1944, 15 May 1944, AA, series A5954, 1, item 289, 10, PMM (44); "Improvements in the Machinery for Empire Cooperation Desired by the Australian Government," 15 May 1945, ibid.; and King diary, 15 May 1944, NAC, W.L.M. King Papers, MG26 J13.

66 King diary, 31 May and 1 June 1944, NAC, W.L.M. King Papers, MG26 J13; "Time for Offensive, Mr. Curtin Says," *Sydney Morning Herald*, 2 June 1944; and COS minutes, 31 May 1944, DHH, DND, Kardex File 193.009 (D31).

67 Pope aide memoirs, 19 February 1944, NAC, RG2, vol. 32, file D-19-1 (Asia), 1943-4; Pope to J.H. Jenkins, 9 February 1944, NAC, Maurice Arthur Pope Papers, MG27 III F4, vol. 1; Pope to Jenkins, 4 April 1944, NAC, RG25, vol. 5749, file 52-C(s), part 1; and Jenkins, "Appreciation of Canadian Participation in the Pacific Theatre of War," 24 April 1944, DHH, DND, Kardex File 193.009 (D32).

68 COS minutes, 7 June 1944, DHH, DND, Kardex File 193.009 (D32); "Memorandum to the Cabinet War Committee: re: Canadian participation in the war against Japan," plus CWC minutes, 14 June 1944, NAC, RG2 7c, vol. 15; and King to Dominions Secretary, 27 June 1944, in *Documents on Canadian External Relations*, vol. 10, *1944-1945*, ed. John F. Hilliker (Ottawa: Department of External Affairs, 1989-90), part 1, 380-1.

69 Paul Malone to Robertson, 5 July 1944, NAC, MG26 J4, vol. 248, file C166565-66; Davis to Robertson, 23 June 1944, NAC, MG26 J4, vol. 234, file C158518-19; Malone to Robertson, 12 July 1944, NAC, RG25, vol. 5699, file 4-G(s), part 2; and "Meeting of Prime Ministers London, May 1944: Review by the Honourable John Curtin, M.P., Prime Minister of Australia," 17 July 1944, GDMF, RG4, reel 588.

70 Canadian embassy Washington to King, 13 July 1944, NAC, RG25, vol. 5756, file 59(s); Wrong to Robertson, 14 July 1944, ibid.; and CWC minutes, 10 August 1944, NAC, RG2 7c, vol. 16.

71 Davis to King, 9 August 1944, NAC, RG2, vol. 32, file D-19-1 (Asia), 1943-4; CWC minutes, 31 August, 13 and 14 September 1944, NAC, RG2 7c, vol. 16; King diary, 14 September 1944, NAC, W.L.M. King Papers, MG26 J13; and Robertson, "War against Japan: participation by Canadian forces," 14 September 1944, NAC, RG25, vol. 5758, file 68-C(s).

72 "Report on Liaison Visit to Canada by Lieut.-Colonel J.G.N. Wilton," 11 September 1944, AWM54, item 937, 6, 2; Lavarack to Blamey, 20 September 1944, AWM3 DRL6643, item 2, 1.2; Glasgow to Evatt, 12 July 1944, AA, Department of External Affairs, series A989, 1, item 44, 125, 8, 10; and Glasgow drafts, September 1944, AA, series A3095, 1, item 35, 9.

73 Col. M. Cosgrave to General A.G.L. McNaughton, 11 December 1944 and 9 January 1945, NAC, A.G.L. McNaughton Papers, MG30 E133, vol. 266, file Cosgrave; and Davis to King, 4 June 1945, NAC, RG25, vol. 3116, file 4533-40.

74 Hilliker, *Canada's Department of External Affairs*, 1:264.

75 F.L.C. Floud to Sir Harry Batterbee, 24 May 1938, PRO, DO35, 586, file G88, 55.

76 Nelson Johnson to Stanley Hornbeck, 20 January 1942, Library of Congress, Nelson T. Johnson Papers, box 66, file Stanley Hornbeck Correspondence August 1941-1942; and Pat Frank to Harold Guinzberg, 25 August 1942, FDRL, Roosevelt Papers, Personal Secretary's file, box 23, file Diplomatic Correspondence Australia: 1939-August 1942.

77 John Robertson, "Australian War Policy 1939-1945," *Historical Studies* 17 (October 1977): 497; Harper, "Threat Perceptions and Politics," 38-9; Alan Renouf, *Let Justice Be Done: The Foreign Policy of Dr. H.V. Evatt* (St. Lucia, Queensland: University of Queensland Press, 1983), 64; and Frei, *Japan's Southward Advance and Australia*, 161-5.

78 J.D.B. Miller, "The Interaction of Economics and Politics in Government Policies," in *Australia's Economic Relations*, ed. J.D.B. Miller (Sydney: Angus and Robertson, 1975); and Norman Hillmer, "The Canadian Diplomatic Tradition," in *Towards a New World: Readings in the History of Canadian Foreign Policy*, ed. J.L. Granatstein (Toronto: Copp Clark Pitman, 1992), 6.

79 Haycock, "The 'Myth' of Imperial Defence," 80.

80 Moffat to Minter, 2 May 1941, Houghton Library, Harvard University (hereinafter HL), Moffat Papers, MS Am 1407. Material quoted from the J. Pierrepont Moffat Papers, MS Am 1407, appears by permission of the Houghton Library, Harvard University.

81 I.P. Garran minute, 27 August 1935, PRO, Foreign Office Records, FO371, 19128, J4117.

82 Burchell to King, 4 September 1940, NAC, RG25, vol. 2789, file 703-40; and Moffat to Ray Atherton, 2 February 1942, NARA, Foreign Service Posts Records, Canada Ottawa 1936-1949, RG84, series 2195A, file 800.

83 Paul Hasluck, *Diplomatic Witness: Australian Foreign Affairs, 1941-47* (Carlton: Melbourne University Press, 1980), 195; Charles Ritchie, *Diplomatic Passport: More Undiplomatic Diaries, 1946-1962* (Toronto: Macmillan, 1981), 8; and Pope, quoted in Arnold Heeney, *The Things That Are Caesar's: Memoirs of a Canadian Public Servant* (Toronto: University of Toronto Press, 1972), 87.

84 Evatt to King, 20 April 1947, AA, Department of External Affairs, series A1068, item P47, 10, 61, ii; Wrong to D. Johnson, 6 May 1947, *Documents on Canadian External Relations*, vol. 13, *1947*, ed. Norman Hillmer and Donald Page (Ottawa: External Affairs and International Trade Canada, 1993), 202-3; Pearson to Louis St. Laurent, "Japanese Peace Settlement," 23 May 1947, ibid., 204-5; and Pearson, "Japanese Peace Settlement; Commonwealth Conference; Canberra," 18 July 1947, ibid., 209.

85 Australian Delegation United Nations to Evatt, 10 January 1946, AA, Department of External Affairs, series A1838 T189, item 854, 4, 2; John English, *Shadow of Heaven: The Life of Lester Pearson*, vol. 1, *1897-1948* (Toronto: Lester and Orpen Dennys, 1989), 289; and "Strength and Organisation of Post-War Defence Forces," 12 March 1947, AA, Council of Defence Minutes, Agendum 1, 1947, series A9787, 1, item 112.

86 Casey to Pearson, 12 June 1951, NAC, Lester B. Pearson Papers, MG26 N1, vol. 2; and Westerman, quoted in Mitchell Sharp, *Which Reminds Me ... A Memoir* (Toronto: University of Toronto Press, 1994), 61.

87 A.R.M. Lower, "National Interests in the Pacific: American and Canadian," June 1939, in *The Road to Ogdensburg: The Queen's/St. Lawrence Conferences on Canadian-American Affairs, 1935-1941*, ed. Frederick W. Gibson and Jonathan G. Rossie (East Lansing, MI: Michigan State University Press, 1993), 114.

6

In the Wake of Canada: Australia's Middle-Power Diplomacy and the Attempt to Join the Atomic Special Relationship, 1943-57

Wayne Reynolds

Australia and Canada have long been contrasted as two so-called middle powers. In the case of Canada, this led to an early spirit of independence within the British Empire that foreshadowed the move toward greater autonomy between the two world wars. After the Second World War, conscious of its powerful neighbour, Ottawa moved to define its middle-power role more specifically by acting as a mediator and a good international citizen. There was also a particular role for Canada to play in the Cold War, a function Canadian diplomats believed they were particularly well qualified to perform. Not only did Canada resist global communism, but it also increasingly found itself "containing the Americans" in a conflict that frequently led to excess in US foreign policy.[1] Mediation, internationalism, and restraint were at the heart of Canada's middle-power identity.

Similarly, there has been a fondness for the view that Canberra, at least under the Labor government from 1941 to 1949, shunned "power politics," seeking instead to pursue a more idealistic view of foreign relations, even if there was a move under their conservative successors to return to a policy of "great and powerful friends." Indeed, Australia's notorious minister for external affairs, Dr. H.V. Evatt, attempted to borrow Canadian declarations over "security power status" made between 1943 and 1944 during the discussions over the UN Security Council. Although the category was never formally recognized by the United Nations, Evatt claimed that Australia fulfilled the role of a "security power" with major responsibilities for policing the postwar Pacific. However, in fleshing out the characteristics of its middle-power identity, Australia lagged behind Canada, which emerged as both a model and a rival for the architects of Australian foreign policy.

There was one aspect of international relations in which Canada was far ahead of Australia: the atomic field. Both Ottawa and Canberra were conscious of the revolutionary changes for warfare and the concomitant implications for their respective roles as "security powers." Of particular significance in all of this was the Quebec Conference in August 1943. There had been much talk at the conference about plans to police the postwar world, prompting Evatt to fire off a cable to the Australian high commission in Ottawa, complaining that it was "most embarrassing" for Canada to make an appearance when Australia "makes no showing at all."[2] The conference went on to pave the way for the construction of an atomic alliance between the Atlantic partners. The British and Canadians were finally given some access to the Manhattan Project, the American atomic bomb program. There was no role for Australia. Exclusion was not acceptable in Canberra. From 1943 to 1957, Australia sought a comparable role to Canada's in the atomic field and in atomic relations. Success or failure would reveal much about the kind of influence Australia could enjoy in an international community dominated by giants. And Canada set the standard by which it could judge whether it fell short or could keep up with the pack.

The Wartime Atomic Program

Canada was well placed strategically to support the British in the development of a future class of atomic weapons. Dispersal of vital research and production centres throughout the British Isles was hardly a sufficient safeguard, given the development of German air power, and it was therefore decided to transfer the project across the Atlantic. Britain and Canada had exchanged information on atomic energy in 1940, and by 1942 they established a joint project at the University of Montreal. The Canadians also hosted an experimental atomic plant at a secure and isolated site at Chalk River, near Ottawa. The location was ideal: "Two facts contribute to making Canada an excellent location for atomic energy projects: the first is the accessibility of uranium ore, and the second is the vast areas of comparatively uninhabited territory where there is likely to be little danger to the general public from radiation and where it is a simple matter to maintain any required degree of secrecy."[3]

The ultimate objective in London, however, was to gain access to the much larger American atomic-bomb effort. The Manhattan Project was to be a military operation that would coordinate everything from the laboratory to the fabrication facility at Los Alamos. The British were particularly keen to participate in the work on plutonium. In April 1943, Lord Cherwell, Churchill's adviser, requested that the team at Montreal undertake a thorough study on the possibility of a large plutonium-producing reactor, a scheme characterized by one of the key participants, the Frenchman Bertram Goldschmidt, as "yet another of the grandiose schemes" designed to produce a British weapon in "four or five years."[4]

The problem was that the US commander of the project, General Leslie Groves, had already decided in 1942 that the United States should not share information on plutonium with the British team. After all, 90 percent of the work was wholly American. The Canadian group, which was working on plutonium and heavy water, could provide "basic data" only for the engineers responsible for their own heavy-water reactor – the Chicago Pile 3. The Quebec Agreement, signed by Roosevelt and Churchill in August 1943, did not alter the situation even if it did promise "full and effective" collaboration. Information was to be exchanged on a range of projects under way in the elaborate Manhattan organization, and British scientists were at last cleared to participate in the work undertaken in the United States. But the Americans refused to give data on large plutonium-producing graphite piles, on plutonium extraction, and on heavy-water production.[5]

The reality was that the Americans would not extend cooperation on the process that promised most on the bomb.[6] Moreover, in denying access to plutonium production techniques, they were undermining the basis of the Montreal group's work. The argument used at the time was one that was to be repeatedly trotted out after the war – Montreal was insecure, and the team there was composed of a mix of nationalities. Not surprisingly, the Quebec Agreement contained an essential clause that Goldschmidt saw as the "basis for the future policy of Anglo-American secrecy after the war" – that of forbidding the communication of atomic information to third parties.[7] This was to deny access to the French, but it was also to recoil on the British later.

In the meantime, the British were integrated into the American program and the Canadian project was effectively put on hold. In 1944, however, the go-ahead was given for the construction of a heavy-water pilot plant in Canada, but the production of plutonium for military purposes was to be satisfied from American reactors. As a result, the Canadian reactor did not go critical until July 1947.

The leading British author on Britain's atomic program, Margaret Gowing, argues that the British intended to pursue their own program, but not so as to prejudice the work carried on at Montreal.[8] But there was more to it than that. The British government was simply not prepared to gamble on the security of plutonium supply from Canadian sources at the end of the war. On the other hand, they wanted the closest possible cooperation with Canada – if that could be achieved. The decision had been made in 1945 to produce a plutonium bomb, and in the opinion of British defence advisers, plutonium was the vital explosive material of the future.[9] The leader of the British team in Canada, Lord Chadwick, therefore implored C.J. Mackenzie, the head of the National Research Council, to put "pep" into the Chalk River project so that they would not be "prejudiced by the Americans running around and doing the job after they have dealt with Japan."[10] In other words, the British wanted the Canadian project to be primarily one based on Empire defence that would deliver the needed supplies of plutonium. Within an imperial atomic scheme, Britain, "which remains the heart and brain of the whole Empire" valued Canada's cooperation above all the other dominions because it was already "so deeply implicated" in the development of atomic weapons.[11]

Had the story ended here, the British Empire would not have figured so largely in London's ambitions to acquire nuclear deterrent weapons before 1957. The problem, however, was that Britain was not the only one offering closer defence relations.

American Hemispheric Defence and the Role of Canada

The first steps toward organizing a more systematic continental defence were foreshadowed by Washington during the Depression. In 1936, Roosevelt warned Canadian prime minister Mackenzie King that the United States might be forced to go into Canada and "defend our neighbourhood" if the Japanese attacked the Canadian west coast. In June 1940, secret military talks made it clear that Washington expected Canadian help in the defence of "this Hemisphere," an assumption that was formalized by the establishment of a Permanent Joint Board on Defence in August of that year. This step drew an immediate response from Churchill, who saw Canada as passing into the American orbit – fears that were indeed realized with the start of the Pacific war.[12]

The advent of atomic weapons in 1945 influenced the relationship between Canada and the United States in two important respects. First, Canada was the second-largest source of uranium after the Belgian Congo, and an infinitely more reliable source as far as the Americans were concerned. It was American money[13] that rescued the Canadian Eldorado Company in 1941, and thereafter the United States succeeded in locking up Canadian Shield ore supplies until the 1960s, albeit with Canadian encouragement. By the time the Roosevelt administration had agreed to the Manhattan Project, Eldorado ore was critical to its future success. The British were to discover the extent of this interdependence when they were rebuffed after attempting to buy between 50 and 100 tons of ore at the end of the war.[14]

Second, the possibility that the United States might be attacked by aircraft or rockets from Soviet sites via the Arctic Circle enormously enhanced Canada's strategic position in American eyes. Washington wanted to integrate Canada into its plans for the defence of the North American continent. In October 1945, following Britain's decision to press ahead with its own nuclear program, the Americans approached the Canadians with a view to convincing them to adopt American defence equipment in preference to that from Britain.[15] The integration of US and Canadian defence was designed to secure the North American continent, and did not make provision for the British Commonwealth. The concept was regional, a point noted by US Secretary of State Dean Acheson when he conceded that the integration of North American defence was, in view of Canada's close association with Britain, "a matter of moment in Canada and one which involves considerable political risk for the present Government."[16]

While the Americans were courting the Canadians, Anglo-Canadian atomic cooperation suffered severe damage at the end of 1945. The usual explanation for this is that Britain wanted to pursue its own program. The step to recall John Cockcroft, the British head at Chalk River, to lead the British experimental establishment in November 1945 – an idea that had been floated in April – sent obvious signals as to Britain's intentions. The move itself occasioned great anger on the part of the Canadians. Indeed, Mackenzie warned Sir John Anderson, a leading figure in the British atomic program, that Cockcroft's withdrawal would create "a very unfavourable impression" and that it would mean that Canada "would have no other alternative than to tie in with the United States."[17]

That, however, had been the problem all along. Mackenzie had come to the conclusion in 1942 that the Montreal laboratory existed at the whim of the Americans, despite its beginning as a British Commonwealth enterprise. The laboratory needed American information and supplies, especially heavy water. Moreover, the Americans could continue their program without the assistance from Montreal, leading Mackenzie to the obvious conclusion that the British had little bargaining strength. If Montreal were to survive, thought Mackenzie, it would be as part of an arrangement with the Americans after the war. As a result, when the vexed question of cooperation with the Americans blew up in 1943, at the time of the partial agreement at Quebec, the minister in charge of the Canadian program, C.D. Howe, argued that the Montreal project "is a relatively small one cast against the entire US-Canadian contracts." A key part of those contracts was the agreement of the Canadians to allocate their entire stock of uranium ore to the Americans until the end of the war. The British could have attempted to get the Canadians to break their contracts to save the Montreal experiments in 1943, but Mackenzie was sent to London with the message that the British must put up with the American terms or "be shut out." Howe himself concluded that the Canadian government "had no interest in competition on such matters with the United States," leading Churchill to accuse the minister of having "sold the British Empire down the river."[18]

The unreliability of the Canadians was also demonstrated to the British over the Halban affair. Hans von Halban, an Austrian refugee who had joined the British research team in Montreal, had already been rebuffed by the Canadians in 1943 when he put to them the idea that the British, and not the Americans, were better qualified to take an interest in European atomic developments after the war. Halban was also working on the use of graphite as an alternative to US-supplied heavy water as a means of moderating plutonium-producing reactors. When Halban returned to London en route to France in 1944, British authorities were anxious to clinch a patents agreement with Halban for his work on graphite. They also wanted to find out whether the French had pursued patent applications in other countries.

Groves was so furious with the British for allowing Halban to leave the project that he ordered his banishment from the Montreal laboratory. Goldschmidt saw a more sinister motive. The occasion of the visit was an opportunity for a "show of strength" against the French and de Gaulle.[19] The historian of the Canadian atomic program, Robert Bothwell, also hints at broader issues being involved. He observed that Halban's departure "ensured that American-supplied heavy water and not graphite would be the moderator" in the development of plutonium-producing reactors.[20] To Howe, however, the British had been responsible for a breach in Canadian-US relations, and as such it was up to them to make restitution. Not surprisingly, Howe agreed with Groves's assessment later that "the US and Canadian partnership is much more important to the United States than the US-UK partnership."[21]

This presented the problem of relying on Canada as a source of atomic weapons in the future. At the time of Cockcroft's recall to Harwell, the centre of atomic energy research in Britain, Ottawa rejected the proposition that the advent of the atomic bomb necessitated the continuation in peacetime of the imperial defence organization set up during the war. The problem, predictably, was Canada. At the 1944 Commonwealth Prime Ministers' Conference, the Canadians had wrecked the possibility of closer Commonwealth defence planning by insisting that they were wary of identifying too closely with imperial schemes as opposed to those of a future UN.[22] Canadian reluctance to participate in Commonwealth schemes – because they threatened to become centralized arrangements in which the dominions' interests would be subordinate to those of Britain – had become a predictable reaction, as David MacKenzie and Francine McKenzie have pointed out in their analyses of Anglo-Canadian relations during the Second World War.

The British high commission in Ottawa reported to London in November 1945 that Hume Wrong, the Canadian assistant secretary of state for external affairs, regarded the "whole concept of imperial defence as unreal." What Canada ideally wanted was "a triangular relationship" in which it would be regarded as an equal by her atomic partners. But if this setup was not feasible, then the choice was clear. Canada's defence was "essentially a North American problem requiring the most complete integration of her defensive arrangements with those of the United States." In the event that "the [UK] and the United States could not get together on these matters (weapons, training, organization) Canada would certainly lean toward the US."[23]

Clearly Canada's priorities in external relations were shifting in response to the unavoidable necessity of close Canadian-American relations. This continental partnership was cemented in 1946, when President Harry Truman announced an ambitious plan to unify the defences of North America and to develop "integrated" long-term plans.[24] Truman later told Mackenzie King that there must be active collaboration in defence because "North America is no longer adequately protected by geography." As such, the American president put to Mackenzie King that "in five years North America must be prepared to meet major enemy capabilities."[25] It is clear that, while Mackenzie King appreciated the need for cooperation with his powerful neighbour, including the standardization of defence equipment and all that that entailed, he also wanted to accommodate the British, if possible. The prime minister put his views to the US ambassador in Ottawa, Ray Atherton, who reported to Washington that "Canadians loyal to the Commonwealth find themselves on the horns of a dilemma." Ottawa had little choice but to work with the United States to defend the continent, and yet "fear such action may lead eventually to withdrawal of Canada from the Commonwealth."[26] Members of the Canadian Department of National Defence also relayed this view to London. For instance, in February 1946 Air Marshal Robert Leckie wrote to Lord Tedder, the chief of the air staff, that he was "very concerned at the growing pressure from the USA to force Canada into the American camp ... The campaign is insidious, obviously directed from high sources."[27]

The Canadian-American defence alignment had implications for atomic cooperation. The British rejected US plans in the United Nations in 1946 designed to establish international controls on atomic weapons, but the Canadians sided with the Americans.[28] Behind the scenes, the priority at Chalk River remained the production of plutonium for military purposes,[29] but this occurred against the backdrop of even greater schemes to coordinate US and Canadian resources. A clue can be gleaned from Truman's defence plan to focus on "industrial mobilisation," which would include the development of "industrial and raw material resources." Not only would the Americans tie up Canadian uranium, but they would also effectively control the whole atomic program.[30]

The American objective was to continue the wartime model of atomic cooperation between the Allies that had enabled the Manhattan Project to secure both materials and manpower from around the world. This would mean that the Project's Combined Policy Committee, on which the British, Canadians, and Americans were represented, would coordinate the acquisition of raw materials, while skilled Allied scientific manpower could fill the large gaps in the program. Indeed, the chair of the US Atomic Energy Commission, David Lilienthal, regarded such shortages as the most serious obstacles in the way of the American program.[31]

While it is clear that Ottawa was prepared to extend full cooperation, leading to the loss of key Canadian personnel to the American atomic program,[32] the British team in the United States still believed that after the war Britain should have its own nuclear deterrent weapons.[33] As a result, there would be competition with the United States for uranium and scientific manpower. When the British government announced in February 1946 that it was going to build a large-scale reactor to produce plutonium, Groves told G.C. Bateman, who directed the search for uranium in Canada, that the United States wanted all the uranium that Canada could produce as well as the supplies from the Congo. Groves even suggested that the United States should have access to Britain's own stockpile at Chalk River "for security reasons," leading Bateman to conclude that in wanting to "protect themselves over too long a period," the Americans had created the conditions for a "tug of war" with the British.[34]

There is even a hint of foul play at this point. A curious aspect of US-Canadian cooperation was the fact that Canada had been the site of the first – and one of the most sensational – spy scandals of the Cold War, which Frank Cain chronicles in greater detail in the next chapter. Elsewhere, as we will see, it was the problem of security that the Americans would use as a basis for denying full intelligence and defence cooperation – especially where modern weapons of mass destruction were concerned. Yet, in Canada, it was after the defection of Igor Gouzenko, the Soviet cipher clerk whose revelations led to the arrest of twenty-two suspected agents, that the United States moved to extend defence cooperation. Britain, however, was not so fortunate. The timing of the spy scandal well served those in the United States who wanted greater secrecy and increased military control of the atomic program. In congress, support for internationalization of atomic energy research and development collapsed, and the passage of the McMahon Act in August ended Anglo-US cooperation.

Where the results of the Gouzenko spy case and the McMahon Act restricted Britain's access to atomic information, the integration of Canada into a system of hemispheric defence removed a major potential supplier of uranium and plutonium. The only path forward offered to the British was to accept the US-Canadian proposal that their reactor would be constructed in Canada and that the United States would exercise the tightest control. This was a position the Americans advocated from 1945 until the formation of the North Atlantic Treaty Organization (NATO) in 1949. They did so because the US Joint Strategic Studies Committee (JSSC) opposed British installations that would be "so close to potential enemy territory." Equally, they did not want Britain's atomic program to develop "until sufficient atomic bombs had been stockpiled to meet US security requirements and until US proposals for international control were accepted." This second objection was at the heart of American opposition to Britain's atomic aspirations. On 26 February 1942 the Joint Chiefs of Staff admitted that if the UK built a large-scale atomic plant, it would be "disadvantageous to the security of the United States," since a British reactor "would probably divert from US manufacturing capacity a large amount of raw material which should be used in producing US atomic weapons ... The point of overriding importance is that all available ore be turned into useable fissionable material available to the US."[35] To that end, in early 1947 Washington invited Canada to seek shelter under the American nuclear umbrella. The records of the Canadian Defence Committee on 9 January reveal that the United States was at that stage preoccupied with hemispheric defence, rather than with global security.[36]

By August the United States and Canada had concerted their defence planning so closely, through a joint board, that the government had to defend itself in the House of Commons from charges that Ottawa's sovereignty was threatened.[37] But the stakes at this point were high for Canada. The Chalk River pile went critical in July and was now in the plutonium business, a development that meant that Canada could supplement US supplies. The plant, in turn, was dependent on US stocks of heavy water.

The bottom line was that the United States was opposed to the development of an atomic program in Britain. The Americans were, however, prepared to see Canada continue as the site of the Commonwealth program. This carried certain consequences that were to prove unacceptable to London.

In October 1946 Britain's Labour prime minister, Clement Attlee, noted the opposition of Canada and the United States to the construction of a plant in Britain and concluded that a plant in Canada would not be an "adequate substitute" for one in Britain "from the point of view of both our national defence and security."[38] But there was progressively less faith in a UK-US-Canada collaborative program. At the British Defence Committee in January 1947, Lord Tedder – a major player in the British program to achieve independent deterrent weapons – took note of the United States' acquisition of bases in Canada, and recorded his hope that the Canadians would not devote "too much of their effort toward development of northern defences."[39] A year later, the Foreign Office reflected on trends after the defence agreement and complained that Britain had not been "kept in the picture." Moreover, the American pressure on the Canadians to either devote more resources to northern defences or to allow a greater measure of control from Washington was stepped up.[40] The British would thus have to rely on their own program, and in January 1947 finally decided to proceed with the construction of their own atomic bomb and delivery systems. This in turn would provide a great opportunity for Australia to assume a role that might have been fulfilled by Canada.

Australia's First Knowledge of the Atomic Program

Canadian work on atomic energy was a crucial factor in bolstering Ottawa's diplomatic credentials. Robert Bothwell has chronicled the wartime role of the Canadian atomic program and has thereby filled out a significant contributing factor in Canada's vital role in the US atomic program. That Australia cherished a similar status and role, however, has not been the subject of historical enquiry. Arguably, it was the prospects of atomic power that guided Australian views on its future status well before the armistice. The source of Australia's knowledge of wartime atomic developments was Professor Marcus Oliphant. Oliphant was to play a major part in the Australian atomic program, but it is also now clear that he played a substantial role in the British wartime program as well. The Australian physicist had the closest personal contact with the leading British scientists in the atomic field well before the war.[41] He worked at the Cavendish Laboratory at Cambridge on high energy accelerators, a field pioneered by Sir John Cockcroft, the director of Britain's first atomic pile at Harwell and another who would play a major role in the development of the Australian atomic dream. In the 1930s, this work put Oliphant on the ground floor of the British nuclear program.

On 10 April 1939 Oliphant's importance to the British bomb program was evidenced by the fact that he was one of just five men who met to consider whether the British wartime atomic program, code-named MAUD, should proceed. It is also apparent that, even at this early stage, he entertained great suspicions about working with the Canadians and Americans. The issue surfaced when London proposed to send two scientists, Hans von Halban and Lew Kowarski, to Canada. Oliphant objected, explaining his position in a letter to Chadwick on 12 July 1940: "I am not at all happy about the question of whether Halban and Kowarski should be allowed to proceed to America. There is nothing more certain that if they go the American continent will know what is happening within a very short time."[42] Oliphant's reference to the "American continent" is significant in light of the fact that Canada was later to be the major site of the "Commonwealth" atomic effort. If Oliphant was assuming that Canada was going to be an accomplice with the United States, his warning was to be prophetic.

It was against this background that Oliphant informed the Australian government about MAUD.[43] Oliphant returned to Australia after Pearl Harbor to help with radar, and warned Prime Minister John Curtin about safeguarding the nation's uranium supplies. The government immediately reserved the control of uranium-bearing ores to the crown and commissioned a survey.[44] In early 1943, Oliphant returned to Britain, where he informed Chadwick that there was "considerable official interest" in Australia in atomic developments.[45]

It was at this stage that the Australians became actively interested in the development of a Tennessee Valley Authority (TVA) type scheme for Australia. The TVA, with its maze of hydroelectric stations in secure inland locations, was to host the first reactors in the Manhattan program. In May 1943, the minister for postwar reconstruction – and later prime minister – Ben Chifley, announced that the Labor government intended to "considerably extend" the policy of the previous government and decentralize munitions production. There would be "an orderly process of decentralisation in the postwar period" which would bring "a new prosperity" to country towns.[46] At that stage, Australia depended for its power on steam-generating units – all of which were within eighty kilometres of the seaboard.[47] A few months later, Evatt argued publicly that Australia would need "abundant power resources" after the war.[48]

These comments were made at the time of the Quebec Agreement, when the United States refused to share plutonium with Britain. In January 1944, at the time of the Anzac Agreement – in which Evatt formally embraced Empire defence[49] – the British team in Canada learned of the American plan to build their own heavy-water reactor, the Chicago Pile 3 (CP-3), which was the basis for the plutonium-producing reactors to be built at Hanford. The British government decided to abandon the Montreal project and develop its own program. Thereafter, there was a strong move by Canberra to become involved in the development of atomic energy. In February, the Australian government received a report from H.P. Moss, the Commonwealth government's controller of electricity, on the future of Australia's electricity supply. Moss noted the strategic importance of an inland site on the Snowy River, which watered a remote mountainous site to the southeast of Canberra, and emphasized that the scheme should be supplied with British power stations: "There is a danger should plant other than British be introduced this would lead ultimately to foreign manufacturers establishing technical and sales organisation to the detriment of Australian and United Kingdom manufacturers."[50]

In August 1944 planning for an inland TVA site was suggested when Evatt showed up in Albury to announce the setting up of a special regional planning committee to examine the potential of the Murray River Basin, to the west of the Great Dividing Range.[51] Evatt stressed that the Murray River Development should follow the TVA, where the US government had control of power development as well as minerals and industrialization. Significantly, the following month Anderson advised that the atom bomb project would be continued indefinitely, and that Australian uranium was essential for "Empire defence."[52] The same month Moss submitted a proposal for the diversion of the Snowy into the Murray.[53]

Within a year Evatt spelled out the precise link between the Snowy and atomic research when he wrote that Australia had a "lively interest in atomic energy" because of its "vast industrial potential" as well as "its military application." Evatt was most reluctant that Australia "enter the new field alone," but thought that Australia could contribute to a Commonwealth program with its thorium resources, scientists for collaborative research, "large open spaces and continually developing resources of hydroelectric power."[54]

The Snowy River Committee, set up in 1944, was from the beginning formulated in the context of major efforts to integrate Empire defence. One document that has recently come to light in the Snowy Mountain Authority archives records the view, in early 1946, that "the advent of uranium, thorium and allied substances as potential sources of power ... might be important factors in deciding the best uses of the Snowy River."[55]

The key to the future lay in British planning. As Oliphant told Evatt after Hiroshima, the Australians could not enter the new field without help. The point of entry was through cooperation with Britain, which, he said, could make the atomic bomb "whenever she had the courage to set to work." Britain had to be particularly careful, he went on, "not to be outstripped in the production of Bombs. We must take care to avoid becoming a lesser power."[56] The problem was, as Oliphant was aware, that the British at that stage still held out hopes for cooperation with the Americans and the Canadians.

Australia and the Canadian Atomic Program

Canada provided Australia with a model for its own atomic development. After all, the project in Canada had been conducted on behalf of the Empire. Furthermore, the location was ideal, since it had access to uranium ore and vast areas of comparatively uninhabited and secure territory.[57] Certainly there is no doubt that the Australian government was later encouraged by their scientific advisers to look to Canada as a possible model for its own atomic program. Oliphant had witnessed first-hand the importance of co-ordinating research between universities and laboratories while he had been in Montreal. There were two universities and various research institutes, but while McGill had a cyclotron, it was essential that scientists also have access to an experimental reactor, which was provided at Chalk River by the National Research Council.[58] The planned role of Chalk River in Canada, under Cockcroft, was to allow university staff from the Commonwealth to undertake advanced experiments in atomic research.[59] Later, following the first British atomic test at Monte Bello in 1952, Oliphant exhorted Australian scientists, "like those of Canada," not to be "discouraged from independent investigation" of atomic problems.[60]

Philip Baxter, then at the NSW University of Technology and later chair of the Australian Atomic Energy Commission (AAEC), said that Australia, "like Canada," should share in atomic development.[61] In a paper that he prepared for the Australian government, he held up Canada as a model: "Canada is a nation of comparable size and situation to Australia. It may be instructive to look at the whole atomic energy program more closely ... Today Chalk

River is a well equipped, largely self-contained, atomic energy research establishment which compares well with those in any other country."[62]

Ernest Titterton, later a leading Australian defence science adviser, also saw Canada as a possible model for Australia in his controversial book, *Facing the Atomic Future*, published in 1956. Titterton pointed to the Canadian Nuclear Research X-perimental (NRX) pile as "one of the most successful ever built," and stressed the value of its role in the production of plutonium – "a vital material for atomic weapons."[63] In fact, the Australian attraction to the Canadian model probably dated from the end of 1945, the moment that they received details about the organization at Chalk River. It may have even been earlier. Correspondence between the British Joint Services Mission in Washington – which was responsible for military liaison – and the Cabinet Office in October 1944 reveals that there was an Australian engineer at Chalk River, Eric Burhop, who had worked with Leslie Martin, the postwar head of the Australian Defence Science organization. Burhop was working on the bombardment of hydrogen obtained from heavy water, and was under pressure to return to the University of Melbourne.[64] The New Zealanders had a more substantial team at Chalk River: four scientists led by Dr. Watson-Munro. Spurred on by the knowledge that the New Zealand group was responsible for the design of a graphite-moderated pile, the Australians were interested in sending physicists to Canada.[65]

The head of the Council for Scientific and Industrial Research (CSIR), David Rivett, entered into an involved correspondence with his counterparts in Ottawa at the beginning of 1946, in an attempt to gain access for Australian scientists to Chalk River. Rivett made no secret of the fact that Australia wanted to build an atomic pile. The CSIR also sent a representative, Allan Whiffen, to speak to the Canadians in February 1946 about the possibilities of a large-scale reactor being constructed in Australia, but had received no encouragement.[66] There were others who displayed a strong interest in developments in Canada. The Scientific Research Liaison officer at the Australian high commission in Ottawa even attempted to secure samples of electronic equipment from Canada's National Research Council. Evatt's people in External Affairs were active in seeking Canadian help in training Australian scientists, and the Australian government sent a direct appeal to Ottawa for atomic cooperation.[67]

There were also attempts to secure direct military representation in strategic discussions held in Canada. On 19 September 1944 Sir John Lavarack – the chief of the Australian military mission in Washington and a key prewar figure in Australian plans to secure an autonomous munitions supply capability – went to the second Quebec Conference on instructions from Curtin. Churchill and Roosevelt confirmed at the conference that the control and use of atomic energy "should continue to be regarded as of the utmost secrecy." That apparently applied to Australia, since Lavarack, who had no official status, did not even have his presence formally announced by the government of Canada, a fact the press at the time put down to "an unfortunate inadvertence."[68]

Australia's atomic diplomacy at the end of the war was devoted to gaining entry into the nuclear club along the same lines as Canada. Mackenzie King attempted to defend Canada's privileged access at Quebec by claiming that his country was a "security power." Beyond that, he stressed that "our country has had some part in bringing about a harmony of sentiment between the United States and the whole British Commonwealth."[69] Churchill himself added to this self-promotion by the Canadians at Quebec by suggesting that they should sit with Britain on a future council of security powers.[70]

Predictably, Evatt reacted by claiming for Australia the same status as that enjoyed by Canada.[71] He complained that "care had been taken" to associate Canada with the UN commission to consider control of atomic energy, and argued that Australia should be accorded a similar role because of its association with the arrangements to provide for a peace treaty in Japan.[72]

His first consideration, however, was not international control of atomic weapons per se. On 13 November 1945, while Evatt was in Washington, the Australian foreign minister reacted strongly to a speech by the influential Republican Senator Stassen, who had proposed that the UN Security Council take control of about twenty five atomic bombs. Evatt told Stassen that Australia would be "threatened" by such an arrangement, emphasizing that "the only countries which would feel the effects of the devastation would be countries which are not members of the Security Council."[73] The Canadians, as Evatt was aware, were well placed to gain privileged entry into the Security Council. At the United Nations, the Canadian delegate on the Atomic Energy Commission, General McNaughton, advised his government that the scientific adviser to the Australian delegation, Herbert Briggs, resisted proposals to place reactors under United Nations Atomic Energy Commission (UNAEC) supervision and stressed the need for further consultations with Canada before Australia could entertain international control of atomic energy.

Ultimately, Australian representation on the Security Council came at the expense of Canada, a turn of events that Canada's diplomats bitterly resented. For Australia, this was a diplomatic victory, but it was hardly what Evatt had intended. His aim was to join Canada as part of the inner circle. Instead, he had to accept a two-year tenure on the Security Council and UNAEC. The Australian representative, James Plimsoll, suggested to Washington informally that "the retiring members should continue ... and thus their experience and knowledge would not be lost." The Americans, who opposed any Australian role other than as a supplier of uranium and thorium, "gave him no encouragement on this idea."[74]

The Canadians were aware of Evatt's policies toward the UN, especially over the question of wanting to "mediate" between the Americans and Soviets over atomic energy. In a "Top Secret" set of instructions for the Canadian representatives on the UNAEC on 7 June 1946, they were advised that, as chair of the UNAEC, Evatt would be likely to "assume a middle-power position" and repeat the performance already witnessed on the Security Council of keeping a close association with the French.[75] While the primary concern of both nations was to preserve the right to have a say in the future disposal of colonies, thereby putting the Americans on notice, it was also likely that Evatt shared French concerns to establish its credentials as a future security power. For the French, this was to lead to the celebrated atomic "force de frappe," and, of course, this brought in its wake the Pacific atomic tests that Labor governments in later ages would roundly condemn.

In any event, the Canadians were not supportive of Australia's requests. Their own atomic future was not going to be materially assisted by the entry of the Australians, who were asking essentially to duplicate Canada's function in the atomic set-up. In the long term, they were to learn in no uncertain terms of America's total opposition to assisting the Australians in carving out a niche in the atomic realm. Privately, the British also opposed a role for the Australians at Chalk River, and advised the Canadians to deflect the overtures. Mackenzie summed up the position to Chadwick in February 1946: "I can assure you that Cockcroft [then the head of Chalk River] has been very careful not to make any arrangements with the Australians and he definitely indicated to Whiffen [CSIR] that any arrangement would have to be negotiated directly with Canada ... I do not know at the moment how far the new arrangement between the United States, the United Kingdom and Canada would bear on the proposal that we receive an Australian team of scientists at our Chalk River plant."[76]

The preferred option, at the time that this letter was sent, was to find the basis for cooperation and agreement among the Quebec partners. That path, however, was uncertain. Britain had to keep its options open. Consequently, London did not entirely discount an Australian atomic program as a substitute for that in Canada.

Britain Gives a Lead: Australia As an Alternative Atomic Site, 1946-57

British defence planners realized that an integrated Commonwealth system was essential. Britain was, without question, "the acknowledged centre" of the Commonwealth, but it was also "the most vulnerable part." The joint planning staff therefore concluded that a Commonwealth-wide system would offset Britain's vulnerability. "It will therefore be necessary so to constitute the overall defence machinery that coordinated direction of the effort of all members can be undertaken from any main part of the Commonwealth." They recognized, however, that while dominions like Australia and South Africa were prepared to closely coordinate their defences with London,[77] the Canadians would not. It was, therefore, considered that the system of Empire Defence be "sufficiently flexible to allow for varying degrees" of cooperation.[78] The British had now identified two ways forward – with dominions like Australia, anxious for Commonwealth integration, and with Canada, whose terms of cooperation would necessarily have to take account of thinking in Washington. The two paths were not to be reconciled.

The British government, as a result, put forward proposals in early 1946 for a much more centrally coordinated system of Empire Defence, which was to be the basis of planning until 1957. The system would use the resources of the Empire to support Britain, the heart of the Empire. The Chiefs of Staff had concluded in early 1946 that, in the event of a "major war the United Kingdom could not be regarded as the sole base for the whole Commonwealth." In the atomic age the Commonwealth would have to act as a unit. The strategic conception for Commonwealth defence, argued the chiefs, was "the security of the United Kingdom, of the Dominions and the communications between them. The security of the United Kingdom was vital, but to limit our strategy to the local defence of this country would permit an enemy to concentrate his entire effort against us, without our being in a position to hit back."[79]

The loss of US assistance in 1946, following the passage of the McMahon Act, confirmed the wisdom and necessity for Britain to look to its Empire in an attempt to replicate the Manhattan Project. Southern Africa offered uranium and the potential for plutonium production, while Australia offered the additional advantage of atomic test sites. As for Australia's hopes of acquiring atomic weapons and technology, Oliphant advised that any attempt to develop atomic energy could only be done on an Empire basis. The undertaking was simply too vast for Britain to proceed alone. Australian defence authorities, from the outset impressed by the possibilities of atomic weapons for a country as underpopulated and exposed as Australia, also understood that any progress in the new field would need British help. At that period, the Australians – like their counterparts in the United States and Britain – were largely assuming that the atomic bomb was a weapon like any other.[80]

The problem was that Australia could not afford the huge costs of developing modern weapons. They therefore did "the next best thing," in the words of Andrew Ross, an historian on Australian defence supply, and prepared "the scientific and production facilities which could equip such forces properly, should war emerge eventually."[81] In June 1945 the Australian Defence Committee conducted a review of postwar policy regarding munitions production and concluded that it was necessary to secure a plan to coordinate production throughout the Commonwealth. In stark contrast to the Canadian position, the committee argued that "a satisfactory agreement along these lines would be of immense benefit to Australia, in common with other parts of the British Commonwealth, in that it would enable production to be maintained at a far higher level than would be the case if it were to be confined to what Australia might require."[82]

On 4 September 1945, Chifley cabled the Australian high commissioner in London, S.M. Bruce, with a request to ascertain Britain's attitude to Australian involvement in development work in the atomic field. He noted the wartime development of Mount Painter, the site in South Australia that had yielded modest amounts of uranium. He conceded that, while details of manufacturing processes could not be given to Australia "at present," the successful use of the bomb against Japan made Australia "most anxious to obtain sufficient information about the uses of uranium for defence and commercial purposes."[83]

The Australian appeals were rewarded. Attlee cabled Chifley on 17 October 1945 with the details of his correspondence with Truman, noting particularly that the production of plutonium would not enable commercial application without the simultaneous production of bomb-grade material. Attlee pointed to Britain's experience in the war when they had to shift industry to "less exposed parts of the island." This thinking also led to the argument to disperse facilities throughout the Empire.[84]

Attlee told the cabinet in February 1946 that it was the intention to continue in peace the "close and thorough full partnership" that had been established in the war in the "field of scientific and technical development, and in the production of munitions and supplies of all kinds."[85] That meant that Britain would assent to Australia's requests to allow scientists to go to Harwell to participate in atomic energy research.[86] But it was to be a two-way street. Chifley wanted Oliphant to return to Australia to advise on steps that could be taken to train scientists within Australia.[87] Formal cooperation on modern deterrent weapons began with a request of the British government in February 1946 for an area 1,600 kilometres long by 300 kilometres wide for trials of rockets and other ordnance. Woomera, in the deserts of South Australia, was to become for the next two decades the primary test site for Britain's rockets and was to be supplemented later by test sites for atomic weapons at Monte Bello, an island site off the West Australian coast and Maralinga, near Woomera. Chifley accepted the "Joint Project" subject to Australia having full access to information and being able to manufacture modern weapons at "a future date in accordance with the need to disperse manufacture through the Empire."[88]

The Defence Committee's "Strategic Appreciation of Australia," prepared for Chifley in February 1946, laid down the guiding principles of Australia's defence that were to serve as the main working policy for the next decade. Empire defence was to be the key: "One of the lessons of the war is that science can exercise a preponderant influence in the face of otherwise superior power – a fact demonstrated by the decisive effect of radar in the Battle of Britain. Superior scientific development can, if secrecy be preserved, redress the balance between a weak nation and a strong one and this is of profound significance to Australia ... There is thus a pressing need for the closest association between the Services and scientific research on the highest plane. Active collaboration with other nations of the British Commonwealth and especially the United Kingdom is essential." There were no doubts, however, about the immediate objectives of a program of atomic research. The defence planners concluded that "development of the use of atomic energy for war purposes may give rise to other applications. This cannot, however, be foreseen and it is therefore not taken into account in our consideration of this problem. Economic and financial implications of the use of atomic energy are not known."[89]

This thinking provides an important backdrop to the high-level British scientific mission, led by General Evetts, that was sent out in April. Evetts informed the Australian government that in the event of another war, Australia would have "full access" to the "secret manufacturing information should it decide to embark on producing the latest weaponry for its own use." Pointedly, Evetts was enthusiastically greeted by the premier of South Australia, Tom Playford, who saw the joint project as a major boost for the industrialization of his state.[90] Playford was also one of the most knowledgeable and ambitious Australian advocates of nuclear power, and proposed that a reactor be built to supply power to the Rocket Range.

Noel Brodribb, the controller general of munitions, had no doubt that the joint project would be the means by which Australia would acquire full knowledge of atomic research and development. This in turn would "without question put Australia in the very forefront of the most modern developments in defence science." Thus Australia would emulate the atomic role that Canada filled for the United States. The only difference was that Australia would reinforce Britain's atomic program.

The strategic partnership between Britain and Australia was forged at the 1946 prime ministers' conference in London.[91] Canadian opposition to a more centralized system of Commonwealth defence was overcome by the acceptance of a principle of regional defence, in which individual dominions were free to make their own arrangements. Australia was to take the lead in planning the defence of the Commonwealth in the Pacific – including the establishment of appropriate defence machinery – and was also to manufacture munitions as well as to develop resources for imperial and local defence. For their part, British delegates stressed that the development of heavy industry, munitions, and aircraft in the dominions was desirable given the vulnerability of the British Isles.[92] Each Commonwealth member was to accept responsibility for the development and defence of their "main support area" and "the strategic zone around it." Between the support areas, members of the Commonwealth were to defend lines of communication. This Commonwealth scheme confirmed a long-held belief in Australia that working with the UK in a reformed Commonwealth could reinforce Australia's efforts to become a more significant player in world affairs, a strategy that their Canadian colleagues did not employ. In stark contrast to Mackenzie King's refusal to become embroiled in Commonwealth defence plans, Henry Tizard, an adviser to the British government on the development of nuclear weapons, held up Commonwealth cooperation as an ideal "of how nations, while still retaining their own sovereignty, could yet set aside these boundaries and work together for the common good."[93] Dr. Solandt, the leader of the Canadian delegation, in good Canadian fashion opposed any "executive" coordination of defence science on a Commonwealth basis. Canada wanted an "advisory" committee only and wanted to be given the freedom of action to collaborate with the United States. He explained his hesitation in terms of the Canadian-American relationship, which put Canada "in a somewhat different position from the remainder of the Commonwealth in that she was a member of the Joint Defence Board which met to discuss the defence of North America ... the existence of the Board practically amounted to an alliance."

On the other hand, the leader of the Australian delegation, General Beavis, said that Australia intended to "devote every effort to making any coordination arrangements a success and to play the fullest part in Commonwealth Defence Research." Given Australia's small population and limited scientific resources, Australia wanted executive coordination of the Commonwealth Defence Science effort.[94] Australia had thus lined up with Britain in granting Tizard's objective – "the fullest cooperation ... and all that such cooperation implied." The path to Maralinga, the Blue Streak Rocket Tests, the production of modern jet bombers, and the Snowy Scheme had been identified at this time.

US Opposition to Imperial Defence

The period between 1946 and 1957 was one in which Washington unswervingly opposed a separate British atomic program and, with it, the possible development of projects in the dominions. As far as Britain and Canada were concerned, however, there could be some accommodation. The former had a crucial role to play in NATO, while the latter was already incorporated into the defence of the North American continent. There was, however, no question of extending such cooperation to other members of the

British Commonwealth. An incident in September 1944 foreshadowed this exclusive approach. Tizard then confided to Mackenzie King that while Commonwealth scientific liaison could be formalized, there was inadequate confidence and trust in the United States to warrant the continuation of a liaison office in Washington. It would only be seen by "the political minded American ... as a method of spying on American industry."[95]

Tizard was right to draw attention to US sensitivity. When the Americans heard from the Canadians about the Ottawa meetings of the Dominion Defence Scientific Liaison Staff, they demanded that they be stopped. Of particular concern was the transmission of technical information to the dominions via the British scientific mission in Washington. For their part, however, the British refused to "dissipate the Dominion enthusiasm for collaboration," but recognized that, in future, defence science talks would have to be held on an "informal" basis.[96]

This situation worsened after the war. As part of the reorganization of atomic research in 1947, the US interdepartmental State-War-Naval Coordinating Committee (SWNCC), on 11 February, considered reports on the disclosure of classified military information to Australia. The US Navy submitted that the release of top-secret information was not justified to Australia "by the probable benefit that will accrue to the US" – the standard criterion in assigning security clearances. Nor, in the Navy view, was the necessity for release borne out by the strategic importance of Australia: "Military interest clearly indicates the desirability of continuing the concept established in SWNCC 206/29, that UK and the British Dominions are to be considered as separate nations. The United States should not subscribe to the principle that UK-Dominion solidarity is to be fostered ... There are no overriding *military* reasons which necessitate release of Top Secret information to Australia/New Zealand."[97]

It was not knowledge of lax security that guided the SWNCC, but policy. The British Commonwealth was not a unit, and the respective members were to discuss matters with Washington bilaterally, an assumption underpinning a range of issues including trade, civil aviation, and regional defence, which other chapters in this volume examine.

The SWNCC was thus according Australia a low priority as the United States moved to establish the Marshall Plan, the Truman Doctrine, and the Joint Defense Board with Canada in the first half of 1947. US interests lay in North America and Europe. Australia had no standing in Washington's emerging global war strategy. Washington was, moreover, rejecting the very basis of the British Commonwealth program by treating the dominions as separate from Britain with respect to training and information. In mid-1948, matters came to a head when classified information was cut off from Australia, ostensibly because there were concerns about security. Yet despite the subsequent attempts by the Chifley and Menzies governments to tighten security, the United States maintained draconian restrictions on atomic information.[98]

In an attempt to get the Americans to relieve the sanctions, the secretary of the Department of Defence, Frederick Shedden, was dispatched abroad in 1949.[99] He was to be treated, however, not so much to lectures on problems of espionage but rather on Canberra's loyalties. He later complained of the anti-imperial sentiment in the United States, recording the remarks by Bernard Baruch that Australia would "do better" if it sold more raw materials to the United States and imported US as opposed to UK manufactured goods. Britain was, said Baruch, "a second-class power without the means to help Australia in the event of need." Shedden also had some interesting – indeed optimistic, from an Australian perspective – views on Canada. He noted that its proximity to the United States was responsible for its past failure to support Commonwealth initiatives, such as that of the conservative Australian prime minister, Joseph Lyons, in 1937 or the Labor prime minister, John Curtin, in 1944. The latter had embraced the notion of a Fourth Empire, as had Shedden himself, and he noted also that Chifley's notion of Empire dispersal in 1946 and subsequent Empire planning "provided some foundation similar to that in Western Europe." He was referring to the establishment of NATO, but the United States, he recorded, did not see that it was yet time for a NATO-type pact in Asia. Shedden therefore saw the solution to be one of "retaining unity" within the Commonwealth.[100]

A central issue at this juncture was the prospect of securing support for the development of nuclear reactors. Australian plans here dated from at least 7 May 1948, when the New Weapons and Equipment Development Committee considered the construction of a large atomic pile in Australia – because of problems in locating these in Britain – in order to produce plutonium for "a substantial number of atomic bombs."[101] South Africa had similar plans.[102]

The problem was that Washington would not share information outside the current nuclear club. It was, however, prepared to be more forthcoming with the Canadians in 1948, whose experimental pile was attracting positive interest from south of the border. Mackenzie indeed was bullish about further US investments in Canadian atomic facilities, and by August 1950 he was advised by the Atomic Energy Commission that if Ottawa wanted to construct a second reactor for military purposes, then Washington would buy plutonium from it.[103]

This was in stark contrast to the view of other Commonwealth members. Tizard himself saw the problem to be US policy on sharing information with "third nations," and that it was for that reason that the British had to "temporarily suspend" the training of scientists in British establishments. Nevertheless, he assured Chifley that dispersal was the best way to proceed: "Taking the long view, many of us are convinced that the responsibility for defence research and development must be gradually dispersed, and that it is of fundamental importance to the future of the British Commonwealth [and] that the scientific organisations of the Dominions should play an ever increasing part in the common problems of defence."[104]

In the wake of US action to restrict information to Britain and the dominions from 1946 to 1948, and with the promise of a change in relations with Washington following the Cold War and the institution of NATO, London did not lend great support to an imperial atomic program. Rather, its former associates in the Manhattan Project might yet provide the support needed, especially with respect to the production of plutonium. In February 1949 the British Technical Committee noted that the Canadians were considering the construction of a natural uranium, heavy-water-moderated reactor that would generate 100 megawatts. This reactor would require large amounts of cooling water, but in the future breeder reactors would operate at even higher temperatures. With their own plans to construct plutonium bombs, the British were, of course, very interested in developments in Canada. They were also prepared, however, to pursue their own program if necessary.[105]

It seems no coincidence then that on 23 February 1950 the Australian secretary of the Defence Department sent a note to his minister stressing the need to press on with work in atomic energy, in keeping with the plans of the previous Chifley government. In fact the Defence Research and Development Policy Committee reaffirmed Chifley's priorities – that is, that the final rate of production of fissionable material would depend on the amount of uranium. Consequently the committee recommended that the search for uranium be accelerated "as a matter of military importance."[106]

The Australians, however, had more than just uranium in mind. The Australian Defence Science adviser, Professor L.H. Martin, who had been in Britain from June to August 1950 to attend meetings of the Commonwealth Advisory Committee on Defence Science, stressed the need for Australia to participate to the fullest degree in work of "first-class" military importance to Britain and Australia. He noted the importance of guided weapons, but went on to argue that "considerable effort" had been expended in Britain to devise means of coping with atomic attack, and that important research had been done in Canada on the dispersal of industry and population. More than that, Canada was on the verge of launching a great collaborative program between Ontario Hydro and the Atomic Energy Authority. The Australians had indeed launched their own hydroelectric scheme in the Snowy Mountains, largely in the hope of replicating the Tennessee Valley Authority's role in the Manhattan Program, but the crucial step to reactor development required support.[107] The stumbling block for the Australians here, noted Martin, was that there was a "great need" for scientific intelligence, which had been cut off in 1948. To Martin, it was vital to restore the pooling of intelligence among those nations covered by the Joint Intelligence Bureau

(JIB) – essentially the dominions and the atomic club.[108] To strengthen this case, and to confirm Canberra's intentions with respect to nuclear weapons, he went on to argue that Australian planning was still based on the organization of "essential deterrent forces" by the United States, Western Europe, and the Commonwealth. Australia was, Martin reminded the committee, a "main support area" by virtue of its manpower, raw material, and industrial resources.[109]

The central question was whether Martin was suggesting the construction of atomic reactors in Australia along the lines of the third step identified by Chifley in 1946. There is reason to assume that, along with the two gas-cooled reactors to be built at Calder Hall, water-cooled reactors of the type planned in Canada would be built in the southern dominions. Just after the start of the Korean War, the British Joint War Production Committee concluded that production should be encouraged in Commonwealth countries "to the greatest practicable extent ... in the interests of strategic dispersal and of increasing the war potential of the Commonwealth."[110] On 18 July 1950, Allan Brown, the secretary of the Australian Prime Minister's Department, explained to the British Treasury that the "Australian Development Plan," which had been announced as a centrepiece of defence preparations, was designed to build industry and "mechanise rural areas with large projects of hydro-electrification." He emphasized the need to increase power production and the essential need for British capital. The Commonwealth-State Consultative Committee had been set up in July to ensure that in the event of war Australia would have at least a 40 percent reserve of electricity-generating capacity. The Snowy power stations would provide this.[111] In considering Australia's role in global war, Menzies, who was then in London, had discussed with Attlee the dispatch of RAAF Lincoln bombers to Malaya and a "long-term program of large-scale development" based on the Snowy which would provide great increases of power.[112]

Menzies was referring here to nuclear power. He made it clear to Attlee that Australia had 600 tons of recoverable uranium and that this could be used in a joint project with Britain. The problem was that, as Menzies had been advised by H.P. Breen, the secretary of the Department of Defence Production, "any further progress brought [Australia's] work into the 'Top Secret' class."[113] It was this that led Attlee to reject, at that point, the Australian request for cooperation, since Britain was bound by agreement with Canada and the United States not to disclose top-secret atomic information. What was crucial in Australian planning, however, was the British prime minister's rider that "we hope soon to receive American proposals for a change in the existing arrangements for collaboration which at present limit us rather narrowly."[114]

However, the Americans still refused to lift the ban on top-secret atomic data. In June 1951 the United States even refused to give Menzies the technology to refine uranium, despite the fact that a year earlier they had done this for Canada.[115] In fact, the prime minister's files reveal that from July 1952, the Australians had a close interest in the new Canadian Heavy Water Reactor (The National Research Universal – NRU) and its rate of plutonium production. Furthermore, the Canadians were assumed to be in a position to operate breeder reactors – the "ultimate source" of power – by 1965.[116] Indeed, the Canadians were on the verge of developing power from reactors built in conjunction with Ontario Hydro. They would start with a small demonstration reactor before proceeding to a large heavy-water reactor capable of producing 20 megawatts by 1958.

The British, however, were to be more forthcoming as a result of the first atomic tests conducted at Monte Bello. By the end of 1952 Britain was ready to test atomic bombs in the 8- to 10-kiloton range, and planned the deployment of ten "Blue Danubes" by 1955. Beyond that, it was clear that the great hydroelectric-atomic power project in Canada would proceed without material support form Britain. In any case, the Board of Trade noted that Canada had imported only $8.5 million worth of heavy electrical plant from Britain in 1954, as opposed to $32.3 million from the United States. Australia, on the other hand, had spent $1.7 million on US equipment as opposed to $19.9 million on British equipment. The comparable figures for South Africa were $1.9 million and $25.8 million.[117] In the words of the official committee on 20 April 1953, Britain "should aim at building up a Commonwealth effort in the industrial atomic energy field, based primarily on Australia and South Africans."[118]

In May 1953 Churchill finally wrote to Menzies, expressing his objection to the American exclusion of Australia from atomic technology and requesting "preferred customer" status with respect to uranium supplies. Australia would get the reactors. Menzies readily agreed to give access to uranium "outside US interference," with the proviso that Britain provide the "technical know-how" denied them since 1948.[119] Australia, as part of this joint project, would supply "uncommitted uranium resources that were surplus to their own requirements."[120] There were some who balked at the scale of Australian commitments at this point. The chief executive director of the Commonwealth Scientific and Industrial Research Organization (CSIRO), F.W.G. White, confided his concerns to Tizard in a confidential note sent in May 1953. "I doubt whether the atomic energy work can be pursued at anything like the level that the Canadians have achieved, but perhaps if we take it slowly it might grow into something reasonably worthwhile."[121] Achieving a similar status to Canada, however, had long been Canberra's ambition, and it overrode more practical reservations.

In January 1954, the British cabinet decided to offer Australia and South Africa[122] technical information on reactor technology in exchange for uranium and possibly plutonium in the future.[123] The paymaster general advised the cabinet that Britain's external policy be adjusted in atomic energy matters. He noted that the restrictive policies of the United States, especially since 1948, had made effective cooperation impossible, but that it was now time to take a "stiffer line" with the United States. Cherwell added that the Australians may well give the British preference over the United States: "There will be direct advantages in having Australian atomic energy developments based on UK equipment and methods. In the next generation or two atomic energy is likely to become an important, if not the main, source of electric power. From the broad economic, political and defence points of view we ought therefore to do what we can to link up Australia closely with ourselves."[124]

In February Menzies signalled his enthusiasm for the offer of technical information and added that Australia would "work on [a] common basis of security in regard to classified information" and would open discussions on this in London and Washington.[125] In March the Australians secured an exchange of notes with Britain that would allow scientists to work in British atomic establishments "with a view to subsequent possible operation in Australia." Specifically, Menzies wanted Australia to draw on British work on plutonium, heavy water, and fission products. Beyond that, the recently established AAEC should have the opportunity to consult with British scientific and technical experts about the possible use of the Snowy Mountains hydroelectric power to operate a diffusion plant to produce enriched fuel elements. They would also want to discuss plans for producing heavy water there, as well as in New Zealand.[126]

The minister of supply, Howard Beale, planned that – in the short term – Australia should build a small material-testing reactor to train industrial and university personnel. The sum of £500,000 was to be set aside by 1957 for erecting and equipping the laboratories, while £1,000,000 would be spent on operating costs.[127] Beale clearly believed that Canberra was about to embark immediately on a major nuclear program. The problem, as he saw it, was to ensure that, when Australia reached the stage of large-scale production of power and plutonium, the division of responsibility would be based on the states' needs for nuclear power, while the Commonwealth would retain control of the reactor "to produce plutonium for military purposes." The Snowy reactor would be built by Australian engineers, who could study the production of plutonium at Windscale, chemical separation techniques at Springfields, the diffusion plant at Capenhurst, production techniques at Risely, and the site for the fast plutonium breeder reactor at Dounreay.[128]

But the scheme came to nothing. Following the Suez Crisis in 1956, and the much larger crisis over controlling the proliferation of nuclear weapons, the United States resurrected the wartime atomic relationship with Britain at Bermuda in March 1957. Britain agreed to gradually phase out the essentials of its independent deterrent program in return for assistance from the United States. Testing would be done in Nevada or the Pacific nuclear test sites and the British armed forces given their own supply of US-made nuclear weapons. Also in March 1957, Britain gained access to Canadian ores after concluding an agreement with Eldorado Mines. Canada itself moved into a much closer partnership with the United States and was to obtain a range of nuclear weapons to allow it to provide for its own northern defences, as well as to participate in NATO.[129]

Given these developments, the role of Australia could only diminish. The atomic bomb sites at Maralinga and Monte Bello were not needed after 1957, while the rockets that were to carry nuclear warheads from Woomera were cancelled in 1960. Atomic research was also considerably restricted after 1957 and Australia left only with the Lucas Heights experimental reactor in Sydney. Ironically, the Canadians were invited to give advice to Australia in 1958 and detailed the development there of "one of the world's great electric power grids." All that the defence adviser could suggest was for Australia to launch a full nuclear power program "in the last quarter of this century."[130] In the meantime the commitment of US forces to Asia and the construction of some of their most secret satellite ground stations on Australian soil gave Australia what Canada had long taken for granted – the US nuclear umbrella.

Conclusion

Canada had a distinct advantage over Australia when it came to influencing the major Anglo-Saxon allies – its geographic location. It was not so much that it was a "middle power," but that it was able to gain privileged access to Washington from the moment the Second World War broke out. Australia, on the other hand, would have readily accepted an arrangement of the type extended to Canada, but all diplomatic attempts to secure this after 1943 failed. The ANZAC Pact was ignored by Washington and later the imperial Australia, New Zealand, and Malaya (ANZAM) defence scheme, which accorded Australia great significance in global war planning, was seen as a "white man's club." Canada, by contrast, was given a major role in US containment strategy and the possibility was held out that NATO allies would have access to nuclear weapons. Moreover, Canada was protected by the US nuclear umbrella. Australia, however, could only secure a weak commitment through the Australia, New Zealand, and United States security pact (ANZUS), and at no time before 1957 was it given assurances about nuclear weapons – despite the Maralinga tests. Indeed, the restoration of the Atlantic Alliance at Bermuda in March 1957 merely confirmed that it had been left out of the nuclear-weapons club and that Britain and Canada were to be accorded special status by virtue of their crucial locations in

American global strategy. In the end, the whole gamble to acquire nuclear weapons from that late war period to 1957 was taken by Canberra not because of its potential to join the special relationship, but because it could act as a substitute for Canada. The atomic program was given impetus by the US ban on atomic sharing with Britain after the McMahon Act of 1946. The Bermuda Conference in 1957 ended it. Australia would have to find alternative ways to become the great middle power it aspired to be.

Notes

1 Norman Hillmer and J.L. Granatstein, *Empire to Umpire: Canada and the World to the 1990s* (Toronto: Copp Clark Longman, 1994), 217.
2 Evatt to Glasgow, cable 143, 24 August 1943, Australian Archives (hereinafter AA), series A3300, item 234.
3 Gessner G. Hawley, *Atomic Energy in War and Peace* (New York: Reinhold Publishing, 1945), 202.
4 Bertrand Goldschmidt, *Atomic Rivals* (New Brunswick, NJ: Rutgers University Press, 1990), 191. Goldschmidt played a seminal role in the Canadian project and later the French nuclear program. To Cherwell, it was a question of Britain's "birthright" to develop atomic energy after the war. R.V. Jones, *Most Secret War: British Scientific Intelligence, 1939-45* (London: Hodder and Stoughton, 1978), 593.
5 Robert Bothwell, *Nucleus: The History of Atomic Energy of Canada Limited* (Toronto: University of Toronto Press, 1988), 47; Goldschmidt, *Atomic Rivals*, 198.
6 It is little wonder that Gowing stresses that "gaseous diffusion" was the "pride and joy of the British atomic project." Margaret Gowing, *Britain and Atomic Energy, 1939-1945* (London: Macmillan, 1964), 250.
7 Goldschmidt, *Atomic Rivals*, 195.
8 Gowing, *Britain and Atomic Energy*, 333.
9 Brian Cathcart, *Tests of Greatness: Britain's Struggle for the Atomic Bomb* (London: John Murray, 1994), 11.
10 Entry 20 June 1945, National Archives of Canada (hereinafter NAC), Chalmers Jack Mackenzie Papers, MG30, B122, vol. 2, Diary no. 19.
11 "Imperial Cooperation in Defence," 12 October 1945, Public Records Office, London, UK (hereinafter PRO), CAB 127, 38, COS(45)614(0).
12 Hillmer and Granatstein, *Empire to Umpire*, ch. 5.
13 The Americans had tied up Canadian uranium and heavy water through a system of commercial companies used as false fronts. The contracts were so carefully and secretly drawn up that C.D. Howe, Canada's powerful minister of munitions and supply, was unable to find out the provisions of the contracts. Reginald Whitaker and Gary Marcuse, *Cold War Canada: The Making of a National Insecurity State, 1945-1957* (Toronto: University of Toronto Press, 1994), 43-4.
14 Robert Bothwell, *Eldorado: Canada's National Uranium Company* (Toronto: University of Toronto Press, 1994).
15 "Post-War Defence Committee: Cooperation with the Dominions on Defence Matters," 22 October 1945, PRO, CAB 127, 38, PWD(45)2.
16 Dean Acheson, "Memorandum by the Acting Secretary of State to President Truman, 1 October 1946," *Foreign Relations of the United States* (hereinafter FRUS), 1946, vol. 5, *The British Commonwealth, Western and Central Europe* (Washington, DC: State Department, 1969), 56.
17 Entry 13 and 15 November 1945, NAC, Chalmers Jack Mackenzie Papers, MG30, B122, vol. 2, Diary no. 21.
18 Bothwell, *Nucleus*, 34-8.
19 Goldschmidt, *Atomic Rivals*, 254.

20 Bothwell, *Nucleus*, 53.
21 Ibid., 68.
22 British delegates concluded that Canada was "anxious to retain a somewhat independent attitude in view of her position on the American continent and her relationship with the USA." Conclusion, Chiefs of Staff Committee, 31 March 1944, PRO, CAB 21, 851, COS(44)58.
23 Unnumbered cable, British High Commission, Ottawa, to Machtig, 10 November 1945, PRO, DO35, 1746. Certainly Canada's first preference was to continue to host the Commonwealth's atomic effort, as the Department of External Affairs optimistically claimed in October 1945: "The Canadian development is the only one in the British Empire." This assessment drew particular comfort from the fact that the "acceptance" of British personnel into American plants during the war "was largely made possible by the existence of our plant in Canada."
24 "Unification of US Armed Forces," 10 January 1946, PRO, CAB 127, 38, PWD(46)2.
25 *FRUS*, 1946, 5:59.
26 *FRUS*, 1946, 5:54.
27 Air Marshal Robert Leckie to Air Marshal A.M. Tedder, 14 February 1946, PRO, AIR 8, 1417.
28 James Gormly, "The Washington Declaration and the 'Poor Relation': Anglo-American Atomic Diplomacy, 1945-46," *Diplomatic History* 8, 2 (1984): 133.
29 Bothwell, *Nucleus*, 111.
30 Conclusion, Post-War Defence Committee, 10 January 1946, PRO, CAB 127, 38, PWD (46)2.
31 "Atomic Energy-International Control," Princeton University, Lilienthal Papers, box 112, 1946 Correspondence: Main Files.
32 Mackenzie complained to Chadwick that the Americans were able to offer salaries that, by Canadian standards, were "fantastically absurd." Mackenzie to Chadwick, 12 February 1946, NAC, Chalmers Jack Mackenzie Papers, MG30, B122, vol. 2.
33 Cathcart, *Tests of Greatness*, ch. 2.
34 "Atomic Energy: Eldorado Mining and Refining," NAC, C.D. Howe Papers, MG27 III B20, vol. 5.
35 Kenneth W. Condit, *History of the Joint Chiefs of Staff*, vol. 6, *The Joint Chiefs of Staff and National Security Policy, 1955-1956* (Washington, DC: Joint Chiefs of Staff, 1992), 297. This was the context for the Baruch plan that, according to the USJSSC, provided the United States with "the maximum international security." "Non Proliferation Policy," 14 July 1947, National Archives and Records Administration (hereinafter NARA), RG128, USJSSC.
36 Cabinet Committees-Defence Committee (Meetings, Minutes, Agenda) – 1945-1947, NAC, RG2, series B-2, vol. 60, file C, 10, 9, M.
37 Cabinet Defence Committee, 12 August 1947, ibid.
38 Mackenzie to undersecretary of state for external affairs, 4 October 1946, NAC, Chalmers Jack Mackenzie Papers, MG30, B122, vol. 2, C, 10, 9, M. The Atomic Energy Committee concluded, in September 1946, that relying on Canada would delay the program in Britain. Minutes of 1st meeting, Atomic Energy Committee, 25 September 1946, Churchill College, Cambridge, Cockcroft Papers, CHAD 4, 10, 44, AE(0)(46).
39 1st meeting, British Defence Committee, 1 January 1947, PRO, CAB 131, 5, DO(47).
40 Note on file, 5 February 1948, and cable 87, High Commission, Ottawa to CRO, "USA-North American Defence," 28 January 1948, PRO, FO 371, 356.
41 Richard Rhodes, *The Making of the Atomic Bomb* (New York: Simon and Schuster, 1986).
42 Oliphant to Chadwick, 12 July 1940, Churchill College, Cambridge, Cockcroft Papers, CHAD 1, box 19, 3.
43 Stewart Cockburn and David Ellyard, *Oliphant: The Life and Times of Sir Mark Oliphant* (Sydney: Axiom, 1981), 112-13.
44 Alice Cawte, *Atomic Australia, 1944-1990* (Sydney: New South Wales University Press, 1992), 3.
45 Oliphant to Chadwick, 10 March 1943, Churchill College, Cambridge, Cockcroft Papers, CHAD 1, box 19, 3.
46 "Statements on the Snowy Mountains Authority," May 1943, AA, series A2618, 1, folder 57.

47 The Australian government also attempted to organize electrical power on a national basis for purposes of defence during the war. State electricity authorities put into effect plans to protect their electricity supplies after the Munich crisis of 1938. In 1942, when the immense importance of electricity to the munitions industry was belatedly recognized by the Curtin government, electricity supply organizations were protected under the National Security Act. These units provided 89 percent of Australia's 1,718,926 kilowatts, and were clustered around east coast ports and coal supplies. David Mellor, *The Role of Science and Industry* (Canberra: Australian Government Publishing Service, 1958), 217-18.

48 Report, *The Argus* (Melbourne), 2 August 1943.

49 Wayne Reynolds, "H.V. Evatt: The Imperial Connection and the Quest for Australian Security, 1941-1945," (PhD diss., University of Newcastle, Australia, 1985), ch. 4.

50 Reports on "Future Supply of Australian Electricity," February 1944, AA, series A2618, 1, items 1001-35. Moss had been aware of the attraction of British capital to any Australian projects to develop hydroelectricity from the days when he was the Chief Electrical Engineer for the NSW government. In April 1935 he lamented that he was unaware of any Australian government interest in such programs. AA, series A659, 1, item 41, 1, 64.

51 Lionel Wigmore, *Struggle for the Snowy* (Oxford: Oxford University Press, 1968), 19. The ultimate objective was to create two large inland cities with a population of about one million people. Brad Collis, *Snowy: The Making of Modern Australia* (Rydalmere: Hodder and Stoughton, 1990), 38. The immediate intention, however, was to locate the power and munitions industries in a safe inland location. Much of the urban development would have followed.

52 Cawte, *Atomic Australia*, 5.

53 H.P. Moss, "History of Investigations into the Snowy," AA, series A2618, 1, items 2165-200.

54 Letter, 14 October 1945, PRO, PREM 8, item 112.

55 Evatt to Attlee, 14 October 1945, AA, series A2618, 1, document 2165, Snowy River.

56 Report, *Sydney Morning Herald*, 17 October 1945, 1.

57 Hawley, *Atomic Energy in War and Peace*, 202.

58 Bothwell, *Nucleus*, 27, 122.

59 Ibid., 122.

60 He was not prepared, however, to mount as large a program as the Canadians were then envisaging. In July he had conceded that the Canadians were in a much stronger position and that Australia would have to "specialize," albeit with the ultimate intention of moving fully into the field "using highly enriched uranium." Entry 16 July 1952, NAC, Chalmers Jack Mackenzie Papers, MG30, B122 vol. 2, Diary no. 33.

61 US Embassy, Canberra, to Department of State, 2 September 1952, NARA, RG59, box 5923, despatch 131. On Baxter's importance in the Australian Atomic Energy program, see S.J. Angyal, "Sir Philip Baxter, 1905-1989," *Historical Records of Australian Science* 8, 3, (1991): 23-4.

62 Professor J.P. Baxter, "Some Observations on the Development of Atomic Power in the World and in Australia," n.d., AA, series A1067, 1, A46, 2, 3, 14.

63 E.W. Titterton, *Facing the Atomic Future*, (London: Macmillan, 1956), 36-7, 131.

64 British Joint Staff Mission, Washington, to Cabinet Office, London, 25 October 1944, Churchill College, Cambridge, Cockcroft Papers, CKFT 25, 8; "Atomic Energy-Research and Production" [1945], AA, series A5954, 1, item 2162, 1.

65 Oliver Franks to Cockcroft, 2 January 1946, Churchill College, Cambridge, Cockcroft Papers, CKFT 25, 8. The New Zealanders, like the Australians, were keen to use the experience to establish a reactor – apparently to be moderated by heavy water – in their own country after the war.

66 Miscellaneous Atomic Energy Papers, Churchill College, Cambridge, Cockcroft Papers, CKFT 25, 8, file 55.

67 Minutes of the [Canadian] Atomic Energy Advisory Panel, 11 June 1946, NAC, C.D. Howe Papers, MG27 III B20, vol. 10; "Correspondence relating to atomic energy, July 1942-December 1945," NAC, Chalmers Jack Mackenzie Papers, MG30 B122, vol. 5.

68 Rhodes, *The Making of the Atomic Bomb*, 537.

69 Nicholas N. Mansergh, ed., *Documents and Speeches on Commonwealth Affairs,* vol. 1 (London: HMSO, 1953), 589.

70 Cabinet Agenda, 21 August 1943, PRO, CAB 66, 40, WP(43)394. The idea was later watered down to the proposal that Canada would have "first claim" to represent the Commonwealth after Britain on the Security Council. Postwar Planning Paper, 6 March 1945, PRO, CAB 122, 605, APW(45)41.

71 Much has been made of Evatt's internationalism and his strong commitment to the United Nations as the means to secure the rights of small powers. This remains an article of faith still for the party faithful. In the words of Ross McMullin, the author of the Australian Labor Party's *The Light on the Hill* (Oxford: Oxford University Press, 1990), published to celebrate its centenary in 1991, Evatt was "a crusading figure on the international stage." What Evatt really wanted, however, was Australia's entry into the ranks of the security powers. In his celebrated work, "Risks of a Big Power Peace" in January 1946, he attacked the great powers not as a representative of the small powers, but for not acknowledging Australia's record "of active and sustained belligerency."

72 Evatt to Makin, cable E66, 9 December 1945, AA, series A1066, H45, 1016, 5, 2.

73 Ken Buckley, Barbara Dale, and Wayne Reynolds, *Doc Evatt: Patriot, Internationalist, Fighter and Scholar* (Sydney: Longmans, 1994), 316.

74 Conversation with Plimsoll, 18 November 1947, NARA, RG84, box 68, file: "Mission to UN Files-Atomic Energy"; "Attitude of Various Delegations in the UNAEC Negotiations," November 1947, NARA, RG84, box 75.

75 Evatt kept very close diplomatically with the French after 1944, possibly even to the extent of orchestrating the timing of the 1944 Australia-New Zealand Agreement with that of the French Conference at Brazzaville. Buckley et al., *Doc Evatt,* 236-7.

76 Mackenzie to Chadwick, 5 February 1946, NAC, Chalmers Jack Mackenzie Papers, MG30, B122, vol. 2.

77 It was at this point that Attlee sent Chifley the details of Britain's wartime vulnerability and stressed the need to disperse industry. He also stressed that "the harnessing of atomic energy as a source of power cannot be achieved without the simultaneous production of material capable of being used in a bomb." Attlee to Chifley, 17 October 1945, AA, series A5954, 1, item 1382, cable 411.

78 "Post-War Organisation for Defence," 24 November 1945, PRO, CAB 127, 38, JP(45)274(Final).

79 22nd meeting, Cabinet Defence Committee, 19 July 1946, PRO, CAB 131/5, DO(46).

80 Wayne Reynolds, "Rethinking the Joint Project: Australia's Bid for the Atomic Bomb 1945-60," *The Historical Journal* (Cambridge) 41, 3 (1998): 853-73.

81 Andrew Ross, "The Arming of Australia: The Politics and Administration of Australia's Self Containment Strategy for Munitions Supply 1901-1945" (PhD diss., Australian Defence Force Academy, Canberra, 1986), 2.

82 "Strategic Deployment throughout the British Empire of Capacity for the Production of Military Requirements," 7 June 1945, AA, series A2031, Defence Committee Minutes no. 219, 1945.

83 Chifley to Bruce, 4 September 1945, AA, series A461, 2, cable 211, item C373, 1, 4, (ii).

84 Attlee to Chifley, 17 October 1945, AA, series A5954, 1, item 1382, cable 411.

85 Cabinet conclusion, 15 February 1946, PRO, CP(46)65. This was endorsed in CM(46)16th conclusions on 18 February 1946, PRO, CAB 129, 7.

86 "Atomic Energy History," Churchill College, Cambridge, Cockcroft Papers, CKFT 25, 8, file 55.

87 Chifley to Attlee, 4 March 1946, PRO, PREM 8, 371.

88 "Establishment of a Guided Projectiles Range and Associated Technical and Industrial Facilities in Australia," Submission 1186, 3 July 1946, AA, series A2700, vol. 27.

89 Defence Committee Report, "Strategic Appreciation of Australia," February 1946, AA, series A5954, 1, item 1662, 4.

90 Peter Morton, *Fire across the Desert: Woomera and the Anglo-Australian Joint Project, 1946-1980* (Canberra: Australian Government Publishing Service, 1989), 14.

91 The briefing paper on defence and security that Sheddon put together for Chifley noted that there had been greatly expanded cooperation between Australia and Britain during the war and that this was going to increase. The section on the formation of the Joint Intelligence Bureau (JIB) has been removed from the Archives file, but it is clear that a mission from Britain to Australia prior to the 1946 Commonwealth Conference had launched significant initiatives here. Intelligence links were to be strengthened, and a Joint Intelligence Bureau was under consideration. Defence science machinery was developed on British lines and a New Weapons and Equipment Development Committee established to chart the new technology. "British Commonwealth Conference 1946: Defence and Security-Outline for Prime Ministers' Use," February 1946, AA, series A5954, 1, item 1662, 1.

92 Report, "Australian Post-War Defence Policy," 23 December 1946, AA, Papers of Sir Frederick Shedden, series A5954, 1, item 1634, 6.

93 Informal Commonwealth Conference on Defence Science (hereinafter ICCDS), 1st meeting, 3 June 1946, PRO, DO 35, 1759.

94 ICCDS, 3rd meeting, 4 June 1946, ibid.

95 Henry Tizard, "Empire Cooperation in Scientific Matters, 1944-1945," Imperial War Museum, London, Tizard Papers, HTT 399.

96 Ibid. It was at this juncture that Chadwick wrote to White, advising that Australia could not be brought into the atomic project "at the present time." The British government "could not act alone in this matter." Chadwick to White, 29 December 1944, Churchill College, Cambridge, Cockcroft Papers, CKFT 25, 8, file 55.

97 Report, State, War, Navy Coordinating Committee, 11 February 1947, NARA, RG59, box 24, SWNCC 206, 29.

98 R. Aldrich and M. Coleman, "The Cold War, the JIC and British Signals Intelligence in 1948," *Intelligence and National Security* 4, 3, (1989): 540-1.

99 130th meeting, COS(49), 7 September 1949, PRO, DEFE 4, 24.

100 "Some General Impressions from a Visit Abroad, 1949," AA, series A5954, 1, item 1687, 15.

101 "Proposed Construction of an Atomic Pile in Australia," May 1948, AA, series A5954, 1, item 1385, 3, 9.

102 Wayne Reynolds, "Planning the Defence of World War III: The Post-War British Empire and the Role of Australia and South Africa, 1943-1957," *Historia* 4, 1 (1998): 72-90.

103 Bothwell, *Nucleus*, 139-43.

104 White to Tizard, 22 December 1948, Imperial War Museum, London, Tizard Papers, HTT 477.

105 Atomic Energy Technical Committee, 9 February 1949, Churchill College, Cambridge, Cockcroft Papers, CHAD 1, box 9, 2 and box 9, 3.

106 Note by secretary of Defence, 23 February 1950, AA, series A816, 1, item 3, 301, 470.

107 Wayne Reynolds, "Atomic War, Empire Strategic Dispersal and the Origins of the Snowy Mountains Scheme," in *War and Society* 14, 1, (1996): 121-44.

108 Note to secretary from Defence Science Adviser, 26 September 1950, AA, series A816, 56, item 11, 301, 746.

109 Council of Defence Agenda 2, 1950, and 3, 1950, PRO, DEFE 11, 325; Meeting with Menzies, 14 July 1950, ibid.

110 "Ability of the Armed Forces to Meet an Emergency," 21 July 1950, PRO, DO(50)58; "Provision of Equipment of Commonwealth Forces," 18 June 1951, PRO, CAB 131, 11, DO(51)72(Revise).

111 Allan Brown, "The Snowy Scheme and National Defence," 18 July 1950, AA, series A2618, 1, item 3063.

112 1st meeting, Cabinet Committee, 14 July 1950, PRO, PREM 8, item 1148, Gen 329. There were parallel developments in Southern Africa, where Britain was moving toward a great scheme of a Central African Federation built around the Kariba and Kafue Schemes that would see the irrigation of 400,000 acres and the provision of power for the copper belt by 1953. PRO, DO35, item 5704.

113 Breen to Menzies, 7 June 1951, AA, series A1209, 23, item 57, 4723, part 1.

114   Attlee to Menzies, 7 April 1950, AA, series A1209, 23, item 57, 4723, part 1, cable 64.
115   Bothwell, *Eldorado*, 343. In September 1951 the McMahon Act was specifically amended to enable Eldorado to build its refinery plant at Port Hope with the cooperation of the Catalytic Construction Company of Philadelphia. The timing was interesting in that Menzies then wanted access to NATO, which the United States refused; in August 1952, the United States also rejected the Australian proposal that ANZUS planners have access to the Joint Chiefs of Staff in Washington, where strategic direction was exercised. The ANZUS powers would be given access to CINCPAC in Hawaii only – the centre for the tactical control of the Pacific. ANZUS Council Meeting, 10 August 1952, PRO, DEFE 11, 56.
116   AA, series A1209, 23, item 57, 4723, part 2.
117   "Overseas Trade Memorandum 9, 56," 10 February 1956, PRO, EG 1, 64. All figures in US dollars.
118   20 April 1953, Nuffield College, Oxford, Cherwell Papers, box J.138.
119   Comments on cable 359, CRO to Canberra, 22 May 1953 by Cherwell for Churchill, Nuffield College, Oxford, Cherwell Papers, box J.123; Official Committee on Defence Science (Atomic Energy), PRO, EG1, 40.
120   "Draft Notes for Bermuda Conference," 19 November 1953, PRO, EG1, 40.
121   White to Tizard, 14 May 1953, Imperial War Museum, London, Tizard Papers, HTT 492. On 30 December 1953 these sentiments were echoed in a letter to Tizard from Ian Clunies Ross from the CSIRO, when he expressed his "very mixed feelings" about Australia's involvement in atomic energy when "there are so many other things to do."
122   CRO to British High Commission, Pretoria, 2 June 1954, PRO, EG1, 126, cable 205. The CRO cabled its assent to Pretoria of cooperation as part of a "wider Commonwealth" program. During the rest of 1954, the British balanced the approach to Australia and South Africa, ensuring the dominions would not get out of step on uranium prices or on the promises of reactor technology. On 15 September, A.W. Snelling in Pretoria sent word to the CRO that the Union was looking at some "hush hush" deposits and was anxious that the CDA did not hear about them, since they would be lost to the Union and the UK for industrial purposes. At that juncture, the Union was tied up with the CDA until 1964 for all uranium. Snelling (UKHC Pretoria) to Sir Saville Garner (CRO), 15 September 1954, PRO, EG1, 126.
123   Cabinet conclusion, 11 February 1954, PRO, CAB 129, 66, C(54)52.
124   Cabinet conclusion, 9 January 1954, PRO, CAB 128, 26, part 1, C(54)7.
125   Cabinet conclusion, 12 February 1954, PRO, EG1, 73, INT, 22, part 2.
126   E.J. Bunting to Sir Edwin Plowden, 30 March 1954, PRO, EG1, 73.
127   Committee on Atomic Energy (International Relations), Notes of Meeting, 16 August 1954, PRO, EG1, 73.
128   Submission 117 and attachments to Cabinet by Howard H. Beale, Minister of Supply, 20 September 1954, AA, series A4906, XM1, vol. 5.
129   John Clearwater, *Canadian Nuclear Weapons: The Untold Story of Canada's Cold War Arsenal*: (Toronto: Dundurn, 1998).
130   *Australian Atomic Energy Symposium: AGPS* (Sydney: Australian Government Publishing Service, 1958).

7

Governments and Defectors: Responses to the Defections of Gouzenko in Canada and Petrov in Australia

Frank Cain

The defection of Igor Gouzenko in Canada in 1945 and of Vladimir Petrov in Australia nearly a decade later, in 1954, had significant impacts on the histories of the two countries. The Cold War tensions in both nations were heightened by the events, and non-left political forces were boosted in the aftermath. The defectors were both portrayed as seeking the freedoms and liberty offered by the democratic West. Each wrote a book on his experiences (or had it ghost written), and Gouzenko had a Hollywood film version made of his. Both men were lowly operators in the Soviet intelligence system, but they were portrayed as leading players; Gouzenko's defection, it was said, "marked the start of the Cold War."[1] Petrov's defection was assessed by local writers as being of genuine importance, and he was described as a Soviet official more knowledgeable than he was ever to reveal.[2] These defections were perceived at the time as representing unexpected intelligence victories against the USSR. The anti-Soviet phobia of the 1930s was renewed against the background of widening divisions that marked the early stages of the Cold War. In Australia the Menzies government was facing defeat, but the significant timing of Petrov's defection helped turn the electoral tide and returned it to office. With the conclusion of the Cold War and the flood of new material from both sides, it is now possible to add new dimensions to these two defections. In both Canada and Australia, it is now clear, US intelligence agencies played a considerable role. American monitoring of the Soviet diplomatic cable traffic provided a more comprehensive picture of Soviet operations in Canada and Australia than was made public at the time. It is also possible, although the jury is still out, that American agents were more involved in the defections than has been suspected.

The most valuable archival material for reassessing Gouzenko and Petrov are the documents known as the Venona papers, released by the National Security Agency (NSA) in the United States in 1996. They reveal the worldwide operations of the US Army in collecting and decoding Soviet cable and wireless messages flowing between Moscow and the various Soviet embassies and consulates throughout the world. The operation commenced in 1939 and signalled the depth of US fears about radical and revolutionary movements and international trade union organizations that American officialdom saw reflected in the functioning of the new Soviet Union. In 1943 the army applied more resources to this program at its main signals intelligence (sigint) base at Arlington Hall outside Washington, DC. The Soviet code was based on a code book and a decoding book with add-on random numbers taken from a one-time pad. The NSA inherited this operation from the army at the end of the war, when it also took over the huge US sigint operation that had emerged by the war's end, and which it currently maintains.

What is of interest for this chapter is that the Venona papers demonstrate how these US intelligence experts watched the unfolding of events in Canada and Australia following the establishment of Soviet embassies in those two countries early in the 1940s. Cables relating to commercial and military matters were decoded, as well as the activities of the military intelligence body, the GRU, and the principal political surveillance body, the KGB.[3] The decoded cables for Australia revealed the connections between the local Communist party officials and the Soviet officials in Canberra, and the Canadian cables mention a Canadian informer code-named "Green" (who has still not been identified). They also reveal that Soviet officials in Ottawa paid particular attention to cultivating friendly relations with Canadian military officers; understandable given the wartime alliance but, given the way in which the Soviets tended to operate, perhaps also an attempt to find friends for a rainier day. Nevertheless, the Australian government knew nothing of these US decodings, and it is unlikely that the Canadian government was informed either. Both governments were in the curious position of having the Soviet officials accredited to their governments and their local communists placed under remote US surveillance. Not only did the two governments remain uninformed about the collecting process, but more importantly, they were unaware of the use the Americans would make of the material they collected.

Another important new source for the Gouzenko and Petrov defections affairs are the papers released by the Federal Bureau of Investigation (FBI). These relate to the wide surveillance, late in the 1930s, maintained by the FBI on American communists (both at home and abroad) and the Soviet officials who were working in the new Soviet embassy and consulates established following the diplomatic recognition of the USSR by the United States in 1933. These documents demonstrate the silent efficiency with which the FBI monitored the activities of the communists and their connections with the Soviet embassy officials. They also show how the FBI leaked the results of its investigations to the press to undermine any plots the communists might hatch. The methods the FBI developed in the late 1930s to turn Soviet officials into informers, how it infiltrated radical organizations, and how it used the press to expose its "enemies" all have a bearing on the defections under discussion. FBI officials were present in Ottawa when Gouzenko defected. It is possible that his arrangements for defection, including his attempted use of the newspapers in the process, indicate the influence of the Bureau. All small- or middle-power countries are beholden to a larger power for their security, military, and trading interests, and this requires them to turn a blind eye to the involvement of the larger power in their internal affairs; the following account of two Soviet defectors in Ottawa and Canberra is no less a demonstration of that political reality. Of course, Canada and Australia also, to a large extent, shared the American perception of the Soviet threat.

Political Times in Canada and Australia
From its inception, the Soviet Union became – for both Canada and Australia – an object of fear. This was driven by the unreal expectation among the governments of both countries in the 1920s that the Soviet revolutionary force would be exported to their shores. Even trade was viewed with suspicion. The Soviet Union purchased a proportion of Australia's annual wool clip in the interwar years, and sought to balance the trade with Soviet exports of petrol, timber, and matches. The Conservative Australian government firmly opposed the importation of petrol from Russia. It consulted MI5 in London on the matter and unquestioningly accepted its recommendation not to allow Soviet tankers into Australian harbours, because the ships' crews might distribute communist propaganda in the Australian port cities. Economic considerations also played a part. The cheaper Russian petrol was already posing a threat to the oil companies in Europe. Stopping its importation to Australia may well have been due less to the local intelligence-driven scares and more to the pressure exerted by the local representatives of the British oil companies on their friends in the Australian Conservative government to ban the imports.

Canada's trading links with the USSR, while more substantial than Australia's, were also affected by political considerations. Canada had joined the British trade agreement with the USSR in 1922, and had terminated it, along with Britain, as a result of the raid on Arcos, the Soviet trading body in London that MI5 believed to be a Soviet source for spying and for channelling funds to the British communists. Against this rising mood of Soviet phobia in government circles, the London police raided the Arcos premises, but little incriminating material was discovered.[4] Canada was nevertheless thereafter slow to renew trade with the USSR, although by September 1932 the Conservative prime minister, R.B. Bennett (never a friend of the Canadian labour movement) agreed to a trade barter valued at £250,000, whereby Canada exchanged aluminium wire for Soviet oil. This deal was at the expense of oil imported from Trinidad, although Bennett announced that temporary jobs for 300 men would be produced as a result. US officials were already hostile to the British Empire's trading alliance – from which the United States was excluded – and they criticized Bennett's actions for abandoning Trinidad and "seeking to break down commodity price levels," which was the aim, they warned, of Soviet policy.[5]

The measures for surveillance by the two governments of their communist parties were similar. Australia established a political surveillance body in May 1919 to monitor the trade unions and the left in general, with the title of the Investigation Branch of the Attorney-General's Department. It took over the work of the wartime Military Intelligence section of the Australian Army, which had reported on and prosecuted anti-conscriptionists, opponents of the war, and the Industrial Workers of the World (IWW). The police departments in the Australian states established special branches to watch the left groups as well. This resulted in numerous investigators in federal and state administrations maintaining surveillance on the many elements of the Australian labour movement, particularly the Communist Party of Australia (CPA). In Canada during the First World War and immediately after, the government began establishing the Security Service of the Royal Canadian Mounted Police (RCMP). As with Australia, this service became preoccupied in watching and prosecuting anti-war activists, the IWW, and later the Communist Party of Canada (CPC). But neither of the communist parties was ever large or threatening. The Australian party's membership was always small, with 280 members in 1925.[6] Its adoption of the more pragmatic policy of the Popular Front after the Great Depression raised its membership to 3,000 by 1935. Similarly, in Canada, the CPC's membership fell to 1,400 members in 1931 (Canada's population has been approximately twice Australia's), but the adoption of the Popular Front policy lifted it to 7,390 in 1935 and 15,000 in 1937. The Investigation Branch in Australia exchanged information with MI5 about Australia's communists and reported to the government how the party was successful in pitching its appeal to parts of the middle class by preaching about anti-Fascism and the possibility of war. The government explored using the Defence Act to reduce the party's influence, but settled for banning its papers and journals from transmission through the post. The RCMP officials kept a close watch on the CPC, and were equally as diligent in compiling reports from agents it placed in party circles.[7]

The commencement of the Second World War on 3 September 1939 presented the opportunity to the Australian Conservative government, led by R.G. Menzies, to implement his long-held desire to ban the CPA. The army supported him with reports of the security threats posed by the party. The more outlandish of these was put forward late in 1939: it suggested that the Finnish-Soviet war could lead to a British-Soviet war, in which the CPA would side with the Soviets and engage in local sabotage. Menzies was urged to take immediate counter measures. But it was the army's report in June 1940, claiming the CPA was behind a coal miners' strike in Newcastle, that helped Menzies to justify the ban he issued on 15 June under the National Security Act. Already anticipating the ban, the party went underground, and distributed pamphlets and newsletters from concealed printing presses. Its members contested state and federal elections as "independents."[8]

In Canada the repression of the CPC was far more drastic, with a ban instituted on 6 June 1940, as well as the internment of 133 members. The RCMP – supported by Cardinal Villeneuve of Quebec, a supporter of General Franco – encouraged the government to introduce the ban. One historian remarked that the party "remained illegal throughout the duration of the war on the advice of the RCMP (as well as the Catholic church and the Quebec Liberal caucus)." By a compromise arrangement the party was permitted to resurface as the Labour Progressive Party, contest elections, and publish its paper under the new title of *Tribune*.[9]

When Germany attacked the Soviet Union in the summer of 1941, a new wartime alliance was born. While the public in Britain, Australia, and Canada – and, later, the United States – were prepared to see a friendly Russian bear, suspicions of communists both at home and abroad never disappeared, especially from official circles. Although the ban on the Communist Party of Australia was removed in December 1942 by a new Labor government, the decision was highly controversial.[10] In Canada the ban on the Communist Party continued throughout the war. By mid-1944 the demands to have the internees released were succeeding – although it took another twelve months for all to be released and another two years for the CPC to regain its legal status.[11] Even so, the realization that Soviet spies were operating during and after the Second World War caused consternation.

Igor Gouzenko in Canada

Gouzenko was born near Moscow in 1919. He entered the Academy of Engineering in Moscow in 1941 and after two months joined the Red Army, following the German invasion of the USSR.[12] He was attached to the Chief Intelligence Directorate of the Soviet General Staff, better known as the GRU, in 1942. He was posted to Ottawa with the rank of Lieutenant in June 1943 as a cipher clerk, and travelled there soon after with his wife, Svetlana. He worked in the Defence Attaché's office in the Soviet embassy, which was established in Ottawa following the agreement in June 1942 between Canada and the USSR to exchange ambassadors. He served under the Soviet Army's attaché, Lieutenant Colonel Zabotin, whose duties were to liaise with the Canadian Army. Zabotin's unacknowledged duties – like those of all military attaché – were to collect military information about his host country by overt and covert means.

By the middle of the war the US Army had broken into the Soviet diplomatic traffic, which it continued to decode from 1943 until 1949, by which time the Soviets had discovered the breach and changed their codes. It can be seen from these cables that the Canadian military commanders welcomed Zabotin. For example, Rear Admiral George C. Jones arranged for him to go to Vancouver in April and May 1944; he was also invited to the army training centre for artillery, infantry, and parachute troops at Winnipeg and the officer training centre at Kingston. The Canadian general staff invited Zabotin to tour an aluminium manufacturing plant, but he politely declined. Brigadier H. Lefebvre of the Canadian army was eager to visit the Soviet front, and Brigadier General V.N. Evstigneev, head of the Foreign Affairs Section of the People's Commissariat for Defence, had an invitation issued via Zabotin for the brigadier's visit.[13] Zabotin also arranged for Major V.M. Rogov, the Soviet Assistant Military Attaché for Air, to be received by the Chief of the Canadian Air Staff, Air Marshall Robert Leckie, who in turn arranged for Rogov to visit air training centres. Zabotin reported on Canadian military operations in Europe to Moscow. These meetings and tours reflected normal military relationships between allies.[14] Zabotin was also responsible for placing orders for equipment with the Canadian government.[15] But US intelligence detected that Zabotin collected additional information relating to munitions production and ship-building involving an informant codenamed "Green."[16] US intelligence paid close attention to the new Soviet embassy in Canada. Even identifying all embassy staff was important, since Soviet intelligence officers were often passed off as minor employees, such as chauffeurs. The Soviet cipher clerk, Igor Gouzenko – identified by the US experts at this stage – was clearly an object of particular interest. (Intelligence agencies usually focus on cipher clerks, because if they can be persuaded to defect, they bring with them access to key diplomatic codes.) His coding errors were noted, along with his subsequent corrections. He was identified as using the code name "Clark." His importance was soon to become apparent.[17]

The Gouzenko Defection

The process by which Gouzenko defected has been recounted by him on many occasions and repeated by numerous writers. Some of the details can be verified, but many of the important facts have remained obscure, and Gouzenko's own behaviour puzzling. Unlike any normal defector – who either negotiated his defection with the security police in the country of defection or simply "walked in" to the local FBI office or police station – Gouzenko deliberately avoided going to the RCMP headquarters in Ottawa. He said that he did not trust them, although he happily placed himself in their hands over twenty-four hours after he commenced to defect.[18] Nor was his defection spontaneous: he had planned it some months previously by identifying the 106 documents he intended to steal from the embassy. Gouzenko was a well-informed foreign resident of Ottawa; he had lived there for two years, merging comfortably into its suburban environment. He had developed some grasp of the English language, rented an apartment, arranged the purchase of household furnishings and effects for it, and commenced a family, with his first child being born in the Ottawa hospital. He could not have failed to understand how Canada's political and legal structures functioned. And yet he tried to defect on 5 September 1945 by leaving his young child with a neighbour and wandering about Ottawa's deserted streets at 8:30 p.m. that evening, accompanied by his pregnant wife. He returned home after failing to persuade staff of the *Ottawa Journal* of the presence of Soviet espionage, only to sally forth the next day, again avoiding the RCMP offices. He, his wife, and his child again appeared at the *Ottawa Journal,* and then went on to the Magistrate's Court and the Ministry of Justice. They returned home to hide in his neighbour's apartment that afternoon; later that evening, he put himself in the hands of the RCMP, to be debriefed by FBI agents. Were these the actions of a frightened young man whose own culture had taught him that the police could not be trusted? Or did Gouzenko intend to create maximum publicity for his defection?

The RCMP had been made aware of Gouzenko's wanderings on 5 September by anonymous informers, and Cecil Bayfield of the police's special branch posted himself outside Gouzenko's apartment in the late afternoon of 6 September.[19] By means still not revealed, the Department of External Affairs also knew of Gouzenko's defection plans. On the morning of 6 September, Hume Wrong and Norman Robertson, senior members of that department, called on Mackenzie King to reveal news of Gouzenko's plans. King informed the United States, and the FBI immediately became involved. The FBI's primary interest in debriefing Gouzenko was to obtain information on the Soviets spying against the US nuclear program. Gouzenko's knowledge extended only to an episode involving the nuclear physicist and communist, Dr. Alan Nunn May, who had been sent to Canada by the British government. Dr. May knew nothing of the US atomic bomb research, but he was contacted by the GRU in Ottawa, to whom he gave samples of uranium 235 enriched and uranium 233, possibly obtained from the Montreal laboratory where he did research. Gouzenko reported that Dr. May was to be posted back to Britain and that the GRU had made arrangements for him to communicate with its representatives in London.[20] The FBI immediately advised the British, so that he could be shadowed in London. Gouzenko's revelations led to May's subsequent prosecution and jailing in Britain. None of the scientists in Canada, including those on loan from

Britain like May, knew about the US atomic bomb process. The United States excluded all these Canadian-based physicists from gaining insights to its nuclear research, while concurrently appropriating the Canadian production of uranium ores for its nuclear developments, as Wayne Reynolds explains in the previous chapter.[21]

Another interest the FBI pursued in the questioning of Gouzenko related to the means by which the communists and Soviet intelligence agents falsely obtained passports. The FBI and the State Department had been monitoring the manner in which US communists obtained American passports to travel on Comintern business in the late 1930s.[22] Of greater concern was their observance of how US citizens suspected of being communists obtained American passports under false names. There was suspicion that such passports were used to smuggle Soviet agents and other communists into the United States. The FBI agents were particularly interested in Gouzenko's documents, indicating that the GRU in Ottawa was involved in the transfer of a stolen Canadian passport into the name of a Soviet agent living in California. The passport had belonged to another Canadian, who had lost it while fighting against the Franco fascist forces in the Spanish Civil War. The passport was thereafter acquired by the Soviets and seemingly inherited by the GRU. The FBI was concerned that, having established Canadian residency, a Soviet agent could more easily obtain a US passport and thereafter become difficult to trace, once merged into the US community.[23]

The FBI agents continued to interview Gouzenko at some length. In reactions typical of a defector, he told his questioners what he thought they wanted to hear. For example, he informed the FBI that the USSR was planning to place agents recruited from eastern, central, and Balkan Europe as espionage workers in its embassies in the United States and Canada. Gouzenko and the FBI agents would have known that Soviet intelligence recruited only from its own Russian-speaking people. He added the prediction that the Soviets were putting all their energies into developing the atomic bomb, and that "the Soviet Union is aiming toward beating the United States and Great Britain in the next war, which will permit the Sovietization of the entire world."[24] However, into all these exaggerations he dropped one pearl of information that pricked up the ears of the Bureau's agents. It was that he had heard in the embassy that an assistant to an assistant secretary of state under Edward Stettinius, the secretary of state, was a spy in the pay of the Soviet Union. After the FBI had debriefed him to their satisfaction, Gouzenko and his family were whisked off to a wartime secret service training base known as Camp X near Whitby, Ontario, guarded by armed RCMP officers. There they remained until March 1946 while Gouzenko assisted the RCMP in analyzing his papers and establishing how various Canadians could be linked to the Soviet spying network.

Vladimir Petrov and His Defection in Australia

The Australian defector Vladimir Petrov was born in 1917 in a Siberian village. The Bolshevik revolution gave him the opportunity for an education that led to him joining the Soviet navy for three years, where he worked in the signals and cipher section. These skills led to his recruitment by the KGB for similar duties, and after a posting to Sweden, he was sent with his wife, Evdokia, to Australia in February 1951 as a cipher clerk in the Canberra KGB office. The Canberra embassy was established in March 1943 following the active lobbying for it by Dr. H.V. Evatt, through his friendship with Vyacheslev Mikhailovich Molotov, the Soviet foreign minister. The previous Conservative government, led by R.G. Menzies, refused to entertain the opening of such relationships, and Dr. Evatt's move to drag Australia into modern diplomatic relationships earned him enmity rather than praise in political circles. Petrov was reluctantly selected by the KGB as the cipher clerk; he was known to have an alcohol problem and to be unreliable. But because Australia's counter-espionage body – the newly established Australian Security Intelligence Organization (ASIO) – objected to other nominations, Petrov was selected (with his acknowledged weaknesses), knowing that ASIO would lack the information to assess him.[25] Soon after arriving, ASIO had one of its part-time agents – Dr. Michael Bialoguski, a Russian-speaking Polish medical doctor – attach himself to Petrov. Australian intelligence agents (like those in Britain or the United States) recognized the value of having a cipher clerk defect because of the secrets he could reveal about coding and decoding. Bialoguski thereby became Petrov's companion for the next three years, reporting the details of Petrov's activities to his ASIO handler.

In contrast to Gouzenko, who began planning his defection close to his posting back to Moscow, Petrov appeared to be signalling to ASIO from approximately a year after he arrived that he would be receptive to an offer to defect. It was necessary to prove to ASIO that he had something to offer, and the following arrangements were put in place. One of his duties was to meet the Soviet diplomatic couriers arriving in Sydney, and on such occasions he stayed overnight in Dr. Bialoguski's flat in Sydney. There he was accustomed to fall into a drunken sleep, during which his doctor friend rifled through his pockets to find slips of papers bearing the names of Australians and others who were in contact with the Soviet embassy for business, social, or other cultural pursuits. The doctor copied the names, which he then gave to his ASIO handler. It was an exercise by which the coding clerk gave ASIO a taste of what it could expect if he was offered a defection package. Certainly Dr. Bialoguski was impressed with the potentiality of his friend's information. This induced him to change his role from informer to "manager" of a source that might produce its own financial rewards. ASIO was displeased with the doctor's new entrepreneurial role, and it attempted to displace him with a new part-time agent in August 1953, an eye specialist then treating Petrov. Dr. Bialoguski responded by travelling in haste to Canberra on 3 September to interview Prime Minister Menzies, also bearing a letter complaining about ASIO's treatment. The prime minister refused to become involved, and Bialoguski had to leave his letter with Menzies's secretary. The immediate result was that Colonel Spry, head of ASIO, dismissed the doctor from ASIO's employment on 22 September. It was a foolish move by Spry, because by then Petrov and his wife had loyally tied themselves to Dr. Bialoguski. As a way of dealing himself back into the game, the doctor informed ASIO on 23 November that both Petrovs intended to defect, and unless ASIO put "him back on his former work," he would take both Petrovs to the newspapers to reveal all. It was a move to which ASIO had no response; it not only reappointed the artful doctor but also increased his remuneration.

The defection plans for Petrov were renewed on 8 December 1953 when Colonel Spry ordered the renting of a house in Sydney as a safe house for Petrov's accommodation, with the contingency plan named "Operation Cabin 11." Petrov wished to become a chicken farmer after defection, and on Saturday 12 December 1953, Dr. Bialoguski took him to such a farm outside Sydney, which ASIO was prepared to buy for him. On 9 January 1954, ASIO gave Petrov £100 to pay the owner a deposit on the purchase price of £7,600. Petrov was closer to committing himself to defecting. The date of 5 April 1954 was set, and the new contingency plan – now labelled "Operation Cabin 12" – was put into play.

The Gouzenko and Petrov defections differed in their operation. Whereas Gouzenko deliberately avoided going to the RCMP with his stolen documents and chose instead to wander about Ottawa on a cold night and the following day, seeking press coverage for his actions, Petrov calmly negotiated with ASIO on the price and contents of the papers he was to bring out. This was a reflection both of the individuals involved and of the changed international context. When Gouzenko defected, the wartime alliance was still relatively intact, although even by September 1945 there had been much to strain it. The hesitations and concern with which the Canadians, King in particular, greeted the news that they had a Soviet defector with top-secret material on their hands, indicates the fluid nature of the East-West relationship. Nine years later, when Petrov planned his defection, the establishment of Soviet control over eastern Europe, the Berlin blockade, and the Korean War had drawn the battle lines firmly. The Venona papers provide another point of comparison. Whereas the Canadian Venona papers gave US officials some insight into the activities of the Soviet officials in Ottawa, including Gouzenko, the Australian Venona papers were much larger and extended over the years 1943 to 1949. Thousands of KGB and GRU messages were collected by the Americans, and while, in contrast to Canada, the Australian GRU messages could not be decoded, much of the KGB traffic was broken into. A better understanding of the background to Petrov's defection can be found in this decoded KGB material. US decoding indicated that in March 1946 the KGB agent in Canberra had been given two British documents by someone in the Australian Foreign Affairs office. These were quickly photographed by the KGB and returned to the office. Rather than inform the Australian Labor government of these security breaches, the Americans decided, in June 1948, to place an embargo on all classified information being sent to Australia. The newly established Central Intelligence Agency (CIA) had heard of the alleged spying in January 1948 and informed Truman of it. Canadian events were fresh in the CIA's mind, even if it was confused about the dates. This leak from Australia, said the CIA report to Truman, "may, in magnitude, approach that of the Canadian expose of last year insofar as high Australian government officials are concerned."[26] Australia sent its secretary of defence to Washington to discover the reason for the embargo. He even spoke to Truman, but was told nothing.

The British were concerned at the US embargo because they were building a missile-testing site in Australia and sought US technical information. The Australian spying was revealed to the British, but only in vague terms. Prime Minister Attlee thereupon sent Sir Percy Sillitoe, director-general of MI5, to brief the Australian prime minister, J.B. Chifley, on the matter in February 1948. Sillitoe could report to Chifley only in the imprecise terms the US officials had given him. The Americans wished to keep their cipher-breaking activities totally secret, particularly from the British, because they had Venona decrypts indicating that a Soviet spy circle operated in Britain as well. The British told the Australians that they had gleaned their information from a mole in the Soviet camp. Chifley had investigations conducted immediately, but all documents could be accounted for and the suspected people had left the government's service. On the basis of the limited US-British information, nothing more could be done.

To demonstrate to the United States their keenness to expand counter-espionage work, the Australians replaced their intelligence body with the ASIO, established under MI5's aegis. It immediately began pursuing the members of the Soviet spy ring. ASIO was given access only to the limited information the American officials had given the British from their Australian Venona decodings. The US officials did not want to give the Australians too much information. Investigations progressed very slowly before the Labor Party lost office in December 1949, replaced by the Conservative government, again led by R.G. Menzies. It was likely that the United States divulged more Venona information to this anti-Labor government of Menzies through R.G. Casey, doyen of the Australian intelligence world and friend of American intelligence leaders such as the Dulles brothers. Even so, US officials would have refused to allow their Venona information to be used by their more amicable Australian friends to prosecute the Venona spies, since it would have to be produced in open court. The Australian government had to find its own means of airing the Venona information without having it attributed to the Americans. One solution was to have Petrov search the Soviet embassy for any record that might contain the names of the Australian Venona spies, which he could then produce on defection, allowing such prosecutions to be launched. This would allow the Australian spies to be jailed – as happened in Canada following Gouzenko's defection – without divulging the US decryption successes. The outcome would be an intelligence coup for ASIO and an endorsement of the proclaimed anti-communist policy of R.G. Menzies, already represented by his attempt to ban the CPA in 1951. Just as importantly, it would vitally assist his government's return at the general elections slated for 29 May 1954. Menzies had already arranged for Queen Elizabeth to visit Australia, and he anticipated that his electoral chances would be improved by the glow radiating from the monarch's presence when he escorted on her visit. Royal protocol dictated that he must wait for Her Majesty to leave Australia before he announced the election date and Petrov's defection. The Queen departed Australia at 5:20 p.m. on 2 April, and Petrov defected near lunchtime on 3 April. On 14 April, the last day of parliament's sitting, Menzies announced the defection and the holding of a royal commission. The timing was perfect.

This question of what papers Petrov was expected to deliver is important for a comparison with Gouzenko's defection, but it also demonstrates the degree of control Petrov had over the planning of his defection, a control seemingly not available to Gouzenko. After Dr. Bialoguski was reappointed as Petrov's go-between on 23 November, ASIO held an important strategy meeting, indicating Petrov's defection was imminent. G.R. Richards, a former policeman turned ASIO agent, was made the liaison person with Petrov. Richards arranged a three-day meeting with Dr. Bialoguski in Sydney from 27 to 30 November 1953, which Petrov also seems to have attended. Meanwhile, Petrov conducted his duties as normal, such as attending a reception given by the Czechoslovakian consul in Sydney and escorting Soviet couriers to and from Canberra. On 27 February 1954, he met Richards for the supposed first time, followed by twelve other meetings either in Sydney or Canberra, during which the details for his defection and the materials he was to produce were agreed upon. ASIO made an offer for Petrov to bring sensitive papers from the embassy for a reward of A$10,000 (A$70,000 in present-day terms) or double that if the papers were revealing about all of the Venona spy ring. How Petrov negotiated over his proposed reward and what papers he showed ASIO from that first meeting with Richards up until his defection in 3 April 1954 is not known. It was clearly evident, however, that ASIO would have been too cautious to hand over such a large amount of money for unseen papers. Its head, Colonel Spry, was a conventional soldier who would not have dreamed of handing over government cash without good grounds. In the negotiations with Petrov, the ASIO, as the buyer, also held the upper hand.

On 9 February 1954, nearly eight weeks before Petrov defected, Spry informed Prime Minister Menzies of the impending event. The contents of Petrov's papers must have been known to Menzies, since he decided then to establish a royal commission to examine the individuals named in the papers. It is rightly said that governments rarely hold royal commissions unless they know the outcome in advance. The Menzies government must have been aware, through ASIO, of what the Petrov papers could be expected to reveal nearly four weeks in advance. On 2 April, the night before defection day, Richards took Petrov to a secret ASIO flat in Sydney, where he met Colonel Spry. Petrov showed them his stolen papers, at which they glanced briefly (more than half were in Russian, which they could not read), and then gave them back to Petrov. Petrov had to bid farewell to two Soviet couriers on 3 April at the Sydney airport. He then had to dash to the shipping port terminal in Sydney to receive his successor, whom he escorted to the airport to put on a flight to Canberra. All the while he carried the stolen papers in a briefcase. He then defected and was taken to a safe house, where he exchanged the documents for the money (the smaller sum), which was put in a safe and the key given to him. ASIO was involved from its founding in pursuing the Venona spies, and it is difficult to believe that its officers had not convinced themselves that there was sufficient material in Petrov's proffered papers to conduct a local exposure of the Venona spies, following the Gouzenko pattern.[27]

A significant difference between Canada and Australia was that the Soviet Union closed its embassy in Australia on 23 April 1954 as an outcome of the Petrov defection and withdrew all the staff. Australia followed by closing its Moscow embassy. Diplomatic relations were not completely severed, and contact thereafter was conducted through the Swedish embassy and the Soviet embassy in New Zealand. The Russians claimed this diplomatic fracture (not occurring in the Canadian case) was caused by Australian breaches of diplomatic privilege. The major incident in this regard was the assault conducted by Commonwealth police officers in Darwin on the two Soviet diplomatic couriers escorting Petrov's wife back to Moscow. Following Petrov's defection, his wife had decided to return to Moscow, and two diplomatic couriers were detailed to escort her. After leaving Sydney, she signalled to the cabin crew on the aircraft that she had changed her mind and wished to remain in Australia. ASIO was advised by radio and arrangement made for her defection. While the aircraft was refuelling at Darwin, the overzealous police at the airport seized the couriers in wrestling-style head-locks – as a measure, they believed, for preventing the couriers from per-suading her from remaining in Australia. Like many diplomatic couriers, they carried pistols, which were removed in the wrestling engagement, but like all couriers, they enjoyed diplomatic privilege and should not have been subjected to such treatment.

Why did the Soviets suspend relations with Australia and not with Canada over the defections? Lacking access to the Russian documents, it can be assumed that the spontaneous nature of the Gouzenko defection caught the Soviets off guard. It could have led them to be anxious to avoid having the exposure of the spying, revealed through the defection, damage the Soviet-Canadian postwar trading relationships. Although the manhandling incident was a factor in the Petrov case, the Soviets may have taken greater umbrage over the Petrov defection on learning post facto that ASIO had been negotiating with him for some time, thereby causing embarrassment in Soviet upper circles. The Soviets were also aware that stopping trade with Australia, particularly the wool trade, would be more damaging to Australia than the USSR.

After the Defections: Canada
Despite the great intelligence victory represented in Gouzenko's defection, the affair was kept secret by the Canadian government. He and his family were held in the RCMP hideout from early September 1945 until 3 February 1946. The defection only then became public after the FBI, as the silent partner in the affair, revealed the defection to the press. Why did the King government suppress news of the defection? Several explanations can be offered. Whitaker and Marcuse argue that the British wished to arrest the physicist, Alan Nunn May, when he arrived in London from Canada early in October 1945, but the US administration and Prime Minister King asked Prime Minister Attlee to hold back so as not to disturb diplomatic relation-ships with the USSR, nor to inflame public opinion against the Soviet Union with these spying revelations.[28] Discussions on postwar diplomacy relating to factors such as the United Nations, the control of nuclear en-ergy, and the formation of an early alliance in the West against the Soviets all dominated these months. King was immersed in the high-level discus-sions because of Canada's early involvement in nuclear research, although this was not related to the atomic bomb. King hoped to use the Gouzenko affair as a bargaining chip with the Soviets, to ensure their cooperation in the diplomatic discussions. This explanation cannot take into account what the FBI was planning.

An alternative explanation lies in the complexity of the material Gouzenko stole from the GRU safe and the time required to sort and appraise it. The 106 documents represented a varied collection of GRU material. Some were "registration" cards showing personal details of the informer, including a photograph and code name. Others were indexes recording details of when Zabotin dispatched to Moscow the documents he received from informers, their code names, and the dates. Others were copies of material handed to Zabotin by informers. These were often copies of official government correspondence. There were also pages Zabotin had torn from his notebook and given to Gouzenko for destruction, but which he retained. There were also handwritten drafts of telegrams given to Gouzenko for coding preparatory to dispatching. This material was mostly written in Russian.[29] The winter months were consumed by the RCMP trying to make sense of Gouzenko's jumbled collection of papers. They had to identify all the informers, the source from which the material came in government circles, collect evidence from the senior officers in those departments, and then knit a case together that was comprehensive enough to ensure successful prosecution of the people concerned. While this was proceeding, the suspects were placed under surveillance by the RCMP – a fact of which they seemed quite unaware. They were further disadvantaged by not being warned by the Soviet officials of Gouzenko's recent defection and the danger they were in. It was not until being seized without explanation five months later, after dawn raids on their homes, that they became aware of the seriousness of their situation.

During this period of planning operations – from late 1945 to early 1946 – the RCMP and the Department of Justice agreed that convictions of the suspects would best be obtained by having them confess or otherwise incriminate themselves. The Justice Department also decided to establish a royal commission that would sit in secret and compel people to confess to breaches of security. Those who confessed would be prosecuted under terms of wartime security legislation, not then repealed. These plans for prosecution and jailings remained in abeyance. But time did not stand still in Washington, and in the belief that events in Ottawa had stalled, the FBI brought the press into play by revealing the defection publicly on 3 February 1946. It demonstrated the degree of proprietary interest the Bureau had in the defection. Why did the FBI select that particular time to reveal the secret? Did J. Edgar Hoover warn King beforehand? These questions will have to await the release of FBI documents for an answer.

With the secret revealed, the Ottawa plans for the royal commission had to be hurriedly implemented. King authorized the suspects to be seized in dawn raids and placed incommunicado in a former military camp under heavy guard. This was a secret operation, and the people were not permitted legal representation. Two Supreme Court justices were appointed royal commissioners: Robert Taschereau and Lindsay Kellock. The prisoners were summoned before them and told that, if they confessed, they would not be prosecuted. This was a callous trick, since they were to be convicted on their own evidence. Whitaker and Marcuse explain how these people were seized, jailed without being charged, denied contact with lawyers, friends, or families, and forced to testify on pain of being prosecuted for contempt. Taschereau and Kellock were allowed to function on the presumption that the accused were guilty until proven innocent. The commissioners conducted their hearings in total secrecy and were permitted to interpret laws to suit themselves and make their own rules.[30] These were dark days in Canadian legal history. Officials knew that Gouzenko and his papers would be unreliable as prosecution evidence and confessions would have to be tricked out of people by the royal commission. They were then prosecuted under the Official Secrets Act of 1939 and the Criminal Code. Some were jailed for long terms. There was no indication that the legal élites opposed the distortion of Canada's legal apparatus in the pursuit and jailing of those people. Nor can it be assessed how much King knew of the circumstances involved in conducting this pattern of legal entrapment and prosecution. Clearly the prime minister was obliged to use the full panoply of Canadian legal power to punish the wrongdoers, if only to demonstrate to the FBI and the Truman administration that the delay of five months had a pattern of intention to it.

Some of the Canadians were put on trial while the royal commission continued on its secret course. Eight were acquitted, but the commissioners remained convinced, when making their final report, that these eight remained guilty of spying. Eleven were convicted, mainly under the swinging provisions of the Official Secrets Act, and charges were withdrawn against two. Squadron Leader Nightingale had been in contact with the Soviet Air Force officer, Major Rogov (identified in the Venona papers as a possible spy), and this, together with Gouzenko's comments, led Taschereau and Kellock to declare him guilty of violating the Official Secrets Act. He was then put on trial, but the court refused to convict him simply for being seen in the company of a Soviet official. Ultimately it was Gouzenko who received the most praise; the royal commissioners concluded in their report that Gouzenko "has rendered great public service to the people of this country, and thereby has placed Canada in his debt."[31]

Protests were made by the Civil Rights Union to the minister of justice, J.L. Isley, about the conduct of the two judges in refusing the witnesses access to counsel. The Union remarked that they "showed strong political bias and prejudice, and by the procedure they adopted they unfairly handicapped the defence of the accused."[32] This Union thereafter began lobbying for a Canadian Bill of Rights.

After the Defections: Australia
Petrov handed over 103 papers to ASIO, nearly the same number as was taken by Gouzenko. But Petrov's were of little importance – except for the one labelled "Document G." This contained a list of sixty-three names of

people with associated code names, some of which were mentioned in the Venona documents. The political manoeuvre by which Menzies managed to have Petrov's defection coincide with the holding of the national general election proved successful. The associated communist scare led to his government being returned with a sizeable majority. The Royal Commission on Espionage (RCE) quickly commenced under three commissioners who were all Supreme Court judges. ASIO was the controlling influence in the RCE, just as the RCMP had been in the Canadian counterpart. ASIO held the Petrovs in its safe houses and determined the topics and the sequence in which they appeared before the RCE. They were then able to rehearse the Petrovs in the responses they were to give before the commissioners.

The Petrovs were as helpful to ASIO and the commission as they could be under the circumstances. Their failing weakness was that, unlike Gouzenko, they were not present when the Venona-revealed spying events occurred. No spying happened while Petrov was the KGB representative. The Venona material related to the years 1943 to 1949, whereas Petrov's term of appointment lasted from 1951 to 1954. He could claim no first-hand experience of the events that were the subject of the Venona decodings. Petrov made good his lack of experience in the events in the Venona papers by claiming to "remember" discussions he had heard when in the Moscow KGB office about events in Australia. His wife assisted by also "recalling" details she, too, had overheard in Moscow about these Australian events. But then "remembering" past conversations was also important in Gouzenko's presentation of his evidence. The importance of Petrov's "remembering" processes was that he could make assertions about events and people incompletely analyzed in the Venona papers. For example, suspicion fell on Ian Milner, an official in the Foreign Affairs Department suspected of having given documents to the Russians. He had left Australia in 1947 and settled in Prague in 1951. The Venona papers contained his name, but they lacked clear evidence of his guilt. But because he lived in Prague, where he was appointed as a lecturer at Charles University, suspicion descended on him. The Petrovs "remembered" receiving a cable (although not produced) from Moscow, inquiring if it was safe for him to return home to New Zealand.[33] The implication was that he feared to travel out of Czechoslovakia lest he be arrested. In fact he travelled to Britain to visit his brother, indicating that fears for his safety in the West were fictitious. The damaging evidence of the Petrovs about Milner, plus his taking up residence behind the Iron Curtain, encouraged the commissioners to find that he might be implicated in spying.

There was also a tendency for the Petrovs' case to unravel on some issues in a manner not occurring with Gouzenko. For example, conflicting evidence was given by the Petrovs about how the KGB list of the names of informers came into their hands. At one time, Petrov held the key to the

KGB safe, but he did not open the unsealed envelope containing the names; at other times, Mrs. Petrov held the key (her normal duty was embassy bookkeeper, not KGB agent), and she but briefly glanced at the names; and then the single envelope was transformed into two envelopes.[34] This conflicting evidence was rationalized away by the commissioners seeking to mask the lack of credibility in the Petrovs' statements.

Another difference between the Canadian and Australian royal commissions was that, whereas the Canadian one examined only those whom the RCMP considered guilty of giving information to the Russians, the Australian one examined over 100 witnesses because their names appeared in Petrov's papers, even though their connection to him was innocuous. Also, the witnesses did not conduct themselves in the same manner. In Canada some openly confessed to giving information, knowing it was for the Russians; others stoutly rejected any connection with spying. In Australia all witnesses denied any involvement in espionage. This led to disbelief among ASIO and the commissioners, which was only heightened by their frustration at being unable to contradict it from the Venona papers. The most notorious case involved the communist activist Walter Clayton, whom the Venona papers revealed as having collected material from informers in the Foreign Affairs Department and passed it to the KGB in 1945 and 1946. He was summoned before the commission because his name and code name appeared on the list from the KGB safe. He denied ever handling any official documents and more firmly denied knowing any Russians. It was a case of blatant lying, but neither ASIO nor the commissioners could contradict him, since they were unable to reveal the details of the Venona case against him.

The royal commission sat from 17 May 1954 until 31 March 1955 and reported finally in September 1955. It could reveal no episode of Soviet espionage (because of the Venona ban), and its final summation was to point the accusatory finger at the distant Ian Milner in Prague for alleged spying, with the phrase, "That he did so [spied for Russia] is supported by other material which we have seen."[35] Mentioning "other material" was a not-so-subtle hint that they had seen the Venona material. The RCE concluded – like the Canadian royal commission report – with unstinting praise for the defectors. The Petrov couple, the judges declared in all solemnity, "were witnesses of truth" and their documents unquestionably "authentic."[36] The government rewarded those who helped sustain the proceedings of the royal commission; the judges all received knighthoods and Colonel Spry of ASIO was awarded an imperial honour. Menzies held another election in 1955 in the shadow of the Petrov affair and increased his parliamentary majority. In contrast to Gouzenko the Petrovs lapsed into obscurity. They adopted the names of Sven and Maria Allyson and lived in a suburb of Melbourne. Colonel Spry placed their names on the "D notice," thus barring the public media from discussing their whereabouts.[37] Dr. Bialoguski wrote a book about his experiences, with the assistance of ASIO, and the Petrovs had a book ghost written about them by an ASIO agent. Written in a pedestrian style and lacking any interesting detail, neither book sold well. Petrov worked as a storeman in a photographic factory and his wife worked with an agricultural machinery company. He died, aged eighty-four, on 14 June 1991. His wife died in 2002.

Gouzenko, in sharp contrast, went on to have a high-profile life in Canada. He had books and films made of his life and he charged heavy fees for the numerous interviews sought from him by newspapers and television stations. He launched successful libel suits against people publishing unflattering articles about him, but squandered these and other earnings. He was regarded as an obnoxious and slightly deranged person, but his initial hero status as a Canadian loyalist led the local wealthy elites to rescue him from the several financial and social disasters he brought on himself. One business executive explained to Mackenzie King in 1949 his motives for aiding Gouzenko and his wife with the following comment: "When Norah [writer's wife] and I consider what this formerly obscure and humble young couple have accomplished for Canada and the democracies there is nothing that we are not prepared to do to aid them."[38] Those close to him, such as his RCMP guards, considered him to be unbalanced and totally egocentric in always seeking financial rewards and in considering himself and Winston Churchill to be the "only two men in the world [who] mattered."[39] Gouzenko died in Toronto after a long illness in June 1982. His wife still lives in Toronto.

Conclusion

One direct outcome of these two defections was the major boost in prestige received by intelligence agencies in both Australia and Canada. ASIO was augmented, and Colonel Spry persuaded Menzies to have the administrative direction under which ASIO functioned replaced by an act of parliament. Spry feared that the Labor Party might seek revenge by curbing the authority of the ASIO he had nurtured. Menzies obliged, and the ASIO Act was passed in 1956.[40] Dr. Evatt, the leader of the Labor Party, justifiably saw the staging of Petrov's defection by Menzies as a political ploy to win the election. As a senior barrister, Dr. Evatt participated in the RCE proceedings, representing some of the parties; by challenging the rulings of the commissioners, he was barred from attending further hearings. Many Catholic members of the Labor Party perceived Dr. Evatt's questioning of the genuineness of Petrov's defection and the conduct of the commission as favouring communism; annoyed by this and his other actions, they split away to form the very small Democratic Labor Party (DLP). The Labor Party thereafter perceived the events relating to Petrov's defection, ASIO's role in it, and the conduct of the RCE as a collective political conspiracy arranged by Menzies for his re-election and for undermining Dr. Evatt's leadership. Substance was offered to such allegations over the following decade; such years witnessed the Menzies government comfortably holding onto office by exploiting fears about the Cold War. Menzies's appeal to the electorate's fear of the Chinese communist army sweeping southward to invade Australia effectively kept the Labor Party from office until 1972.

The RCMP was boosted by Gouzenko's defection with increased numbers and expanded powers to investigate communists and to subject civil servants to security clearances. Commissioner S.T. Wood of the RCMP declared to the local press early in 1946 that his force was "weeding out ... Communists, persons of doubtful loyalty and fellow travellers" in a "purge" parallel to that ordered by Truman in the United States.[41] Whereas in Australia the left remained intact and sometimes gave support to the communists in union elections, in Canada the left moved toward the centre and embraced a coalition with the Liberals and the right. The communists remained the sole occupant of the extreme left of Canadian politics, and as all supporters drifted away and its remaining members were politically ostracized, the party withered away. The provinces also witnessed the continuing effect of the Gouzenko defection. In British Columbia the conservative forces – led by John Hart, among others – expanded their decades-old fight against trade unions; in Quebec, the deep-seated fears of the Catholics about communism were exploited further by the premier, Maurice Duplessis, as a measure for maintaining his hold on power and as a cynical measure for vote buying. The term "witch hunt" has been applied by historians to the events following Gouzenko's defection, as scientists, writers, academics, film makers, and some trade union leaders were put on notice that their loyalties were suspect and they would have to pay a heavy price for retaining their social and political beliefs.[42]

The Canadian defection could also have been a contributing factor in the US decision to establish the Central Intelligence Agency (CIA), under the National Security Act, in 1947. They took the Gouzenko affair, together with their Venona transcripts, as a manifestation of Soviet espionage remaining a permanent feature in the postwar world. And while Hoover of the FBI showed that the Bureau was capable of continuing to operate outside US borders against the communist foe, that continuing role would only serve to distract it from pursuing the communist enemy within the gates. The possibility that the FBI had manipulated events within Canada to effect Gouzenko's defection may also have demonstrated the advantage of the new CIA having an operations arm as a measure for countering the wily Soviet influence inside other countries.

How useful were the documents produced by the two defectors? On the basis of the information Gouzenko produced (and released thus far by the Canadian government), the Soviets did not seem to gain any considerable advantage from what their informers provided. No nuclear information was forthcoming from Dr. Nunn May because, as the commissioners declared, "no one in Canada had that information."[43] Statistics given to the Soviets by J.S. Benning on the Canadian production of military equipment – such as tanks, planes, and ships, built either locally or in the United States – would have been of no more than indirect importance.[44] These statistical reports showed a continually expanding production, and while they may have made the Soviet military envious of such a huge output, they would also have confirmed to the Soviets that the North Americans were dedicated to the war and that the combined Allied resources could not fail to win the war. The formula for making the explosive known as RDX – first developed by the Germans in 1904, further refined by the United States and Canadians, and passed to the Russians by Professor Raymond Boyer – may have been useful to the Soviets. Boyer passed it on in 1943, knowing that the United States was withholding it from them. Boyer, who was not a communist, was motivated by the belief that the overwhelming necessity to beat the enemy should displace any reluctance among the Allies to pool their scientific knowledge.[45] It was a policy to be applauded and, as applied in many other spheres of Allied cooperation, a policy that helped win the war.

Of the two sets of papers passed to the Soviets in Australia, those of Petrov would have been of no use. The problematic nature of Document G has already been discussed, and the other material – such as Document J, written by a communist journalist, that summarized economic and political life in Australia, and Document H, providing personal details about journalists – would have amused their Moscow readers but provided no intelligence information. The other set of Australian papers relating to the RCE – that is, the Venona papers that were made available in 1996 – are disappointingly thin; it would be difficult to perceive how their contents would have benefited the Soviets. Thousands of these Soviet cables were collected by the United States, but only the KGB messages could be translated, and then only partially. Of those, the British government asked for 189 messages to be withheld, leaving 218 that we can read. Most of them seem to be reports sent from the Dominions Office in London, giving news of events derived from the British embassies overseas. This could have been of some value to the Soviets, but it could also have duplicated what they already knew. We shall have to await the release of Soviet documents to judge whether the Australian Venona cables were of use to them at the time. Those papers that were removed from the office, photographed, and returned were considered to be important by the Russians. These were papers prepared by the Post Hostilities Planning Committee in Britain. The committee was established to plan the surrender of the enemy in a war clearly about to be won, but it also prepared other papers on what the postwar world would be like. They were, in fact, not policy documents, but simply discussion papers to which the dominions, such as Australia, were invited to contribute. They were labelled secret to prevent them being judged as policy papers. This misled not only the KGB chief in Canberra at the time (S.I. Makarov), but also the recent Australian writers on the topic. Makarov believed them to be valuable, but he lacked a thorough knowledge of English. He sent them in lengthy cables to Moscow, where they were also considered valuable – again by people with poor English skills. The US decoding experts intercepted the cables and, realizing that they were copies of British documents, they obtained the London copies and thereby broke into the KGB's Canberra code. What were unimportant papers at the time went on to have important ramifications.[46]

The outcome of the defections was a win-win situation for the Americans. They seemed to know more about events concerning Soviet activities in Canada than did the Canadian government. And it seemed to take some time for the Canadian government to become aware of the vast US Army and FBI intelligence apparatus that surveilled the Canadians, and the possible impacts this could have on governmental affairs. The same considerations applied to Australia. The Australian Labor government was not treated frankly by the US government with regard to Venona. Evidence is emerging that this default was not so much due to deliberate action by the Truman government as it was to unilateral action by the US intelligence bodies, which kept the US government in the dark on the matter. The succeeding Australian government tried to prove its anti-communist credentials to the United States by, for example, attempting to legally proscribe the communist party and to bring the Venona traitors to book via a royal commission linked to the Petrov affair. It received no additional support from the US authorities in the following years, other than what was given to the US allies. Meanwhile, the United States maintained its wide-sweeping intelligence surveillance of the Soviet Union. From the details discussed in this chapter, it can be appreciated how inherently weak were the Soviet intelligence institutions, about which US intelligence must have been fully aware. Why the Cold War continued for another forty years against a heavily embattled Soviet state will be answered as more archival deposits are released by the main players in those decades. If the explanation commences with the Gouzenko and Petrov defections, this chapter will become a good starting point for that analysis.

Notes

1 J.L. Granatstein and David Stafford, *Spy Wars: Espionage and Canada from Gouzenko to Glasnost* (Toronto: Key Porter Books, 1990). See chapter 3 on Gouzenko, "The Man Who Started the Cold War."

2 Robert Manne, *The Petrov Affair: Politics and Espionage* (Sydney: Allen and Unwin, 1987), 227. He asserts that "the genuine importance of the Petrovs [has] been persistently misunderstood."

3 This organization was known, prewar, as OGPU, then NKGB by 1941, MGB by 1946, and KGB by 1954. For consistency, the name KGB will be used in this chapter.

4 "Decode of telegram received by H.E., the governor general from Secretary of State for Dominion Affairs" 27 May 1927, Australian Archives (hereinafter AA), series A981, 1, item Soviet Union 37A, part 3.

5 "Trade between Canada and the U.S.S.R.," 20 September 1932, National Archives and Records Administration (hereinafter NARA), RG489.

6 For a history of the CPA, see Stuart Macintyre, *The Reds: The Communist Party of Australia from Origins to Illegality* (Sydney: Allen and Unwin, 1998).

7 Some of these R.C.M.P. Security Bulletins, as they were called, have been located and published by the Committee on Canadian Labour History. Gregory S. Kealey and Reginald Whitaker, eds., *R.C.M.P. Security Bulletins: The War Series*, vol. 1, *1939-1941* and vol. 2, *1942-45* (St. John's, NF: Committee on Canadian Labour History, 1989-93).

8 Frank Cain, *The Origins of Political Surveillance in Australia* (Sydney: Angus and Robertson, 1983), ch. 7.

9 Kealey and Whitaker, eds., 1:17.

10 Cain, *Origins of Political Surveillance in Australia*, ch. 7.

11 Norman Penner, *Canadian Communism: The Stalin Years and Beyond* (Toronto: Methuen, 1988), 179.

12 *Report of the Royal Commission to Investigate the Facts Relating to the Circumstances Surrounding the Communication by Public Officials and Others in Positions of Trust of Secret and Confidential Information to Agents of a Foreign Power* (hereinafter *RRC*) (Ottawa: Government Printer, 1946), 647.

13 National Security Agency, Central Security Service (hereinafter NSA), report 29 January 1944, Fifth Venona Release.

14 NSA, reports 31 January and 4 February 1944, Fifth Venona Release.

15 NSA, report 25 January 1944, Fifth Venona Release.

16 NSA, report 22 January 1944, Fifth Venona Release. "Green" was not identified by the royal commission; see *RRC*, 685.

17 NSA, report 25 January 1944, Fifth Venona Release.

18 Sam Cohen, counsel for Fred Rose, raised this important point in court, saying that it was extraordinary that a "person who has knowledge of what is going on in Ottawa ... did not know that he should go to no other place" than the RCMP. Transcript of *Rex vs. Fred Rose*, 22 March 1946, National Archives of Canada (hereinafter NAC), Jacob Lawrence Cohen Papers, MG30 A94, vol. 45.

19 John Sawatsky, *Gouzenko: The Untold Story* (Toronto: Macmillan of Canada, 1989), 39.

20 Hoover to State Department, 18 September 1945, NARA, RG59.

21 Reginald Whitaker and Gary Marcuse, *Cold War Canada: The Making of a National Insecurity State, 1945-1957* (Toronto: University of Toronto Press, 1994), 46-8.

22 See file "International Communist Agent," 1930-1939, NARA, RG59, dealing with a US citizen arrested by the Austrian police for being a communist and being in connection with Austrian communists. Communism was then banned in Austria.

23 The RCMP devoted many resources to tracing how this passport was transferred into the name of a Soviet citizen living in California.

24 John Edgar Hoover to State Department, 24 September 1945, NARA, RG59.

25 Author interview with former KGB officer, Lt. Gen. Sergei A. Kondrachev, Strasberg, Germany, 3 May 1997.

26 CIA to Truman, 27 January 1948, Harry S. Truman Library.

27 Frank Cain, *A.S.I.O.: An Unofficial History* (London and Melbourne: Frank Cass and Spectrum, 1994), ch. 7.

28 Whitaker and Marcuse, *Cold War Canada*, 40.

29 This limited description of Gouzenko's papers is derived from the *RRC*.

30 Whitaker and Marcuse, *Cold War Canada*, 58.

31 *RRC*, 648.

32 Civil Rights Union to Rt. Hon. J.L. Ilsley, 5 February 1947, NAC, W.L.M. King Papers, MG 26L, vol. 19, USSR Espionage in Canada, 1947-1948, 100-9.

33 "Interview with Petrov Tuesday, 6.4.54.," AA, series A6119, XR1, item 18, (ASIO file).
34 For a full explanation of how the KGB safe key wandered from person to person and the KGB list was copied, see Cain, *A.S.I.O.*, 181-2.
35 *Royal Commission on Espionage Official Transcript of Proceedings*, 9 vols. (Sydney: NSW Government Printer, 1955), 146.
36 Ibid., 148.
37 The "D notice" system was the British invention whereby the public media joined in a gentlemen's agreement with the government not to discuss technical defence issues or matters dealing with state intelligence.
38 Frank Ahearn, President Wallace Reality Co. Ltd., to Mackenzie King, 13 January 1949, NAC, W.L.M. King Papers, MG26 J4, vol. 417, Gouzenko, Corresp. 1949.
39 Comment by RCMP Deputy Commissioner William Kelly in Sawatsky, *Gouzenko*, 10.
40 Cain, *A.S.I.O.*, 252-3.
41 Whitaker and Marcuse, *Cold War Canada*, 164.
42 Ibid., 80.
43 *RRC*, 617.
44 Ibid., 403.
45 For the May, Benning, and Boyer cases, see ibid., 375-458.
46 See Frank Cain, "Venona in Australia and Its Long-Term Ramifications," *Journal of Contemporary History* 35, 2 (April 2000): 231-48.

8
Diplomacy in Easy Chairs: Casey, Pearson, and Australian-Canadian Relations, 1951-7
Christopher Waters

At first glance, Australian-Canadian relations during the 1950s would not seem to be fertile ground for study by an international historian. While Australia and Canada were firmly entrenched in the Western bloc in these Cold War years, they had different foreign policy agendas. Both of these nations were members of the Commonwealth of Nations and were closely allied to the United States, but they shared few major foreign policy problems and interests, except perhaps in the field of international economic policy. Placed on opposite corners of the vast Pacific Basin, Canada and Australia had few demanding reasons for extensive diplomatic exchanges. The first half of the 1950s saw the focus of Australian foreign policy turn away from Europe and the Middle East toward East Asia, while for Canada, its commitment to the security of Western Europe through membership in the North Atlantic Treaty Organization became the major focus of Canadian diplomacy. There were no great clashes between these two friendly nations, no difficult diplomatic problems, and certainly no possibility of military conflict. The Australian-Canadian relationship was extremely cordial, but not of crucial importance to either nation. Yet, this combination of friendly yet distant relations was the very factor that provides some important insights – not only into the foreign policy of each of these nations, but also into the underlying influences that shaped their foreign policies.

The major Australian figures with responsibility for international policy in the 1950s – such as Robert Menzies, the Australian prime minister from 1949 to 1966, and Richard Casey, Australia's external affairs minister from 1951 to 1960 – very much enjoyed visiting Ottawa as a pleasant interlude during their many journeys to Washington and London. They also enjoyed exchanging ideas and information with their Canadian counterparts, such as Louis St. Laurent, the Canadian prime minister from 1948 to 1957, and Lester Pearson, the Canadian minister for external affairs for those same years. In Ottawa (Canadian ministers rarely visited Australia), both the Canadians and the Australians could compare notes on the state of the world and on the actions and policies of the United States and United Kingdom without fear of stepping on great and powerful toes. Arthur Menzies, the head of the Far Eastern Division in the Canadian Department of External Affairs, explained that "Although, from a geographic point of view, we look at the Pacific from opposite corners and do not have identical national security problems there is great benefit to us in an intimate exchange of views with our Australian cousins."[1] The freedom of their private exchanges and the intimacy of the relationship resulted in archival records that contain many interesting insights into the thinking and policies of these two governments, and provide rich material for the international historian.

There were several elements that fostered close relations between the two governments during these years. Canada and Australia were members of the Commonwealth, and accordingly both had close historical, economic, cultural, military, and diplomatic ties with Britain. For both nations, however, the United States – as the only superpower in the Western bloc – was, by the 1950s, their most important ally and strongest influence on their international policies. During the period from 1951 to 1957, both Australia and Canada had Liberal parties in power – albeit, in Australia, the Liberal Party was in government in a coalition with the Country Party. While there were important differences in the political cultures of the Canadian and Australian Liberal parties, the men who led these governments shared many values, many ideas, and held a broadly similar view of the state of the world in the 1950s and, just as importantly, what the world should be like. There was also considerable like-mindedness between the officials in the departments of External Affairs in Ottawa and Canberra.[2] Another development that drew the two countries closer together in the 1950s was that, during these years, Australia began to grapple with a problem that had been engaging Canadian diplomats deeply since the 1920s. This was the question of how to maintain good relations and develop appropriate policies when being pulled in different directions on certain policy issues by the United States and Britain. Differences between the United States and Britain over successive crises in East Asia, and later over the Suez Crisis, created the desire by Australian ministers and officials for more intimate consultations with Canada about how to manage these Anglo-American arguments.[3]

There is, then, good reason for the international historian to explore the Canadian-Australian relationship during these years. The major subject I wish to examine in this chapter is the relationship between the two ministers of external affairs for this period – Lester Pearson and Richard Casey. I will examine briefly their backgrounds, their personal relationship, and their broad attitudes to international affairs, before looking in more detail at Australian and Canadian attitudes and policies toward the revolutionary change that swept through South and East Asia during this tumultuous decade. This chapter will explore those attitudes and policies, identify similarities and differences, and attempt to explain any differences – not only in terms of these nations' different geographical locations and security interests, but also in terms of the different political cultures and imperial inheritances of the St. Laurent and Menzies governments. In common with several other chapters in this book, the contrasting Canadian and Australian experiences of the evolution from dominion status to nationhood emerges as an important theme of this study of Australian-Canadian relations during the 1950s.

Casey and Pearson

From the very beginning of his tenure as minister for external affairs in 1951, Casey attempted to establish a special relationship between Australia and Canada, and in particular with Pearson.[4] Casey was later to tell Arthur Irwin, the high commissioner for Canada in Canberra, that when tackling a major foreign policy issue he felt very much alone. By way of explanation Casey said his senior officials – such as Arthur Tange, secretary of the Department of External Affairs, and Jim Plimsoll, a first assistant secretary – were so caught up in day-to-day problems that they had little time for fundamental thinking on policy. He added that most of his cabinet colleagues were too consumed with domestic issues to be seriously interested in foreign policy. Casey believed that he was "no good at battling this kind of thing through by himself." Irwin noted that Casey "had to have somebody with whom he could bat the ball back and forth. That was the way to get at these things. 'You have to bat the ball and Mike's [Pearson] the kind of man you can do that with.'"[5] There was a degree of reciprocity from Pearson, who "found his exchanges of ideas with Casey both reassuring and stimulating."[6] Casey placed considerable importance on his relationship with Pearson. As he said when struggling with the thorny question of changing the direction of Australian policy toward Asia in 1956: "If only Mike and I could get alone somewhere and think it through. Mike and I are in the same kind of job, we have similar backgrounds, we are both in politics and have to think in political terms."[7]

Did Casey and Pearson in fact have similar backgrounds? In some ways there are remarkable parallels in the paths of their lives, but in others they were worlds apart. Both of these men were born in the 1890s during the height of the age of new imperialism; Casey being seven years older than his counterpart, Pearson. Richard Casey was born into a very wealthy and well-connected Melbourne family, the son of a successful businessman. Lester Pearson was born into a family of modest means in a village outside Toronto, the son of a Methodist minister. Casey had a privileged childhood, being educated in private schools, including one of Melbourne's leading private schools, Melbourne Church of England Grammar School. Pearson was brought up in genteel poverty, but through the sacrifices of his father, his ability to gain scholarships, and family connections he received a good education. In the years just before the First World War, Casey attended Melbourne University before transferring to the University of Cambridge, where he studied engineering. Pearson studied history as an undergraduate at the University of Toronto and, after many interruptions for war service and a brief business career, he continued his historical studies at Oxford University with the benefit of a scholarship. Both men thus had the common experience of many future leaders within the Commonwealth – the Oxbridge experience. Their education was in different fields, with Casey's lying in the sciences and engineering and Pearson's in the humanities. Both men served in the First World War; Casey as a staff officer in the Gallipoli campaign and on the western front, Pearson as first a medical orderly in Salonika, later as an officer pilot in the Royal Flying Corps who was injured and sent home before seeing combat. Both men had short spells in the commercial world after the war before entering government service – the British ideal of public service being a common theme in the lives of both men.

In 1924 Casey was selected as one of Australia's first diplomats, based for the next eight years in the British Cabinet Office in London, with the task of reporting directly to the Australian prime minister about all issues of international policy. After his time at Oxford, Pearson became a history professor at the University of Toronto before also entering the world of diplomacy as a first secretary in the Canadian Department of External Affairs. Pearson, like Casey, was to enjoy a lengthy spell as a diplomat in London, his service being from 1935 to 1941. During the Second World War, both men served as their respective countries' minister in Washington (Pearson later served as ambassador). In the late 1940s both men made the decision to go into domestic politics, with Pearson becoming his nation's external affairs minister in 1948 and Casey achieving the same portfolio in 1951. Casey failed to achieve his ultimate ambition of becoming Australian prime minister; by contrast, Pearson succeeded in holding the office of prime minister from 1963 to 1968.

The two men had followed a similar trajectory to reach their respective positions as minister for external affairs, but there were significant differences in outlook and experience between the two men. Casey has been described accurately by his biographer, W.J. Hudson, as one of the last great Anglo-Australians.[8] By contrast Pearson – while to some extent an Anglophile in his early years – tended as he grew older to emphasize his Canadian nationalism more and more. During the Second World War Casey served first as the British resident minister in the Middle East and later as British governor in Bengal in the last years of the British Raj. It is impossible to believe that Pearson would have considered such positions suitable for a Canadian. In their political outlooks Pearson was a liberal but Casey was more a conservative, with some liberal tendencies. Neither man had any time for socialism, although in the aftermath of the Great Depression and the Second World War, both were prepared to accept that there was a legitimate role for the state to take positive action in maintaining high levels of employment and adequate standards of health care, welfare, and education. Pearson was prepared to put more emphasis in his foreign policy on the tenets of liberal internationalism and the role of law than Casey, who tended to base his policy on a realist view of the world and hence emphasize alliance diplomacy and the rule of power politics rather than international governance. However, these differences in approach to international relations should not be exaggerated, as both men were ultimately realists; the differences between them were more a question of emphasis than fundamental divergence of philosophy. These two men shared much in terms of experience, attitudes, and sensibilities, and for Casey, at least, Pearson was a valued and respected, if distant, confrere.

Prior to the 1950s, Casey and Pearson do not seem to have had a long history of friendship, although both families knew each other in Washington during the war.[9] As external affairs ministers, their relationship was initially quite formal, but soon became more intimate, with their correspondence headed "My dear Dick" and "My dear Mike."[10] There was growing intimacy in their limited, but significant correspondence. On one occasion Pearson wrote affectionately on reading an extract from Casey's diary that Casey was a "vivid reporter because his almost Boswellian ingenuousness makes him a good deal more honest than more subtle people would be."[11] It is important not to over-emphasize the closeness of their relationship – Pearson only briefly mentions Casey twice in his memoirs – but they enjoyed and profited from their meetings and exchanges. An example of this can be seen in Pearson's expression of delight to Arthur Irwin in 1956 that Irwin had established an intimate relationship with Casey, "because it is particularly good for Canadian-Australian relations that they should be conducted to a considerable extent in easy chairs. We have a good deal more in common than is generally realized and a good deal to learn from each other."[12] Pearson also noted a distinct difference in Casey's diplomatic style from his predecessors, writing after one of their first meetings as ministers in 1951: "Casey is obviously going to do the job – at least at international conferences – in a very different way from his predecessors, and I think he will be more successful in making friends and influencing people; even though his old Etonian, striped pants manner may put off some of the rougher exponents of the new diplomacy."[13]

Casey had a markedly different diplomatic style to the thrusting and bold approaches of his two predecessors, Dr. Herbert Vere Evatt, minister for external affairs from 1941 to 1949, and Percy Spender, minister for external affairs from 1949 to 1951. With the advantage of hindsight, however, there is little doubt that both Evatt and Spender achieved far more in the field of international affairs with their noisy styles than Casey did with his more quiet approach and behind-the-scenes style of diplomacy, more in line with the practices of the British Foreign Office. Pearson and his officials certainly preferred Casey's diplomatic style and personality to those of his two stormy predecessors. By 1954 the closeness of their relationship was reflected in Pearson's privately expressed wish for a Menzies victory in the Australian federal election of 1954 and Casey's continuance in office, which "will cause no disappointment in the Canadian Department of External Affairs, and especially with its Minister."[14]

The Cold War Years and the Anglo-American Relationship

By 1950 Europe was divided by the Iron Curtain, mainland China had gone communist, and the contest between the Cold War blocs had begun for the hearts and minds of the peoples of the decolonizing world. The early 1950s was a time of almost continuous crisis, with the Korean War fought to a bloody stalemate and the arms race between the superpowers accelerating dangerously as they both expanded and deployed their nuclear arsenals. These, too, were the years of McCarthyism in the United States, with anti-communist campaigns and purges confining American political culture and international policy within narrow boundaries. In Eastern Europe the Soviet Union crushed any internal opposition to the new communist governments. As the decade passed, however, there was a shift in the Cold War from this state of almost continuing crisis to the beginning of a period that became known as the time of "competitive co-existence." This transformation began with the death of Stalin in 1953 and took on particular strength in Asia with the Korean settlement in 1954 and the Geneva summits of 1955. Tension was to remain high, however, as was demonstrated by the Soviet invasion of Hungary in 1956. Across the world throughout these years, the Cold War defined international, national, and personal politics. Yet in this period, it was not only the Cold War that was redrawing the global map. With the rise of nationalist movements throughout Asia and Africa, the European empires were disintegrating, and by 1950 major colonies such as India and Indonesia had already won independence. As part of this broad decolonization process, the British Empire was transforming itself into a new Commonwealth of Nations. It was a time of great change. For men born in the decade before the twentieth century, who had lived through two world wars, it seemed to be a potentially very dangerous world.

Both Casey's and Pearson's understandings of world affairs in the postwar period were dominated by the Cold War. Pearson as a liberal and Casey as a conservative both saw communism as the greatest threat to peace in the world and to the world order they cherished. The Cold War, for them, was not only a clash of the superpowers, but also a clash of ideologies and values. Communism posed a direct threat to the principles, values, and ideas that were so much a part of their respective characters. In their eyes the threat to world peace came directly from the Soviet Union. For both of these men, the Kremlin was engaged in an aggressive, expansionist campaign that threatened world peace. As Pearson wrote in his memoirs, in a critique of the revisionist interpretation of the Cold War, "But the fact, the indisputable fact, remains that the main and very real threat to world peace during the first years of the Cold War was the armed might, the aggressive ideology, and the totalitarian despotism of the Communist empire of the USSR and its satellite states under the iron hand of one of the most ruthless tyrants of all time."[15] Casey, in his writings in the 1950s, presented a similar analysis: "In spite of the events of recent years, I believe it can be said that the basic objectives of Russian policy have not changed. Their aim continues to be world domination, directly or indirectly ... The primary aim of Soviet foreign policy remains the destruction of democratic unity."[16]

In the late 1940s Pearson had been one of the chief architects of Canada's commitment to the security of Western Europe through its membership in the North Atlantic Treaty Organization. This was a complete reversal of Canada's prewar policy of rejecting any military commitment to the defence of Western Europe in peacetime. It was the fear of communism in general and the Soviet Union in particular that pushed Canadian political and public opinion to adopt this radical new course. Foreign and defence policy under the Menzies government was also largely shaped by the fear of the Soviet threat. If anything, the Menzies government was more hawkish in its anti-communist views and policies than the St. Laurent government, although perhaps not by so much. Despite their political differences, Casey and Pearson did broadly share the same world view, which had at its core the driving force of anti-communism.

This meeting of minds was reflected in the two men's early exchanges. Casey wrote to Pearson in June 1951 that their two nations were passing through "one of our most difficult and dangerous periods."[17] Casey argued that the solution to the problem of the expansion of communism since the Second World War lay in united resistance by the English-speaking peoples of the world, and this required a powerful alliance between the United States and Britain. The relationship between the United States and the British Commonwealth, Casey stressed, was "now more important than any time in the past."[18] He believed that both Canada and Australia had a special responsibility – indeed, an obligation – to foster a sturdy and lasting relationship between the United States and Britain. In this letter Casey summed up for Pearson his vision for Australian-Canadian relations in the following terms: "What I hope could happen is that a working relationship could be developed between us which would enable each of our countries to make its full and positive contribution towards better understanding in the Anglo-American or English speaking world. It seems to me that both of our countries have special opportunities for influencing the opinions of London and Washington."[19] Casey saw their special task as working together as "an effective force for the reconciliation of interests between the United States and Britain and an element of stability in the United Nations and the world in general."[20] Noting that he had read Pearson's public statements on this subject, Casey heartily agreed with Pearson's views. In his reply Pearson welcomed the idea of closer cooperation between their two countries and agreed that the two governments – but more particularly their two departments – could play a very useful part in facilitating a stable relationship between the British Commonwealth and the United States in the days ahead, which he agreed were bound to be difficult ones.[21] His was a warm, but realistic response. Pearson believed that the best approach, one he had already been following, was for nations such as Canada and Australia to explain the Commonwealth view to Washington and the American view to London. Yet, as Pearson warned, given the agitated state of American public and political opinion, which was being whipped up by anti-communist zealots, even advice from the friendliest neighbour was liable to be misunderstood.[22] Wayne Reynolds demonstrates that, in the 1950s, the Menzies government wanted Australia to develop a similar role to that of Canada in the field of atomic energy, in both peaceful and military spheres. In the field of international affairs, Casey, too, wanted Australia to play a similar role to that of Canada: that of a friendly conciliator that could help settle any disagreements between the United States and Britain.

There were substantial differences over policy between Britain and the United States during the first half of the 1950s, which caused tension in the Anglo-American relationship. The recognition of the People's Republic of China, the possible use of atomic weapons in the Korean War, the proposal for Western military intervention in Indochina in 1954, and the Offshore Islands crisis of 1955 were just some of the issues over which major rifts occurred. The Anglo-American relationship plummeted to its nadir over the Suez Crisis in 1956. Casey and Pearson had plenty of scope, therefore, for their role as conciliators between Washington and London. It is significant that both Casey and Pearson opposed the Anglo-French invasion of Egypt in 1956 – not only because they believed, rightly, that it was doomed to fail, but also because it threatened to split the Commonwealth and, more importantly, shatter the Anglo-American special relationship. Apart from the Suez Crisis, it was Asia that was the location for most of these Anglo-American disputes. It was also in East and South Asia where there were some subtle, but significant differences between the approach and policy of Canada and Australia.

From the early years of their relationship as ministers, Casey attempted to get Pearson more interested in events in Southeast Asia. In May 1952 Casey sent Pearson extracts from his personal diary, which he had kept for a number of years. The extracts were about the trip he had made around East and South Asia in July 1951. This tour of the region had a major impact on Casey's overall approach to Australian foreign policy, as his experiences of travelling through Asia led him to make the decision that South and East Asia, not Europe and the Middle East, must now be the major focus for Australian foreign policy. In his letter forwarding these extracts, Casey recognized that "South East Asia is only on the fringe of Canada's area of particular interest – whereas to us it is of very real interest."[23] Indeed this was the case, with Pearson showing only polite interest, but Casey did not give up. In January 1955, in an attempt to engage Pearson more deeply in Australia's neighbouring region, Casey wrote what he described in his own words as "a rambling personal letter from me on the subject that is most prominent in our minds in this country – the situation in South-East Asia and the area generally to the north of Australia."[24] While East and South Asia were not areas of prime concern for Canadian policy makers, neither did they ignore them completely. There were several avenues of contact and involvement by the Canadian government in Asia: through the Commonwealth, Canada had close relations with India, Pakistan, and Ceylon; through its membership on the International Supervisory Commission, Canada was directly involved in Indochina; through the Colombo Plan, Canada gave aid to the region; through the opening of an embassy in Jakarta, relations with the Indonesian Republic were initiated; through its involvement in the Korean War, Canada had close links to South Korea; and through trade and diplomatic ties, Canada was closely interested in Japan. So, although Casey could not get the Canadians deeply engaged in Southeast Asian affairs, there were many points of joint concern in Asia.

General Approach to Asia

The major foreign policy problem in relation to Asia in the decade after the Second World War was to make a judgment about the nature of the revolutions that swept through Asia in the late 1940s and 1950s, and to develop appropriate policies in response to these revolutions. Were these nationalist rebellions against hundreds of years of European rule? Were they rebellions of the masses against the terrible economic, social, and political conditions in which they lived? Or were they communist revolutions inspired and fomented by the Soviet Union and its communist allies? The Canadian and Australian governments came to much the same answers to these questions. In the 1950s Canadian ministers and officials had much the same attitude toward communism in Asia as their Australian counterparts.[25] The St. Laurent and Menzies governments both recognized that nationalism was a major force that had led to the independence of India, Pakistan, Ceylon, Burma, and Indonesia, but by the 1950s both saw a communist conspiracy in progress that was seeking control of Southeast Asia. Pearson, in a speech to parliament on 28 May 1954, noted that the urge for national freedom and economic and social reform, not devotion to communism, was the mainspring of the revolutions in Asia, but he warned that communist imperialism from Moscow and Peking had been too successful in exploiting and, in some cases, capturing these forces for it to be ignored. He argued that the communist conspiracy was making progress in securing control of Southeast Asia.[26] This was an analysis that could equally have been uttered by Casey.[27]

The Canadian and Australian governments opposed what they considered the expansion of communist rule and influence throughout Asia. They viewed the revolutionary movements in China and Vietnam as being dominated by the communists, with the moderate nationalist elements being purged soon after independence was secured. Consequently, both governments were opposed to Mao's government in the People's Republic of China and Ho Chi Minh's government in the Democratic Republic of Vietnam, although they recognized that, in the short term, there was little that could, indeed should, be done to topple these new communist governments. Casey and Pearson were firm opponents of the communist nations of Asia, but they were prepared to adopt a more *realpolitik* approach to dealing with these nations than the United States. In the mid-1950s, for example, both were prepared to recognize the People's Republic of China as a matter of pragmatic international politics, but neither could persuade their governments to act, given the fierce opposition of the United States and divided public opinion at home.[28] Both Canada and Australia had willingly made significant contributions to the American-led United Nations force in Korea, but both governments had been concerned about any American action that would have spread the war beyond Korea, such as the use of atomic weapons or taking the offensive to mainland China.[29] Canadian diplomats had been horrified by the stubborn reluctance of the United States to negotiate with the People's Republic of China to find some sort of compromise on the major issues, such as ending the Korean War and the future of Formosa. The Menzies government and its officials took a tougher line against China than Canada, but Casey, if not his ministerial colleagues, was prepared to consider recognition as a matter of practical diplomacy. Both nations recognized that, of the anti-communist nations, only the United States had sufficient power to influence events in East Asia, and consequently prime responsibility for Western action and policy in that region had to lie with the American government. Therefore – for the most part – they kept any disagreement they had with the policies of successive American administrations toward China out of the public arena.[30] Despite some misgivings about particular aspects of American policy in East Asia, both Pearson and Casey agreed with the Americans' fundamental assumption that communist China was a threat to Southeast Asia, either by means of internal subversion or, less likely, by overt aggression.

Events in Vietnam also captured the attention of both Pearson and Casey. In early 1954 the victory of the Viet Minh forces over the French colonial forces in the battle of Dien Bien Phu brought about the end of French colonial rule of Vietnam and, as part of the Geneva settlement, brought northern Vietnam under the direct rule of the Democratic Republic of Vietnam. These developments heightened the fears of the Menzies government about the consequences of the continuing withdrawal of European power from the region, and the course of the Cold War in Asia. The response of the Menzies government was to take both diplomatic and military measures. In 1955 Australian ground and naval forces were sent to Malaya to be part of the Commonwealth Strategic Reserve, which was intended primarily to be a deterrent against communist Chinese aggression into Southeast Asia.[31] At the same time the Menzies government initiated a diplomatic campaign to discover American military plans for the defence of Southeast Asia. Menzies had little success, as the administration of President Eisenhower was extremely reluctant to divulge its top-secret military plans, even to close allies such as Australia.[32] The other major response of the Menzies government to the events of 1954 was to commit Australia wholeheartedly to the South East Asian Treaty Organization (SEATO), which had been established under the terms of the Manila treaty. The Menzies government wanted SEATO to be an anti-communist security pact, backed by significant military forces, for the defence of Southeast Asia. It saw SEATO as the means to tie both the United States and Britain into the defence of Southeast Asia. The Menzies government wanted SEATO to be a military organization under which members, including the United States, would make ironclad commitments to deploy a set number of forces for the defence of Southeast Asia.[33]

As it turned out, the Menzies government was destined to be disappointed by the toothless tiger that SEATO turned out to be. A new series of non-military anti-communist measures for Southeast Asia – relating to educational, cultural, political, trade union, intelligence, and anti-subversive matters – was also launched.[34] Another part of the Menzies government's defence strategy was its agreement with Britain to test British nuclear weapons in Australia. The Menzies government's defence strategy for Southeast Asia was therefore based on close alignment with the American-led bloc in the Cold War, a forward defence strategy including the permanent stationing of forces in the region, the willingness to make military responses to events in Southeast Asia, the placement of American and British power, through SEATO, in the region between China and Australia's northern shores, and active cooperation with Britain on nuclear weapons testing in

Australia. It was this wide range of action and the development of these new policies that encouraged Casey to write to Pearson in early 1955 to inform him of this activity and to attempt to engage Canadian interest in the region.

For the St. Laurent government, the security of Southeast Asia was a low priority in its foreign policy. While Pearson and the Canadian government acknowledged the need for SEATO, and supported it as a collective security arrangement for Southeast Asia that would act as a deterrent against communist Chinese aggression, they neither desired nor sought to make any concrete contribution. The view of the St. Laurent government was that Canada's military resources were not unlimited and that they should be used to fulfil Canada's already heavy obligations under the North Atlantic Treaty Organization and the United Nations. In any case, Canada would have been precluded from membership of SEATO by its membership in the International Supervisory Commission for Indochina, part of the diplomatic machinery established to oversee the implementation of the Geneva settlement. So while Canada fully supported the establishment of SEATO, it did not seek membership or any informal connection. There was another subtle difference in the Canadian attitude toward SEATO compared to that of the Menzies government. Pearson called for SEATO to be developed in a way that would least alienate countries such as India, Indonesia, and Burma, which had all expressed opposition to the Manila treaty.[35] By contrast the Menzies government, while seeking as many Asian members of SEATO as possible, saw the collective security arrangement primarily as a means of tying its two great and powerful friends – the United States and Britain – into the defence of the region to Australia's north. The Menzies government was much less sensitive to the views of India, Indonesia, and Burma than the St. Laurent government, and in this area of foreign policy lay the major divergence in Canadian and Australian policy toward Asia.

India and the New Commonwealth
As to the nations that lay along the southern rim of the communist world in Asia – those nations not committed to either side in the Cold War – there were significant differences in attitude between Canadian and Australian policy makers. The key example of these differences was in their relations with India and its prime minister, Jawaharlal Nehru. In meetings with Pearson in Ottawa in September 1955, Casey raised the issue of their governments' relations with India. Noting that Canada had a much better relationship with India than Australia, Casey said he had been giving much thought as to how Australian-Indian relations could be improved. The poor state of those relations was due in part, Casey explained, to "a certain lack of sympathy and rapport between Mr. Nehru and Mr. Menzies."[36] This was not the only reason, however. There were several fundamental differences

in attitude and foreign policy between the governments of Menzies and Nehru, which had led to an alarming deterioration in Australian-Indian relations. Many Australian conservatives, including Menzies, had been appalled by and had therefore opposed the decision of the 1949 Commonwealth prime ministers meeting to allow India to remain in the Commonwealth when it became a republic. Menzies described the decision to allow India to remain in the Commonwealth on such terms as "merely continuing a process of disintegration and retreat."[37] Indeed Menzies was personally opposed to the evolution of the old British Commonwealth of the prewar era into a much enlarged, multiracial Commonwealth consisting of both crown dominions and republics.[38] Another source of friction between the Menzies and Nehru governments arose from their starkly different approaches to the Cold War. The Menzies government was very critical of Nehru's pursuit of the concept of non-alignment and his support for the idea of peaceful coexistence with the communist bloc. The Menzies government also saw the emergence of the non-aligned movement, under the leadership of Nehru, as a threat to its plans for the defence of Southeast Asia. Nehru, for his part, was very critical of the establishment of the South East Asian Treaty Organization, which he saw as a military alliance with little connection to most Asian nations, and which would only be a threat to peace and stability in the region. The Menzies government, on the other hand, saw SEATO as an essential element of its defence plans in Southeast Asia. The Menzies government was also fiercely critical of the Indian interpretation that the victory of the Viet Minh in northern Vietnam was a nationalist rather than a communist triumph. Of course, the Menzies government was also one of the few nations to support the Anglo-French invasion of the Suez Canal zone in 1956, while Nehru was one of Britain's fiercest critics.

The impact of these policy conflicts damaged Australian-Indian relations to such an extent that Paul Hasluck, the Australian minister for territories, advised Irwin in April 1956 that "current Australian-Indian relations were "'not good' to 'bad' and that Australia's relations with India were worse than those with any other country, including Russia!" As Irwin noted, Hasluck was a "thoughtful, liberal-minded person" and "one of the more intelligent members of the Cabinet" and the fact that he held such strong views about the Indian government was "both revealing and disturbing."[39] In a conversation with Pearson in March 1955, Menzies mentioned how distressed he was at the anti-American attitude of Nehru and his ministers, which he attributed mainly to "Nehru's Asianness and to his distrust of U.S. leadership."[40] Nehru, in return, was highly critical of Menzies. The Canadian high commission in New Delhi reported in November 1956 that Nehru did not believe that Menzies belonged in the twentieth century, that Nehru contemplated the Australian prime minister's speeches with "wry amusement," and that, even before the Suez debacle, Nehru considered that Menzies was a fit subject for a "Victorian museum."[41]

By contrast Canada had friendly relations with India. Canada, most notably through Pearson's activities at the 1949 Commonwealth prime ministers meeting, had been one of the strongest supporters of the proposal that India, as a republic, be allowed to continue its membership in the Commonwealth. Nehru had been very grateful to Pearson for his constructive contribution to solving this problem. As Hector Mackenzie, in his study of Canada's role in this important moment in Commonwealth history, concludes, "the attitude of the Canadian government to the New Commonwealth was a positive one."[42] While the St. Laurent government held much the same view as Casey and Menzies about the threat from communism in Asia, the nature of the Viet Minh victory in Vietnam, and the need for SEATO, it was far more willing to "agree to disagree" with the Indian government about the value of non-alignment, to at least acknowledge that there was another side to the argument, and, most importantly, to accept – indeed, promote – the new multiracial Commonwealth.

This difference in approach was reflected in the two countries' attitudes toward the meeting of twenty-nine Afro-Asian nations held in Bandung in April 1955. The Menzies government was fearful of this new development in international relations, which it considered would damage SEATO, advance the position of the People's Republic of China, and further the communist advance into Asia.[43] Pearson, by contrast, was prepared to engage with this new movement, and sent a message of good wishes to the organizers. The overall result of Canada's approach was that Nehru had "a very great respect" for St. Laurent and Pearson. The Canadian high commission in New Delhi reported that Nehru trusted the judgment of the two Canadians and looked on both of them with something close to affection. The report went on to state that Nehru "considers, to use his highest term of praise, that Canada is 'a good country' and the Prime Minister [St. Laurent] and Mr. Pearson are 'good men.'"[44] The contrast between the state of Indian-Australian and Indian-Canadian relations could not have been starker. Canadian diplomats saw India as the key to the future of the whole of non-communist Asia, which lay in a large crescent from Turkey right around to Japan. They saw that part of the answer for turning India from a potential ally of the western anti-communist bloc into a real ally was by means of the Commonwealth connection, but to be successful, they understood that all notions of the old Empire had to be abandoned and the new Commonwealth had to be embraced with enthusiasm. In complete contradiction to the Canadian position, Menzies, Casey, and at least some Australian officials saw Nehru as the destroyer of the unity of the old British Commonwealth and Empire, which they believed had been vital to the security of not only Australia, but of the entire Western bloc. While they, too, recognized the strategic importance of India, Menzies and Casey believed Nehru was soft on communism and that his policy of non-alignment and peaceful coexistence with the communist bloc only provided further opportunities for the advance of communism.[45]

By March 1956 Casey was deeply dissatisfied with the general direction of Australian policy toward Asia. It is perhaps symptomatic of the isolation, almost alienation, Casey felt from his cabinet colleagues by this time that it was to the Canadian high commissioner, Arthur Irwin, rather than to his colleagues and officials, that he poured out his concern. At a private dinner with Irwin on 22 March, Casey spent almost three hours discussing Australian policy toward Asia. Casey believed a new approach by Australia was necessary if satisfactory relations were to be established with the new nations of South and East Asia, but he told Irwin he felt he was not succeeding in his search for such an approach. Mike Pearson, Casey told Irwin, was the one person who – if they could get together for long enough – might help him "re-think his way through the problem." The stark contrast between the frosty Australia-Indian relationship and the warmth of the Canadian-Indian relationship – a major policy failure in Casey's eyes – was one factor that had prompted Casey to fundamentally question Australia's overall approach to Asia. Another was Casey's pessimism about Britain's initiative to give independence to Malaya and Singapore in 1957. Casey felt that the British government was being too orthodox about the coming independence of these two colonies, and that Britain should be doing more to leave a stable, united, and non-communist nation behind. He told Irwin he could not understand why the Canadians managed to get on so well with the Indians while the Australians did not. Irwin suggested that it might have something to do with Canadian history, "which had taught us something about how to get along with people with whom we disagreed." Casey agreed that there might be something in this. Irwin somewhat boldly suggested that "Australian security demanded establishment of mutually satisfactory relationships between Asia and Australia and that Australia had not really come to grips with the problem." Casey replied "That's it exactly old man."[46]

In his report of this conversation to Pearson, Irwin concluded that Casey was a very frustrated man. On the one hand, Casey knew that Australia's overall approach was ineffective and needed to be changed; on the other, Irwin wrote: "Another part of him, however, is still emotionally, and to some extent intellectually, nostalgically involved in the colonial era." This made it very difficult, Irwin concluded, for Casey to really face up to the implications of the end of the European imperial era. An example of this problem Irwin cited was Casey's exposition on the future defence arrangements for Malaya and Singapore, which Irwin argued was a revealing sidelight on his basic approach to foreign policy. Irwin wrote, "He [Casey] is still willing to let Mother [the United Kingdom] make the deal for him."[47]

Pearson wrote an insightful reply, in which he generally agreed with Irwin's analysis. He told Irwin that he believed Casey did see the need "for a change of mind and perhaps a change of heart, but he does not seem able to see what is wrong." Pearson noted that Casey's instincts were usually right, but that he was very much a prisoner of the past. While Casey's writings often revealed, Pearson wrote, "a genuine and generous sympathy for South East Asians ... He does, however, betray from time to time a difficulty – where again he is not unique – in comprehending the nature of nationalist feeling." Pearson found Casey's preoccupation with the decline of British power in Asia "disturbing." He acknowledged that Casey had challenged Selwyn Lloyd, the British foreign secretary, on this very point, but added that Casey's diary was full of sad reflections on the sudden decline of Britain's role in Asia. Pearson felt that it was in the area of attitudes toward the decline of British power and the evolution of the Empire into Commonwealth that lay the answer to Casey's query as to why the Canadians got on so well with the Indians. Pearson believed that the secret to establishing good relations with countries such as India, Pakistan, and Ceylon was to adopt the attitude that "'empire' has progressed into a higher rather than a lower existence." Unlike the Australians, Pearson believed a majority of Canadians in positions of authority "honestly believe that, to cope with the problems of to-day, the new type of Commonwealth is an infinitely better institution than the old." Consequently, Canada's relations with countries such as India were much better than they had been in the past. Pearson recognized that the other major feature that assisted the St. Laurent government in this regard was that Canadians "never feel in our bones the fears and anxieties which Australians must have when they look towards their Near north." The absence of immediate pressures and problems, Pearson conceded, was "always a great asset, in becoming popular: or at least in avoiding dislike and suspicion."[48]

Conclusion

While the St. Laurent and Menzies governments followed a very similar overall approach to the great events unfolding in Asia, how can we explain the differences in attitude and policy toward India and the new Commonwealth? The analyses by both Irwin and Pearson of Casey's dilemma in rethinking Australian-Asian relations go right to the core of the answer to this question. First, as Pearson recognized, Canada did have the luxury of distance, which enabled the St. Laurent government to develop a policy of sympathetic support for the new nations of South and Southeast Asia, free from the pressures, both real and imagined, that beset the Menzies government in making its policies toward the region. The revolutionary change that swept through Asia in the 1940s and 1950s did fundamentally change Australia's place in the world, and it provided a very difficult policy and political challenge to the Menzies government that could not be ignored. For Canada, the future of South and Southeast Asia had neither the seriousness nor the immediacy as an international policy issue that it did for Australia. Second, in many ways, men such as Casey and Menzies were "still emotionally, and to some extent intellectually, nostalgically involved in the colonial era," as Irwin had put it, and this did make it very difficult for them to accept the evolution of Empire into the new Commonwealth. In the 1950s there was a fundamental difference in approach by the Canadian and Australian governments to the end of Empire and the dawn of the new Commonwealth. While conservatives and many liberals in the Menzies government mourned the decline of the European empires and feared for the future, the liberals in the St. Laurent government and in the Canadian Department of External Affairs saw this as an advance on the past and as an opportunity for the future.

The divergence in approach between the Australian and Canadian governments was summed up by the differences in their rhetoric about the imperial relationship with Britain. The Canadians accepted the term Commonwealth of Nations, but as a Canadian report noted in November 1956, "Menzies and some of his colleagues in the Government have showed an outmoded affection for the term 'Empire' and do not seem to realize its unsuitability for the present Commonwealth structure."[49] The use of these terms was symptomatic of more profound differences in their approach to the evolving imperial saga. The St. Laurent government was prepared to embrace the new Commonwealth; the Menzies government tried to resist it. The St. Laurent government was prepared to use the new Commonwealth as a policy tool for establishing new and profitable relationships with countries such as India. In complete contrast, the Menzies government saw little advantage in the new Commonwealth and blamed India for destroying the organic unity of what Menzies called the "Crown empire."

The difference in approach to the new Commonwealth went right to the heart of the political cultures of the Liberal parties in Australia and Canada. The Liberal parties in Canada and Australia inherited very different legacies from their nations' colonial pasts. The Australian Liberal Party was, in large part, a party of the Anglo-Australians: those Australians who carried an imperial identity and observed the world through an imperial imagination. The Liberal and Country parties in Australia had always been home for the most fervent pro-imperial section of the Australian population. In Canada these pro-imperialists were more likely to be found in the Conservative Party than in the Liberal Party. The Canadian Liberal Party was more likely to be the home of those Canadians who wished to carve out a separate role for Canada in the world and who wanted to modernize Canada's relationship with Britain. The political landscape in each country played an important role in shaping the different approaches of the Australian and Canadian

Liberal parties to the end of Empire. While in Canada the alternative governing party to the Liberal Party was the Conservative Party, in Australia the alternative government was the Australian Labor Party. In contrast to the Anglo-Australian identity of Menzies's Liberal Party, the Australian Labor Party was the party of the progressive nationalists, with its base of trade unionists and Irish Catholics. The Liberal and Country parties in Australia encompassed the centre to the right of the political spectrum, including all those from small "l" liberals to the conservative Tory right. The Liberal Party in Canada, by contrast, dominated the middle ground of politics and included many who, in Australia, might have found their political home in the Australian Labor Party. The Canadian Liberal Party did not include the conservative Tory constituency, which made up such a significant part of the Australian Liberal and Country parties.

The differences in attitude to the British Empire between the Australian Liberal and Labor parties had been pinpointed by T.C. Davis, the Canadian high commissioner in Canberra during the later years of the Second World War. Davis reported to Ottawa in October 1943 that there had "been a distinct cleavage with regard to certain matters of foreign policy as between the Labour Party, on the one side, and the United Australia Party and the Country Party on the other side."[50] Davis described the anti-Labor forces in Australia as "very much akin to the viewpoint of the group in Canada usually described as the ultra-Imperialistic section of our population."[51] He noted that they always championed the continuation of the British connection, supported the "theory that when Britain is at war, Australia is automatically at war," and called for the greatest assistance that was possible, in terms of men and materials, to be provided for Britain.[52] Davis considered that the Liberal Party that Menzies had created out of the ruins of the United Australia Party during the later years of the war was more accurately depicted as "conservative" rather than "liberal."[53] Davis was, of course, applying the Canadian template of politics to the Australian scene. By contrast Davis described the Labor group as "'Isolationist' in viewpoint," somewhat along the line of thought followed by the French-speaking people in the Province of Quebec – that is, French Canada. The Labor group, he argued, were English speaking, and were of British stock, and did accept the British connection and membership of the British Commonwealth of Nations, but they insisted upon "Australia's status as an independent nation within the Commonwealth." Davis believed that the Labor Party, unlike the conservative parties, did not support the maxim "When Britain is at war, Australia is at war."[54] Davis was reporting the cleavage within Australian society between the nationalist strand within the Labor Party and its supporters and the more pro-Empire attitude of the Anglo-Australian elite who dominated the conservative side of politics. By contrast in Canada the Conservative Party was the natural home of the pro-Empire constituency and was therefore the more imperially minded political party. The Liberal Party in Canada, while by no means anti-British or adopting the same approach as the Australian Labor Party, was the home of those who wished to redefine and modernize the traditional imperial links with Britain. These differences in composition and political culture were of great significance for determining the attitudes and policies of the Menzies and St. Laurent governments toward the evolution of Empire into new Commonwealth in the 1950s.

The two nations' different imperial histories also shaped the approaches to world affairs of Pearson and Casey and their different governments in another way. As Francine McKenzie demonstrates, Canada started the process of redefining its international status during the interwar years, when it was one of the dominions that pressed hardest for constitutional change within the British Commonwealth. By contrast Australia, as McKenzie writes, either resisted or only reluctantly accepted the constitutional changes won by the other dominions, such as Canada and Eire, during this period. Consequently, while McKenzie argues both Australia and Canada emerged from the Second World War as sovereign nations, she recognizes that the process of evolution toward full nationhood was, in both countries, an ongoing, not a finished process that had reached different stages in the two countries. By the 1950s Canada was perhaps twenty years further down the path than Australia in its evolution from colony to dominion to nation. Australians had only begun to fully grapple with the issue of Australia's international status during the time of the Labor governments of the 1940s, a process that men such as Menzies and Casey had attempted to halt on their return to power in 1949. Pearson's analysis that Casey was not historically, politically, or intellectually well equipped to deal with the evolving Commonwealth and the emergence of new nations such as India identifies the still partial nature of Australia's decolonization process in the 1950s. Certainly Australian conservatives such as Menzies and Casey were not as well equipped as Pearson and other Canadian liberals to deal with the disintegration of the British Empire and its transformation into a Commonwealth of Nations. As Margaret MacMillan argues, Canada and Australia can be viewed as "imagined communities," but then so, too, can empires. Men such as Menzies and Casey still viewed the world with an imperial imagination. Their imagined community was of the prewar British Commonwealth, made up of the old white dominions of Australia, Canada, New Zealand, and South Africa, with Great Britain at the centre. When it came to issues such as the decolonization of the European empires in Asia and the evolution of the British Empire into a new Commonwealth, Menzies and Casey – with their fixed imperial imaginations – were very much prisoners of the past.[55]

The different imperial inheritances and political cultures of the men in the Liberal parties of Canada and Australia are essential to an understanding of what differences there were between the Australian and Canadian governments in the 1950s.[56] In conclusion, however, it is important to stress that the differences between Casey and Pearson – and in the broader sense, between the St. Laurent and Menzies governments – over certain policy issues, such as the evolution of the Commonwealth and relations with India, were the exception rather than the rule. By and large these men and their governments shared similar world views and similar analyses of the great events that were changing the face of Asia. They both shared an appreciation that communism was a major threat to non-communist Asia and that the danger was orchestrated from Hanoi, Peking, and ultimately Moscow. They both supported collective security arrangements to oppose what they viewed as the spread of communism in Asia. They both believed a continuing strong partnership between the English-speaking nations would be crucial to a successful outcome of the Cold War, and as a result worked persistently at improving the state of Anglo-American relations. They both recognized that the largest burden for defending the non-communist world lay with the United States, and that in the final account it was crucial to keep in-step with successive American administrations. Accordingly, they publicly supported major American policies in Asia, and – for the most part – expressed their misgivings about any particular American action behind closed diplomatic doors. In the final analysis Casey and Pearson were both part of a diplomatic elite across the English-speaking nations that shared many of the same values and understandings of the world. They also shared a diplomatic style. It was the fact that the similarities in view, policy, and style between these two men and their governments far outweighed their differences that enabled Australian-Canadian diplomacy in the 1950s to be so very comfortably exercised in "easy chairs."

Notes
1 Menzies to Irwin, 30 March 1955, National Archives of Canada (hereinafter NAC), W. Arthur Irwin Papers, MG31 E97, folder 24-3.
2 Author interview with Arthur Menzies, Ottawa, 15 January 1999.
3 Irwin to Menzies, 7 April 1955, NAC, W. Arthur Irwin Papers, MG31 E97, folder 24-3.
4 Casey to Pearson, 12 June 1951, NAC, Lester B. Pearson Papers, MG26 N1, vol. 2, file R.G. Casey.
5 Arthur Irwin to Pearson, 28 March 1956, NAC, Lester B. Pearson Papers, MG26 N1, vol. 2, file R.G. Casey.
6 Arthur Menzies to Irwin, 30 March 1955, NAC, W. Arthur Irwin Papers, MG31 E97, folder 24-3.
7 Arthur Irwin to Pearson, 28 March 1956, NAC, Lester B. Pearson Papers, MG26 N1, vol. 2, file R.G. Casey.
8 W.J. Hudson, *Casey* (Melbourne: Oxford University Press, 1986). The major biography of Pearson is the two-volume work by John English, *Shadow of Heaven: The Life of Lester Pearson*, vol. 1, *1897-1948* (Toronto: Lester and Orpen Dennys, 1989), and *The Worldly Years: The Life of Lester Pearson*, vol. 2, *1949-1972* (New York: A.A. Knopf Canada, 1992). For Pearson as external affairs minister, also see Geoffrey Pearson, *Seize the Day: Lester B. Pearson and Crisis Diplomacy* (Ottawa: Carleton University Press, 1993).

9 Casey to Pearson, 12 June 1951, NAC, Lester B. Pearson Papers, MG26 N1, vol. 2, file R.G. Casey.
10 See the correspondence between Pearson and Casey in NAC, Lester B. Pearson Papers, MG26 N1, vol. 2, file R.G. Casey.
11 Pearson to Irwin, 25 April 1956, NAC, Lester B. Pearson Papers, MG26 N1, vol. 2, file R.G. Casey.
12 Ibid.
13 Memorandum, Pearson to acting secretary of state for external affairs, 7 November 1951, NAC, RG25, vol. 8164, file 5870.40 part 4.2.
14 Pearson to Casey, 1 March 1954, NAC, Lester B. Pearson Papers, MG26 N1, vol. 2, file R.G. Casey.
15 Lester Pearson, *Mike: The Memoirs of the Right Honourable Lester B. Pearson, vol. 2, 1948-1957*, ed. John A. Munro and Alex I. Inglis (Toronto: Quadrangle, 1973), 25.
16 R.G. Casey, *Friends and Neighbours* (East Lansing, MI: Michigan State University Press, 1958), 49.
17 Casey to Pearson, 12 June 1951, NAC, Lester B. Pearson Papers, MG26 N1, vol. 2, file R.G. Casey.
18 Ibid.
19 Ibid.
20 Quoted in ibid.
21 Pearson to Casey, 29 June 1951, NAC, Lester B. Pearson Papers, MG26 N1, vol. 2, file R.G. Casey.
22 Ibid.
23 Casey to Pearson, 19 May 1952, NAC, Lester B. Pearson Papers, MG26 N1, vol. 2, file R.G. Casey.
24 Casey to Pearson, 28 January 1955, NAC, Lester B. Pearson Papers, MG26 N1, vol. 2, file R.G. Casey.
25 Author interview with Arthur Menzies, Ottawa, 15 January 1999.
26 See extract of speech in memorandum, "The Canadian Attitude to the Manila Treaty," 21 July 1955, NAC, RG25, vol. 6022, file 50273-40 part 9.
27 For the Menzies government's relations with Asia, see Gregory J. Pemberton, *All the Way: Australia's Road to Vietnam* (Sydney: Allen and Unwin, 1987); Peter Edwards with Gregory Pemberton, *Crises and Commitments: The Politics and Diplomacy of Australia's Involvement in Southeast Asian Conflicts 1948-1965* (Sydney: Allen and Unwin, 1992); John Murphy, *Harvest of Fear: A History of Australia's Vietnam War* (Sydney: Allen and Unwin, 1993); and David Lowe, ed., *Australia and the End of Empires: The Impact of Decolonisation in Australia's Near North, 1945-1965* (Geelong: Deakin University Press, 1996).
28 For Canadian policy on recognition, see NAC, Lester B. Pearson Papers, MG26 N1, vol. 20, file "China – recognition of China," and for Australian policy and attitudes, see Lachlan Strahan, *Australia's China: 1937-1994* (Cambridge: Cambridge University Press, 1996) and Notes of meeting with Rt. Hon. R.G. Casey, 6 October 1954, NAC, RG25, vol. 6022, file 50273-40 part 7.3.
29 For Canadian caution as to American policy in the Far East, see NAC, RG25, vol. 6031, file 50293-40 parts 1-4.
30 For the Canadian attitude, see Memorandum, "U.S. Pre-eminence in the Far East," A.R. Menzies to J.W. Holmes, 21 May 1957, NAC, RG25, vol. 6032, file 50293-40 part 5.1.
31 Edwards with Pemberton, *Crises and Commitments*, 162-8.
32 David Lee, "Australia and Allied Strategy in the Far East, 1952-1957," *Journal of Strategic Studies* 16, 4 (1993): 511-38.
33 "Memorandum for the Minister: Australian Views on SEATO," 1 September 1954, NAC, RG25, vol. 6022, file 50273-40 part 7.
34 Christopher Waters, "An Exercise of the Imagination: R.G. Casey and Australian Plans for Counter-Subversion in Asia, 1954-1956," *Australian Journal of Politics and History* 45, 3 (1999): 347-61.
35 Memorandum, "The Canadian Attitude to the Manila Treaty," 21 July 1955, NAC, RG25, vol. 6022, file 50273-40 part 9.

36 Memorandum, Pearson to the undersecretary for external affairs, 18 September 1955, NAC, RG25, vol. 6379, file 4533-40 part 2.2.
37 Greene, Canberra, to secretary of state, Ottawa, 6 May 1949, NAC, RG25, vol. 4479, file 50017-40 part 3, despatch 288.
38 David Goldsworthy, "Menzies, Britain and the Commonwealth: The Old Order Changeth" in *Menzies in War and Peace,* ed. Frank Cain (Sydney: Allen and Unwin, 1997), 99-115.
39 Irwin to Pearson, 26 April 1956, NAC, RG25, vol. 3726, file 5860-40 part 1, despatch 206.
40 See record of conversation in NAC, RG25, vol. 6647, file 11562-41-40.
41 "Mr Nehru's Visit to Canada: December 22-23, 1956," prepared by Canada House, New Delhi, 26 November 1956, 2 and 58, NAC, Lester B. Pearson Papers, MG26 N1, vol. 34, Visit of Nehru to Ottawa file, top-secret brief.
42 Hector Mackenzie, "An Old Dominion and the New Commonwealth: Canadian Policy on the Question of India's Membership, 1947-49," *Journal of Imperial and Commonwealth History* 27, 3 (1999): 104.
43 For the Australian attitude toward the Bandung conference, see Christopher Waters, "After Decolonization: Australia and the Emergence of the Non-aligned Movement in Asia, 1954-55," *Diplomacy and Statecraft* 12, 2 (2001): 153-74, and for the Canadian attitude see NAC, RG25, vol. 7220, file 12173-40 parts 2 and 3.
44 "Mr Nehru's Visit to Canada," 2.
45 For a study of Australia-Indian relations, see Meg Gurry, *India: Australia's Neglected Neighbour? 1947-1996* (Brisbane: Centre for Australian-Asian Studies, Griffith University, 1996); also see Australian Archives (hereinafter AA), series CRS A1838, 2, file 229, 10, 1, 6 part 1. For a memoir of Canadian-Indian relations, see Escott Reid, *Envoy to India* (Delhi: Oxford University Press, 1981).
46 Arthur Irwin to Pearson, 28 March 1956, NAC, Lester B. Pearson Papers, MG26 N1, vol. 2, file R.G. Casey.
47 Ibid.
48 Pearson to Irwin, 25 April 1956, NAC, Lester B. Pearson Papers, MG26 N1, vol. 2, file R.G. Casey.
49 Report entitled "Australia," unsigned, 5 November 1956, NAC, RG25, vol. 6750, file 329-40, part 9.2.
50 T.C. Davis to the secretary of state for external affairs, 16 October 1943, NAC, RG25, vol. 3244, file 5870-40C, part 1, letter 385.
51 Ibid.
52 Ibid.
53 Memorandum for the prime minister, 7 November 1944, NAC, RG25, vol. 5699, file 4-G(S), part 2.
54 T.C. Davis to the secretary of state for external affairs, 16 October 1943, NAC, RG25, vol. 3244, file 5870-40C, part 1, letter 385.
55 Gregory Pemberton, "An Imperial Imagination: Explaining the Post-1945 Foreign Policy of Robert Gordon Menzies" in *Menzies in War and Peace,* ed. Cain, 154-75.
56 Of course there were many other factors at play in both Canada and Australia that shaped attitudes to the Empire and Commonwealth: for example, Canada had its large French-Canadian population and its proximity to the United States, while Australia had its large Irish-Catholic population and its isolation from Britain.

9
The Limits of Like-Mindedness: Australia, Canada, and Multilateral Trade
Ann Capling and Kim Richard Nossal

As "non-great" powers, Australia and Canada are often assumed to be bound together by a mutual interest in ensuring that the multilateral trade system is rules-based rather than power-based. Certainly both countries have been prominent and active players in the creation and maintenance of the international trade system, particularly the General Agreement on Tariffs and Trade (GATT) and its successor, the World Trade Organization (WTO). And both countries have a clear shared desire to impose disciplines that curb the use of brute economic and political power by the United States, and to a lesser extent by the countries of Western Europe. But for all their assumed like-mindedness, it is nonetheless clear that, as the Australian and Canadian governments pursued their respective interests, they revealed deeply divergent approaches to the multilateral trade system. More often than not, these divergences produced conflict in their bilateral relationship, often accompanied by considerable ill-feeling on both sides.

In this chapter we survey two cases of conflict in the Australian-Canadian relationship that illustrate the degree to which a shared interest in the multilateral trade system was not enough to bridge the divergence in policy bred by the pursuit of self-interest. The first is the case of the negotiations over the International Trade Organization immediately after the Second World War. The second is the case of the often bitter divergence that occurred some four decades later, when the two countries found themselves engaged in an effort to promote the liberalization of agricultural trade.

These cases remind us that the conflictual face of the Australian-Canadian relationship is not merely an historical phenomenon, a function of a kind of adolescence that both countries were experiencing in international affairs as they emerged from "dominion status" to fully sovereign states and engaged in what has been described as "a mix of affection and bickering" that is the mark of "sibling rivalry,"[1] the analogy so frequently used in the context of the Australian-Canadian relationship. On the contrary: the kind of quarrels surveyed by Margaret MacMillan, David MacKenzie, Francine McKenzie, and

Galen Perras did not eventually give way to the maturity that, to use John W. Holmes's tongue-in-cheek characterization, comes to countries in middle age.[2] Rather, the differences over the multilateral trade system suggest that conflict arising from the pursuit of self-interest will always be a feature of the Australian-Canadian relationship, however tempered that conflict may be by the kind of factors identified by Andrew F. Cooper in his chapter. In short, while these two countries will frequently cooperate and retain an essential friendliness, there are clear limits to like-mindedness.

Competitors since the Creation: The Case of the ITO

The international institutions established after the Second World War have been rather loftily likened by Dean Acheson in his memoirs to the creation of the world.[3] As John Holmes reminds us, there were, of course, others also present at the creation, even if they do not loom as large in the American retelling of the story.[4] But it is important to note that those small countries that also participated in the negotiations on the post-1945 international order had a deep interest in the shape of the multilateral trade system. According to Michael Hart, "No country expected more of GATT than Canada, and no delegation was more enthusiastic about the prospect of a sound basis for international trade cooperation than that of Canada."[5] In the minds of officials in Ottawa, the establishment of a multilateral system for trade and payments was the best means of guaranteeing Canada's future prosperity, because it would allow countries to overcome the problem of bilateral trade imbalances. The Liberal government of Mackenzie King had never been a fan of the Ottawa Agreements of 1932, which had entrenched the imperial preferential system and curtailed Canada's ability to negotiate with the United States. Although bilateral trade agreements with the United States and Britain in 1938 provided some relief from the straitjacket of the bilateral preferential system, Canada's capacity to trade with the United States remained limited by its inability to convert its chronic sterling surpluses to US dollars. Under a multilateral monetary system with convertible currencies, Canada would be able to use the proceeds of its trade surplus with Britain in order to finance its regular trade deficit with the United States.[6]

Canada's enthusiasm for multilateralism became particularly evident during the Anglo-American negotiations that led to the establishment of the Bretton Woods international monetary system in July 1944. In the difficult months of negotiations prior to the Bretton Woods conference, a clutch of Canadian postwar planners, led by Louis Rasminsky of the Bank of Canada, played an influential role in brokering the conflict between the competing US and British plans.[7]

From a purely domestic perspective, multilateralism would allow Canada to resolve its chronic trade imbalances with its two major trade partners.

But multilateralism was attractive for other reasons as well. First, Canadian bureaucrats and political leaders shared the American view that a multilateral system, underwritten by strong US leadership, would prevent a retreat to the aggressive mercantilism and beggar-thy-neighbour policies of the interwar period.[8] Second, they hoped that multilateralism would provide a useful framework within which Canada could pursue other trade objectives, especially in terms of its burgeoning bilateral relationship with the United States.[9] Finally, they believed that multilateral institutions would provide a forum where Canada could influence the policies of the major powers and the shape of the postwar international order.[10] Indeed Canada already had a privileged seat at the negotiating table by virtue of being included in the Anglo-American discussions in 1944 and 1945, which prepared the ground for the US proposals for the postwar trade system. No other country was included in these "conversations," and the Canadian government was able to make use of its position to try to broker a compromise between Britain and the United States on the nature of the postwar monetary architecture.[11]

Australia was far less enthusiastic about the American vision for a multilateral trade system. The US proposals committed national governments to promoting the reduction of tariffs and other trade barriers and the elimination of all forms of discrimination in international commerce. These objectives constituted a challenge to the fundamental elements of Australia's trade and development strategy – imperial preference and industry protection. In particular there was a far greater degree of skepticism about the alleged merits of non-discriminatory multilateralism compared to the certainty provided by bilateral trade agreements. Indeed no aspect of the US proposals caused more anguish among Australian cabinet ministers and their policy advisers than the future of imperial preference in a multilateral system.

The most ardent advocates for the retention of imperial preference were, not surprisingly, its principal beneficiaries – the horticulture industries of Victoria and Tasmania. Any threat to the preferential system was a threat to the viability of the fruit growers and preservers who benefited from preferential access to Commonwealth markets, especially Britain and Canada. In parliament they were supported by the opposition Liberal and Country parties, which had been responsible for establishing returned soldiers in the fruit-growing industries after the First World War. They also had powerful support within the bureaucracy, primarily within the Department of Trade and Customs, which was responsible for the administration of the tariff system. The official view in Trade and Customs was that imperial preference had been a justifiable response to "mistaken and selfish measures" such as the US Smoot-Hawley tariff of 1930.[12] There was no reason to believe that such actions would not recur in the future, and so the principle of discriminatory bilateralism among "friends" was just as valid now as it had been then.

By contrast officials in the departments of Commerce and Agriculture, External Affairs, and Postwar Reconstruction believed that the preferential system had not only outlived its usefulness but had now become detrimental to Australia's trade interests. In their view trade diversion was counterproductive for a country like Australia, which relied on foreign markets for the disposal of a large part of its agricultural production. Not only that, but by limiting Australia's ability to offer concessions to non-Commonwealth countries, it had prevented Australia from concluding trade agreements with its other important trade partners, especially the United States.[13] The Australian Labor government of J.B. Chifley tended toward that view as well. After all, like Canada, Australia had always made clear its willingness to pare back its special trade relationship with Britain, Canada, and the other members of the imperial preferential system, in return for the guarantee of better access to the US market for Australia's major exports – wool, meat, and dairy products. Indeed in the early years of the Second World War, Australia had tried unsuccessfully to reach a bilateral trade agreement with the United States similar to Canada's 1938 trade agreements.[14] But once the war ended, Chifley seriously doubted the ability of the administration of Harry S. Truman to make sufficient trade concessions to warrant a reduction of Australia's preferential access to Commonwealth markets. In congress the mood was already swinging away from liberal internationalism back toward protectionism, and it was rumoured that Truman had assured members of congress that there would be no tariff reductions on wool, Australia's most important export to the United States.[15] For that reason, the Labor government was deeply skeptical about the US ability to negotiate a sufficient level of market access to compensate for the loss of preferences in Commonwealth markets. In other words they feared that there might be very little to gain from the multilateral trade negotiation process envisaged in the US proposals.

A second concern was the apparent threat to Australia's policy of industrial diversification and development through tariffs and other protective measures. The US program envisioned limits on the use of these measures through the negotiated reduction and "binding" of tariffs, restrictions on subsidies for protective purposes, and bans on quantitative import restrictions. This was entirely at odds with Australia's traditional approach to industrial development, which depended on the Tariff Board's autonomy to recommend protective measures on a "scientific" basis.[16] In fact the Australian government's commitment to industrial development was growing, not waning, in this period. The recent experience of war had amply justified the claims of protectionists, who argued that industrial diversification was vital to Australia's capacity to defend itself. Protectionist sentiments had been further strengthened by the Keynesian turn in Labor's postwar development policy, which drew a direct connection between economic security and welfare and the expansion of production and consumption through industrial development. In other words the US proposals promoted tariff reductions at precisely the time that Australia more than ever before was committed to the use of interventionist measures to promote industrialization.

Indeed a fundamental shortcoming of the US proposals was that they failed to recognize or make provision for the industrial ambitions of less-developed countries like Australia. This was not just a threat to Australia's ambitions for industrial development, but to its economic growth and export prospects more generally, which depended on the industrialization of developing countries in the East Asian region to provide new markets for Australia's raw material exports. Australia's concern, shared by other countries with a relatively small industrial base, was that the US proposals would freeze the existing international division of labour in favour of the wealthy industrialized countries of the northern hemisphere. Indeed Australia's fundamental criticism of the US approach was that it placed too much emphasis on the removal of trade barriers as a means of promoting trade and too little emphasis on the responsibility of governments to maintain full employment and, therefore, a high volume of demand. In addition, there were no provisions for the economic development of countries outside the industrialized world. Instead it assumed that some countries were naturally primary producers and would never industrialize. The net effect of the US draft would be to "fossilize" existing patterns of production and trade, ultimately stifling rather than expanding world trade.[17] Australia wanted to see more positive commitments in the charter, including specific undertakings on employment and economic development. This would restore the balance between the "thou shalt nots" and the "thou shalts."[18]

A final concern looming in the minds of the Chifley government and its trade negotiators was the problem of American hegemony. In Australia there was deep skepticism about the self-serving aspects of the US proposals for trade and its capacity to exert political and economic pressure on virtually every other country in the capitalist world. This partly explains Australia's initial refusal to join the International Monetary Fund (IMF).[19] The acid observations of one of Australia's most eminent economists, J.B. Brigden, were typical of the dominant view in Canberra. Brigden characterized the World Bank and the IMF as "flabby vehicles of Uncle Sam's patronage" that "cannot help being dominated by the U.S.A., and the primitive habits and criteria that determine U.S.A. policies in Washington. The experienced countries must play minor parts, and, indeed, play up to and flatter the U.S.A. ego, for the sake of the world, in this business as in all other United Nations' activities."[20]

Paradoxically, this situation opened up a diplomatic opportunity for Australia to play an influential role in the establishment of the multilateral trade system. Despite its relative lack of bargaining power, Australia was in a unique position in terms of its ability to manoeuvre on the international stage. Unlike the war-ravaged countries of Western Europe, Australia was not directly dependent on American trade and aid to feed and shelter its own people. Nor was Australia in Britain's position of being so seriously in debt to the United States that it had little muscle to bring to negotiations. And unlike Canada, Australia did not have close economic and political ties with the United States. So, for Australia, there was little to be lost in making its demands heard on the international stage. Thus Australia behaved very much as the "enfant terrible" at the postwar conferences that culminated in the establishment of the postwar trading system.

Australia and Canada were among the eighteen countries that participated in the Preparatory Committee meetings, which prepared the ground for the UN Trade and Employment Conference that was scheduled to open in Havana in 1947. The first session of the Preparatory Committee was held in London in late 1946, where a draft charter for a new International Trade Organization (ITO) was substantially worked out. The second session, in Geneva in 1947, produced the first round of multilateral trade negotiations and established the GATT to incorporate these results into a temporary treaty. At these meetings, Australia and Canada found themselves pitted against each other on virtually every major aspect of the negotiations. In essence Canada had lined up in close support of the US proposals for a draft ITO charter, while Australia spearheaded the opposition.

In London the lines were drawn between those who supported the US draft, those sharply critical of it, and those who were neutral. The supporters were a small but commercially powerful group, including Canada, Britain, and of course, the United States – all major exporters of manufactured goods that would derive immediate benefits from trade liberalization. The neutral group included the industrialized countries of Western Europe, which supported the general thrust of the US position but wanted to secure some assurances on issues such as full employment. Australia was in the vanguard of the remaining group of countries – including Brazil, Chile, Colombia, China, Czechoslovakia, India, Lebanon, and New Zealand – which all opposed many elements of the draft charter. As one contemporary US account observed, Australia was the "leader of the underdeveloped countries,"[21] an outgrowth of the postwar search for new diplomatic niches explored in more detail in Francine McKenzie's chapter. This was quite a remarkable departure for Australia, especially in terms of what it indicated about where the government in Canberra saw the country in the postwar international economy. Instead of adopting the position of its major trade partners and military allies, Australia found that it had much more affinity with other newly industrializing primary producers. While Australia otherwise had little in common with these countries, they were united by a common problem in an emerging system of trade rules tipped in favour of industrial countries. This new self-identification as a developing country became a central feature of Australian multilateral trade policy in the postwar period, which served to fundamentally distinguish its attitude and approach from that of Canada.

On virtually every major issue at the London meeting, Canada and Australia found themselves at loggerheads. The US version of the draft charter set out a number of basic rules and principles to be observed by every ITO member. First, and most important, were the rules relating to non-discrimination: most-favoured-nation (MFN) treatment and national treatment. MFN is the principle that ITO-member countries apply tariffs and other trade barriers equally to imports from all other members. Closely related is the rule of national treatment, which holds that imports must be treated no less favourably than domestic goods once tariffs and other allowable border measures have been applied to imports. The second rule concerned transparency and the notion that trade restrictions should be open to scrutiny. In the interests of transparency, the draft charter advocated the abolition of non-tariff restrictions, such as import quotas and administrative arrangements that often served as a cloak for discriminatory treatment. The third rule concerned the elimination of preferences, and was embodied in the rule that members neither increase preferences nor introduce new ones (the "no new preference rule"). In addition, the US draft proposed that tariff reductions should automatically reduce margins of preference. Finally, the draft charter expressed a normative commitment to trade liberalization and the reduction of barriers to trade.[22] It is interesting to compare the Australian and Canadian positions on each of these principles. Apart from anything else, it is instructive to see how closely allied the Canadian position was to the American vision.

In the first instance Australian negotiators argued that their government's acceptance of these commercial policy obligations depended on the outcome of tariff negotiations and the extent to which the charter entrenched an international commitment by governments to maintain domestic Keynesian strategies for full employment.[23] Australia was hardly unique in embracing the case for full employment as a domestic policy objective. The Chifley government's 1945 White Paper on Full Employment in Australia was very similar in tone and substance to those issued at the same time in Canada and Britain, except in one key respect: the latter emphasized the importance of tariff cuts in achieving the conditions for economic growth and employment, whereas the Australian White Paper was completely mute on the importance of trade liberalization. While Canada supported the US view that trade liberalization would create employment and growth,

Australia argued the opposite position, claiming it could not liberalize until full employment and steady growth were achieved. At the heart of this argument was Australia's fear that the United States and Britain could slump back into depression and, through deflationary strategies, pass on its effects to the Australian economy. At the Commonwealth economic conference in London in February 1944, Australia had tried to enlist Canadian and British support for an international employment agreement – with little success. To them, it seemed that Australia was seeking all gain and no pain.[24] Despite these rebuffs, Canberra argued strongly for full employment as an international policy, and this became the centrepiece of Australia's trade diplomacy in the postwar period.[25]

At the 1946 London conference, the Australian delegation "took the lead in advocating the strongest possible employment undertakings and the inclusion in the Charter of provisions for affirmative action of an expansionist character for the maintenance of employment."[26] Australia had gained a valuable ally when British negotiators signalled their support for much more detailed employment provisions in the charter. But the Canadians and Americans continued to reject any notion of an international agreement to maintain full employment through Keynesian measures.[27] In the end, and only after a considerable struggle, Australia was instrumental in securing an extension of the "nullification and impairment of benefits" provision, which would allow the ITO to release a member from its charter obligations if it was found that it was being adversely affected by another member failing to live up to its undertakings.[28]

Canada and Australia also found themselves opposed on the issue of economic development, with Ottawa lining up with the other industrialized countries and Canberra spearheading the developing countries' demands for special rights. Australia's view was that countries with industrial aspirations should be exempt from commercial policy rules regarding the use of quantitative restrictions and tariff bindings, and advocated the inclusion of positive measures to promote development. By contrast Canada and the United States remained opposed to any notion of special rights for these developing countries. In these debates a central issue was the rule regarding the use of quantitative restrictions. The US draft charter proposed to ban the use of import quotas, with special exceptions for trade in agriculture and countries experiencing balance-of-payments difficulties. Most countries agreed with the general principle that tariffs, and not import restrictions, should be the basic instrument of border protection, but there was deep conflict over the extent and nature of exceptions to this rule.[29] In particular Australia joined with countries like India in demanding a "developing country exception," to allow the use of quantitative restrictions for the purpose of economic and industrial development. Australian negotiators also argued that, in some instances, quotas might have to be applied selectively against imports from specific countries – a violation of the most-favoured-nation rule. The rationale behind this was the need to protect full employment in Australia against a persistent trade deficit with the United States or the deflationary consequences of an American depression.[30]

Given the difference in the draft charter's treatment of industrial products and agricultural products, Australia and the developing countries had a very strong case. For domestic political reasons, the US draft excluded agricultural products from the general rules of commercial policy. American agriculture policy allowed the use of quantitative restrictions (to protect the sugar industry), and export subsidies (to support cotton and wheat growers), and any threat to these measures would mean the end of congressional support for the charter. In general Canada supported the United States in arguing for the "agriculture exception,"[31] since Ottawa had an interest in entrenching the price-support mechanisms that had been introduced in Canada in 1944 to ensure that prices for dairy products, eggs, and hogs remained stable once the war ended and did not collapse – as they had done after the First World War.[32] Thus there was an imbalance in the draft charter that quite clearly favoured the industrial nations over the commodity-exporting nations. As a primary product exporter, Australia was deeply critical of the "agriculture exception," but – given the US position – it was impossible to oppose it without wrecking the negotiations. So, instead, Australia and other commodity-exporting countries sought to expand the commercial policy exceptions in order to promote their economic and industrial development objectives. Australia led this effort by advocating the insertion of a whole new chapter in the charter on economic development, which was approved and adopted.[33]

The final major point of divergence between Australia and Canada was the future of the imperial preferential system. The restoration of multilateralism and elimination of the imperial preferential system was the sine qua non of the US proposals. From that, the United States was insistent that all tariff negotiations should automatically reduce margins of preference. For its part, Australia strongly resisted the US formula, arguing that it violated the principle that trade concessions be mutually advantageous.[34] Practically, imperial preferences were Australia's only real bargaining chip, and it was staunchly opposed to any notion of a "formula" approach to preference reductions. In addition, the Australian government wanted to retain the capacity to increase preferences, especially if it failed to secure satisfactory US market access in the trade negotiations. However, this demand was anathema to both the United States and Canadian governments. Canada was more than willing to bargain away its preferences, which had inhibited its ability to cut deals with the United States; indeed, Canada and Britain had released each other from their contractual obligations with respect to preferences in order to allow each greater scope to conclude deals with the United States. In response to Australia's demands, Canada and the United States worked closely together to produce a formula that would allow Australia to renegotiate, but not under any circumstances increase its preferential margins.[35]

Despite their conflicting and competing interests in the establishment of the multilateral trade system, the Canadian and Australian delegations, particularly at the senior officials level, maintained cordial and cooperative relations. The Australian delegation had expected Canada's views to be virtually identical to those of the United States, and they were pleasantly surprised on those occasions when this was disproved. More importantly, the Australian negotiators recognized the importance of establishing good working relationships, since "so much of the detailed work of the Committees in Conferences of this character depends on personal relationships. Agreement comes much more readily when personal goodwill exists on both sides."[36]

We have focused on the immediate postwar period in order to nuance the general observation that Australia and Canada were active participants in the creation of the contemporary multilateral trade system. To be sure, both countries shared an interest in using the GATT to secure their own domestic policy objectives, particularly in the way that the GATT provided a forum in which both countries could secure better market access to the all-important US market. But otherwise, as we have explained, their interests diverged greatly, with Canada moving virtually in lockstep with the US administration while Australia led the opposition. This comparison is particularly instructive in both highlighting the closeness of the US-Canadian relationship at the time, and in demonstrating how Australia's self-identification dramatically diverged from its other Commonwealth "cousins" in the immediate postwar period.

To a great extent, these themes shape the trajectory of the Australian and Canadian multilateral trade diplomacy down to the present day. Both nations came to rue the exclusion of agriculture from the GATT. As efficient, export-dependent producers of a broad range of temperate-zone products, Australia and Canada suffered greatly from mounting agricultural protectionism being embraced by the United States, the European Economic Community (EEC), and Japan. Through the 1950s, 1960s, and 1970s, both Canberra and Ottawa made frequent and vigorous representations within the GATT to establish some disciplines on agricultural protectionism and export subsidies. But their relatively weak bargaining power vis-à-vis the United States and the EEC meant that such initiatives produced few tangible results. Similarly, Australian and Canadian support for formal intergovernmental action to stabilize international commodity prices failed to garner enthusiasm from the United States, the other major temperate-zone producer and exporter. As a result, Australia and Canada sought special treatment within the GATT, formally exempting themselves from the Kennedy

Round formula tariff cuts on industrial products due to the failure of the GATT to address the problem of agricultural protectionism.

Although Australia and Canada were in similar straits, the Canadian government was able to obtain some relief from its difficulties not available to Australia, notably by negotiating bilaterally with the United States. For instance, during the Kennedy Round, Canada managed to secure mutual tariff reductions on farm products traded within North America, whereas Australia had little success in trying to reduce American barriers to its meat, wool, and sugar exports.[37] This is indicative of a long-term pattern whereby Canada's close economic relationship with the United States enabled it to cut bilateral deals of the sort that were not available to the Australians. Eventually Canberra would be moved to abandon the bilateral route, and instead organized a multilateral coalition to press for the liberalization of agricultural trade.

Irreconcilable Differences: The Case of the Cairns Group

The differences between the Australian and Canadian approaches to multilateral trade, evident in the ITO case, reflected a divergence in approach but produced no serious conflict in the relationship between the two countries. In the late 1940s Canberra and Ottawa were competitors, each backing an alternative vision for the postwar international trade system. By contrast the differences in how both countries approached multilateral trade negotiations in the late 1980s produced not only a divergence in vision, but acrimony in the bilateral relationship.

The roots of the Australian-Canadian divergence over the issue of trade liberalization in agriculture – during the Uruguay Round of multilateral trade negotiations – lay in the sharp differences in each country's interests in agriculture, and can also be found in the way in which each government chose to try to advance their interests in the context of a multilateral coalition, the Cairns Group.

The Group of Fair Traders in Agriculture – or Cairns Group – had its origins in a multilateral meeting that was called by the Australian government of Bob Hawke, to coincide with the opening of the Uruguay Round. The meeting, held in the Queensland town of Cairns in August 1986, involved a coalition of fourteen governments with an expressed interest in liberalizing trade in agriculture: Argentina, Australia, Brazil, Canada, Chile, Colombia, Fiji, Hungary, Indonesia, Malaysia, New Zealand, the Philippines, Thailand, and Uruguay. The story of the Cairns Group and its role in the Uruguay Round negotiations has been told elsewhere;[38] our interest here is in highlighting the divergent approaches of Australia and Canada, and examining the conflict between Canberra and Ottawa that plagued the Group.

The Hawke government's initiative in pulling together a group of like-minded countries to press for liberalization in global agricultural trade was driven by an increasing concern in Canberra over the deleterious effects of illiberal trading practices in agriculture by the United States, the European Community (as the European Union then was), and, to a lesser extent, Japan. These countries not only maintained a variety of restrictions on agricultural imports, but also routinely subsidized exports of their agricultural surpluses, often undercutting more efficient Australian producers. Throughout the post-1945 period, the Australian government had persistently expressed concerns about such trading practices, voicing its views both through bilateral channels and in multilateral fora. But by the early 1980s, the illiberalism that persisted in international agricultural trade – even as international trade was being increasingly liberalized – was having profoundly negative consequences for Australian agricultural exports, and thus for Australian producers themselves. By this time the sector was in crisis – hard hit by recession, a persistent rise in costs of production, a severe drought, dramatic declines in global prices for primary commodities, and the "side-swipe" effects of a growing trade war in agriculture between the United States and the European Community (EC).[39] The Liberal-Country party coalition government of Malcolm Fraser, facing rising anger in rural Australia, tried to put reform of multilateral trade in agriculture on the international agenda, but without success. For example, at the GATT ministerial meeting in Geneva in November 1982, appeals by Doug Anthony – leader of the Country Party – to put agriculture on the agenda were rebuffed, prompting Anthony to angrily walk out of the meeting in protest.[40]

One of the reasons the Fraser government's appeals for liberalization in agricultural trade could be so readily dismissed by protectionist Americans and Europeans was that the Australian government's approach to international trade was, in fact, highly inconsistent. While Australia embraced a liberal approach to its highly efficient agricultural sector, it was deeply attached to illiberal protectionism for most other sectors of the economy. Indeed the "protective state" had been a central feature of government policy throughout the twentieth century,[41] and Fraser's government was merely the latest in a succession of governments that had preached liberalism in agriculture while practising protectionism everywhere else. All of this changed after the Australian Labor Party, under Bob Hawke, formed a government following the March 1983 general elections, however. Over the course of the 1980s, the Hawke government began a process of dismantling the various elements of the "protective state," liberalizing Australia's manufacturing sector.

While the Hawke reforms focused on the industrial manufacturing sector, the government was no less concerned about the crisis in agricultural trade that continued to have such an impact on rural Australia (and thereby on the ALP's electoral prospects).[42] As a result, the government renewed its efforts to liberalize agricultural trade, though it employed very different tactics from those used by the Fraser government. No longer was the emphasis on "megaphone diplomacy" and confrontation. Rather, the Hawke government decided to try a multilateral approach to global agricultural trade reform that sought to gather together a number of like-minded, middle-sized agricultural producers that had all been harmed by the restrictive policies of the United States and the European Community in the 1980s. The result was a heterogeneous grouping drawn from a full range of the economic spectrum, all points of the global political compass – East and West, North and South – and five continents. The idea was that this group would put forward a long-term reform package for the liberalization of global agricultural trade, including the progressive elimination of existing tariffs, the conversion of non-tariff barriers into tariffs that would also eventually be eliminated, the elimination of domestic support measures, and the elimination of agricultural export subsidies. Such a broad-based coalition would act as a "third force" in the Uruguay Round of GATT multilateral trade negotiations (1986-94), seeking – in the words of one official who participated in the process – "to embarrass the Americans and the Europeans into some kind of action."[43]

The Australians invited the Canadian government to the meeting at Cairns in August 1986 – partly because of Canada's position as an export-oriented, middle-sized agricultural power, partly because of the relationship between Hawke and Mulroney,[44] but mostly because Canada was a member of the G7, and the Australians hoped that the Canadian government would carry the message of the Cairns Group into that forum. However, the government in Ottawa had none of the commitment to liberalization in all aspects of international trade that marked the Hawke government's approach. On the contrary, the Canadians remained essentially Janus-faced when it came to international trade in agricultural products. On the one hand, Canadian governments have traditionally been committed to the liberalization of trade in certain agricultural sectors, a reflection of the fact that approximately one-third of Canadian agricultural production is exported, and that those exports regularly contributed to Canada's overall positive trade balance. But only *some* agricultural sectors are export-oriented, such as grains, oilseeds, and red meats. Wheat is particularly important, with some 75 percent of Canadian wheat being exported annually. On the other hand, however, some other agricultural sectors – notably the dairy, poultry, fruit, and vegetable industries – were not export-oriented, but heavily protected by supply management schemes and import quotas. More importantly, each of these sectors was concentrated in particular regions of the country. The government in Ottawa therefore had a deep electoral interest in protecting the fruit industry in British Columbia and the dairy and feather industries in Quebec and Ontario, but pressing for liberalized trade in the grain and red meat industries centred in the prairie provinces.[45]

Given this structure of essentially contradictory interests, it is perhaps not surprising that Canada's membership in the Cairns Group was deeply problematic – the Canadian government was an advocate of both free trade and protectionism at the same time. Ottawa's approach to agricultural trade in the Uruguay Round was thus to try to have it both ways: to press for liberalization in agricultural trade while at the same time protecting the status of the supply management schemes and import quotas so important for the Ontario and Quebec dairy and poultry industries. The essence of the Canadian policy was to avoid having to make a choice in its approaches. Rather, as an internal Canadian report put it, the question was "how both avenues can be pursued in a mutually reinforcing manner."[46] The search for mutual reinforcement would lead the Progressive Conservative government of Brian Mulroney to try to keep all of these domestic groups satisfied by playing a multifaceted hand, and refusing to be embarrassed by all of the deep contradictions of promoting multilateral liberalization in grains but protectionism in other agricultural products. On the contrary, the Canadians were unapologetic. "What's wrong with staking out a Canadian position?" asked Don Mazankowski, the deputy prime minister and minister of agriculture. "We should be applauded for that."[47] And they were: in the November 1988 general elections, the Mulroney Conservatives swept the rural seats in both central and western Canada.

Because the Mulroney government's eye was so firmly fixed on maintaining this transregional electoral coalition, it could never bring itself to abandon the principle of protectionism for central Canadian agriculture and embrace the ideals of the Cairns Group. On the other hand, Ottawa never entertained the idea of resolving the contradiction in its position by leaving the Cairns Group. While, as we will show below, there were a number of reasons why the Canadian government chose not to leave, one important reason was that Canada's membership in that group was an important signal to western producers that the Progressive Conservative government in Ottawa was looking out for their interests.

As a result, the Canadian government consistently found itself the odd country out in the Cairns Group, unable to embrace the liberal proposals put forward by the other members and unwilling to embrace the idea of the group as a tight coalition that required solidarity from all of its members. On the contrary: the Canadians kept making it quite clear that they did not feel bound by the Cairns Group's perspectives, and that they saw the Cairns exercise in purely instrumental terms – in other words, a means to pursue Canada's other trade agenda items. Likewise, Ottawa was willing to convey the Cairns Group message to the G7 summit, but it refused to press the group's perspective. And on a number of occasions, the Canadians openly broke ranks with the other members of the coalition – issuing separate press releases after every Cairns Group meeting, tabling its own separate proposal at a GATT negotiating meeting in 1987, and failing to sign on to a Cairns Group proposal in 1988. Likewise, Ottawa went so far as to refuse to sign the proposal for the tariffication of non-tariff import measures, advanced by all other members of the Cairns Group in October 1990. Instead Canada issued its own proposal later in the month, arguing that import restrictions should continue to be permitted. Not surprisingly, this kind of defection created considerable annoyance among other members of the Group, particularly among the Australians, who had hoped that coalition solidarity would buttress the efforts of the Group to forge a "third force" in the Uruguay Round.[48]

But it can also be argued that it was not simply the huge and deeply structural divergence in approaches that created such bitter feelings between Australia and Canada over the course of the Uruguay Round. Rather, it can be suggested that it was the Canadian attitude toward the Australian role in the Cairns Group, and the implications of Australian leadership for Canada's own self-perceived role as a middle-power intermediary between the great powers, that produced the most friction in the relationship during this period.

Richard A. Higgott and Andrew F. Cooper identified the two features of Australia's leadership role in the Cairns Group. One feature was the entrepreneurial leadership demonstrated by the Hawke government in taking the initiative to organize a coalition of the like-minded, in order to push for a rules-based solution to the increasing problem of protectionism in international agricultural trade. The second was the technical leadership involved in using the experienced and sizeable Australian trade bureaucracy to bolster the position of the Group.[49] Both elements of leadership were crucial for any attempt to forge a "third force" in the Uruguay Round. Not only did one need a government to take the initiative to gather the coalition together, but one also needed the expertise that allowed the Group to develop well-researched positions and, as one participant in the process put it, to "do the sums."

But there was also another kind of leadership at work in the Cairns case: intermediary leadership, or a willingness to try to mediate a resolution to the burgeoning conflict between the great powers, which was creating such harm to the smaller countries engaged in the agricultural export trade and "side-swiped" by the feuds of the Americans and the Europeans. It was in this area that the Australians also managed to play an important role, recognized by the majors as the spokesman for a "third force." For the first time since the 1950s, the Australians were taken seriously enough to be accorded a central role in both the formal and informal processes of negotiations. Following the failure of the mid-term review meeting in Montreal in

1988, the United States and the EC invited Australia to participate in secret trilateral negotiations on agriculture. This trilateral process was crucial in providing a low-profile way of making progress away from media scrutiny. By 1990 these negotiations had produced agreement on the three pillars of reform: export subsidies, domestic support mechanisms, and import restrictions. Following the abortive Brussels ministerial meeting in 1990, Japan was invited to join the secret negotiations. It was in this G4 group that the major breakthrough on agreement for tariffication was achieved in October 1991.[50]

There can be little doubt that Australia's new-found prominence in the international trade area irked the Canadians, and provides yet another example of the kind of sibling rivalry over status examined by Margaret MacMillan in her chapter. The annoyance manifested itself in large and small ways. For example, the Canadians were annoyed that Australia retained the chairmanship of the Cairns Group rather than it being rotated.[51] While a small matter, the lack of rotation ensured not only that the spotlight would always be on the Australians (and not, inter alia, on the Canadians), but also that the Australian government would be able to set the agenda.

More important to Canadian officials was the perception that Australian activism was threatening Canada's traditional role of insider and interlocutor between the great powers. In particular the Canadians were concerned about the involvement of Australia in summit diplomacy to which Canada had not been invited. The Canadians responded in the first instance by trying to replace Australia as the spokesman for the Cairns Group in the G4 "inner" negotiations. When the United States proved unreceptive to this idea, the Canadians enthusiastically endorsed the creation of another summit, comprising the agriculture ministers of the G4 countries plus Canada. Dubbed the Quint, this group first met in Florida in January 1989. However, the Quint met only twice and was not reconvened: by all accounts, the United States pulled the plug on this summit because it was widely perceived as a means by which protectionist elements in agriculture departments and governments could slow down progress on negotiations.[52]

By 1988 the split between Canada and the other Cairns Group members was out in the open, and although the Canadian government refused to leave the group, it was no longer seen as part of the coalition by either the other Cairns members or the major agricultural powers. The unedifying dénouement came in 1991, when the Canadian government actually tried to put together a counter-coalition of countries keen on strengthening GATT Article XI protections, which allowed governments to apply quantitative import restrictions to agricultural imports. This campaign was, quite predictably, regarded as anathema by Australians.

Conclusion

The two cases examined in this chapter confirm the general observation made by the editors of this book – that the Australian-Canadian relationship is marked by an overall friendliness and closeness that makes the use of the "family" analogy so common among those who write about it. As L. Michael Berry, the Canadian high commissioner in Canberra in the mid-1990s put it, the "comfort level" in the relationship is very high,[53] an observation that confirms Christopher Waters's characterization of "easy-chair" diplomacy. Our examination of the approaches of both countries to the multilateral trading system in the late 1940s and late 1980s reveals that high comfort level in dealing with one another.

At the same time, however, these cases suggest that there are limits to how far such attributes as like-mindedness, friendliness, trust, and high comfort levels will go to mitigate the effects of divergent calculations of national interest. In both cases surveyed in this chapter, the like-mindedness of these two Commonwealth partners was veneer-thin. In both cases governments in Canberra and Ottawa were led in dramatically different directions by the assessments of ministers and bureaucrats about the most appropriate approach to take.

The major difference between the ITO case in the late 1940s and the Cairns case in the late 1980s seems to be the degree of exasperation and bitterness generated by these divergences. In the late 1940s there appeared to be a recognition that the divergence in approach was entirely understandable; officials went their separate ways in the trade area without the kind of personal acrimony that was infecting the diplomatic relationship between the two countries at the time.[54] In the Cairns case, by contrast, the acrimony in the relationship appeared to emerge not because of the divergence in approaches per se, but because both sides regarded the other's behaviour as inappropriate. Australians might have understood the reasons for Canada's Janus-faced stand on agriculture, but they found the Canadian refusal to leave the group to be both hypocritical and also damaging to the efforts to forge a compromise over agriculture. For their part, Canadians might have understood why Australia was embracing the liberalization agenda so ardently, but they found the Australians to be manipulative and pushy – "free trade zealots," in the words of one Canadian official.[55]

This acrimony continues to spill over into other aspects of the trade relationship: since the end of the Uruguay Round, there have been bitter bilateral disputes over beef, pork, and salmon, with the latter culminating in a WTO dispute in 1998. What is equally important, however, is that the deep annoyance experienced by officials and ministers at each other's behaviour over the Cairns Group and in bilateral trade disputes since has not spread to other areas of the relationship.

Notes

We are grateful to the Australian Research Council of Australia (grant A79802876), the Arts Research Board of McMaster University, and the Social Sciences and Humanities Research Council of Canada (grant 410-95-1085) for support that made the research for this chapter possible.

1 Andrew F. Cooper, *In between Countries: Australia, Canada, and the Search for Order in Agricultural Trade* (Montreal and Kingston: McGill-Queen's University Press, 1997), 14.
2 John W. Holmes, *Canada: A Middle-Aged Power* (Toronto: McClelland and Stewart, 1976).
3 Dean Acheson, *Present at the Creation: My Years at the State Department* (New York: Norton, 1969); the epigraph quotes Alfonso the Wise of Castille: "Had I been present at the creation I would have given some useful hints for the better ordering of the universe."
4 John W. Holmes, *The Shaping of Peace: Canada and the Search for World Order, 1943-1957*, vol. 1 (Toronto: University of Toronto Press, 1979), 27.
5 Michael Hart, "Twenty Years of Canadian Tradecraft: Canada at GATT, 1947-1967," *International Journal* 52, 4 (Autumn 1997): 581; see also Michael Hart, *Also Present at the Creation: Dana Wilgress and the United Nations Conference on Trade and Employment at Havana* (Ottawa: Centre for Trade Policy and Law, 1995).
6 A.F.W. Plumptre, *Three Decades of Decision: Canada and the World Monetary System, 1944-75* (Toronto: McClelland and Stewart, 1977), 28.
7 J.L. Granatstein, *The Ottawa Men: The Civil Service Mandarins, 1935-1957*, 2nd ed. (Toronto: University of Toronto Press, 1998), 139-53; Tom Keating, *Canada and World Order: The Multilateralist Tradition in Canadian Foreign Policy* (Toronto: McClelland and Stewart, 1993), ch. 2.
8 Clair Wilcox, *A Charter for World Trade* (New York: Macmillan, 1949), 26. Wilcox headed the US delegation to the 1947 GATT talks in Geneva.
9 Australian Trade Policy – Article VII, Summary of Discussions on Post-War Commercial Policy, London, June 1943, National Library of Australia (hereinafter NLA), Sir John Crawford Papers, ms 4514, box 1, f.
10 Frank Stone, *Canada, the GATT and the International Trade System*, 2nd ed. (Montreal: Institute for Research on Public Policy, 1992), 21.
11 Canada, Department of External Affairs, *Documents on Canadian External Relations*, vol. 9, *1942-1943*, ed. John F. Hilliker (Ottawa: Department of External Affairs, 1980), 651-5.
12 Trade and Customs Memorandum, 3 January 1944, NLA, Sir John Crawford Papers, box 1.
13 "Review of the Progress of Inter-Imperial Trade," by L.F. Steele, Department of Commerce, 6 October 1944, Australian Archives (hereinafter AA), series A9879, 1, file 2913.
14 Trade Relations with the United States of America, 13 December 1943, AA, series A9879, 1, file 2930.
15 Chifley to Attlee, 23 October 1945, *Documents on Australian Foreign Policy 1937-49* (hereinafter *DAFP*), vol. 8, *1945*, ed. W.J. Hudson and Wendy Way (Canberra: Australian Government Publishing Service, 1989), doc. 331.
16 This process is outlined in Ann Capling and Brian Galligan, *Beyond the Protective State: The Political Economy of Australia's Manufacturing Industry Policy* (Melbourne: Cambridge University Press, 1992), especially ch. 3.
17 Extract from Discussions on Draft Charter for an ITO between US and Australian Representatives, 30 August to 2 September 1946, NLA, Sir John Crawford Papers, box 1. An extract of this is found in *DAFP*, vol. 10, *July-December 1946*, ed. W.J. Hudson and Wendy Way (Canberra: Australian Government Publishing Service, 1993), doc. 95, but it omits the comments made by the US spokesman, Winthrop G. Brown of the State Department.
18 The biblical allusion is B.W. Hartnell's, assistant director to Secondary Industries Division, Department of Post-War Reconstruction. See transcript of Hartnell's oral report on the London conference, 18 December 1946, NLA, Sir John Crawford Papers, box 3, doc. S56.
19 Crisp's biography of Chifley devotes a chapter to the prime minister's "Homeric struggle" to secure Australian ratification of the Bretton Woods agreement. See L.F. Crisp, *Ben Chifley* (Croydon: Longmans, 1960), ch. 14.
20 Confidential memo on "The International Monetary Fund," by J.B. Brigden, 8 April 1946, AA, series A9879, 1, file 9300, 105A, part 3. This document is also included in *DAFP*, vol. 9,

January-June 1946, ed. W.L. Hudson and Wendy Way (Canberra: Australian Government Publishing Service, 1991), but some sections quoted here have been omitted from the published version.

21 W.A. Brown Jr., *The United States and the Restoration of World Trade* (Washington: Brookings Institution, 1950), 99.

22 An excellent exposition of the rules and norms of the multilateral trade system is found in Jock A. Finlayson and Mark W. Zacher, "GATT and the Regulation of Trade Barriers: Regime Dynamics and Functions," *International Organization* 35 (Autumn 1981): 561-602.

23 Australian Memorandum on Article 1 of US Draft Charter, 7 November 1946, Economic and Social Council of the United Nations (hereinafter ECOSOC), London, E, PC, T, C.V, 19.

24 S.J. Butlin and C.B. Schedvin, *Australia in the War,* series 4, vol. 4, *The War Economy, 1942-45* (Canberra: Australian War Memorial, 1977), 658.

25 For a comprehensive account of Australia's "full employment diplomacy," known also as the "positive approach," see Tim Rowse's forthcoming biography of Nugget Coombs, to be published by Cambridge University Press; also see Butlin and Schedvin, *Australia in the War,* chs. 5 and 21.

26 Brown, *The United States and the Restoration of World Trade,* 95.

27 British Commonwealth Talks, "Full Employment," 24 October 1946, AA, series A9879, 1, file 9346, 37.

28 Address by B.W. Hartnell, assistant director to Secondary Industries Division, Post-War Reconstruction, 18 December 1946, NLA, Sir John Crawford Papers, box 3. In the US draft charter the chapter on commercial policy had provided for a complaint procedure if any member believed that the actions of another member led to the "nullification and impairment" of benefits derived from the commercial policy provisions. As a result of Australian pressure, the nullification and impairment of benefits rule was extended to include all aspects of the charter, including employment obligations.

29 Brown, *The United States and the Restoration of World Trade,* 78-89, 98.

30 The 1945 White Paper outlined the government's intent to use quantitative restrictions on imports in the event of a chronic balance of payments deficit arising from a "prolonged and severe" fall in export income. However, the government also wanted to reserve the right to apply import restrictions "selectively," which also meant on a discriminatory basis. "Full Employment in Australia," 30 May 1945, Commonwealth of Australia, *Parliamentary Papers,* Session 1945-46, vol. 4, 1191-213. See also G.G. Firth, "Commercial Policy," 26 September 1945, NLA, Sir John Crawford Papers, box 16.

31 Brown, *The Restoration of World Trade,* 116.

32 It should be noted that the Canadian government's support for US exemptionalism was not absolute. When, in 1955, the United States managed to secure an unlimited exemption from its Article XI GATT obligations, Ottawa strongly criticized the move. Canada consistently maintained its opposition to such exemptions; indeed, in 1987 it was still arguing for an end to the 1955 American exemption.

33 "Chapter Relating to Proposed International Agreement on Industrial Development suggested by the Australian Delegation," 21 October 1946, ECOSOC, London, E, PC, TCI&II, 1.

34 Australia did not budge from this position, which it adopted in late 1945. See for instance, "Modification of Preferences in Return for United States Financial Aid to Britain," n.d. [late 1945], AA, series A9879, 1, file 9317.

35 Brown, *The Restoration of World Trade,* 75.

36 "Trade and Employment Conference," unofficial report by Representative of Department of External Affairs, January 1947, AA, series A1938, 1, file 711, 1, 3, item 2. The Australians thought that the Canadian delegation, led by Hector McKinnon, chair of the Tariff Board, was "competent and sound, but without any notable flair or very distinct influence on the course of proceedings."

37 Gerard and Victoria Curzon, "The Management of Trade Relations in the GATT," in *International Economic Relations of the Western World 1959-1971,* ed. Andrew Shonfield (London: Oxford University Press, 1970), 324.

38 See, for example, Andrew F. Cooper, Richard A. Higgott, and Kim Richard Nossal, *Relocating Middle Powers: Australia and Canada in a Changing World Order* (Vancouver: UBC Press, 1993), ch. 3; Cooper, *In between Countries*; Diane Tussie, "Holding the Balance: The Cairns Group," in *The Developing Countries in World Trade: Policies and Bargaining Strategies,* ed. Diane Tussie and David Glover (Boulder, CO: Lynne Rienner, 1993); also Peter W. Gallagher, "Setting the Agenda for Trade Negotiations: Australia and the Cairns Group," *Australian Outlook* 42 (1988); Gareth Evans and Bruce Grant, *Australia's Foreign Relations in the World of the 1990s* (Carlton: Melbourne University Press, 1991), 116-19.

39 For an overview, see Stuart Harris, "Australia in the Global Economy in the 1980s," in *Diplomacy in the Marketplace: Australia in World Affairs, 1981-90,* ed. P.J. Boyce and J.R. Angel (Melbourne: Longman Cheshire, 1992), 30-50.

40 For an acerbic assessment of the efforts of the Fraser government to do battle with the EC over agriculture, see Alan Renouf, *Malcolm Fraser and Australian Foreign Policy* (Sydney: Australian Professional Publications, 1986), 161-3. See also Cooper, *In between Countries*, 106-7.

41 Capling and Galligan, *Beyond the Protective State*, esp. ch. 4.

42 As John Kerin, Hawke's minister for primary industry, said bluntly of the ALP's rural seats in 1986, "We cannot hold government without these seats." Quoted in Cooper, *In between Countries*, 148.

43 Author interview, confidential, Sydney, 4 February 1997.

44 Cooper, *In between Countries*, 119.

45 For a survey, see Theodore H. Cohn, "Canada and the Ongoing Impasse over Agricultural Protectionism," in *Canadian Foreign Policy and International Economic Regimes,* ed. A. Claire Cutler and Mark W. Zacher (Vancouver: UBC Press, 1992), 62-88.

46 Quoted in Cooper, *In between Countries*, 183.

47 Quoted in ibid., 140.

48 A senior negotiator recalls one Cairns Group meeting outside Geneva where the Australian and Argentine officials "hammered" the Canadians throughout the night. Similar pressure was also frequently applied at the diplomatic and ministerial levels. Author interview, confidential, Sydney, 4 February 1997.

49 Richard A. Higgott and Andrew F. Cooper, "Middle Power Leadership and Coalition Building: Australia, the Cairns Group and the Uruguay Round of Trade Negotiations," *International Organization* 44 (Autumn 1990): 589-632.

50 Author interviews, confidential, Sydney, 4 February 1997, and Melbourne, 9 March 1999.

51 Cooper, *In between Countries*, 212.

52 Ann Capling, *Australia and the Global Trade System: From Havana to Seattle* (Cambridge: Cambridge University Press 2001), 135.

53 L. Michael Berry, "Canada and Australia: Pacific Partners – Past, Present, Future," in *Canada-Australia: Towards a Second Century of Partnership,* ed. Kate Burridge, Lois Foster, and Gerry Turcotte (Ottawa: Carleton University Press, 1997), 6.

54 See Greg Donaghy, *Parallel Paths: Canadian-Australian Relations since the 1890s* (Ottawa: Department of Foreign Affairs and International Trade, 1995), 12. One measure of this acrimony was the willingness of the Australian minister for external affairs, H.V. Evatt, to dismiss his Canadian counterpart as "an American stooge."

55 Author interview, confidential, Ottawa, 13 August 1997.

10
Keeping in Touch: Patterns of Networking in the Canadian-Australian Diplomatic Relationship
Andrew F. Cooper

The analogy of the family is a convenient – if rather simplistic – way of getting a fix on the Canadian-Australian relationship. Built into the pattern of interaction between these two countries persists a complexity and an intensity that belies the geographic distance between them. Sometimes described as a "sibling rivalry,"[1] the relationship has been characterized by periodic bickering. Despite the relative frequency and public nature of such outbursts, however, the connection between Australia and Canada has not become a dysfunctional one. Although the two countries reveal different and competitive personalities when dealing with each other, there remains a sense of familiarity vis-à-vis their operational habits and world view that allows them to work together on a wide range of issues. On top of the affinities built up through their formal set of ties and associations, there is embedded within the Canadian-Australian relationship a willingness and ability to operate more informally on a like-minded basis in the international arena. This established pattern of networking between Canada and Australia is most pronounced in the context of multilateral activity through the United Nations (UN) system.

Locating the Differences between Canada and Australia
The differences between Canada and Australia have two very different dimensions. Consistent with the family analogy, the most publicized difficulties in the relationship are strongly associated with rifts between key individuals. The Evatt-Pearson relationship in the late 1940s was marked by a tension-ridden quality bordering on the obsessive and extreme. In the early 1990s the simmering tension between the Canadian Progressive Conservative government and its Australian Labor Party (ALP) counterpart on trade questions boiled over in a highly contentious and personalized fashion. Finance Minister Don Mazankowsi (former deputy prime minister) engaged in what was termed an "unwarranted intervention" in Australian politics, for writing a letter to then Opposition leader John Hewson accusing

Prime Minister Paul Keating of misrepresenting Brian Mulroney's decision to retire from politics. Responding to Keating's claim that Mulroney had been forced to quit because of the introduction of the new Goods and Service Tax (which Hewson wanted to replicate), Mazankowsi stated that this interpretation was not only "unfortunate" but "beneath contempt."[2]

These personal and personality problems, however, are supplemented and accentuated by a number of other stylistic and substantive differences. As recognized by a number of contributors to this volume, there are acute differences in the way Canada and Australia have played the diplomatic game. The traditional hallmark of Canadian diplomacy is its low-key or "quiet" nature, with activity being carried out with a minimum of fanfare. Australia's diplomacy featured a more zealous quality. In contrast to Canada's reliance on patient, behind-the-scenes activity, Australia has periodically utilized louder and often abrasive tactics designed to draw attention to the issue at hand. As one Australian academic stated, Australia has had a well-deserved reputation as the "loudest, most demanding, least diplomatic" of the older dominions.[3]

In the immediate post-1945 era Australia's willingness to "have a go" at the great powers was highlighted by H.V. Evatt's efforts at the 1945 San Francisco Conference on World Organization to "liberalise and democratise" the design of the new international system.[4] Denouncing the veto in the UN Security Council as conferring excessive privileges on the great powers, Evatt demanded that the international system be made more equitable through the granting of a wider jurisdiction for the General Assembly, and the elevation of the Economic and Social Council into a principal organ of the world organization.

More recently, this robust diplomatic style has been captured in the continuous Australian campaign to liberalize international agricultural trade. As practised by Prime Minister Malcolm Fraser in the 1970s, Australia's "bullish" diplomacy was cast in a negative light. Indeed one of Fraser's own diplomats criticized the approach for its "talk, bluster and international exhibitionism."[5] In the 1980s and early 1990s this struggle was interpreted in a more positive and constructive light. While remaining highly focused on this issue at the political level, the government of Bob Hawke sold its plan not in the impulsive take-it-or-leave-it style favoured by Fraser, but as part of a detailed, step by step, approach to the GATT negotiations.

These differences in style are shaped not only by the character of influential leaders, but by the tremendous – and longstanding – structural differences between Canada and Australia in terms of their international economic and political weight. Diplomatically, Canada had the advantage of being an insider in the international system, with access to many of the key decision-making forums. At the "creation" of the postwar architecture, Canada became a major player. During the negotiations on the establishment of a new trade organization, for example, Canada was referred to as one of the "Big 3."[6] Geography reinforced Canada's ascendant position; being closer to the United States helped enhance Canada's diplomatic status during the Cold War era. Canada's strategic location also ensured its entry into the North Atlantic Treaty Organization (NATO), as well as the North American Aerospace Defence Command (NORAD) and the Defence Production Sharing Agreement. By way of contrast Australia remained very much on the outside of this magic circle. The form and structure of Australia's economy was beset by problems not much different from those faced by less-developed countries.[7] While Australia and Canada shared similar sensitivities – due to their resource-based economies, their level of foreign investment, and their relative lack of research and development – Australia did not have Canada's variety of options in foreign economic strategy. Whereas Canada had the choice of building a special relationship with its leading trading partner (the United States), Australia was left, through the 1950s and 1960s, a "misplaced" continent caught between the past (Britain) and the future (Asia-Pacific).[8] With the explicit backing of the United States, Canada gained elevation into the Group of 7 leading industrial countries. Notwithstanding some expressions of Japanese support, Australia was denied entry into this exclusive club.

This set of characteristics exaggerated some of the fundamental differences between Canada and Australia. Enjoying its position of comparative comfort, Canada presented itself as a mature and responsible actor in international affairs. Rather than distinguishing itself as a critic, Canada adopted a problem-solving orientation. Instead of being categorized as a system reformer, Canada is best labelled as a system maintainer. Canada concentrated on making a difference in the actual workings of the system as it stood, not on ambitious initiatives designed to reshape the international system. Ideas or idealism were deemed to be inadequate. The key was in delivering results when and where it mattered.[9] Australia remained resentful and suspicious of Canada's pre-eminence, especially when this differentiation in status appeared to exclude Australia from participation on an equal footing. Grounded in the junior position, Australia remained susceptible to the compensatory lure offered by more adventurous methods and radical solutions. Only by raising its voice and its demands could Australia be an effective player. In some select cases, as Christopher Waters attests, this approach could prove effective. In many other cases, though, the resort to loudness bred frustration.

The full extent of these differences surfaced in the two episodes noted above. In the construction of the postwar institutional architecture, Evatt portrayed himself as the champion of the medium and smaller countries in mobilizing his campaign for an equitable international system in the immediate aftermath of the Second World War. This campaign of "constructive criticism"[10] was directed in particular at the imbalance in the system established via the veto powers granted to the great powers, and the lack of recognition of the contribution of many of the non-great powers to the war effort. In stark contrast Canada's diplomatic focus at the meetings concentrated on what was possible rather than what was right. The Canadian delegation orchestrated its activities on laying out the scaffolding of a solid and lasting institutional structure, not on the promotion of plans for a visionary model for the future.

From Evatt's point of view, Canadian pragmatism was a sign not of good sense but of timidity. Canada's cautious approach – demonstrated most clearly by its refusal to join with Australia in either the fight to curtail the veto power or to increase the powers for the UN General Assembly – was roundly criticized as displaying a lack of courage.[11] Alternatively, from the Canadian point of view, the Australian crusade on the veto was viewed as not only quixotic but counterproductive. While admitting some grudging admiration for Evatt's tenacity, Pearson "puzzled at his apparent lack of concern over some of the plain facts of world politics." From a Canadian perspective, Evatt's behaviour at San Francisco showed not only vanity and arrogance but also a complete lack of understanding of how international relations operated.[12]

Similar sorts of tension, as Ann Capling and Kim Nossal point out, came to the fore during the campaign for the reform of the multilateral trade system, through the Cairns Group of agricultural traders. As the host country of its first meeting in Cairns, Queensland, in August 1986, Australia took on the role of intellectual-strategic leader of this group of "non-subsidizing" middle and smaller countries opposed to the export practices of the United States and the European Community (EC). Not only did Australia move ahead of Canada in defining the mission of this coalition, it pressed all the member countries to make concessions themselves. Cushioned by its G-7 status, Canada did not see itself as one among equals within the coalition. Canada made it clear from the outset that, although it was willing to act as a messenger for the Cairns Group to the G-7 summits, it was not willing to represent the Cairns Group interests at the G-7 or in any way restrict its own freedom of independent action. Suspicious of a concentration of the leadership of the group in Australian hands, Canada pressed for a process by which the chair (if not the secretariat) of the group was rotated among its members.

At one level, the unravelling of the Canadian-Australian partnership over the Cairns Group fit the longstanding model of disagreements between the two countries. As in the case of the Evatt-Pearson rift, these problems highlighted the differences contained in the stylistic expression of Australian and Canadian diplomacy. Consistent with its past behaviour, Australia was willing to push hard for institutional reform. Equally steadfastly, Canada remained far more modest and incremental in its approach. At another level, however, the Cairns Group episode was fundamentally different from the Evatt-Pearson rift. The differences between Canada and Australia on the crafting of the UN architecture intruded little into domestic politics. By way of contrast the agricultural trade issue had the potential for a considerable spillover effect, from the international to the domestic. The ALP government tried to lead the campaign for international reform by going out ahead of other countries in terms of its commitment to domestic restructuring. Seeking to downplay its own domestic responsibility for international change, Canada played for time, mindful of the need to retain its own flexibility in terms of policy options. Influenced by the process of this deepening connection between international roles and internal setting, therefore, the image is offered up of a more volatile, if not substantively disconnected, relationship between Canada and Australia.

Reinterpreting (and Smoothing over) Differences

Having built up the impression that the Canada-Australia relationship remains beset by a number of serious problems, it is necessary to take another more nuanced look at this interpretation. For a counterargument can be made that the impact of these distinctive sources of tension between the two countries has become exaggerated. While in no way denying the manner in which Canada and Australia have rubbed up against each other in an irritating fashion, this conflictual take on the relationship still appears to be an incomplete and inaccurate one. Although these disagreements were noisy, they caused only a temporary disturbance in what was, at base, a solid relationship.

A number of alternative forms of analysis are salient here. For one thing, it may be argued that the implications of these issue-specific differences have commonly been overstated. On the issue of the veto, Pearson and his colleagues tried to moderate the tenor of, and manage the fallout from, Evatt's approach. After one of Evatt's many outbursts against the United States, Great Britain, and the Soviet Union, Pearson personally intervened to try to defuse tensions. As Norman Robertson, the undersecretary of state of external affairs, reported to Prime Minister Mackenzie King after this episode: "Pearson and I are seeing Evatt this evening and will endeavour to ascertain just what object he hopes to achieve by the tactics he is pursuing."[13] Moreover, it must be mentioned that Evatt did not represent the totality of the Australian approach. Although the split between Evatt and the Canadian delegation during the San Francisco conference cast a long shadow over Canadian and Australian statecraft, these personality-driven references do not provide a completely accurate signpost for the Australian-Canadian connection. While Canadians Pearson and John Holmes drew uncharacteristically harsh portraits of Evatt's activities, for example, they also went out of their way to praise other members of the Australian delegation. Nor was

Evatt immune from partisan criticism for his behaviour at home. Robert Menzies, as the leader of the Liberal opposition, attacked Evatt as severely as the Canadians did, ridiculing the minister of foreign affairs' "passion ... for words and formulae."[14]

The agricultural trade issue of the 1980s and early 1990s may also be re-examined through a more positive lens. From this perspective, the relationship between Canada and Australia within the Cairns Group is seen in much more constructive – if idiosyncratic – terms. Far from being a predetermined or "natural" fit, the involvement of Canada in the coalition represented a tangible spillover from the friendship enjoyed between Mulroney and Hawke. Abetted by their participation at the Commonwealth heads of state meetings, the two leaders became, in Australian parlance, good mates. Hawke was even invited to be a keynote speaker at Mulroney's national economic summit conference in early 1985.[15]

With the nature of its predetermined or "natural" fit strongly contested, the split within the Cairns Group must be seen against a wider backdrop. This interpretation shifts the onus for the split within the Cairns Group away from the negative interplay between Canada and Australia to other aspects of the coalition-building exercise. From this wider perspective, one significant factor was the strong and persistent sense of suspicion among the Latin Americans (and, in particular, Brazil) concerning Canadian participation. As a member of the hardline G-10, Brazil retained quite different priorities and interests in the GATT than Canada on a wide range of issues, including services and intellectual property. There was a huge gap as well between the positions of Brazil and Canada on the issue of "special" and "differential" treatment for developing countries. As Sylvia Ostry, Canada's ambassador for multilateral trade negotiations, declared in testimony to the House of Commons Committee on Foreign Affairs: "I thought [the Cairns group] was a useful group to negotiate the wording that allowed us to get into it [the Uruguay Round], but I said to myself that once the round started all the other agenda items on which they were very divided – Canada and Brazil do not have the same views on many issues, to put it mildly – would cause it to break up."[16]

Even when the Canadian participation in the Cairns Group did start to fray, the process of disconnection was relatively painless in a number of ways. On the one hand, the continuing importance of personal diplomacy at the leadership level needs to be examined. The visit by Deputy Prime Minister Mazankowski to Expo '88 in Brisbane, as part of the Australian bicentennial celebrations, served as the most notable illustration of this sort of activity. Although, in fact, the possibility of Canada taking itself out of – or being ejected from – the group had been discussed in Ottawa (a scenario much speculated on in the Australian media), this trip led to a burst of high-level crisis-management diplomacy that, in effect, papered over the dispute. A meeting between Mazankowski and Prime Minister Hawke and a number of his cabinet ministers resulted in an agreement to disagree on the issue, with Australia expressing its determination to push forward with its own proposals, but not at the expense of a public break with Canada.

Moreover, the rift between Canada and Australia and the Cairns Group did not constitute a formal split. Despite all the tension between them over the mode of operation in the Cairns Group, the bond between Canada and Australia continued to be strong in many ways. While beset by irreconcilable differences over the issue of agricultural trade reform, the two countries were in no hurry to decisively break up. Canada kept its place in the group, even if it could no longer be considered part of the group, in the sense of contributing substantively to its activities on policy. This nebulous state of affairs was perhaps best summed up by the reply from a spokesperson for the Canadian trade minister, when asked at the end of 1990 whether Canada continued to be a member of the group: "We're part of it, but we're not part of it."[17] Communiqués from the group continued to note Canada's opting out of the Cairns Group formula for "comprehensive tariffication."[18] In reply to questions about the unity of the coalition, state officials replied that Canada was "a different member of the Cairns group."

Canada continued to take on some specific tasks of import to the group, specifically that of delivering a message to the 1990 Houston G-7 summit concerning the need for substantive progress on the GATT round. At the same time, Canada offered a good deal of compensatory activity for its shift away from comprehensive agricultural reform (in order to defend its own structure in terms of marketing boards and supply management). Canada's proposal for a new International Trade Organization (ITO) looms large as an illustration of this type of positive action. Canada also was out in front of the other Cairns Group members with respect to the attempt to improve international disciplines on countervail duties.

From a completely different angle, the contrasting diplomatic styles of Australia and Canada continued to be seen as complementary rather than at odds with each other. This theme of complementarity was touched on by members of both the Australian and Canadian delegations in the Evatt-Pearson years. Paul Hasluck, the well-respected Australian diplomat and Liberal foreign minister, acknowledged that there existed "a certain Canadian-Australian community of feeling" even during this earlier period, in that "thought concerning the postwar world seemed to be moving along several common lines."[19] This theme of cooperation in the midst of tension is echoed in a review of Hasluck's memoirs by John Holmes, the Canadian diplomat-scholar who had some extensive first-hand experience of the differences in the Canadian-Australian relationship during the 1940s. While Holmes poured scorn on Evatt's methods – with his emphasis on stirring things up rather than quietly building consensus – he suggested at the same time that this divergence simply confirmed that Australia's behaviour was the flip side to Canada's own diplomatic style. From this perspective, Evatt and the loud Australians provided perfect foils for the quiet Canadians. Holmes elaborated eloquently on this theme: "This brilliant, pugnacious, unlovable man made, without doubt a laudable contribution to the new world order, especially at San Francisco, where someone of his graceless zeal was probably needed to rally the lesser powers and convince the great powers that their rule was not the law. Whether his raucous diplomacy was more effective than the quieter methods of the Canadians is an open question. There is an argument that they made a complementary team."[20]

The irritations and sense of competition between Canada and Australia should not hide a similar dynamic within the Cairns Group coalition. To resort to a well-worn notion, Canada played the nurturing "nice cop," with Australia performing the role of the disciplinarian "tough cop." This division of labour stands out in the Canadian and Australian response to the United States' subsidized sales to the USSR in August 1986. In launching the coalition of "fair traders," Hawke echoed the determination of Fraser, accusing the Americans of sacrificing their own principles of integrity and liberty by escalating the "ridiculous" trade war to "ludicrous proportions."[21] Mulroney's muted criticism of the United States was a study in contrast. While calling the action "unhelpful," Mulroney maintained a low profile approach in seeking redress. Rather than resorting to megaphone diplomacy, Canadians emphasized the prime minister's personal ties and communication channels with President Reagan.[22]

This contrast in style was also evident in the way Canada and Australia conducted their diplomacy in the context of the G-7 summits. Comfortably in place within this institutional setting, Canada was an active player in these forums with respect to policy dialogue and agenda setting. By necessity Australia was restricted to providing a new dimension to the role of outsider. As foils the two countries could play to their own strengths. Mulroney, in hosting the economic summit in 1988, confirmed Canada's position as a consummate insider. Hawke, alternatively, tried to get an invitation to the Toronto site. When this request was denied, he did not back away but chose instead to be as close as possible to the summit without actually participating in it. As Mulroney opened the summit, Hawke delivered a speech to the Chicago Economic Club on the other side of the Great Lakes.

The Other (More Cooperative) Face of the Canadian-Australian Relationship

The focus on these key irritations and points of difference during the Evatt-Pearson and Hawke-Mulroney years presents only one side of the Canadian-Australian relationship – and a distorted and unidimensional side at that.

While not wanting to tilt the balance between their similarities and differences too far the other way, a strong case can be made for the significance of like-mindedness in the Australian and Canadian context. At the domestic level, many of the preconditions have long existed for this sense of like-mindedness. Not only do Canada and Australia share the institutional and constitutional framework associated with the Westminster model, their shared histories as "settler societies," as well as their federal structures of governance, are points of convergence. At least one academic goes so far as to say that: "There are few countries in the world that have as much in common as Australia and Canada."[23]

At the international level, this notion of like-mindedness parallels in many respects the concept of Australia and Canada as middle powers. As has been well profiled in this volume, a dominant point that runs through all of the analysis on the positions of Australia and Canada in international affairs is that they belong to a special category of countries that lie in between the greater and lesser powers.[24]

While not a substitute for the middle-power mode of analysis, like-mindedness provides a valuable tool to get around some of the intellectual baggage and excesses attached with the term. To begin with, there are the well-known normative biases in the middle-power approach. The conventional method of looking at middle powers privileges an underlying set of idealistic impulses. Central to this perspective is the article of faith that middle powers act as good international citizens.[25] Such interpretations, to be sure, have some considerable element of relevance. Still, the emphasis on the morality and "good works" incorporated in these analyses of Canadian and Australian international performance has the tendency to blur as much as it clarifies. For all of its strengths, the notion of good international citizenship is highly prone to distortions, ambiguity, and nostalgic mythology. Despite the implicit claim of moral superiority, neither Canada nor Australia has an unblemished record with respect to international issues. The foreign policy performance of both countries has been criticized on a number of occasions for their passivity and/or abdication of responsibility in responding to international crises.

There are also some methodological problems. In examining Canada and Australia as middle powers, there has been a tendency to deal with them in two-country, single-issue case studies – that is to say, as separate exercises with minimal connection in terms of analysis. The parallelism between Canadian and Australian responses to issues such as foreign aid and immigration (to take just two examples) is detailed. But in cases such as these, there have been few attempts to coordinate policies.[26]

The notion of like-mindedness circumvents some of these difficulties, shifting the attention away from an exclusive emphasis on issue-specific instances of contact to a more generalized pattern of dialogue and consultation. In doing so the common view of the Canadian-Australian relationship, as defined by their contrasting (and often competitive) attitudes to well-defined initiatives and/or "crusades," is not entirely discarded. But an attempt is made to situate this behaviour in the context of an ongoing pattern of networking at both the formal and informal level.

This pattern features multiple channels and contacts. In a variety of ways networking between Canada and Australia has taken on a formal status, featuring a regular schedule of meetings at the ministerial level and top-level bureaucratic contacts around the Association of Southeast Asian Nations (ASEAN) regional forum and a host of other organizations. To give one illustration of this pattern at the political level, the bilateral meetings held between André Ouellet and Gareth Evans in June 1994 featured exchanges on a wide variety of topics, ranging from US policy on East Asia to industry's commitment to trade and investment in the Asia Pacific Economic Cooperation (APEC) context. At the bureaucratic level, the main forum of contact has been the Canada-Australia Senior Officials Consultations (SOC). In a wider framework this system of networking tapped into the Canada-Australia-New Zealand (CANZ) ministerial trilateral and the CANZ senior officials meetings. The establishment of the 1989 Canada-Australia consular sharing agreement has buttressed this apparatus. Under this agreement, the two countries began to share consular responsibilities in selected countries. Raymond Chan, Canada's secretary of state (Asia-Pacific), described this division of responsibility in an address at Australian National University in August 1994: "We get along so well that we have even begun to share diplomatic premises abroad – the Canadian Ambassador to Cambodia works in the Australian Embassy; the Australian High Commission in Barbados shares the Canadian High Commission offices in Bridgetown."[27]

More informally, a pervasive form of social (and idea) networking has developed, ranging from widespread exchanges of officials to the sharing of information to the interaction between non-state actors. This interaction has many dimensions. One important source of interaction is through the shared experiences of Australian and Canadian peacekeepers, as witnessed in their joint involvement in the Cambodian peace process and the planning of the UN force for East Timor. Another significant source is the quantity and quality of the exchanges of officials – from personnel seconded to the prime ministers' offices to middle-level Department of Foreign Affairs and International Trade (DFAIT) officials, to statisticians and a variety of technical workers. This extensive network is buttressed by the extensive set of contacts and cooperation built up in the post-1945 period within the intelligence and military domains.

The Australian and Canadian business communities have also deepened their ties. Triggered largely by the emergence of APEC, Canadian companies have used Australia to penetrate Southeast Asian markets. Australian companies, in turn, have expanded their presence in Canada. While much of this investment is concentrated in the resource sector (BHP, for example), other companies have been encouraged to use Canada as a bridgehead into North America. In recognition of these growing ties, an Australian-Canadian Chamber of Commerce has been established. As one business journalist said, "For two countries that compete strongly in world commodity markets, trade and investment ties between Canada and Australia are surprisingly vigorous."[28]

Consistent with the tradition of "a bottom up or private sector approach,"[29] members of the Australian and Canadian business communities have actively participated in the Pacific Trade and Development Conference (PAFTAD), the Pacific Economic Cooperation Conference (PECC), and the Pacific Basin Economic Conference (PBEC), as well as APEC. Australian and Canadian NGOs have, by way of contrast, worked together to try to open up the APEC process and to rebalance the forum away from a narrow "APEC means Business" orientation toward a more inclusive agenda encompassing human rights and environmental issues.

Networking in the domain of ideas is also extensive, and helps to capture the breadth of the Canadian-Australian relationship. It may be true, as Bruce Grant writes, that Australia borrows reluctantly from Canada: "The model closest to the Australian experience, Canada, is rarely mentioned in public debate. Australians do not wish to be told that they can learn from Canada's experience, possibly because it is too close to their own ... possibly because they feel ... competitive with Canadians."[30] But this dynamic, as Wayne Reynolds reminds us in his chapter, is longstanding. Conscious or not, it also remains pervasive. This process of borrowing, however, is no longer one way. Australia may have learned and extracted from the Canadian experience on issues as diverse as the recognition of the People's Republic of China, the scrutiny of foreign investment, immigration reform, and Aboriginal land claims. But Canada has taken lessons from the Australian experience as well. One sign of this crossover came in the area of "national consultation" in the Hawke-Mulroney period. Another sign has come with the increased interest of Canadian universities and colleges in the Australian "model" for attracting overseas students from the Asia-Pacific region. In contrast to the extensive array of mechanisms Australia has put in place, Canada has had a comparative lack of these structures (with the Asia-Pacific Foundation a notable exception). Indeed, with the Australian experience in mind, Canada has made some recent effort to catch up. In the last few years Canadian education centres have been set up in Seoul, Taipei, and Jakarta. But this effort still falls short in comparative terms. Not only is the Australian educational centre in Jakarta much bigger, it has a well-proven track record. At the bilateral level, the extension of this type of networking as a two-way process is best captured in reference to the acceleration of educational exchanges between Australian and Canadian universities. Ryerson University has an increasingly popular exchange program with the Royal Melbourne Institute of Technology. The University of Waterloo has several exchange programs in place, including one between Environment and Resource Studies and Griffith University.

The UN Dimension of Canadian-Australian "Like-Mindedness"

The site where the notion of Canadian-Australian like-mindedness continues to be most ingrained and relevant is within the UN domain. The dominant side of both Australian and Canadian diplomacy has been support for their alliance partners, as expressed through association and joint activity with the United States and the other pivotal members within NATO and ANZUS, the Australia, New Zealand, and US security pact.[31] In its classic form this approach signifies "going along" with the United States and the larger alliance in cases such as the Gulf War of 1991. These are not the only connections that matter for Canada and Australia, though. From an alternative perspective, the tendency of Australia and Canada to cluster together with each other and a number of other like-minded countries – the traditional candidates being New Zealand and the Nordic countries – is given considerably more weight. Relocated in this fashion, Australia and Canada share an embedded sense of identity not only on the basis of middle-power values and sentiments concerning the rules of the game within the international system, but because they have traditionally seen themselves as "floaters" within the international system. In other words Australia and Canada share a perception that they are not attached to a single regional home, but straddle regions.

On top of these generalized motivations come a number of more specific and instrumental reasons to work together. For one thing, there is the institutional rationale. The structural design of the United Nations itself has encouraged close contact on a wide number of issues. Because Australia and Canada (with New Zealand) were placed in the catch-all "Western Europe and Others Group" (WEOG), these countries had some considerable incentive for adhering to a practical application of like-mindedness. To deliver results through lobbying, and the sponsoring of resolutions at the UN, Australia and Canada needed to operate in tandem with other countries with which they shared some degree of collective outlook on ideas and values on an ongoing basis.

There is also the organizational expertise rationale. It is one thing for a group of countries to have the will to engage in cooperative practices. It is quite another thing for these countries to have the *ability* to do so. Like-mindedness in practice necessitates an elevated skill level consistent with a strong level of administrative capacity and diplomatic expertise. Working with others requires particular forms of statecraft, with a focus on international institutions and agreements. Albeit often expressed in contrasting styles, Canada and Australia have long possessed the ability to act as catalysts with respect to diplomatic efforts, in the sense of triggering initiatives, the planning and convening of meetings, setting priorities, and drawing up and fleshing out proposals, as well as a wide range of more routine activity surrounding liaison efforts and shuttle diplomacy. But the engagement of these skills has become even more a point of reference (and distinction) in the 1990s. As Richard Higgott suggests, "the number of states that can provide entrepreneurial inputs into post Cold War diplomacy will always be limited [although not] as small as many observers ... instinctively assume."[32]

In tracing the evolution of this like-mindedness, a considerable degree of continuity can be found built into this behaviour. Akin to their middle-power status, the like-minded notion provided some space for Australia and Canada to manoeuvre around their role as supporters of the United States and the Western alliance. As Arthur Andrew noted in a retrospective look at Canadian diplomacy, after a long career in the Department of External Affairs: "No Great power is going to encourage any country to play the role of gadfly, but the role is a necessary one and it can be played with an effect out of all proportion to the importance of the country doing it ... [This was a role Canada played] very effectively in cooperation with like-minded countries – the Scandinavians, Australia, New Zealand and others."[33]

The operational arrangement of like-mindedness nonetheless allowed flexibility and the retention of distinctive styles of diplomacy. Despite the occasional bursts of higher-profile activity, like-mindedness did not translate into a deep form of engagement. The bulk of this activity appears to have been directed toward sharing information, exchanging views, explaining positions, and bouncing ideas off one another. The main ingredient was the development of a habit of consultation through the CANZ caucus within the UN system. The character of the organizational structure of this caucus was extremely loose, with some considerable leeway for differences and rival ambitions. No secretariat existed; the obligations were minimal.

The notion of like-mindedness, in the context of the Australian-Canadian relationship has a considerable degree of continuity built into it. Although the traditional paradigm of like-mindedness is strongly identified with the 1950s and early 1960s, it is misleading to conclude that this notion faded away completely in later years. Amid all the other controversies and tilts associated with the years in which Pierre Trudeau (1968-79, 1980-4) and Gough Whitlam (1972-5) served as prime ministers of Canada and Australia, respectively, a sense of like-mindedness not only survived but – at least on particular issues – actually flourished. A case in point was the Law of the Sea (LOS). Low on the priority level in the 1950s, this protracted round of multilateral negotiations came to the fore of Australian and Canadian foreign policy in the 1970s. In terms of coalition building Canada and Australia placed much store in working through a loose assembly of countries, the so-called Group of 12 (also known as the "good Samaritans"), which included Austria, Denmark, Finland, Iceland, Ireland, the Netherlands, Norway, Sweden, Switzerland, and New Zealand.[34]

This pattern of networking was replicated during the Mulroney-Hawke years. One illustration that comes to mind revolved around the issue of UN reform and the "new world order." As part of its effort to help Boutros Boutros-Ghali, the UN secretary general, develop *An Agenda for Peace*, Canada associated with the familiar like-minded countries. In January 1992 the CANZ and Nordic countries submitted a joint brief to the UN Secretary General. This brief focused on both the need for forward-looking assessments about potential crisis situations and for the Security Council to make greater efforts to involve other UN member states in its deliberations.[35]

Another illustration of extensive networking along these lines is provided by the diplomatic activities of Australia and Canada on human rights. On women's rights, for instance, Canada and Australia – together with New Zealand and Nordic countries (and sometimes with the United States) – worked closely together at all the major UN-sponsored "mega" conferences of the early 1990s. During the 1992 UN Conference on Environment and Development, or Rio Earth Summit, the CANZ delegations combined with an informal coalition of women delegates to co-sponsor a general resolution highlighting the need to consider the gender dimensions of environment and development issues. A larger group of like-minded countries tried to have the wording of the population, health, and poverty texts accepted into the women's chapter of the Rio declaration.

The 1993 UN Vienna World Conference on Human Rights reinforced this practical application of like-mindedness. Much of the emphasis in this forum focused on procedural matters. Helped by the willingness of Canada, Australia, and many of the smaller European countries to push for greater institutional "openness" within the Vienna process, a good number of NGOs became conference insiders. Not only did the Canadian and Australian governments work with the other like-minded countries to champion increasing the access available to NGOs to key drafting committees, Australian and Canadian NGOs extended their own links within the NGO community via the newly established NGO WEOG.

Nor, it may be added, are there signs that this notion of like-mindedness is becoming a spent force during the years since Jean Chrétien (1993-) and John Howard (1996-) have become prime ministers of Canada and Australia. At the heart of two of the most heavily publicized "coalitions of the willing" of the 1990s is the traditional grouping of like-minded countries. Australia was out in front with Canada, New Zealand, and the Nordic states pushing for the establishment of an International Criminal Court. Canada and Australia – together with Belgium, the Netherlands, Austria, Norway,

Denmark, Ireland, New Zealand, Germany, and Switzerland – were also part of the core group in the campaign to ban anti-personnel land mines.

The Future of Like-Mindedness

The extent and ongoing impact of this alternative side of Australian and Canadian diplomacy should not be exaggerated. Neither Canada nor Australia wants to elevate the notion of like-mindedness to a dominant position in their approach to international affairs. It is interesting to recall here that in the 1970s and early 1980s, neither of these countries shared the enthusiasm of their like-minded allies (led by Norway and the Netherlands, with support from Sweden and Denmark) for the establishment of a formal structure for "the Like-Minded Group of States."[36] The proposed agenda of this more coherent like-minded group was an ambitious one: support for the New International Economic Order (NIEO), advocated by the Group of 77 developing countries generally; and policies such as the Common Fund (centred on a redistribution from the industrial North to the industrializing South) more specifically.

The situational and structural changes associated with the end of the Cold War have thrown up additional barriers to the development of like-mindedness. A flatter power structure may not necessarily enhance co-operation between the traditional like-minded countries. While there may be some room for them to operate, these countries have been forced to adapt to a situation of relative economic decline. In consequence they may be pushed toward competitive forms of status-seeking activity. New initiatives have brought not only new opportunities for cooperation but new challenges in terms of competition between Canada and Australia. Even the land-mines episode was marred by signs of bickering between Australia and Canada about tactics and the relevance of using or bypassing the Convention on Conventional Weapons.

The ascendant forces of regionalism have also played a part in prying the traditional like-minded countries apart. Faced with an exposure to an increasingly regionally based international system, both Australia and Canada have had to reassess their positions as traditional "floaters" in the international system. Australia has been especially ambivalent about its location within the UN system. Institutionally Australia's geographic relocation was underscored by its push away from the WEOG toward fuller participation in the Asian regional meetings (although this push kept being resisted by several of the key Asian countries). In policy terms Australia has broken with the rest of the Western group on a number of issues relating to the principle of universalism on human rights. Canada has also gone through a process of relocating itself. Through the North American Free Trade Agreement (NAFTA) and the Organization of American States (OAS), Canada has embraced the American hemisphere in a multidimensional manner. With this shift has come an attempt to jig the notion of like-mindedness to embrace Latin American countries.[37]

Still, the relevance and value of like-minded diplomatic activity in the context of the Australia-Canada relationship should not be underestimated. Networking with each other reinforces many of the positive attributes of Australian and Canadian diplomacy, namely support for the international order, multilateralism, diplomatic initiatives, conflict reduction, and constraint on the larger powers. Amid all the challenges of the post-Cold War era, the potential space of operation for these problem-solving endeavours has appreciably expanded as well. Held back by the restricted boundaries of the post-1945 international system, with its tight definition of the boundaries of activity and legitimate actors in world politics, like-minded contact was largely confined to specific areas (largely centred on conciliation). The freeing up of the structural limitations and disciplines of the Cold War era allows a more thorough release not only of Australian and Canadian skills, but reputational attributes in international affairs.

Moreover, the tendency of Australia and Canada to continue to work together may be reinforced as much by default as design. The rearrangement of the global hierarchy and the potent forces of regionalism present the prospect of Australia and Canada being distanced – if not completely isolated from each other – as like-minded partners. While this pessimistic scenario remains a possible outcome, nevertheless, more positive countervailing tendencies remain in play as well. For Canada, the prospect of using a NAFTA-plus arrangement as a new way of counterbalancing the United States and its other dominant pattern of association remains dim. Canada has neither the same sense of familiarity or ease of working together with countries from Latin America as it has had with Australia and other more traditional like-minded countries. In the Australian case the experience of the 1997-8 Asian financial crisis (or Asian "flu") has been salutary in warding off choices that imply putting all its eggs in one basket. While any attempt to counterbalance Australia's deeper engagement with the Asian countries will no doubt privilege the United States and Western Europe, a spillover effect will be felt in terms of a strengthening of like-mindedness with Canada.

The bottom line is that there continues to be room and some impetus for like-minded activity. The endurance of the close connection between Australia and Canada has been bent by the transformation of the international system, as well as by the accumulated effect of the many irritations between these two countries. Still, this set of problems has not broken the will or the capacity of either country to keep up a close connection, especially in the UN domain. Despite the (sibling or not) rivalry between them, and their divergent needs and interests, a solid pattern of diplomatic contact continues to exist. Indeed the forces of transnationalism and the widening of the international agenda have enlarged the range of networking opportunities in the past decade. This is not to say that either Australia or Canada should be tempted to overplay the like-minded card. If widened, the connection has not deepened. Other relationships remain not only paramount but more vibrant. By itself the connection does not provide either country with undue leverage. Moreover, as the irritations on the Cairns Group and a variety of other issue-specific episodes signal, there is a brittleness to the relationship that should breed caution with respect to shared activity. The like-minded card is valuable to hold only if it is played with moderation and care. Its very endurance, nonetheless, provides ample testimony to the salience of the cooperative face of Australian-Canadian relations.

Notes

I am grateful for the support of the Social Sciences and Humanities Research Council of Canada.

1 This theme goes back to such works as Alexander Brady's *Democracy in the Dominions: A Comparative Study in Institutions* (Toronto: University of Toronto Press, 1947).
2 Quoted in Peter Goodspeed, "Mazankowski Letter Sparks Aussie Row," *Toronto Star*, 9 March 1993.
3 T.B. Millar, *Australia in Peace and War: External Relations, 1788-1977* (London: C. Hurst, 1978).
4 H.V. Evatt, "The United Nations," The Oliver Wendell Holmes Lectures 1947 (Cambridge, MA: Harvard University Press, 1948), 4. See also Norman Harper, *A Great and Powerful Friend: A Study of Australian-American Relations between 1900 and 1975* (St. Lucia, Queensland: University of Queensland Press, 1987), ch. 10; Neville Meany, "Australia, The Great Powers and the Coming of the Cold War," *Australian Journal of Politics and History* 38, 3 (1992): 316-33.
5 Alan Renouf, *The Frightened Country* (Melbourne: Macmillan, 1979), 497.
6 B.W. Muirhead, *The Development of Postwar Canadian Trade Policy: The Failure of the Anglo-European Option* (Montreal and Kingston: McGill-Queen's University Press, 1992), 50.
7 See, for example, H.W. Arndt, "Australia: Developed, Developing or Midway?" in *A Small Rich Industrial Country: Studies in Australian Development, Aid and Trade*, H.W. Arndt (Melbourne: F.W. Cheshire, 1968).
8 On Australia's geographic dilemma, see Geoffrey Blainey, *The Tyranny of Distance: How Distance Shaped Australia's History* (Melbourne: Sun Books, 1966). For the best-known comparative study of the Canada-US and Australia-US relationship, see Robert O. Keohane and Joseph S. Nye Jr., *Power and Interdependence: World Politics in Transition* (Boston: Little, Brown, 1977).
9 John W. Holmes, *The Shaping of Peace: Canada and the Search for World Order*, vol. 1 (Toronto: University of Toronto Press, 1979), 237. For an elaboration on the themes of reputation and skill in Canadian foreign policy, see Andrew F. Cooper, *Canadian Foreign Policy: Old Habits and New Directions* (Scarborough, ON: Prentice Hall Allyn and Bacon, 1997).
10 Evatt, "The United Nations," 4.
11 See Paul Hasluck, *Diplomatic Witness: Australian Foreign Affairs 1941-1947* (Carlton: Melbourne University Press, 1980), 195.
12 John A. Munro and Alex I. Inglis, eds., *Mike: The Memoirs of the Right Honourable Lester B. Pearson*, vol. 2, *1948-1957* (Toronto: University of Toronto Press, 1973), 277. See also Holmes, *The Shaping of Peace*, 1:247-59.
13 Robertson to King, 10 June 1945, Canadian Institute of International Affairs, John Holmes Papers.
14 See, for example, Menzies quoted in "Forde-Evatt Proposal at UNICO Attacked," *Sydney Morning Herald*, 17 May 1945.

15 Laurie Oakes, "A Domestic Victory in Hawke's Ottawa Triumph," *The Bulletin*, 2 April 1985, 34, 37.
16 Testimony to the Standing Senate Committee on Foreign Affairs, Canada, *Proceedings*, 13 June 1989, 5:19.
17 Quoted in Madelaine Drohan, "Canada at Odds with Trade Group," *Globe and Mail*, 24 October 1990.
18 Helen Trinka, "Canada Rains on Team Parade," *The Australian*, 20 October 1989, 6.
19 Paul Hasluck, *Diplomatic Witness*, 80.
20 John W. Holmes, review of *Diplomatic Witness*, *International Journal* (Summer 1982): 493.
21 Quoted in Paul Samuel, "Hawke Flays US Hypocrites over Cheap Wheat for Russia," *The Australian,* 1 August 1986.
22 "Reagan Deaf to PM's Protest in Approving Soviet Wheat Sale," *Toronto Star,* 23 August 1986.
23 Tom Symons, "Closing Remarks: Two Federations," in *Public Policies in Two Federal Countries: Canada and Australia,* ed. R.L. Matthews (Canberra: Centre for Research on Federal Financial Relations, ANU, 1982), 10. See also Malcolm Alexander and Brian Galligan, "Australian and Canadian Comparative Political Studies," and Robert J. Jackson, "Australian and Canadian Comparative Political Research," in *Comparative Political Studies: Australia and Canada,* ed. Malcolm Alexander and Brian Galligan (Melbourne: Pitman, 1992).
24 Annette Baker Fox, "The Range of Choice for Middle Powers: Australia and Canada Compared," *Australian Journal of Politics and History* 26, 2 (1980): 193-203. See also Andrew F. Cooper, Richard A. Higgott, and Kim Richard Nossal, *Relocating Middle Powers: Australia and Canada in an Evolving World Order* (Vancouver and Melbourne: UBC Press and University of Melbourne Press, 1993).
25 See, for example, Bernard Wood, *The Middle Powers and the General Interest* (Ottawa: The North-South Institute, 1988).
26 The only extended exceptions prior to this publication have been Kim Richard Nossal's work on economic sanctions, *Rain Dancing: Sanctions in Canadian and Australian Foreign Policy* (Toronto: University of Toronto Press, 1994), and my own work on agricultural trade policy, Andrew F. Cooper, *In between Countries: Australia, Canada and the Search for Order in Agricultural Trade* (Montreal and Kingston: McGill-Queen's University Press, 1997).
27 Notes for an address by the Honourable Raymond Chan, secretary of state (Asia-Pacific), at the Australian National University, "Canada and the Asia-Pacific Region," 4 August 1994, Canberra, Australia, 94, 41.
28 Neville Nankivell, "Freeing up Trans-Pacific Trade," *Financial Post*, 25 July 1995.
29 L.T. Woods, "The Business of Canada's Pacific Relations," *Canadian Journal of Administrative Sciences* 4 (1987): 418.
30 Bruce Grant, *The Australian Dilemma: A New Kind of Western Society* (Rushcutters Bay, NSW: Mcdonald Futura Australia, 1983), 66.
31 On these themes, see Andrew Fenton Cooper, Richard A. Higgott, and Kim Richard Nossal, "Bound to Follow? Leadership and Followership in the Gulf Conflict," *Political Science Quarterly* 106, 3 (Fall 1991): 391-410; Cooper et al., *Relocating Middle Powers*.
32 Richard Higgott, "Issues, Institutions and Middle-Power Diplomacy: Action and Agendas in the Post-Cold War Era" in *Niche Diplomacy: Middle Powers after the Cold War,* ed. Andrew F. Cooper (London: Macmillan, 1997), 37.
33 Arthur Andrew, *The Rise and Fall of a Middle Power: Canadian Diplomacy from King to Mulroney* (Toronto: James Lorimer, 1993), 166.
34 Clyde Sanger, *Ordering the Oceans* (Toronto: University of Toronto Press, 1987), 25.
35 David Cox, "Canada and the United Nations: Pursuing Common Security," *Canadian Foreign Policy* 2, 1 (Spring 1994): 63-78.
36 Asbjørn Løvbraek, "International Reform and the Like-Minded Countries and the North-South Dialogue 1975-1985," in *Middle Power Internationalism: The North-South Dimension,* ed. Cranford Pratt (Montreal and Kingston: McGill-Queen's University Press, 1990), 44.
37 See, for example, Canada-Caribbean-Central America Policy Alternatives, *Report Card on Canada's First Year in the OAS in the Light of Hemispheric Relations,* CAPA occasional paper, July 1990, 21.

Conclusion
Francine McKenzie and Margaret MacMillan

We have tried to do two things in this volume: trace the relations between Australia and Canada, and compare their historical development. In the course of preparing our chapters we have found it difficult to disentangle these two approaches; indeed, it became clear that we should not necessarily try to separate them. Some chapters deal primarily with relations (MacMillan, Perras, Waters, Nossal and Capling, Cooper); others concentrate on comparative developments (McKenzie, Russell, MacKenzie, Cain, Reynolds) – although all address both aspects. The sum of these chapters points to several preliminary conclusions about the direct relationship, as well as their respective foreign policy traditions.

The common colonial past within the British Empire was the first point of contact between Canada and Australia, and continued to define their relationship as it unfolded. It is, therefore, not surprising that there have been numerous attempts in this volume to define the Canadian-Australian relationship in familial terms: as siblings engaged in a natural rivalry, or as distant cousins. Explaining international relations in humanizing concepts is a ploy familiar to academics, especially those who study the Commonwealth and Empire. In this larger context scholars regularly invoke a family construct, with Britain as the mother country (it was all the parent the dominions needed) and the dominions forever categorized as children, no matter how grown up they might become. In this respect the anthropomorphization of the dominions – Canada and Australia in particular – has been an impediment to understanding their evolutions. They have been cast in moulds from which it is difficult to escape. And yet, the family metaphor captures an historical reality (that Canada and Australia were to a large extent the offspring of Britain) that left an indelible impression on the nations they would become. Several of the contributors to *Parties Long Estranged* admit that there are limitations to the family trope, although they cannot resist it in trying to capture, in a succinct form, the complexity of Australian-Canadian relations. That is because family metaphors convey a deep-seated connection and profoundly felt familiarity, despite the fact the two countries' formal relationship was slow to develop. In the late nineteenth century they depended on technological advances to make direct contact possible. Over the course of the twentieth century, their relations broadened incrementally, without any sense of urgency. A relationship existed despite the absence of official and tangible bonds because of their convergence as self-governing colonies in the British Empire. There was a recognition that they were connected, even if individual Canadians and Australians would be hard-pressed to define the basis for that belief. As Christopher Waters points out, empires – like nations – are imagined communities. The absence of direct contact, limitations on the knowledge Australians and Canadians had of one another, and the demise of the British Empire have not weakened the feeling and belief that Canada and Australia are part of an enduring imagined community.

One familial label not used, but suggested by the studies in this volume, is of Canada and Australia as fraternal twins, always judged relative to the other. Since the end of the Second World War, Canada and Australia have both emerged as middle powers in the international community. Neither country ever came close to possessing the economic strength, political influence, or military might necessary to become great powers, let alone superpowers. Still, Canadian and Australian governments since 1945 have fought for the right to be heard in international affairs, assumed leading roles in international organizations such as the United Nations, lobbied for access to élite councils, and demanded the respect of their more powerful allies. Most of the chapters in the second section of this volume were conceived of within the middle-power paradigm. This approach lends itself to comparisons of policy makers and politicians, who could and did judge their progress against one another, as well as scholars seeking to understand how they operated within a polarized international system dominated by superpowers. The middle-power approach also helps contemporary players and scholars looking at the past to understand a relationship that was simultaneously competitive and based on a close understanding of the other's tactics, goals, and challenges.

The history of Canadian-Australian relations in the twentieth century encompasses a broad spectrum of attitudes, including disagreement, disdain, disappointment, envy, incomprehension, admiration, ease, familiarity, and cooperation. Almost every chapter in this volume examines the acrimonious side of Australian-Canadian relations, which touch economic (GATT, the Cairns Group), diplomatic (planning the peace after the First and Second World Wars, atomic weapons), and military (failed cooperation in defence) issues. Differences bred frustration, evident in the gratuitous insults exchanged between Canadian and Australian officials, from T.C. Davis's prescription that all Australians needed "a few beatings and a bit of kicking around and then you couldn't beat them"[1] to Evatt's characterization of Canada's best and brightest diplomats, sent to the San Francisco conference of 1945, as "stooges." Yet the authors never conclude that low opinions and conflicting interests damaged that relationship. The value both Canadian and Australian governments attached to their relationship, no matter how understated, ensured that disputation never deteriorated into rupture. Consequently, differences were compartmentalized and prioritized. That meant that communication was ongoing and collaboration always a possibility. In fact it was often an actuality. The extent of cooperation and durability of cordiality in Canadian-Australian relations is another theme traced throughout this volume, from the comfortable conversations of foreign ministers to common participation in international forums to bilateral networks established between universities, governments, and individual politicians. Discord and lack of interest are not, therefore, the defining characteristics of this relationship. Rather, they are one side of a relationship that cannot be fully understood or accurately represented without the goodwill, respect, easy familiarity, emulation, and cooperation that persisted and deepened over the course of the twentieth century. Indeed the relationship appears to have gained in importance to both Ottawa and Canberra – from ignorance and detachment evident at the start of the twentieth century to interest and engagement at its close. Although cooperation is not always possible, and rarely uncomplicated, the commitment to try to work together and the belief that an effort toward cooperation is worthwhile is more evident now than ever before. These ten chapters do not cover all possible case studies, but they do move from one end of the spectrum to the other, from the futility of cooperation over civil aviation to the relaxed and far-reaching consultation between Pearson and Casey. Consequently, they identify the wide parameters within which this relationship played itself out. It is our hope that other scholars who examine this relationship will try to explain why it functions at such extremes.

The chapters in this volume demonstrate that, at the comparative level, there are fundamental similarities and differences in the national histories of Canada and Australia. It is clear that in their evolution from colonies to dominions to fully sovereign states, Australia and Canada followed similar paths, confronting common issues, even though they did not move at the same speed. Canadians were more willing – although not necessarily enthusiastic – to dilute the formal side of their relationship with Britain than Australia. Having a French-Canadian prime minister at the end of the nineteenth century brought home the reality that Canada was not populated solely by British expatriates and descendants, and that the tie to Britain was a divisive force in domestic politics. Australia, in contrast, had to wait until the Second World War for a representative of the Irish minority to come to power. When John Curtin became prime minister in 1941, Australia made up for lost time and dramatically redefined the expectations and limitations of its relationship with Britain. The different paces of the Canadian and Australian shift to independence also reflected different experiences, with Canada early on laying out clear boundaries for British involvement in Canadian political life, following the King-Byng affair of 1926. Australia would not undergo a comparable crisis over the authority and responsibility of its governor-general until the 1970s. The reaction, then, was much more bitter than it had been in Canada in the 1920s. What becomes clear is that Australians and Canadians had different expectations of Britain, a difference that was nakedly apparent during the Second World War. Australia expected more, and therefore Britain had farther to fall in the estimation of Australian citizens. The recent republican crisis in Australia is the outcome of sharp disappointment, the like of which was never experienced in Canada, where the Queen's position as head of state is not seriously challenged.[2] Canada and Australia have also confronted similar internal challenges, such as dealing with the First Nations within their borders, which revealed the cultural, social, and legal values of these two societies. As Peter Russell has explained, there were obvious differences, as well as some overlap, in the reactions of governments, politicians, and citizens to the land claims of Native groups. There has also been a desire on Australia's part to learn from the less acrimonious, although far from ideal, Canadian experience.

The contributors to this book have all been trained in the tradition of a single national history. One of the benefits of this exercise in collaboration has been to draw us out of our own accustomed paths. Comparative analysis does not paint national histories in identical colours, or merely identify commonalities, but it helps to understand those factors that make histories unique. We end up by better understanding our particular traditions; writing these chapters has been the means to an end. It has also been an end in itself. It is hoped that this volume will serve as a justification, if any is needed, for other scholars to take up a detailed comparative analysis of the national histories of Canada and Australia.

There are many areas still left to explore. How did federalism develop in each country? What is the pattern of relations between the national government and provinces and states? How have changing patterns of immigration affected each society? What does multiculturalism mean in each country? What are the great themes in the arts? What role do sports play? And how much have developments in the one country affected those in the other? Above all, there is the great question of what it meant and now means to be part of the imagined community of Australia or Canada. Clearly, as a number of us have suggested, membership in the British Empire and the plantation of British people and their institutions on different soils were both crucial in shaping the new societies. So was geography. Both peoples inhabited a vast and often terrifying land. But what about the differences, even then: the significant proportion of convicts in Australia in the early nineteenth century and the equally significant proportion of Loyalists in Canada – and, in the case of the latter, the presence of the French? We need to identify and understand the impact of particular determinants on the histories of these two nations. And, of course, we need to go wider as well as deeper: to consider the other white dominions. New Zealand's relationship with Australia, Newfoundland's with Canada, South Africa's with the Empire as a whole – all offer much opportunity for fruitful comparisons.

This is obviously not the first analysis of Canadian-Australian relations or their comparative development, and we are confident it will not be the last. As we have outlined in the introduction, and as the endnotes of our contributors reveal, there is a wealth of information on this subject. However, this volume belongs to a small existing corpus. It is our hope that the corpus will grow, and that *Parties Long Estranged* will help to orient the next group of scholars who take up this fascinating subject.

Notes
1   T.C. David to N.A. Robertson, 27 December 1945, Saskatchewan Provincial Archives, James G. Gardiner Papers, reel X, 41887-90.
2   On 17 May 2001 John Manley aired his belief that Canada possessed the maturity "to have a truly Canadian head of state," and opined that the monarchy would be gone within fifty years. The reaction to his comments was notably lacklustre. Although more Canadians support the abolition of the monarchy than its retention (48 percent to 39 percent in a 1998 Pollara poll), this is not an issue that Canadians believe is worth discussing. It is not now a political priority, nor is it likely to become so in the near, middle, or distant future. See Campbell Clark, "Manley Revives Debate on Allegiance to Monarchy," *Globe and Mail*, 19 May 2001, A5.

Select Bibliography

Because Canada and Australia have common legal and political systems, parallel economic development, and similar demographics and patterns of settlement, as well as interconnected histories within the British Empire and Commonwealth, scholars in many disciplines have long realized the benefits of using these two countries as comparators across a wide range of subjects, including immigration, public policy, the environment, Aboriginal studies, women's studies, culture, trade, legal traditions, and national identities.

The literature comparing Canadian and Australian foreign policy and foreign relations is more limited. One of the earliest articles on the subject is K.A. MacKirdy, "Canadian and Australian Self-Interest, the American Fact, and the Development of the Commonwealth Idea" in *Empire and Nations: Essays in Honour of Frederic H. Soward,* ed. Harvey L. Dyck and H. Peter Krosby (Toronto: University of Toronto Press, 1969). A small group of scholars have examined the Canadian and Australian experiences as middle powers in the international community. Annette Baker Fox, *The Politics of Attraction: Four Middle Powers and the United States* (New York: Columbia University Press, 1977) is one of the earliest such works. More recently, Andrew F. Cooper, Richard A. Higgott, and Kim Richard Nossal have compared and contrasted Canada and Australia in *Relocating Middle Powers: Australia and Canada in a Changing World* (Vancouver: UBC Press, 1993). Andrew Cooper has also compared Canadian and Australian efforts to establish liberal trading practices in agricultural commodities: *In between Countries: Australia, Canada and the Search for Order in Agricultural Trade* (Montreal and Kingston: McGill-Queen's University Press, 1997). Kim Nossal has examined the attitudes of Ottawa and Canberra toward the use of sanctions to register opposition to tyrannical regimes in *Rain Dancing: Sanctions in Canadian and Australian Foreign Policy* (Toronto: University of Toronto Press, 1994).

Scholarly works on foreign relations have tended to focus on Australian and Canadian relations with Great Britain and the United States. In Australia's case considerable attention is also paid to relations with New Zealand. Works on the direct Canadian-Australian bilateral relationship form a small subset of these larger literatures. John Hilliker examined their wartime relationship in "Distant Ally: Canadian Relations with Australia during the Second World War," *The Journal of Imperial and Commonwealth History* 13, 1 (October 1984). Greg Donaghy sketched out the relationship over a hundred years in a twenty-five-page booklet: *Parallel Paths: Canadian-Australian Relations since the 1890s* (Ottawa: Department of Foreign Affairs, 1995). Donaghy's article in particular served as a starting point for many of our contributors' analyses. There are several articles on the trade relationship between the two countries in Kate Burridge, Lois Foster, and Gerry Turcotte, eds., *Canada-Australia: Towards a Second Century of Partnership* (Ottawa, 1997). On balance, however, this last work falls more readily in the category of Canadian studies than that of Canadian-Australian relations.

Histories of the British Commonwealth are a useful, if slightly circuitous, way to approach the Canadian-Australian relationship. Because the Commonwealth was one of the earliest, most frequent, and persistent venues for Canadian and Australian politicians and diplomats to meet at, much can be learned about that particular bilateral relationship, even though they tended to be situated in the larger context of the Commonwealth and therefore are a part of a complex of relationships. For the early period, see John Kendle, *The Colonial and Imperial Conferences, 1887-1911* (London: Longmans, 1967). Philip Wigley, *Canada and the Transition to Commonwealth: British-Canadian Relations 1917-1926* (Cambridge: Cambridge University Press, 1977) is especially helpful for relations between Canada and two Australian prime ministers, Stanley Bruce and Billy Hughes. R.F. Holland, *Britain and the Commonwealth Alliance, 1918-1939* (London: Macmillan 1981) and Nicholas Mansergh, *Survey of British Commonwealth Affairs,* vol. 3, *Problems of External Policy 1931-1939* (London: Oxford University Press, 1952) cover the interwar period. W.K. Hancock also gives some consideration to the development of dominion nationalism in *Survey of British Commonwealth Affairs,* vol. 1, *Problems of Nationality 1918-1936* (Oxford: Oxford University Press, 1937). There is more written for the years after 1939. Nicholas Mansergh's many scholarly monographs provide much information on Canada and Australia, although his accounts of the Commonwealth tend to be British-centred. See *The Commonwealth Experience* (London: Weidenfeld and Nicolson, 1969) and *Survey of British Commonwealth Affairs,* vol. 4, *Problems of Wartime Co-operation and Post-war Change 1939-1952* (London: Oxford University Press, 1958). More recently, Francine McKenzie has examined Canadian and Australian (as well as New Zealand and South African) relations with Britain, the United States, their direct relationship, as well as their respective involvement in planning for the peace after 1945 in *Redefining the Bonds of Commonwealth, 1939-1948: The Politics of Preference* (Basingstoke: Palgrave, 2002).

Political and diplomatic memoirs compensate somewhat for the dearth of scholarly analysis. Canadian and Australian diplomats were certainly aware of one another's goals, interests, and tactics. Scholar-diplomat John Holmes comments on the tension and rivalry in Canadian-Australian relations in his insightful two-volume study, *The Shaping of Peace: Canada and the Search for World Order, 1943-1957* (Toronto: University of Toronto Press, 1979 and 1982). Indeed Holmes's private papers at Trinity College, Toronto, are filled with articles and speeches on the Commonwealth. Charles Ritchie, whose diplomatic diaries are much loved for their impudence and wit, commented in 1946 how much he enjoyed the company of his Australian counterparts: "They are such pungently lively company and don't give a damn for the proprieties." See *Diplomatic Passport: More Undiplomatic Diaries, 1946-1962* (Toronto: Macmillan of Canada, 1981), 8. However, he clearly didn't enjoy them enough to write about them with any frequency. References are fleeting and hint at, rather than analyze systematically, the relationship. Escott Reid, *On Duty: A Canadian at the Making of the United Nations 1945-1946* (Toronto: McClelland and Stewart, 1983) provides evidence of the rivalry and competitiveness of these two emerging middle powers. *Mike: The Memoirs of the Right Honourable Lester B. Pearson*, vol. 2, *1948-1957*, ed. John A. Munro and Alex I. Inglis (Toronto: University of Toronto Press, 1973) offers useful insights on the differences between the Canadian and Australian reactions to the Suez Crisis of 1956. Richard Casey's diaries also reveal the range of subjects discussed by Australian and Canadian officials: Richard Casey, *Australian Foreign Minister: The Diaries of R.G. Casey 1951-1960* (London: Collins, 1972).

Canadian and Australian involvement and interests also overlapped on specific issues, including the South African War (1899-1902), as well as the wars in Korea (1950-3) and Vietnam (1954-75), the Suez Crisis of 1956, and trade. Scholarly analyses of these subjects in Canada and Australia generally employ a national focus, meaning there are accounts of Australian or Canadian involvement. Because of the convergence of interest, and the corresponding opportunity for contact, such studies of one country's international relations are filled with information about the other country, even though the works were not conceived of as comparative analyses or studies in the Canadian-Australian relationship. See, for example, Carman Miller, *Painting the Map Red: Canada and the South African War 1899-1902* (Montreal and Kingston: McGill-Queen's University Press, 1993); Steven Lee, *Outposts of Empire: Korea, Vietnam, and the Origins of the Cold War in Asia, 1949-1954* (Montreal and Kingston: McGill-Queen's University Press, 1995), which briefly compares the difference in outlook of Ottawa and Canberra to the growing communist threat in Asia; W.J. Hudson, *Blind Loyalty: Australia and the Suez Crisis, 1956* (Carlton: Melbourne University Press, 1989); Ann Capling, *Australia and the Global Trade System: From Havana to Seattle* (Cambridge: Cambridge University Press, 2001); John Singleton and Paul L. Robertson, *Economic Relations between Britain and Australasia 1945-1970* (Basingstoke: Palgrave, 2002).

Finally, official document collections for both Canada and Australia contain a significant amount of material on the Canadian-Australian relationship. These collections give a good idea of the range of topics on which Canada and Australia consulted, from atomic energy to the communist triumph in China, the General Agreement on Tariffs and Trade, and aid policy. There are currently sixteen volumes in *Documents on Australian Foreign Policy*, covering the period 1937-49. (There is also a special volume dealing with Indonesia and East Timor, 1974-6.) The Canadian equivalent, *Documents on Canadian External Relations*, covers the years 1909-57 in twenty-three volumes. Both document series are ongoing.

Contributors

Frank Cain teaches twentieth-century Australian history and intelligence history at the University of New South Wales. He researches and publishes in political history, intelligence history, the history of the United States in the Cold War, and labour history. He is the author of *Menzies at War and Peace* (1997). His most recent publication is *Arming the Nation: A History of Defence, Science and Technology in Australia* (1999).

Ann Capling teaches politics at the University of Melbourne, and is Associate Dean (Academic Programs) in the Arts Faculty. She is the co-author of *Beyond the Protective State: the Political Economy of Australian Industry Policy* (1992) and *Australian Politics in the Global Era* (1998) and the author of *Australia and the Global Trade System: From Havana to Seattle* (2001).

Andrew F. Cooper teaches political science at the University of Waterloo. He is a former Fulbright scholar and current assistant editor of the *Canadian Journal of Political Science*. His books include *In between Countries: Australia, Canada and the Search for Order in Agricultural Trade* (1997) and *Canadian Foreign Policy: Old Habits and New Directions* (1997); as co-author, *Relocating Middle Powers: Australia and Canada in a Changing World Order* (1993); as editor, *Niche Diplomacy: Middle Powers after the Cold War* (1997); and as co-editor, *Worthwhile Initiatives? Canadian Mission-Oriented Diplomacy* (2000), and *Enhancing Global Governance: Towards a New Diplomacy* (2002).

David MacKenzie teaches history at Ryerson University. He is the author of *Inside the North Atlantic Triangle: Canada and the Entrance of Newfoundland into Confederation, 1939-1949* (1986), *Canada and International Civil Aviation, 1932-1948* (1989), and *Arthur Irwin: A Biography* (1993).

Francine McKenzie teaches history at the University of Western Ontario. She is the author of *Redefining the Bonds of Commonwealth 1939-1948: The Politics of Preference* (2002).

Margaret MacMillan is Provost of Trinity College and teaches history at the University of Toronto. She is the author of *Women of the Raj* (1988, 1997) and *Peacemakers: The Paris Peace Conference of 1919 and Its Attempt to end War* (2001), and the co-editor of *Canada and NATO: Uneasy Past, Uncertain Future* (1990), as well as *The Uneasy Century: International Relations 1900-1990* (1996). She is a former co-editor of *International Journal*.

Kim Richard Nossal is chair of the Department of Political Studies at Queen's University. He is the author of *Rain Dancing: Sanctions in Canadian and Australian Foreign Policy* (1994), co-author of *A Brief Madness: Australia and the Resumption of French Nuclear Testing* (1997), and co-editor of *Diplomatic Departures: The Conservative Era in Canadian Foreign Policy, 1984-93* (2001).

Galen Perras is an archivist at the National Archives of Canada. He is the author of *Franklin Delano Roosevelt and the Origins of the Canadian-American Security Alliance, 1939-1945: Necessary, but not Necessary Enough* (1998) and *Stepping Stones to Nowhere: The Aleutian Islands, Alaska, and American Military Strategy, 1867-1945* (UBC Press, 2003).

Wayne Reynolds teaches history at the University of Newcastle. He is the biographer of H.V. Evatt (1994) and author of *Australia's Bid for the Atomic Bomb* (2001).

Peter Russell is University Professor Emeritus at the University of Toronto, where he taught political science for forty years. He has published widely in judicial, constitutional, and Aboriginal politics. His essay here is based on research for a book he is writing entitled *Recovering Terra Nullius: Mabo and the Decolonization of Indigenous Peoples*.

Christopher Waters teaches international history in the School of Australian and International Studies at Deakin University, Melbourne. He is the author of *The Empire Fractures: Anglo-Australian Conflict in the 1940s* (1995), co-author of *Ministers, Mandarins and Diplomats: Australian Foreign Policy Making, 1941-1969* (2002), and co-editor of *Evatt to Evans: The Labor Tradition in Australian Foreign Policy* (1997).

Index

Holmes, John W., 138, 230, 253, 255-6
Hong Kong, in Second World War, 108, 128, 129, 130
Hoover, J. Edgar, 197, 202
Horner, D.M., 132
House, Edward, 13, 29, 30
Howard, John, 79, 82-3, 84, 88, 89, 90, 262
Howe, C.D., 111, 114, 133, 134, 140, 155, 156
Hudson, W.J., 210
Hughes, Robert, 67
Hughes, William (Billy): on annexation of Pacific islands, 28-9; and Borden, 14, 19-20, 22, 26-7; and Chanak crisis, 36; on Council of Ten, 23; and department of external affairs, 15; and Imperial War Cabinet, 20; and Paris Peace Conference, 21, 24, 25-7; on racial equality clause in League Covenant, 27-8; and Treaty of Versailles, 24, 26, 30; on United States in First World War, 25; and Wilson, 20, 25-6, 29-30
Hull, Cordell, 126
Human rights, 263
Hungary, Soviet invasion of, 212
Hyde Park Agreement, 49

ICAO. *See* International Civil Aviation Organization
Imperial Airways, 104, 109
Imperial conferences, 16-17; 1907, 37; 1937, 39-40, 106, 107; during 1930s, 39-40; Imperial Economic Conference of 1932, 40
Imperial defence, 18, 166, 168-9
Imperial foreign policy, 18, 19, 36-7, 42
Imperial preference, 40, 230, 231-2
Imperial secretariat, 17
Imperial War Cabinet (IWC), 13, 20, 21, 25, 127
India, 216; Australian/Canadian relations with, 220-1; in British Commonwealth, 219, 220; and British Empire, 223; Canada's policy toward, 218, 220; independence, 212; at Paris Peace Conference, 21; self-government, 13
Indian Trans-Continental Airways, 105
Indians (North American). *See under* Aboriginal peoples
Indigenous peoples. *See* Aboriginal peoples
Indochina, 214, 215
Indonesia, 212, 215, 216
Industrial Workers of the World (IWW), 186
Inquiry into Aboriginal Deaths in Custody (Australia), 83
Inter-allied economic conference, Paris (1916), 20
International Air Transport Authority, 99
International Civil Aviation Conference, Chicago (1944), 112, 113

International Civil Aviation Organization (ICAO), 97, 99, 113, 114, 117
International Criminal Court, 262
International Monetary Fund (IMF), 234
International Supervisory Commission for Indochina, 215, 218
International Trade Organization (ITO), 229, 230-9, 234, 245, 255
Inuit, 88
Ireland, civil aviation in, 105, 106
Irish Free State, 34
Irwin, Arthur, 209, 211, 219, 221-2, 223
Isley, J.L., 198
Italy, invasion of Ethiopia, 38-9
ITO. *See* International Trade Organization
IWC. *See* Imperial War Cabinet

Jameson, Starr, 17
Japan: agricultural trade, 238, 240; air service to, 115; Anglo-Japanese alliance, 24-5; and Australia, 15, 25, 27, 43, 108, 125, 128-9, 132; Canada's attitude toward, 25, 138; in the G-4, 244; and League Covenant, 27-8; and North American coast, 131-2, 154; in Second World War, 43, 108, 125, 128, 131-2, 154
Jebb, Richard, 16, 17
Jenkins, J.H., 139
Johnson, Nelson, 142
Johnston, William, 67
Joint Chiefs of Staff, 158-9
Joint Intelligence Bureau, 172-3
Joint Operating Company, for transatlantic air service, 105
Joint Strategic Studies Committee (JSSC), 158
Joint War Production Committee, 173
Jones, George C., 188

Keating, Paul, 81, 89-90, 250
Keenleyside, Hugh, 138
Kellock, Lindsay, 197, 198
Kerr, Philip, 23, 30
KGB, 184, 192-3, 199-200
King, William Lyon Mackenzie, 125; and Anglo-Canadian connection, 36, 107, 157; and atomic energy, 164; on Australia in United Nations, 53; and Canadian sovereignty, 41; and Chanak crisis, 35; on Commonwealth, 40, 44, 47; and cooperation with United States, 154, 157; on Evatt, 253; and Gouzenko defection, 189, 196, 201; and Italian invasion of Ethiopia, 39; and Japanese threat, 131-2, 139, 154; on League of Nations, 39; on Menzies, 127; and military aid to Australia, 129, 134-6, 137, 140, 141, 142; retirement, 144; and Treaty of Versailles, 24; on war with Germany, 41, 42

Kiska (Aleutian Islands), 136, 137
Korean War, 212, 214, 215, 216
Kowarski, Lew, 160

Lamer, Chief Justice Antonio, 84
Land mines, 262
Lands, Aboriginal (Australia), 70, 73, 81-3; cultivation of, 66; granted to settlers, 70; mining of, 82, 83; pastoral leases of, 82; uninhabited, 66. *See also Mabo* case; *Terra nullius* doctrine; *Wik* case
Lands, Aboriginal (Canada): Native title to, 84-5; of Nisga'a people, 77-8, 85-6
Lands, Aboriginal (North America): in Canada vs United States, 71; Royal Proclamation (1763) and, 65, 69
Laurier, Wilfrid, 17, 18
Lavarack, Sir John, 141, 163-4
Law of the Sea (LOS), 261
League of Nations, 22, 23-4, 25, 27-8, 38-9
Leckie, Robert, 157, 188
Lefebvre, H., 188
Liberal party, 208, 223-5
Like-Minded Group of States, 263
Lilienthal, David, 157
Lloyd George, David, 20, 21, 23, 25, 26, 28, 29
Lloyd, Selwyn, 222
Lloyd, Sir William, 21
Locke, John, *Second Treatise of Government,* 66
Lower, A.R.M., 144
Loyalists, 68
Lucas Heights (Australia), 176
Luck, Leslie, 90
Lyons, Joseph, 171

MAB. *See* Munitions Assignment Board
Mabo case, 63, 67, 68, 73, 78, 81, 88, 89
McCarthy, Leighton, 134
McCarthyism, 212
Macdonald, Angus, 132, 141
McIntosh, Alister, 43
Mackenzie, C.J., 153, 155, 165, 171
Mackenzie, Hector, 220
McMahon Act, 158, 166, 177
McNaughton, General, 164
Makarov, S.I., 204
Malaya, 128, 131, 217, 221
Maliseet people, 86
Manchurian crisis, 38
Manhattan Project. *See* United States: atomic program
Manning, Preston, 85
Mao Tse-Tung, 216
Maralinga (Australia), 176
Marcuse, Gary, 196, 198
Marshall case, 86

Marshall, Chief Justice John, 69, 70
Marshall Plan, 170
Martin, Leslie H., 163, 172-3
Massey, Vincent, 28, 125
MAUD, 160
May, Alan Nunn, 189, 196, 203
Mazankowski, Don, 242, 249-50, 254-5
Menzies, Arthur, 208
Menzies, Robert G.: on Afro-Asian nations' conference, 220; anti-communism policy, 186-7, 194; and atomic program, 173-4, 175; on Evatt, 254; on evolution of British Empire, 223; on India in Commonwealth, 219; and Mackenzie King, 127; and Nehru, 218, 219-21; and Petrov defection, 192, 194, 195, 200, 201; and Southeast Asia, 217-18; and Soviet embassy, 192; on Statute of Westminster, 41; visits to Canada, 207; on war with Germany, 42, 125
Métis, 74
MI5, contact with Australia, 185, 186, 194
Middle powers, 52, 55-7, 108, 151, 176, 252, 257, 268
Midway Island, 142
Mi'kmaq people, 86
Miller, J.D.B., 142
Milner, Ian, 199, 200
Milner, Lord, 23, 24, 27, 30
Moffat, Jay Pierrepont, 41, 143
Mohawk people, 83
Molotov, Vyacheslav Mikhailovich, 191
Monk, Justice, 70
Monte Bello, 162, 167, 174, 176
Moss, H.P., 161
Mulroney, Brian, 83, 84, 241, 242, 250, 254, 256
Munitions Assignment Board (MAB), 133, 134-5
Munro-Ferguson, Sir Ronald, 30
Murdoch, Keith, 30

NAFTA, 263
National Indigenous Working Group on Native Title (Australia), 82
National Research Council, 162, 163
National Research Universal (NRU), 174
Native peoples. *See* Aboriginal peoples
NATO. *See* North Atlantic Treaty Organization
Nehru, Jawaharlal, 218; anti-American attitude, 219; and Cold War, 219; and Commonwealth, 220-1; and Menzies, 218, 219-21; on Pearson, 220; on St. Laurent, 220; and SEATO, 219; and Suez crisis, 219
New Caledonia, 132
New Guinea, 27, 28, 132
New Zealand, 56, 67, 112, 260, 262